# Kamisama Kiss

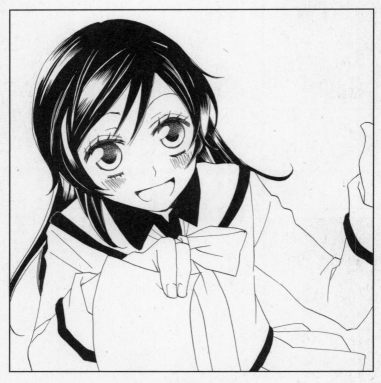

**Story & Art by**

*Julietta Suzuki*

# Kamisama Kiss

## Volume 14
## CONTENTS

Chapter 79   004

Chapter 80   035

Chapter 81   065

Chapter 82   095

Chapter 83   131

Chapter 84   161

End Notes   191

# CHARACTERS

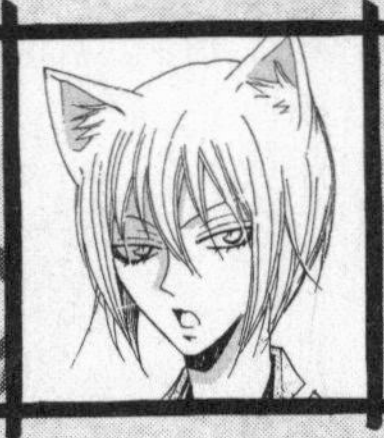

## Tomoe
The shinshi who serves Nanami now that she's a tochigami. Originally a wild fox ayakashi. He controls powerful kitsunebi.

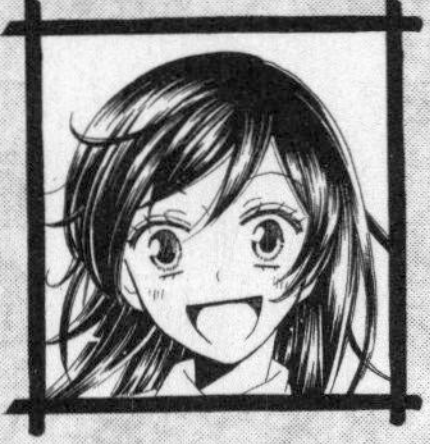

## Nanami Momozono
A high school student who was turned into a kamisama by the tochigami Mikage. She likes Tomoe.

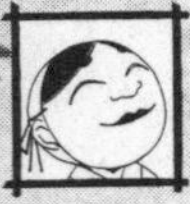

## Onikiri
Onibi-warashi, spirits of the shrine.

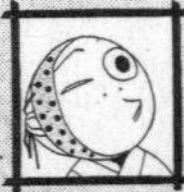

## Kotetsu
Onibi-warashi, spirits of the shrine.

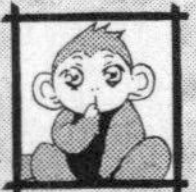

## Mamoru
Nanami's shikigami. He can create a spiritual barrier to keep out evil.

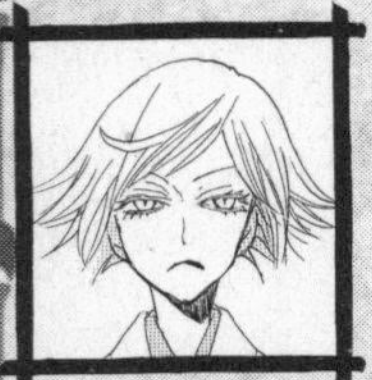

## Mizuki
Nanami's second shinshi. The incarnation of a white snake. Used to be the shinshi of Yonomori shrine.

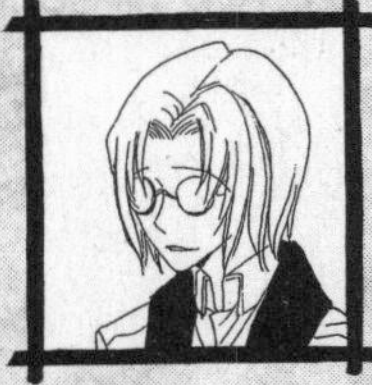

## Mikage
A kamisama who ran away from home. He turned Nanami into a tochigami and left his shrine in her care.

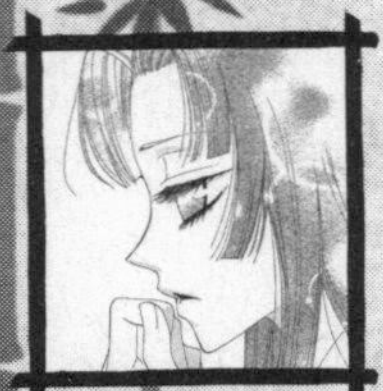

## Yukiji
A human woman from more than 500 years ago who was somehow connected to Tomoe.

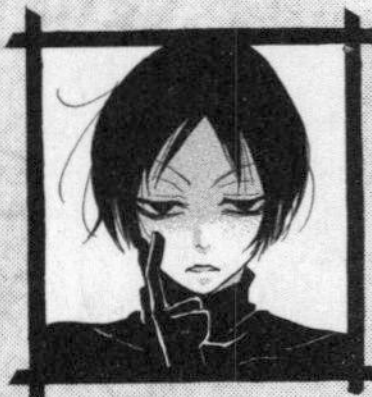

## Kirihito
A human whose body was taken over by the great yokai Akura-oh. He is attended by shikigami minions.

## Story so far

Nanami Momozono is a high school student who was evicted from her home when her dad skipped town.
She meets the tochigami Mikage in a park, and he leaves his shrine and his kami powers to her.
Now Nanami spends her days with Tomoe and Mizuki, her shinshi, and with Onikiri and Kotetsu, the onibi-warashi spirits of the shrine.
Nanami has been slowly gaining powers as a kamisama by holding a festival at her shrine, attending a big kami conference, and getting embroiled in the succession fight at the tengu village.
When Nanami manages to help Himemiko, a catfish yokai, and the human Kotaro realizer their love, her own love for Tomoe grows. And Tomoe's feelings for Nanami are also increasing.
But suddenly strange marks begin to appear in Tomoe's body…!

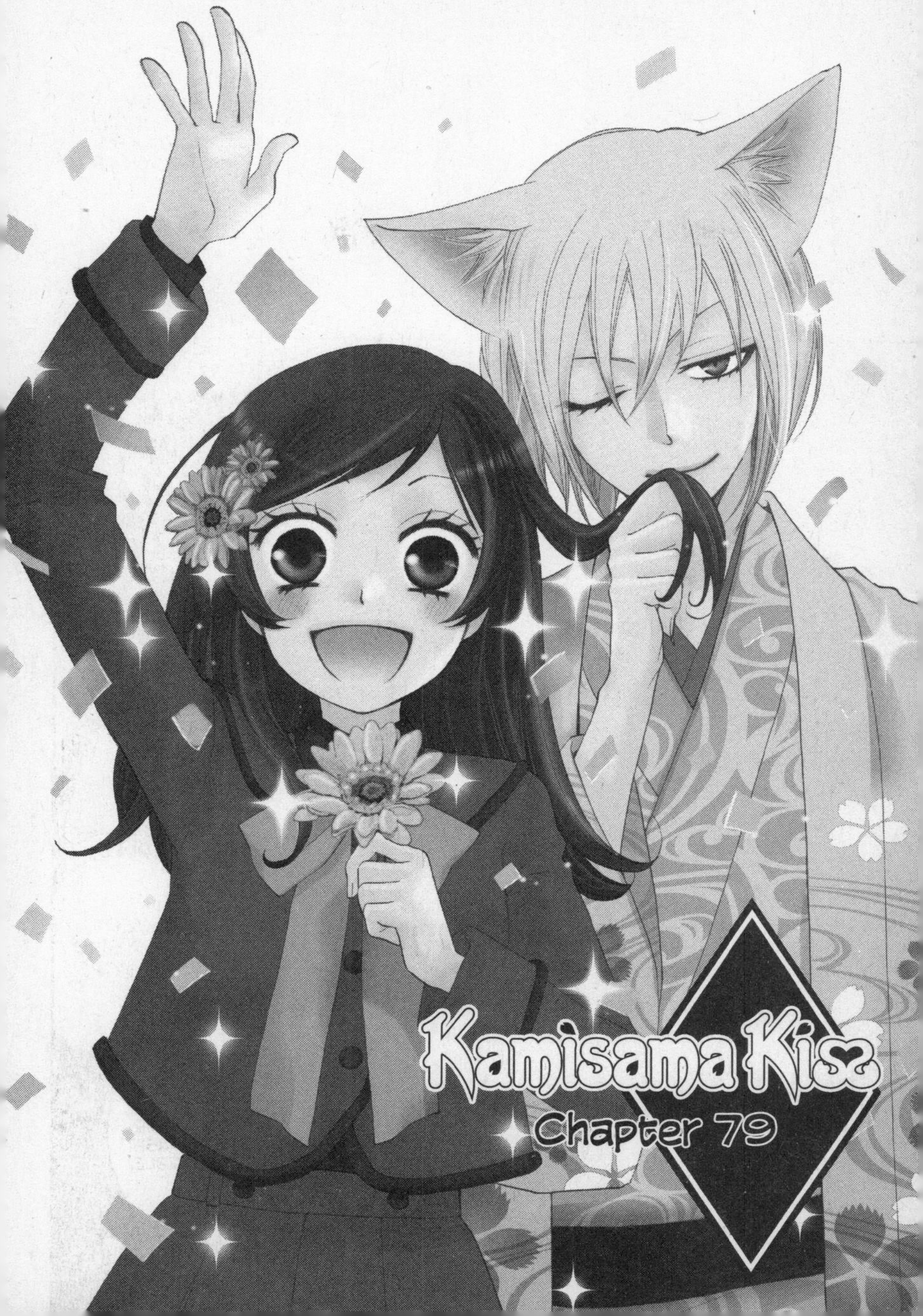
Kamisama Kiss
Chapter 79

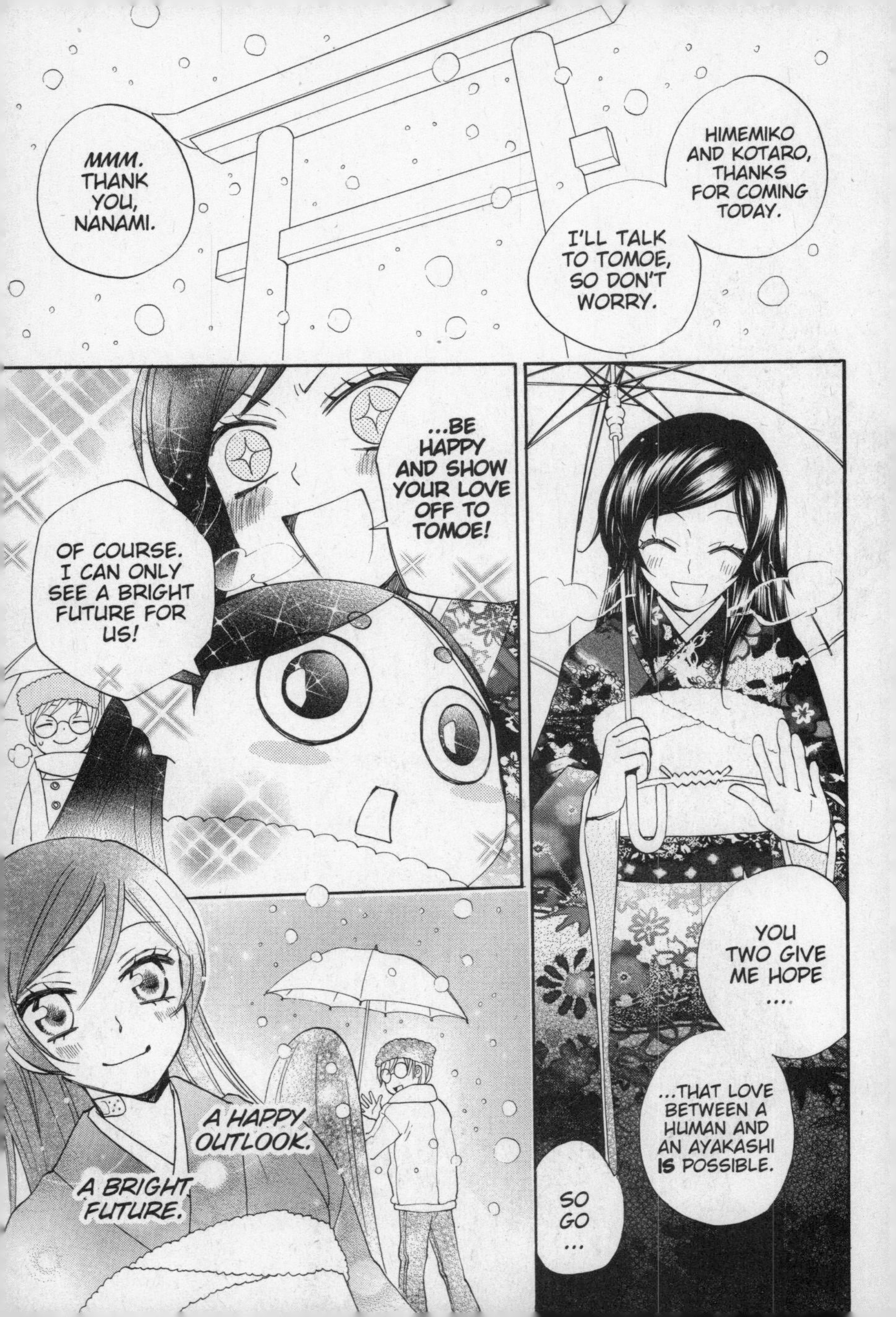
HIMEMIKO AND KOTARO, THANKS FOR COMING TODAY.
I'LL TALK TO TOMOE, SO DON'T WORRY.
MMM. THANK YOU, NANAMI.
YOU TWO GIVE ME HOPE ...
...THAT LOVE BETWEEN A HUMAN AND AN AYAKASHI **IS** POSSIBLE.
SO GO ...
...BE HAPPY AND SHOW YOUR LOVE OFF TO TOMOE!
OF COURSE. I CAN ONLY SEE A BRIGHT FUTURE FOR US!
A HAPPY OUTLOOK.
A BRIGHT FUTURE.

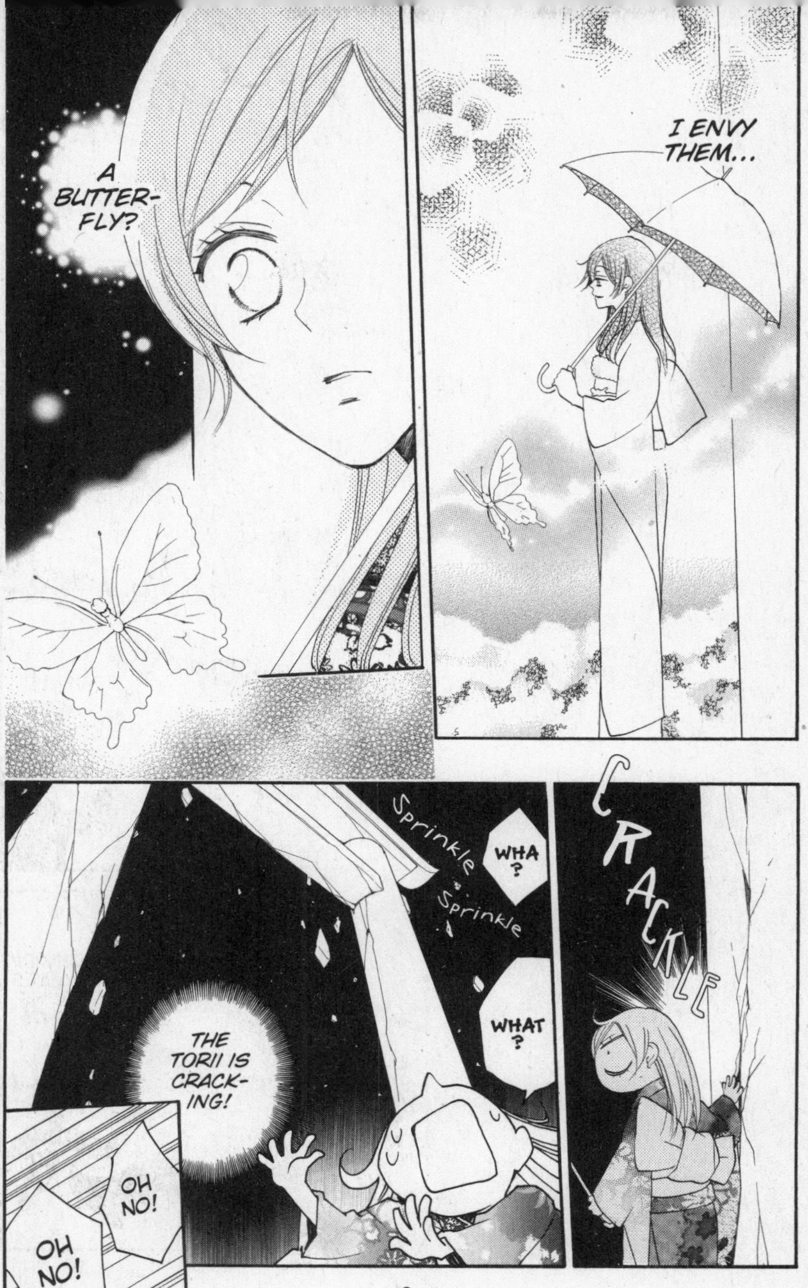
I ENVY THEM...
A BUTTER-FLY?
CRACKLE
WHA?
Sprinkle Sprinkle
WHAT?
THE TORII IS CRACK-ING!
OH NO!
OH NO!

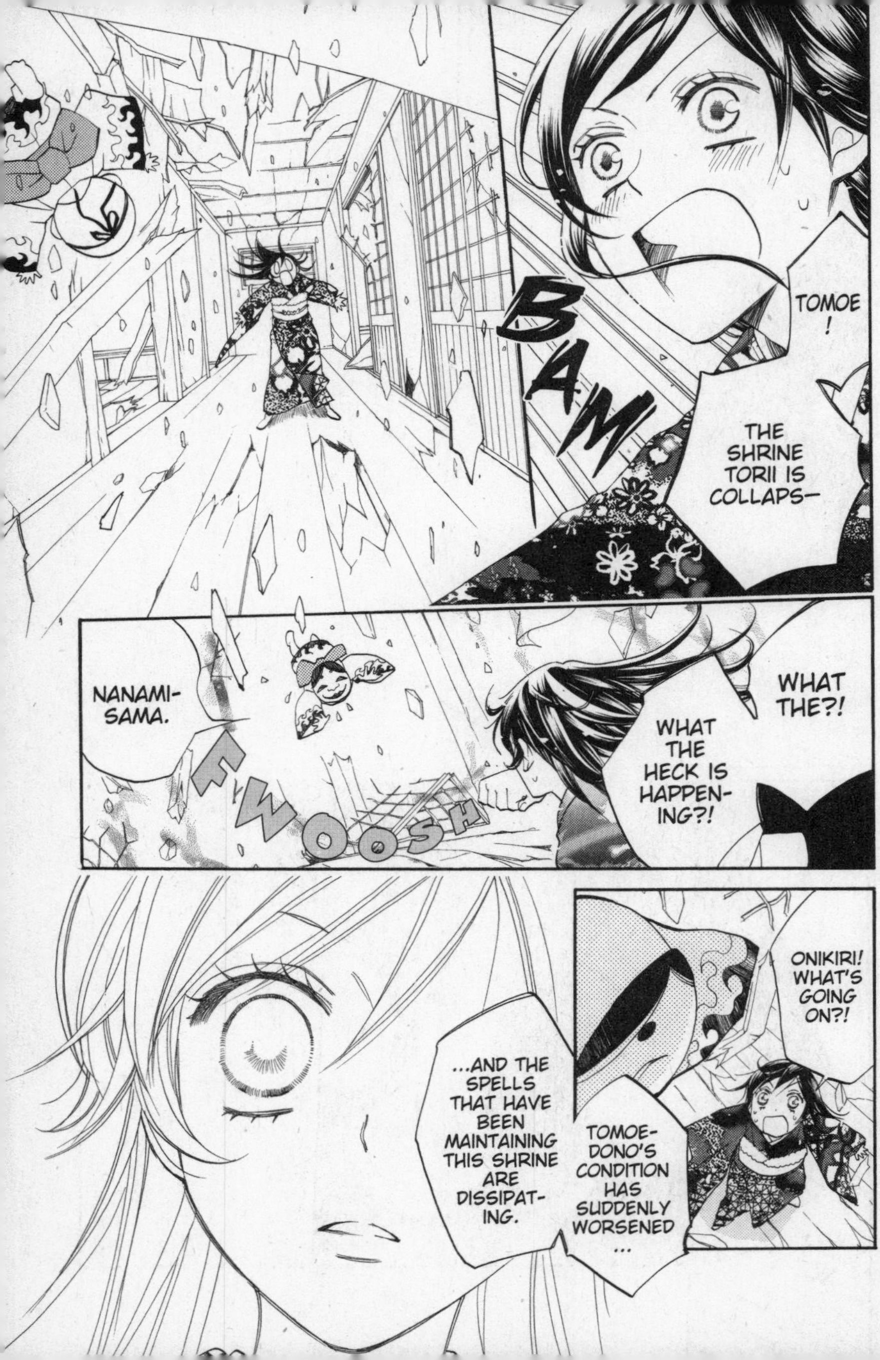
TOMOE!
BAM
THE SHRINE TORII IS COLLAPS—
WHAT THE?!
WHAT THE HECK IS HAPPENING?!
NANAMI-SAMA.
FWOOSH
ONIKIRI! WHAT'S GOING ON?!
TOMOE-DONO'S CONDITION HAS SUDDENLY WORSENED...
...AND THE SPELLS THAT HAVE BEEN MAINTAINING THIS SHRINE ARE DISSIPATING.

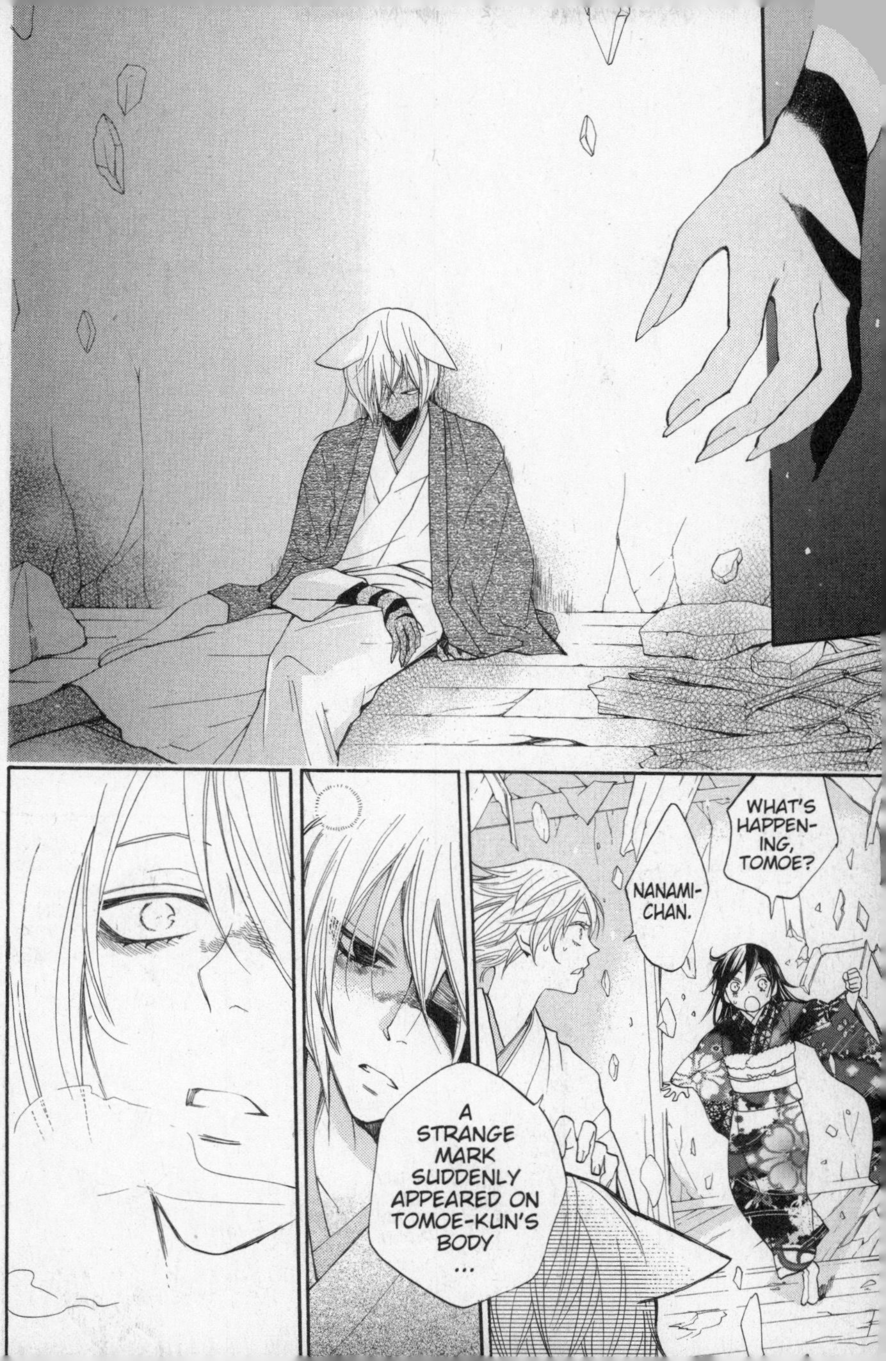
WHAT'S HAPPEN-ING, TOMOE?
NANAMI-CHAN.
A STRANGE MARK SUDDENLY APPEARED ON TOMOE-KUN'S BODY ...

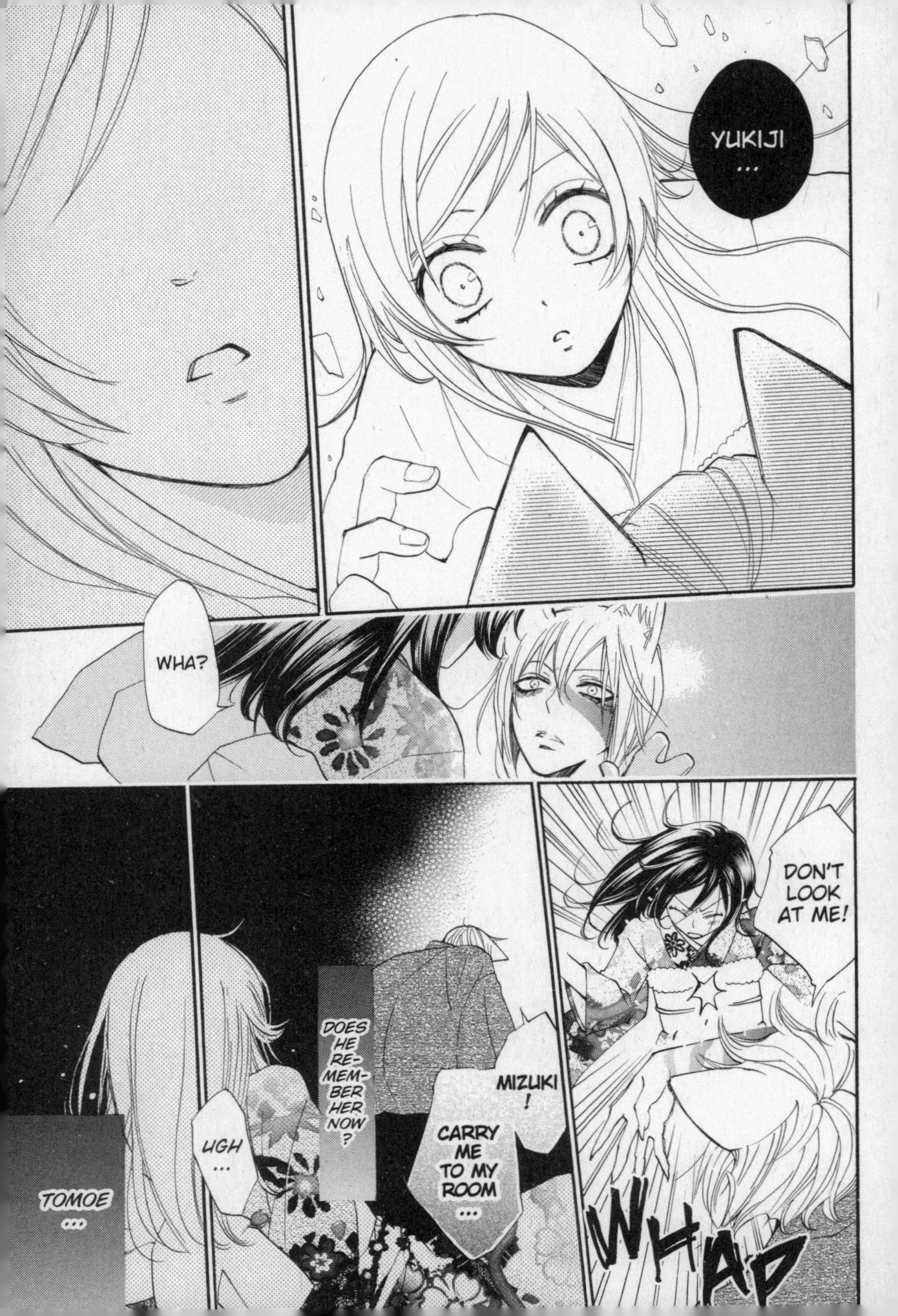
YUKIJI ...
WHA?
DON'T LOOK AT ME!
MIZUKI!
CARRY ME TO MY ROOM ...
WHAP
DOES HE REMEMBER HER NOW?
UGH ...
TOMOE ...

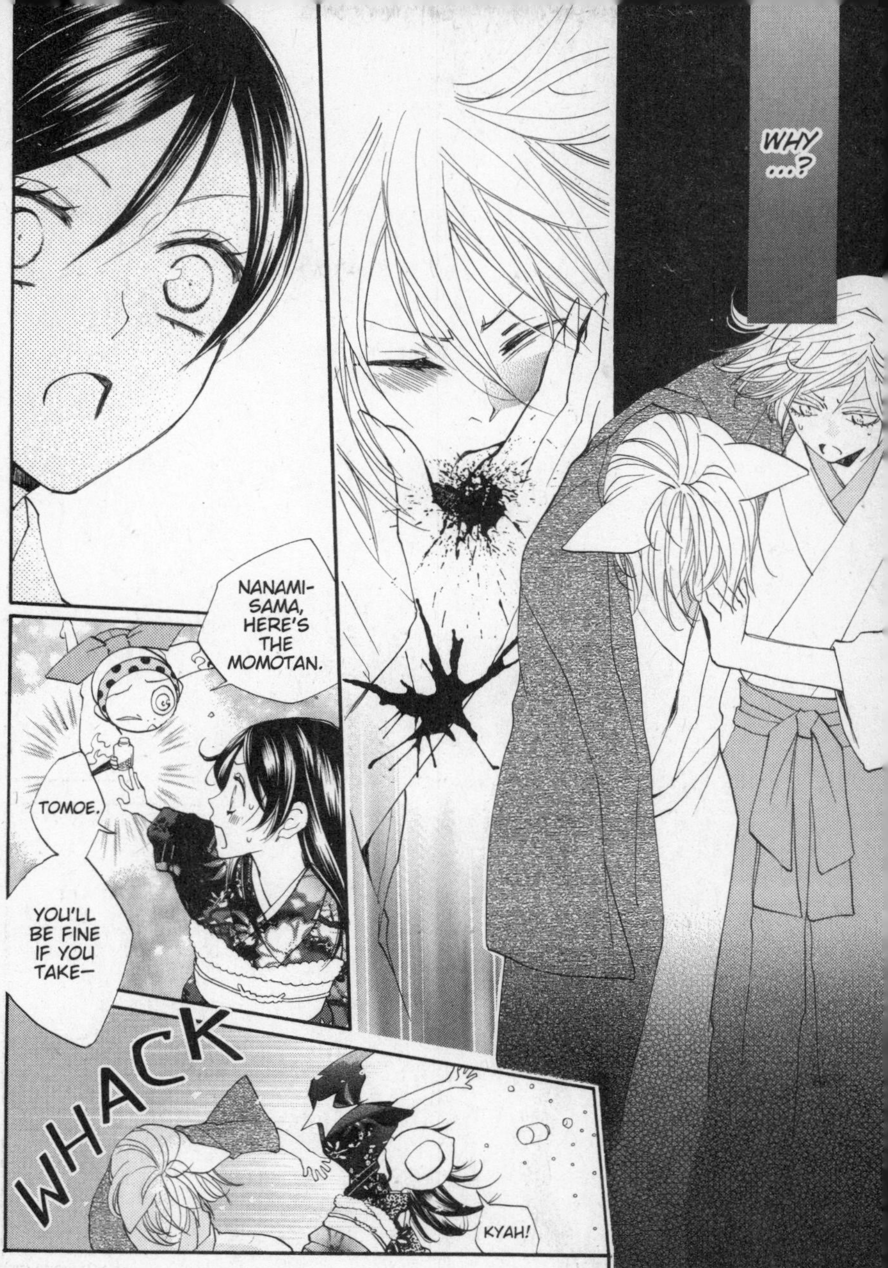
WHY ...?
NANAMI-SAMA, HERE'S THE MOMOTAN.
TOMOE.
YOU'LL BE FINE IF YOU TAKE—
WHACK
KYAH!

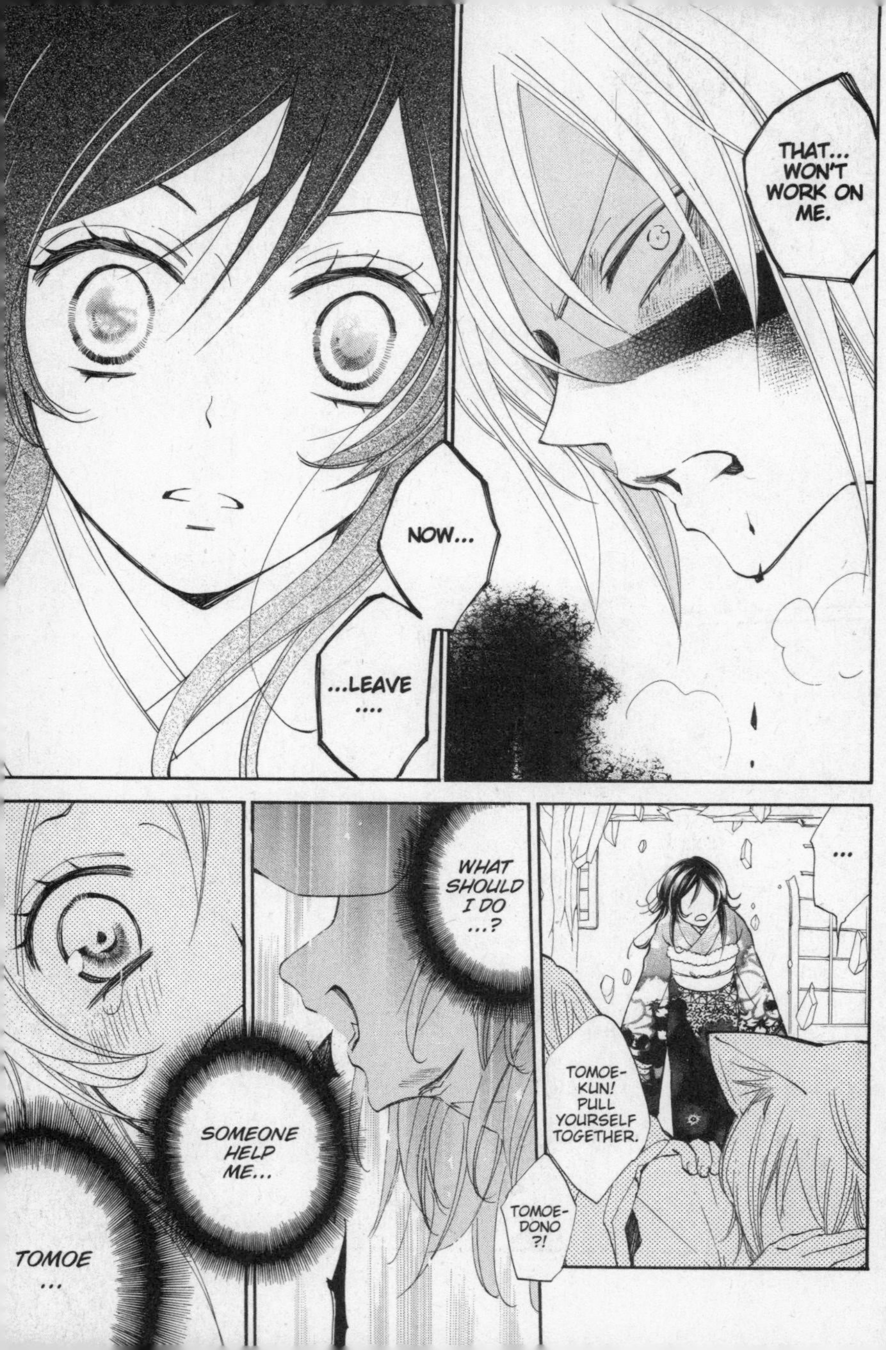
THAT... WON'T WORK ON ME.
NOW...
...LEAVE ....
...
TOMOE-KUN! PULL YOURSELF TOGETHER.
TOMOE-DONO ?!
WHAT SHOULD I DO ...?
SOMEONE HELP ME...
TOMOE ...

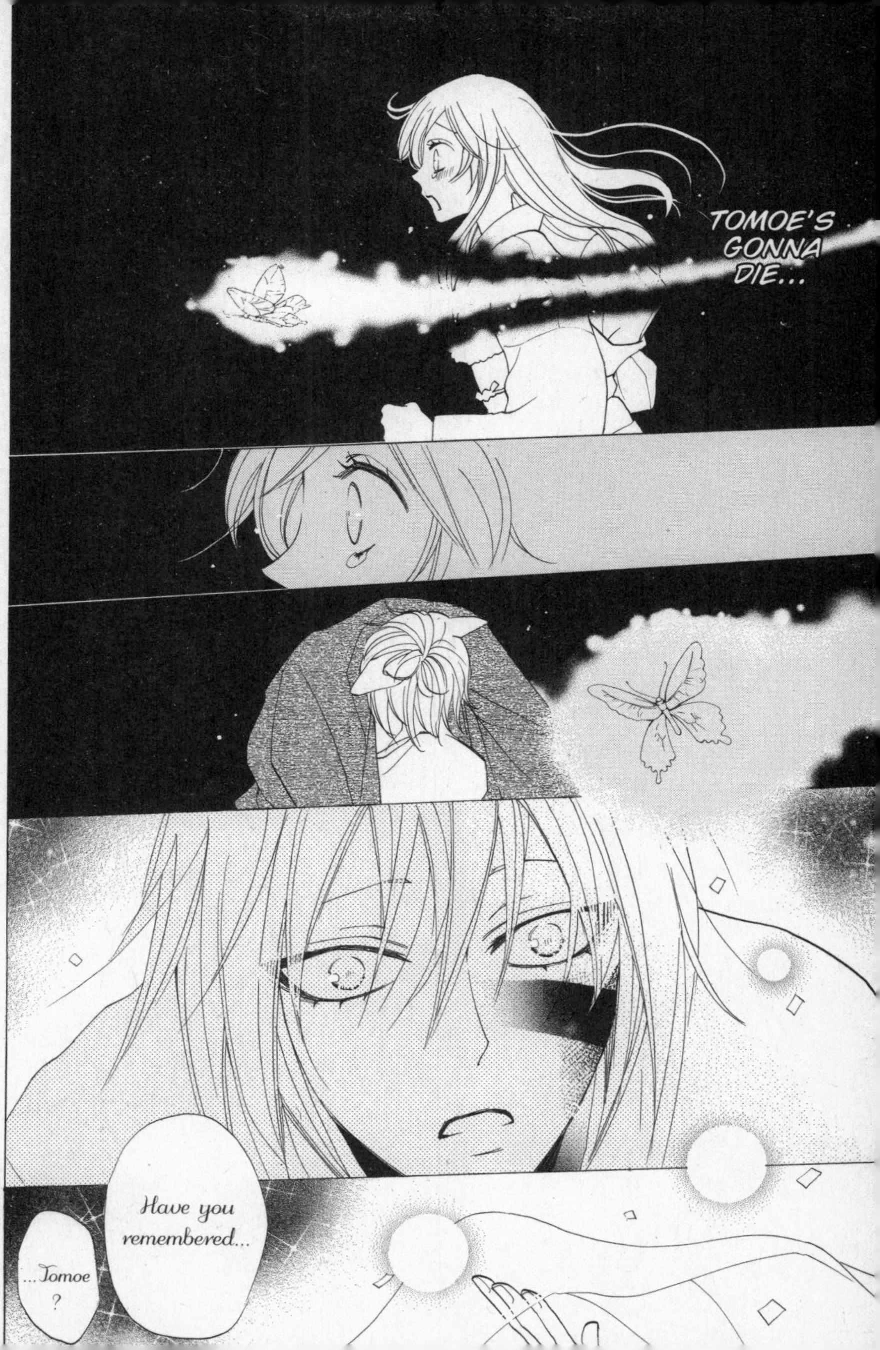
TOMOE'S GONNA DIE...
Have you remembered...
...Tomoe?

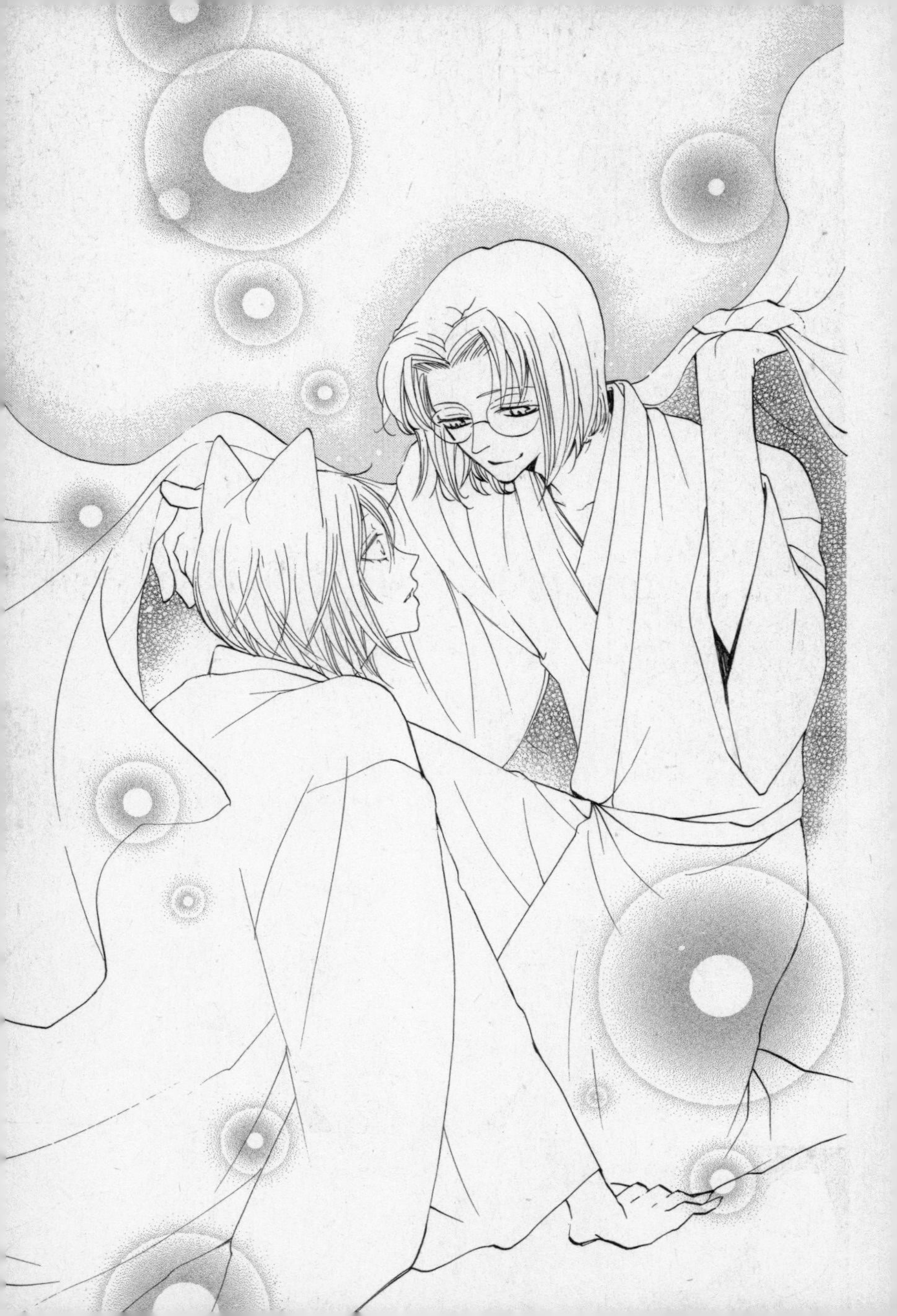

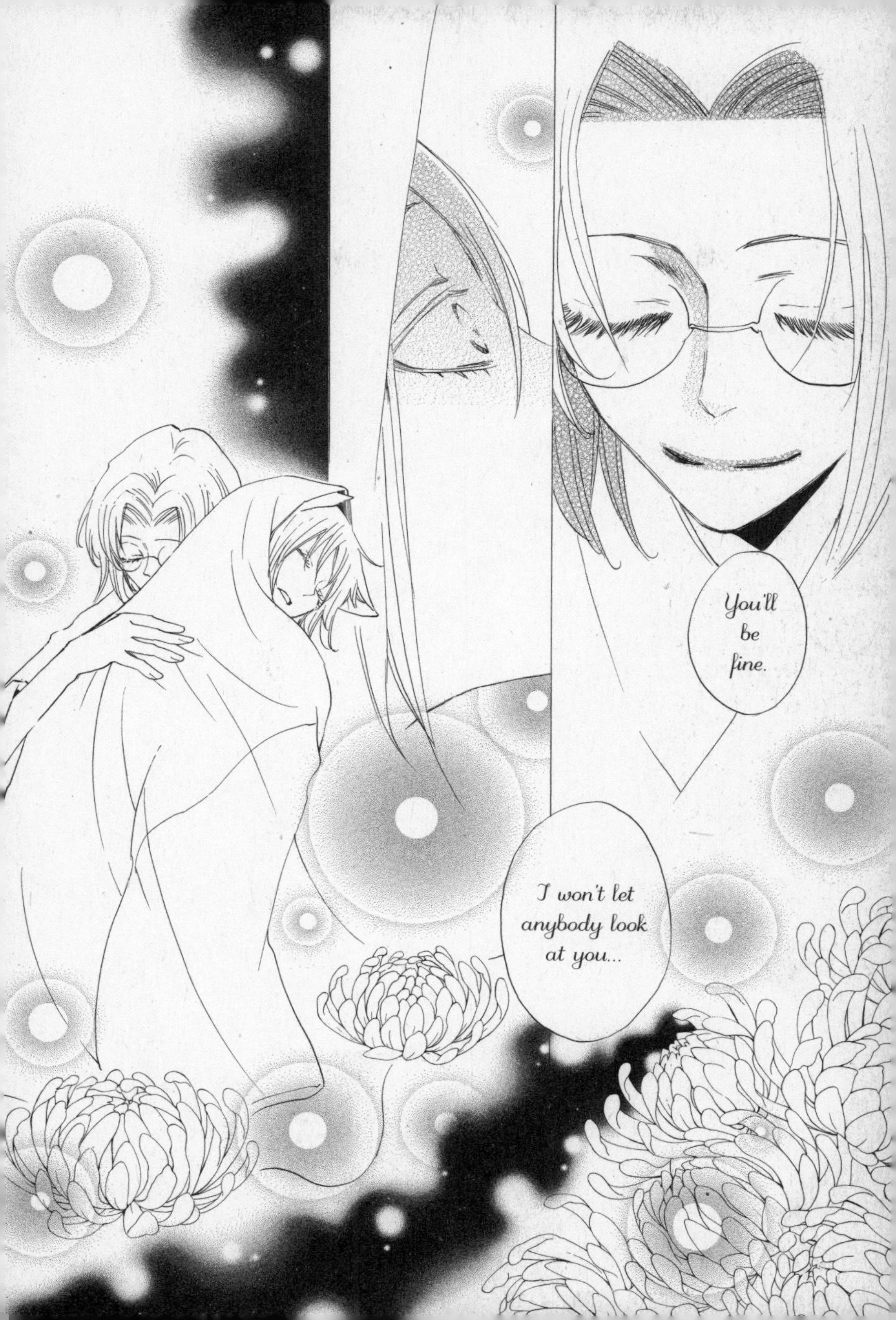
You'll be fine.
I won't let anybody look at you...

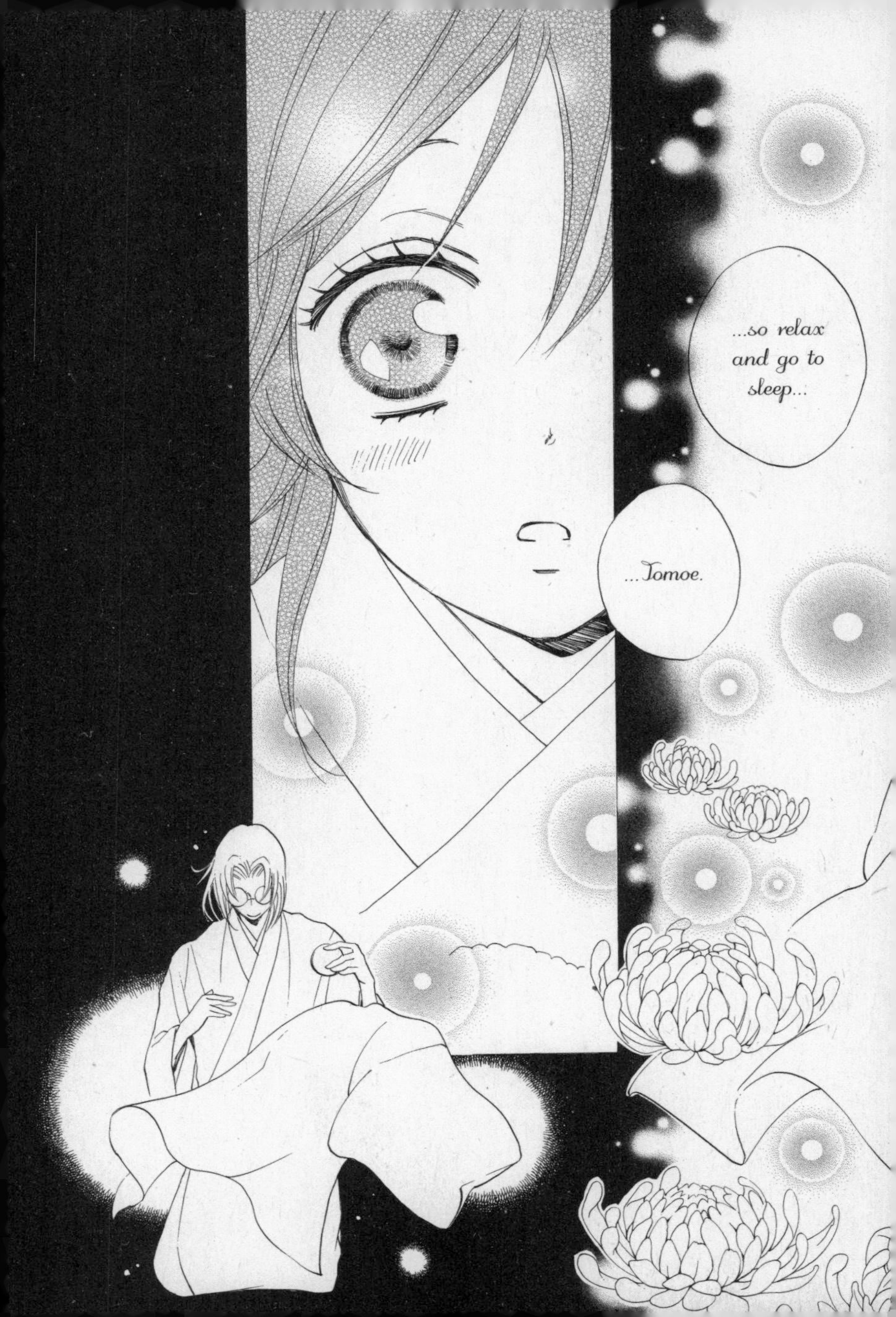
...so relax and go to sleep...
...Tomoe.

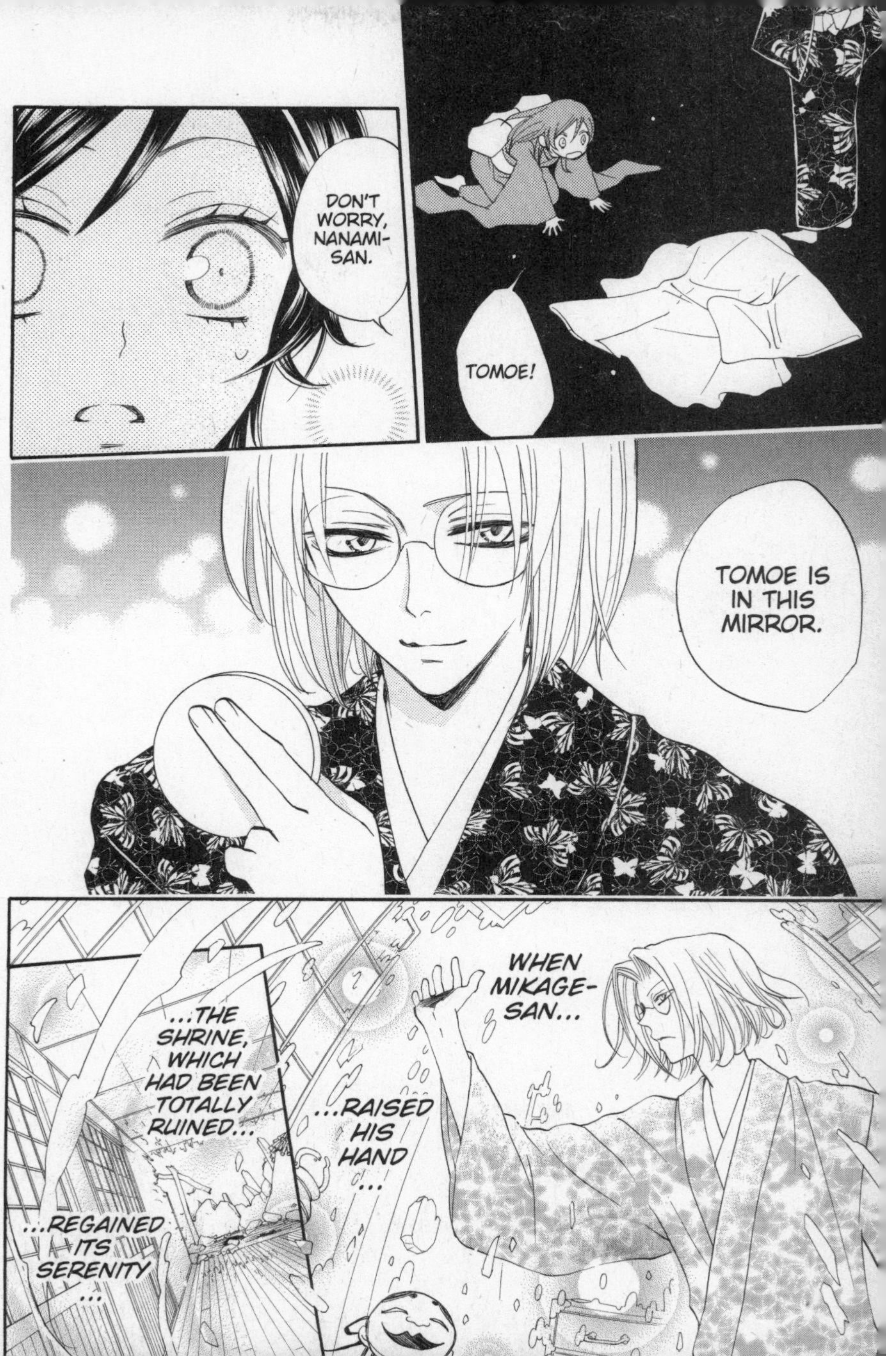
TOMOE!
DON'T WORRY, NANAMI-SAN.
TOMOE IS IN THIS MIRROR.
WHEN MIKAGE-SAN...
...RAISED HIS HAND...
...THE SHRINE, WHICH HAD BEEN TOTALLY RUINED...
...REGAINED ITS SERENITY...

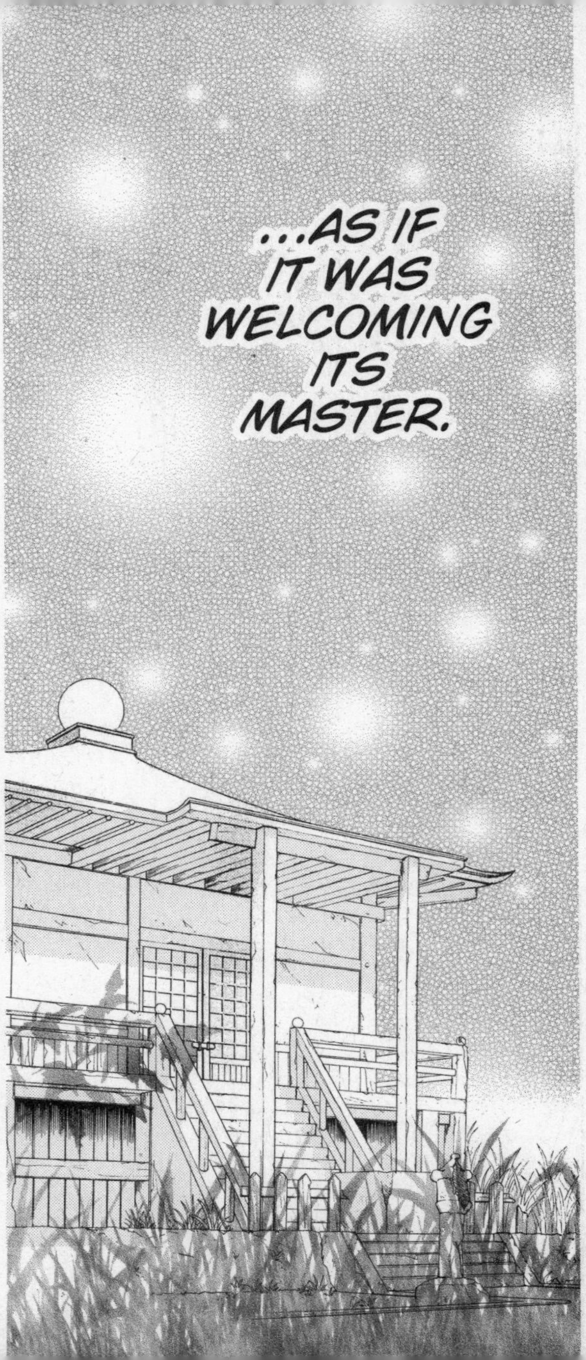
...AS IF IT WAS WELCOMING ITS MASTER.

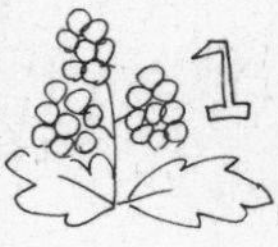

Hello!

Thank you for picking up volume 14 of Kamisama Kiss!

This is already the 14th volume. For some reason, time has really flown.

I hope you enjoy reading it!

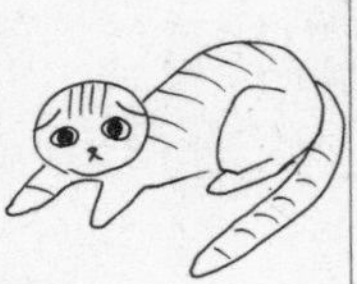

My cat celebrated its sixth birthday today. It's grown up in an instant.

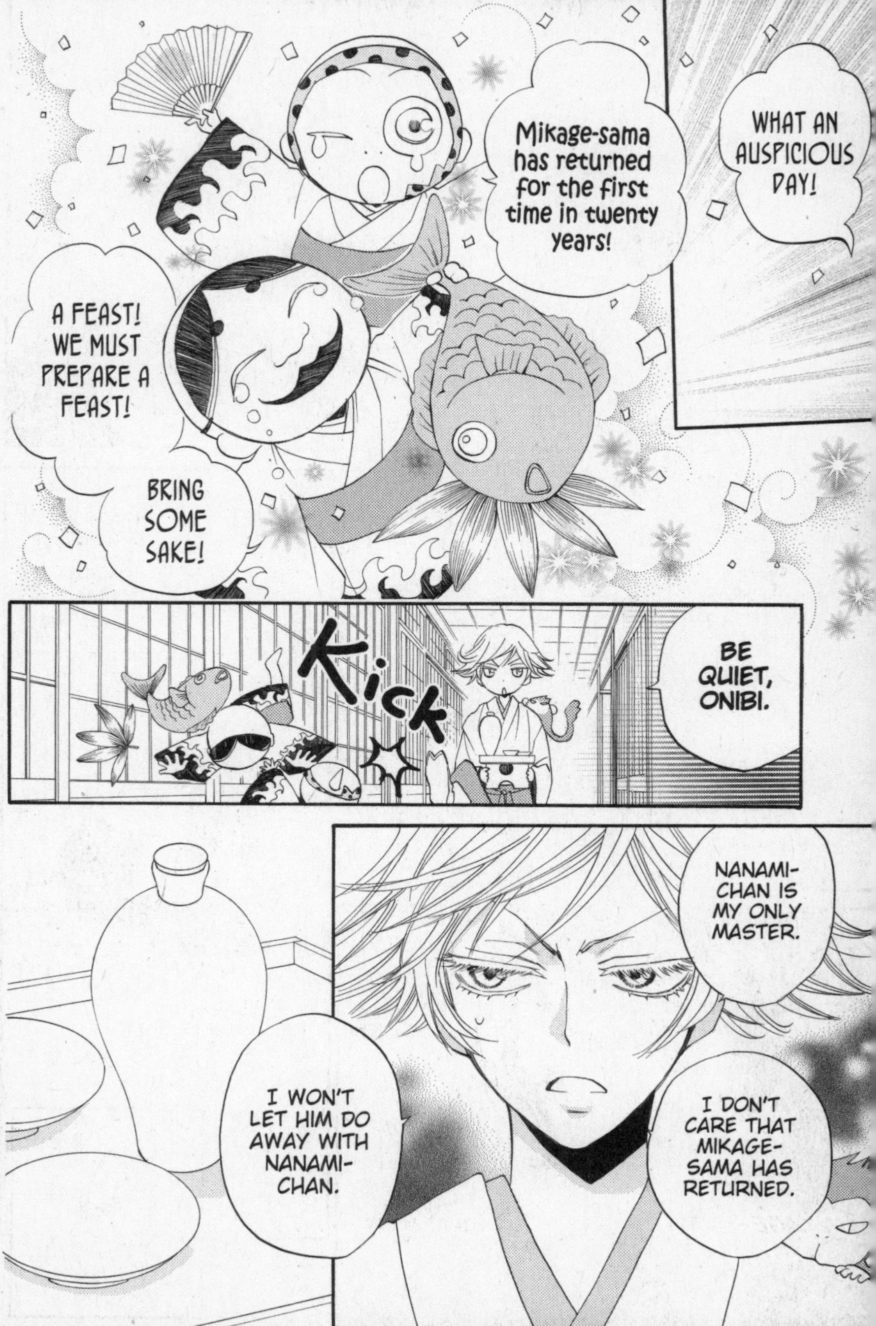
WHAT AN AUSPICIOUS DAY!
Mikage-sama has returned for the first time in twenty years!
A FEAST! WE MUST PREPARE A FEAST!
BRING SOME SAKE!
BE QUIET, ONIBI.
Kick
NANAMI-CHAN IS MY ONLY MASTER.
I DON'T CARE THAT MIKAGE-SAMA HAS RETURNED.
I WON'T LET HIM DO AWAY WITH NANAMI-CHAN.

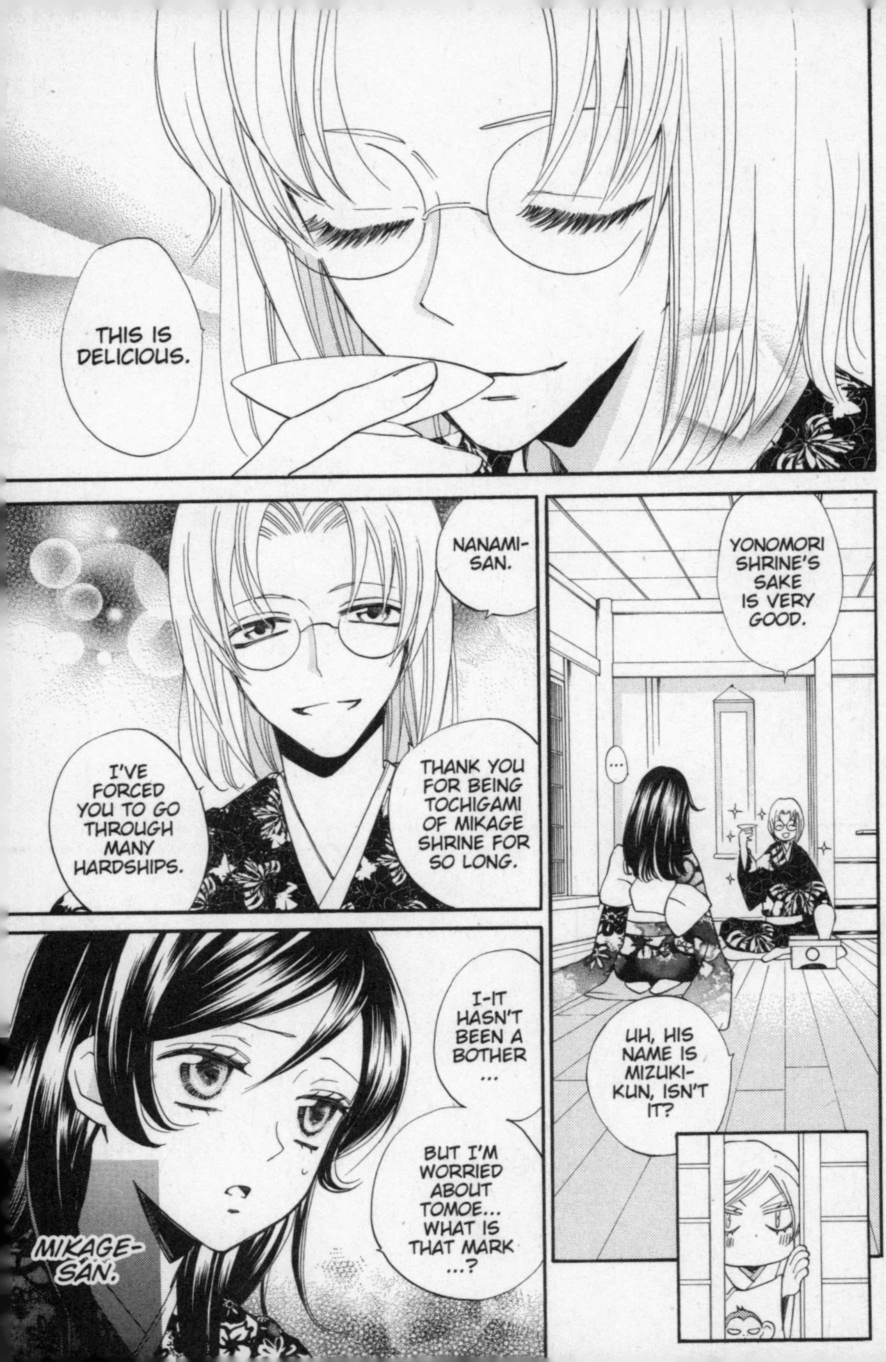
THIS IS DELICIOUS.
YONOMORI SHRINE'S SAKE IS VERY GOOD.
...
UH, HIS NAME IS MIZUKI-KUN, ISN'T IT?
NANAMI-SAN.
THANK YOU FOR BEING TOCHIGAMI OF MIKAGE SHRINE FOR SO LONG.
I'VE FORCED YOU TO GO THROUGH MANY HARDSHIPS.
I-IT HASN'T BEEN A BOTHER ...
BUT I'M WORRIED ABOUT TOMOE... WHAT IS THAT MARK ...?
MIKAGE-SAN.

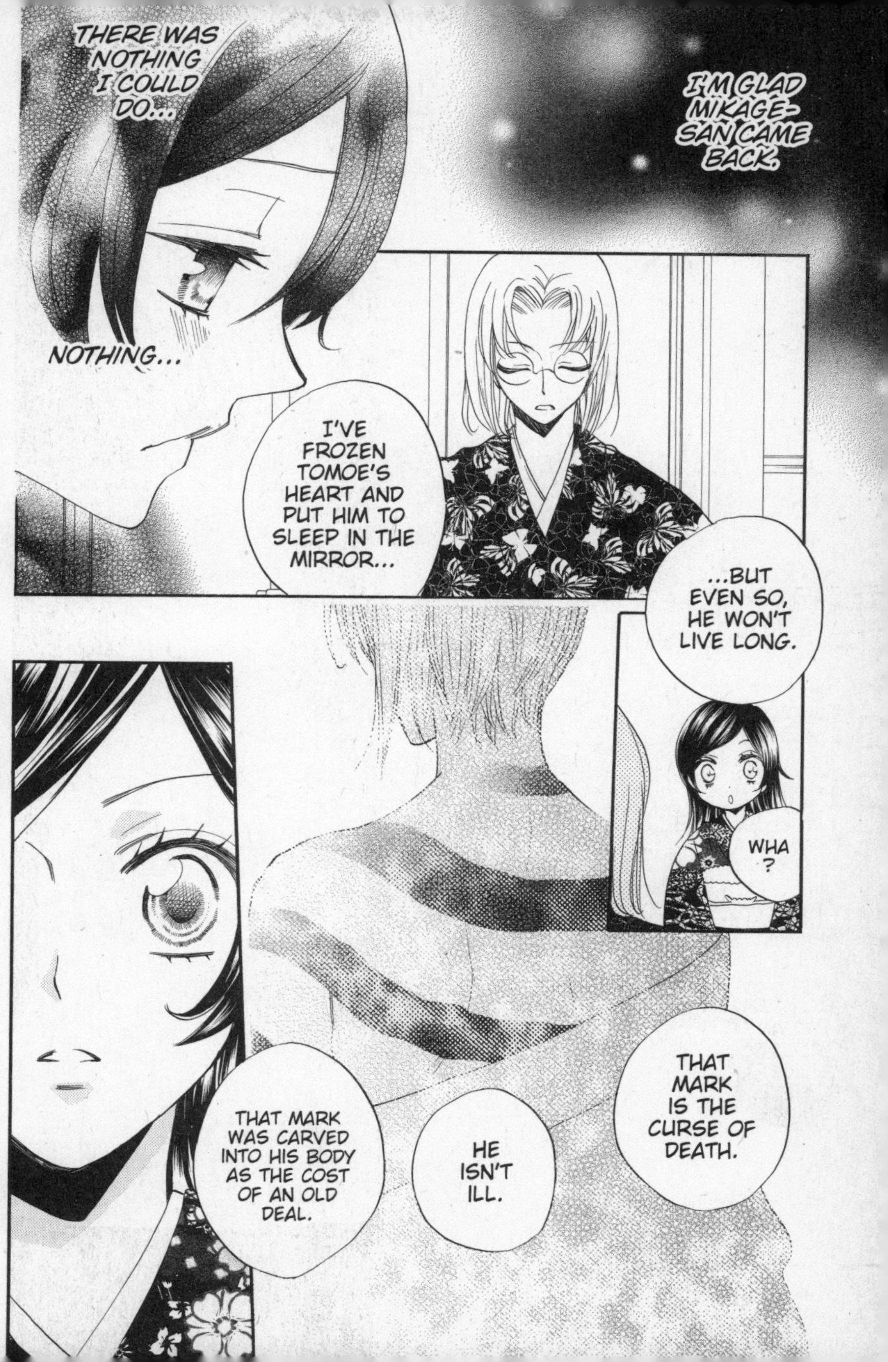
I'M GLAD MIKAGE-SAN CAME BACK.
THERE WAS NOTHING I COULD DO...
NOTHING...
I'VE FROZEN TOMOE'S HEART AND PUT HIM TO SLEEP IN THE MIRROR...
...BUT EVEN SO, HE WON'T LIVE LONG.
WHA?
THAT MARK IS THE CURSE OF DEATH.
HE ISN'T ILL.
THAT MARK WAS CARVED INTO HIS BODY AS THE COST OF AN OLD DEAL.

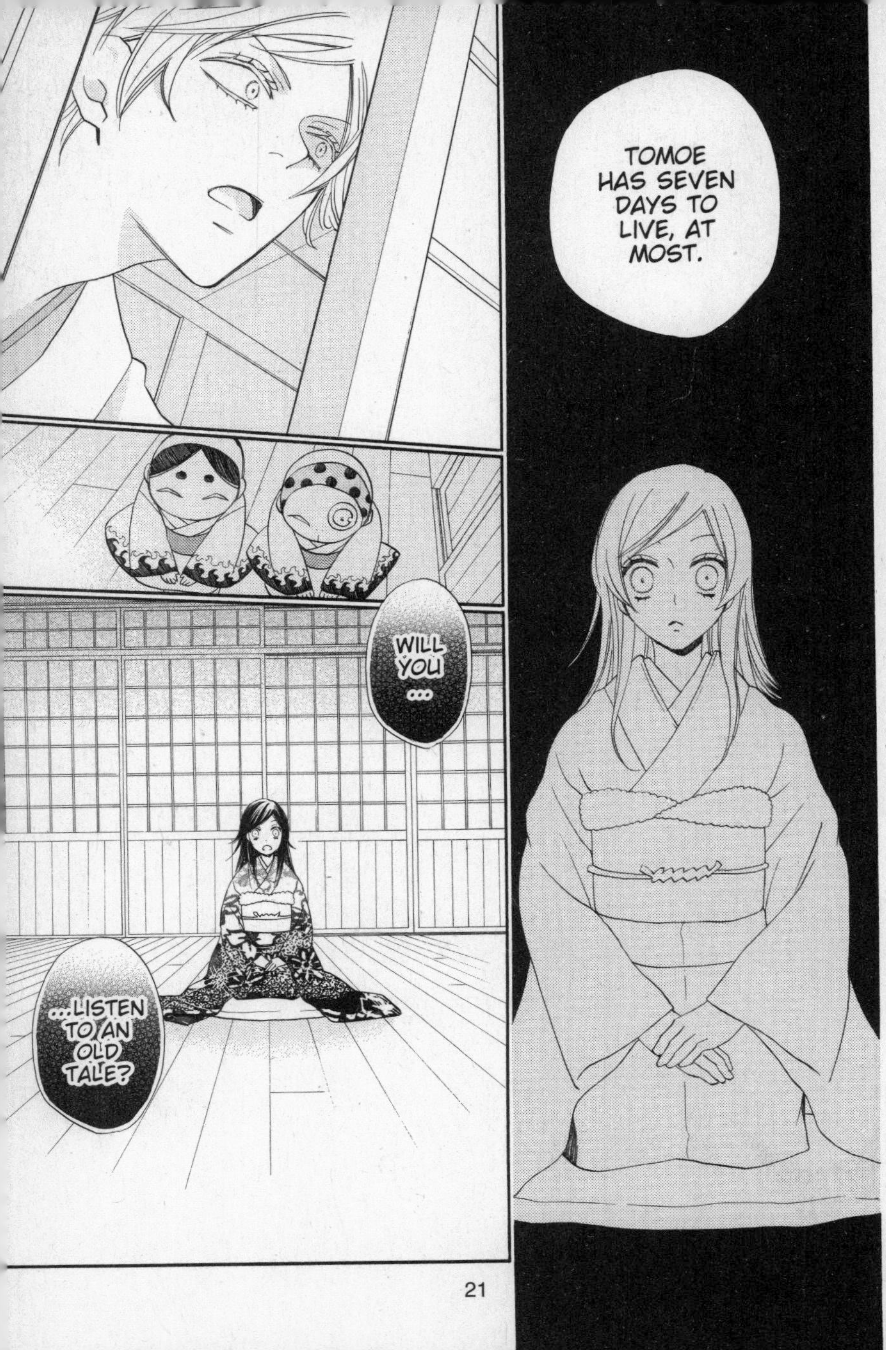
TOMOE HAS SEVEN DAYS TO LIVE, AT MOST.
WILL YOU...
...LISTEN TO AN OLD TALE?

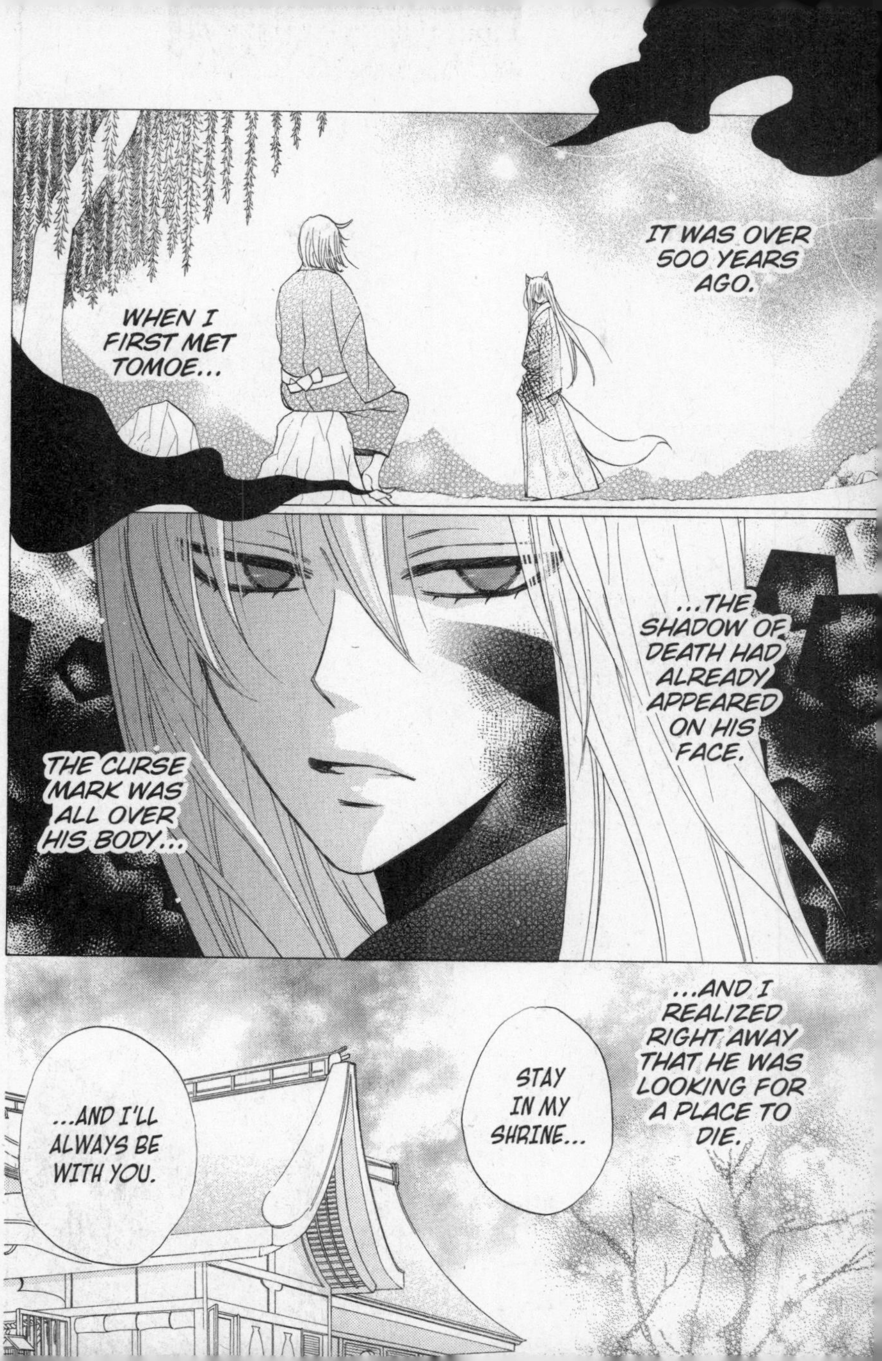
IT WAS OVER 500 YEARS AGO.
WHEN I FIRST MET TOMOE...
...THE SHADOW OF DEATH HAD ALREADY APPEARED ON HIS FACE.
THE CURSE MARK WAS ALL OVER HIS BODY...
...AND I REALIZED RIGHT AWAY THAT HE WAS LOOKING FOR A PLACE TO DIE.
STAY IN MY SHRINE...
...AND I'LL ALWAYS BE WITH YOU.

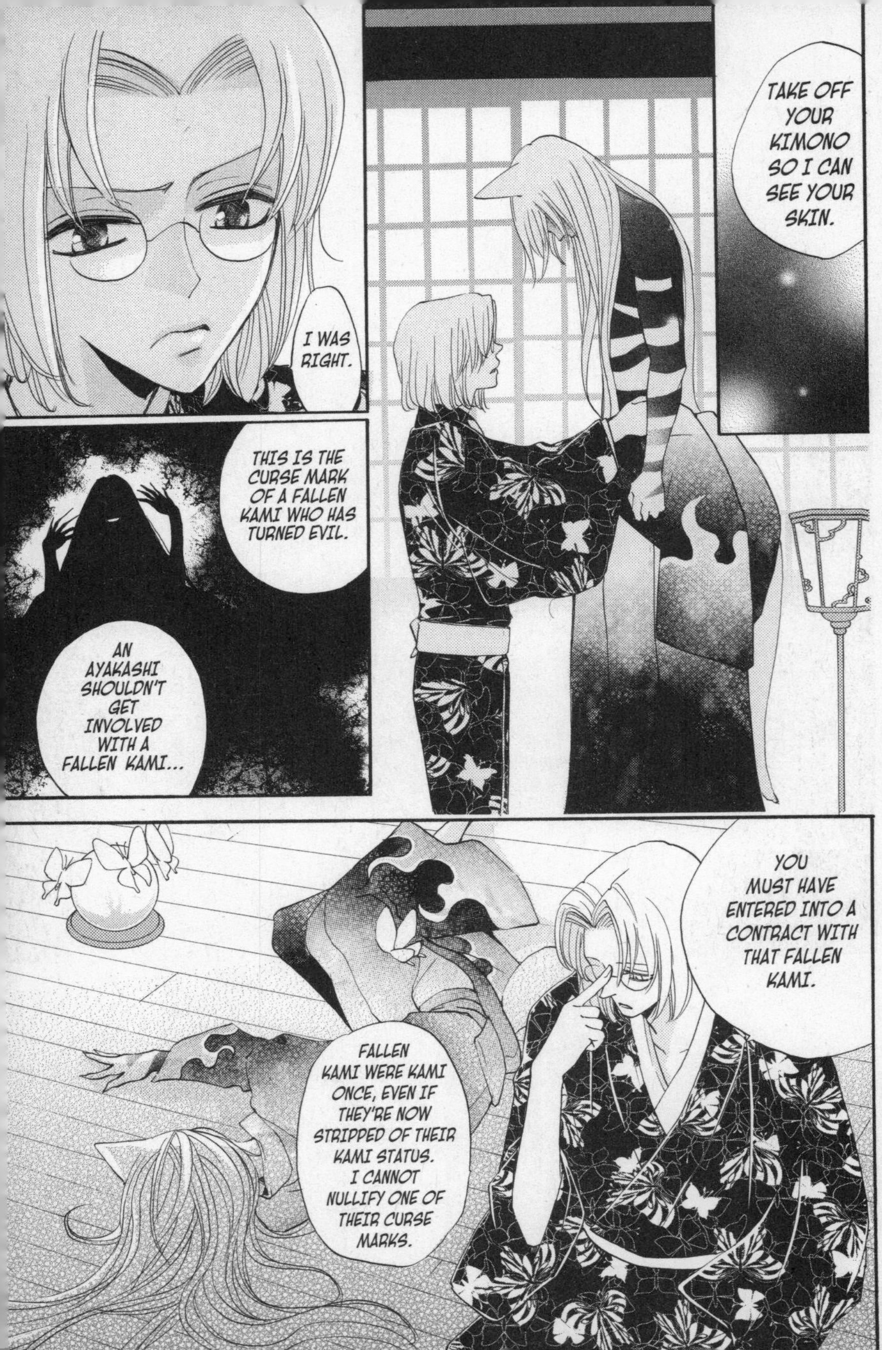
TAKE OFF YOUR KIMONO SO I CAN SEE YOUR SKIN.
I WAS RIGHT.
THIS IS THE CURSE MARK OF A FALLEN KAMI WHO HAS TURNED EVIL.
AN AYAKASHI SHOULDN'T GET INVOLVED WITH A FALLEN KAMI...
YOU MUST HAVE ENTERED INTO A CONTRACT WITH THAT FALLEN KAMI.
FALLEN KAMI WERE KAMI ONCE, EVEN IF THEY'RE NOW STRIPPED OF THEIR KAMI STATUS. I CANNOT NULLIFY ONE OF THEIR CURSE MARKS.

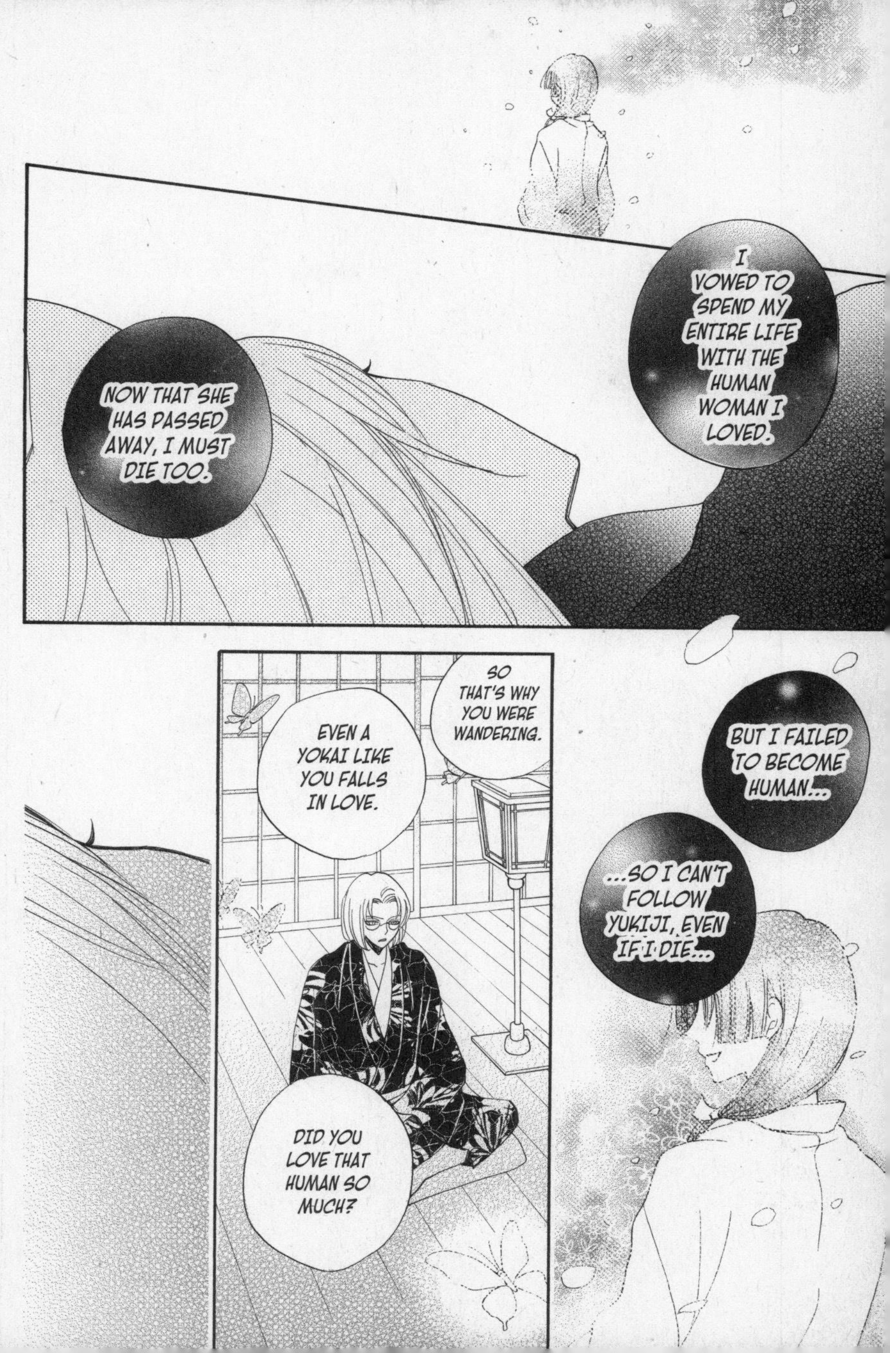
I VOWED TO SPEND MY ENTIRE LIFE WITH THE HUMAN WOMAN I LOVED.
NOW THAT SHE HAS PASSED AWAY, I MUST DIE TOO.
BUT I FAILED TO BECOME HUMAN...
...SO I CAN'T FOLLOW YUKIJI, EVEN IF I DIE...
SO THAT'S WHY YOU WERE WANDERING.
EVEN A YOKAI LIKE YOU FALLS IN LOVE.
DID YOU LOVE THAT HUMAN SO MUCH?

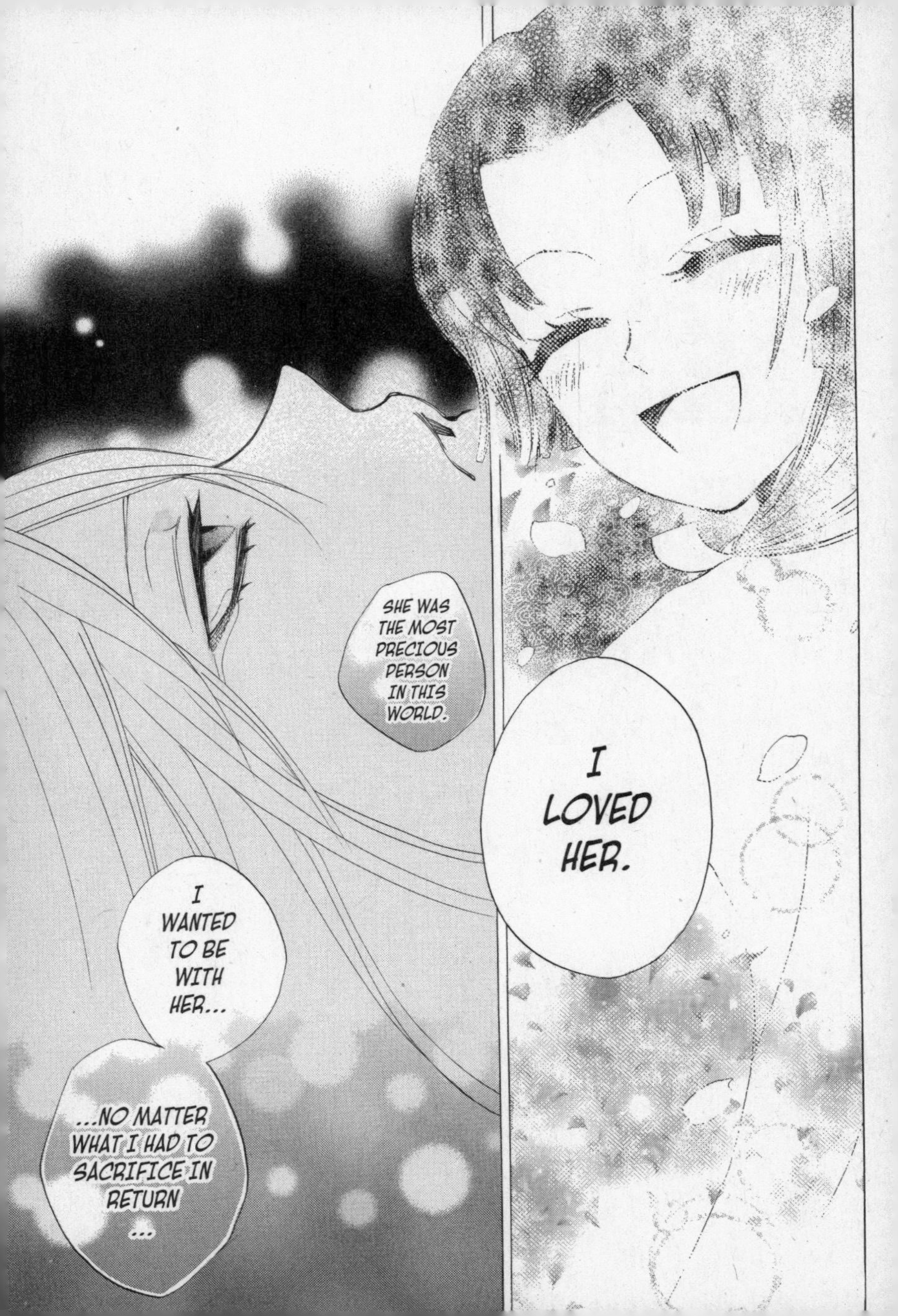
I LOVED HER.
SHE WAS THE MOST PRECIOUS PERSON IN THIS WORLD.
I WANTED TO BE WITH HER...
...NO MATTER WHAT I HAD TO SACRIFICE IN RETURN...

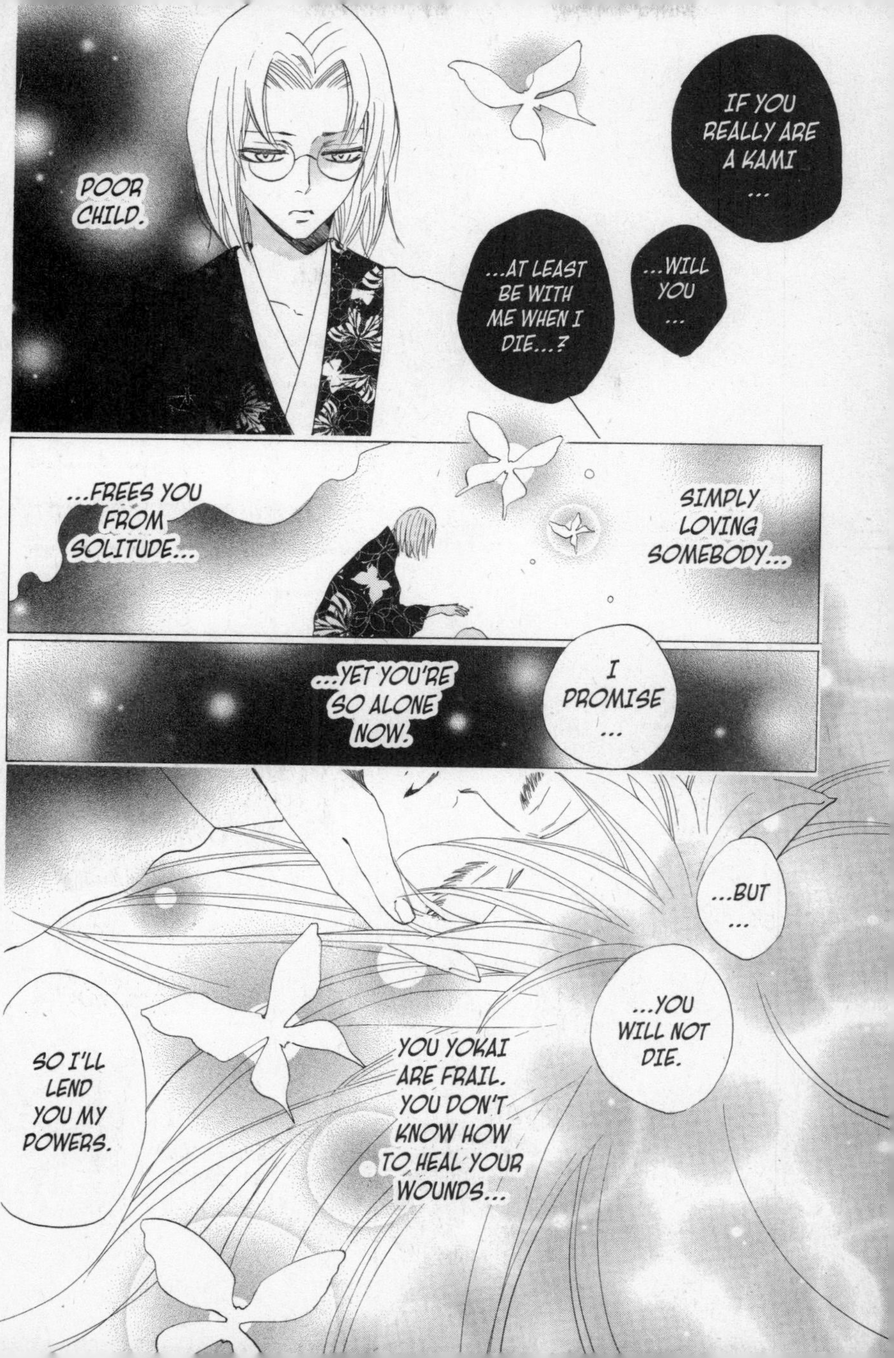
IF YOU REALLY ARE A KAMI ...
...WILL YOU ...
...AT LEAST BE WITH ME WHEN I DIE...?
POOR CHILD.
SIMPLY LOVING SOMEBODY...
...FREES YOU FROM SOLITUDE...
I PROMISE ...
...YET YOU'RE SO ALONE NOW.
...BUT ...
...YOU WILL NOT DIE.
YOU YOKAI ARE FRAIL. YOU DON'T KNOW HOW TO HEAL YOUR WOUNDS...
SO I'LL LEND YOU MY POWERS.

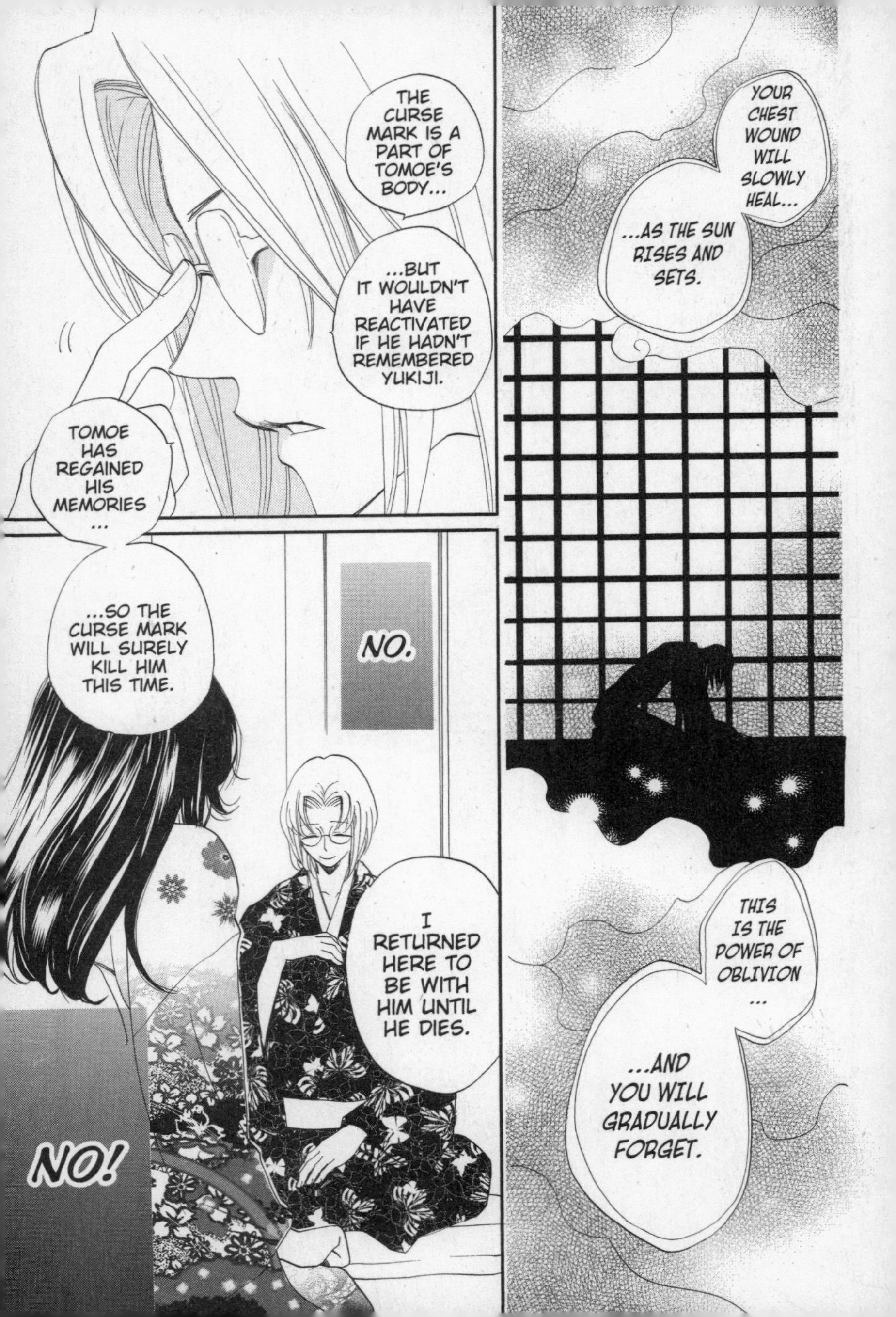
YOUR CHEST WOUND WILL SLOWLY HEAL...
...AS THE SUN RISES AND SETS.
THIS IS THE POWER OF OBLIVION...
...AND YOU WILL GRADUALLY FORGET.
THE CURSE MARK IS A PART OF TOMOE'S BODY...
...BUT IT WOULDN'T HAVE REACTIVATED IF HE HADN'T REMEMBERED YUKIJI.
TOMOE HAS REGAINED HIS MEMORIES...
...SO THE CURSE MARK WILL SURELY KILL HIM THIS TIME.
NO.
I RETURNED HERE TO BE WITH HIM UNTIL HE DIES.
NO!

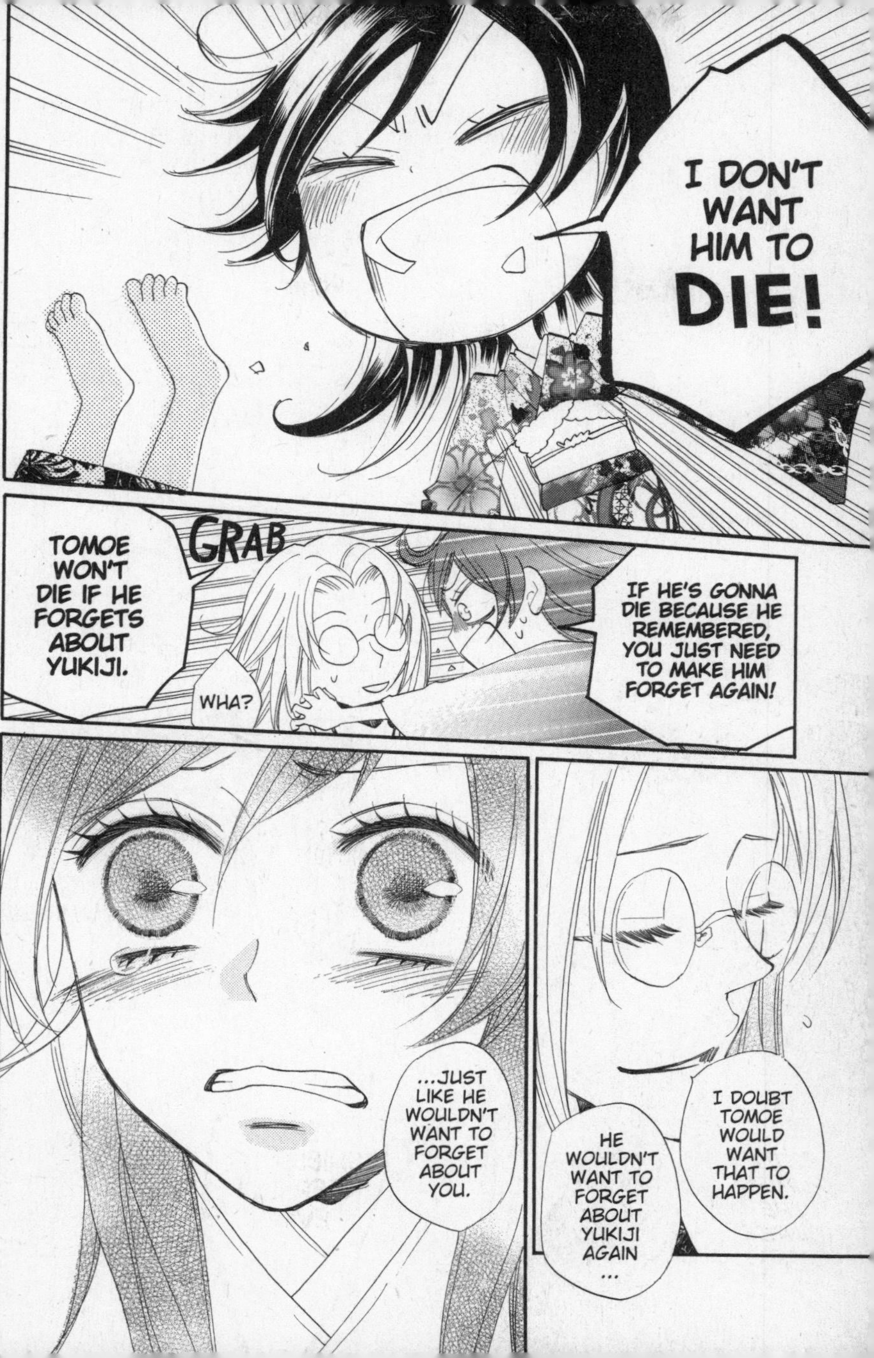
I DON'T WANT HIM TO DIE!
IF HE'S GONNA DIE BECAUSE HE REMEMBERED, YOU JUST NEED TO MAKE HIM FORGET AGAIN!
GRAB
WHA?
TOMOE WON'T DIE IF HE FORGETS ABOUT YUKIJI.
I DOUBT TOMOE WOULD WANT THAT TO HAPPEN.
HE WOULDN'T WANT TO FORGET ABOUT YUKIJI AGAIN ...
...JUST LIKE HE WOULDN'T WANT TO FORGET ABOUT YOU.

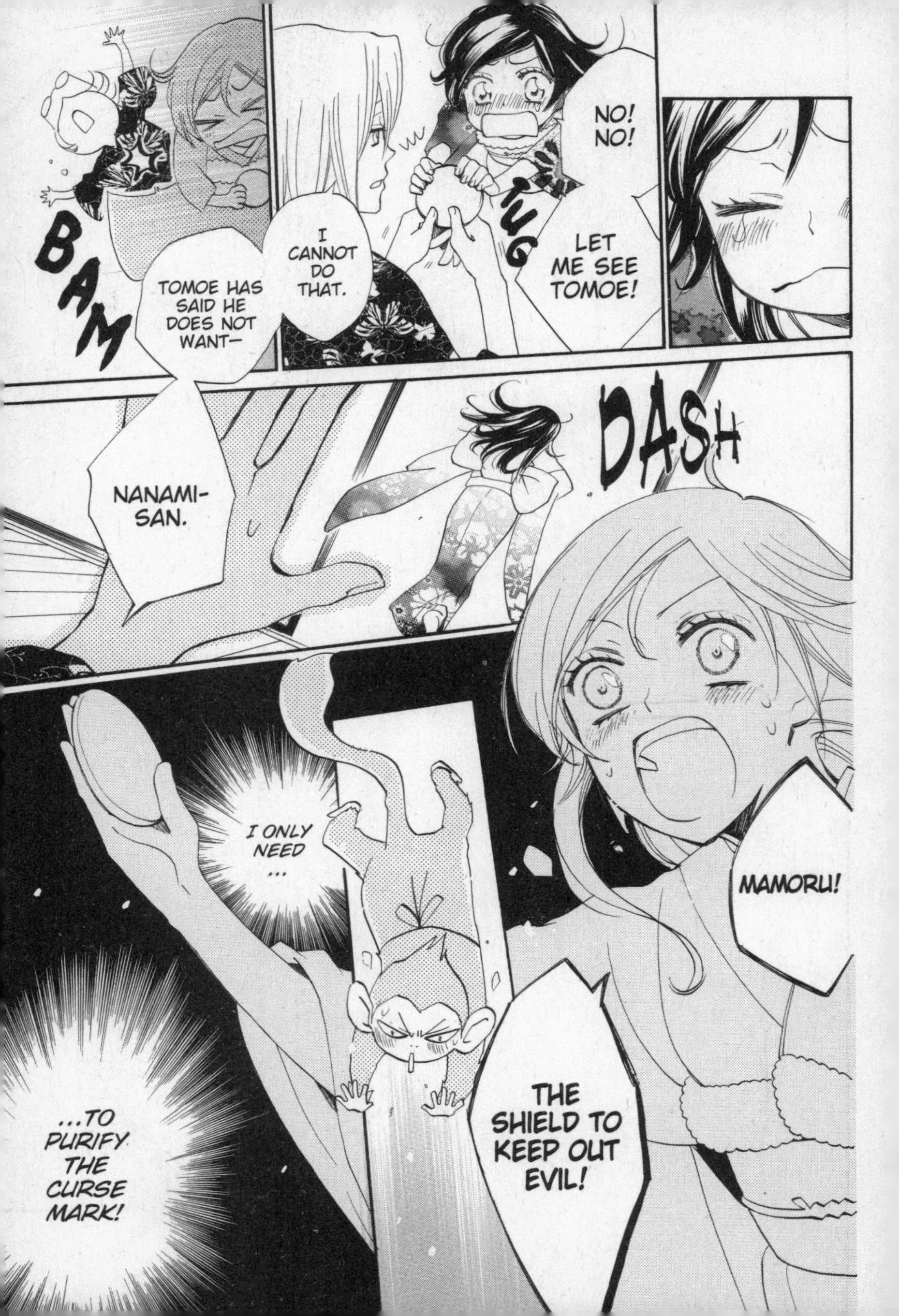
NO! NO!
LET ME SEE TOMOE!
TUG
I CANNOT DO THAT.
TOMOE HAS SAID HE DOES NOT WANT—
BAM
DASH
NANAMI-SAN.
MAMORU!
THE SHIELD TO KEEP OUT EVIL!
I ONLY NEED ...
...TO PURIFY THE CURSE MARK!

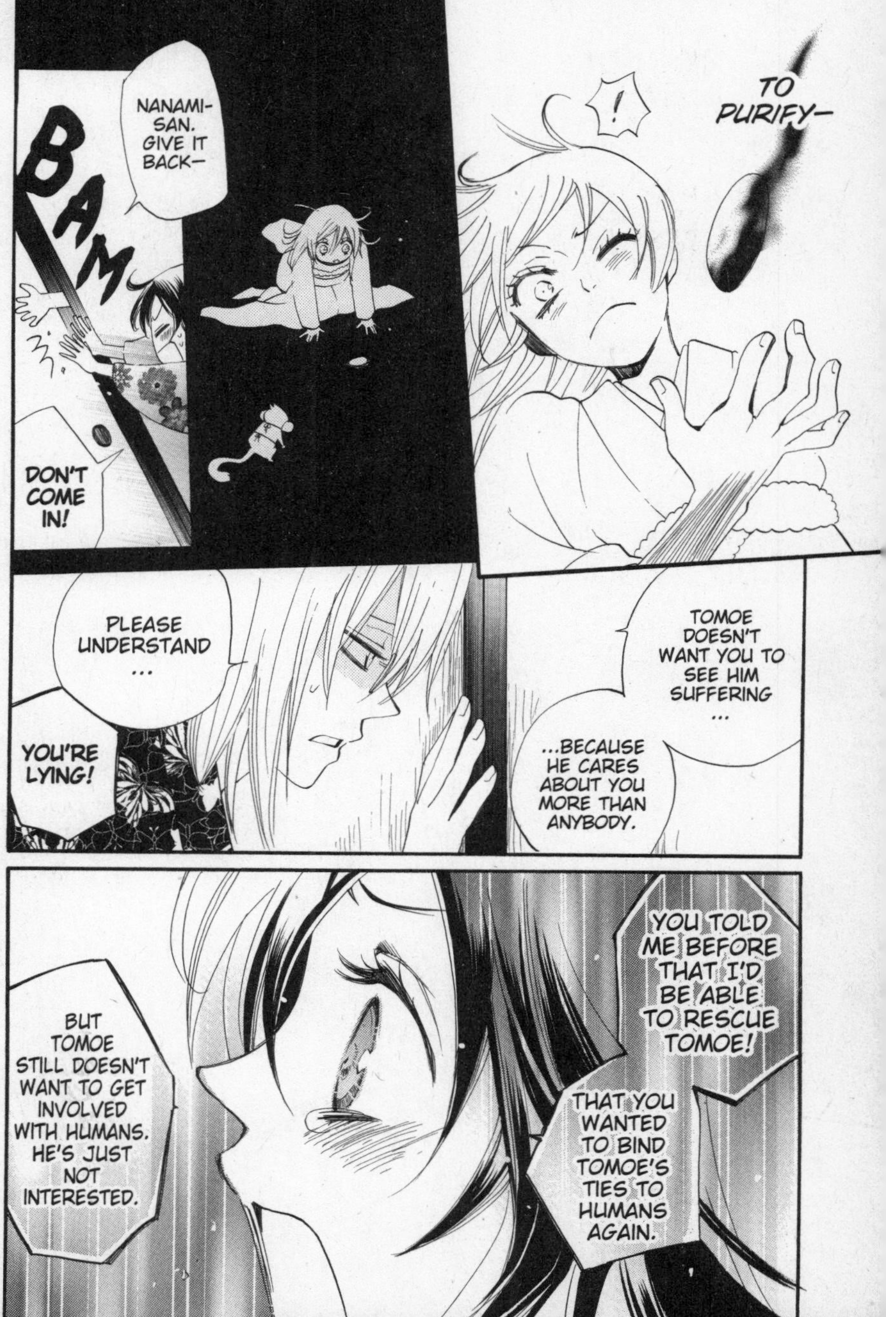
!
TO PURIFY—
NANAMI-SAN. GIVE IT BACK—
BAM
DON'T COME IN!
TOMOE DOESN'T WANT YOU TO SEE HIM SUFFERING ...
...BECAUSE HE CARES ABOUT YOU MORE THAN ANYBODY.
PLEASE UNDERSTAND ...
YOU'RE LYING!
YOU TOLD ME BEFORE THAT I'D BE ABLE TO RESCUE TOMOE!
THAT YOU WANTED TO BIND TOMOE'S TIES TO HUMANS AGAIN.
BUT TOMOE STILL DOESN'T WANT TO GET INVOLVED WITH HUMANS. HE'S JUST NOT INTERESTED.

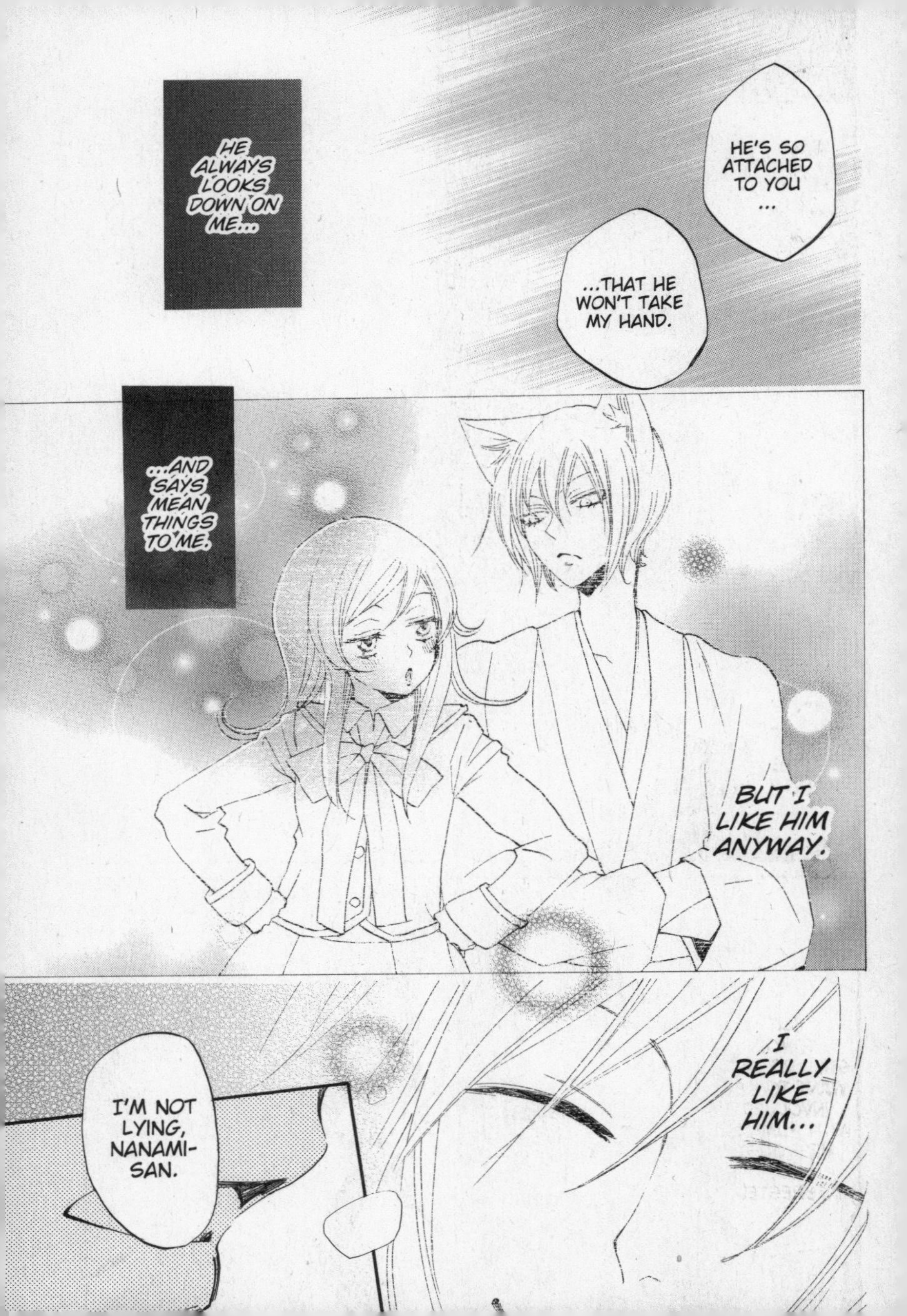
HE'S SO ATTACHED TO YOU ...
...THAT HE WON'T TAKE MY HAND.
HE ALWAYS LOOKS DOWN ON ME...
...AND SAYS MEAN THINGS TO ME.
BUT I LIKE HIM ANYWAY.
I REALLY LIKE HIM...
I'M NOT LYING, NANAMI-SAN.

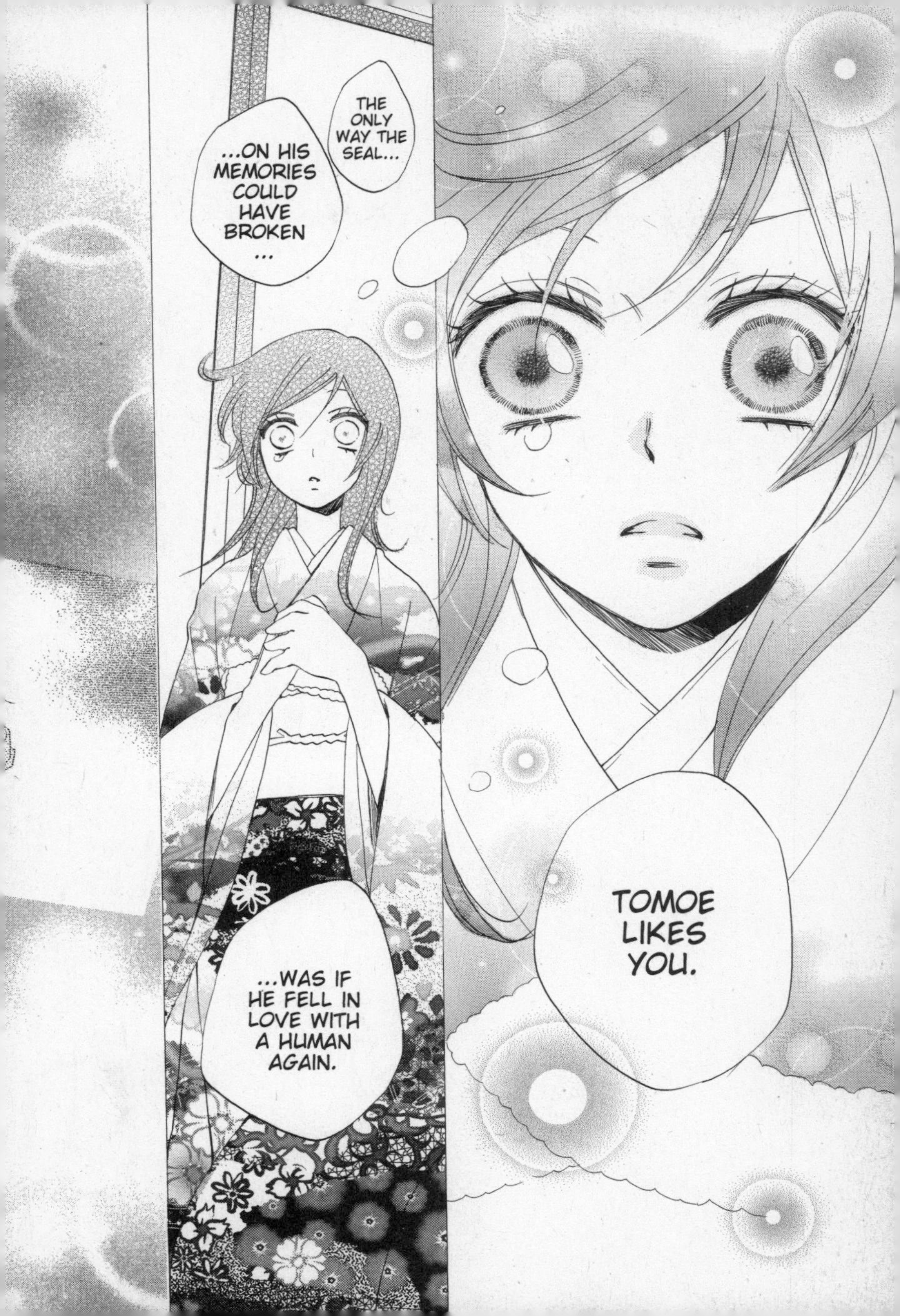
TOMOE LIKES YOU.
THE ONLY WAY THE SEAL...
...ON HIS MEMORIES COULD HAVE BROKEN...
...WAS IF HE FELL IN LOVE WITH A HUMAN AGAIN.

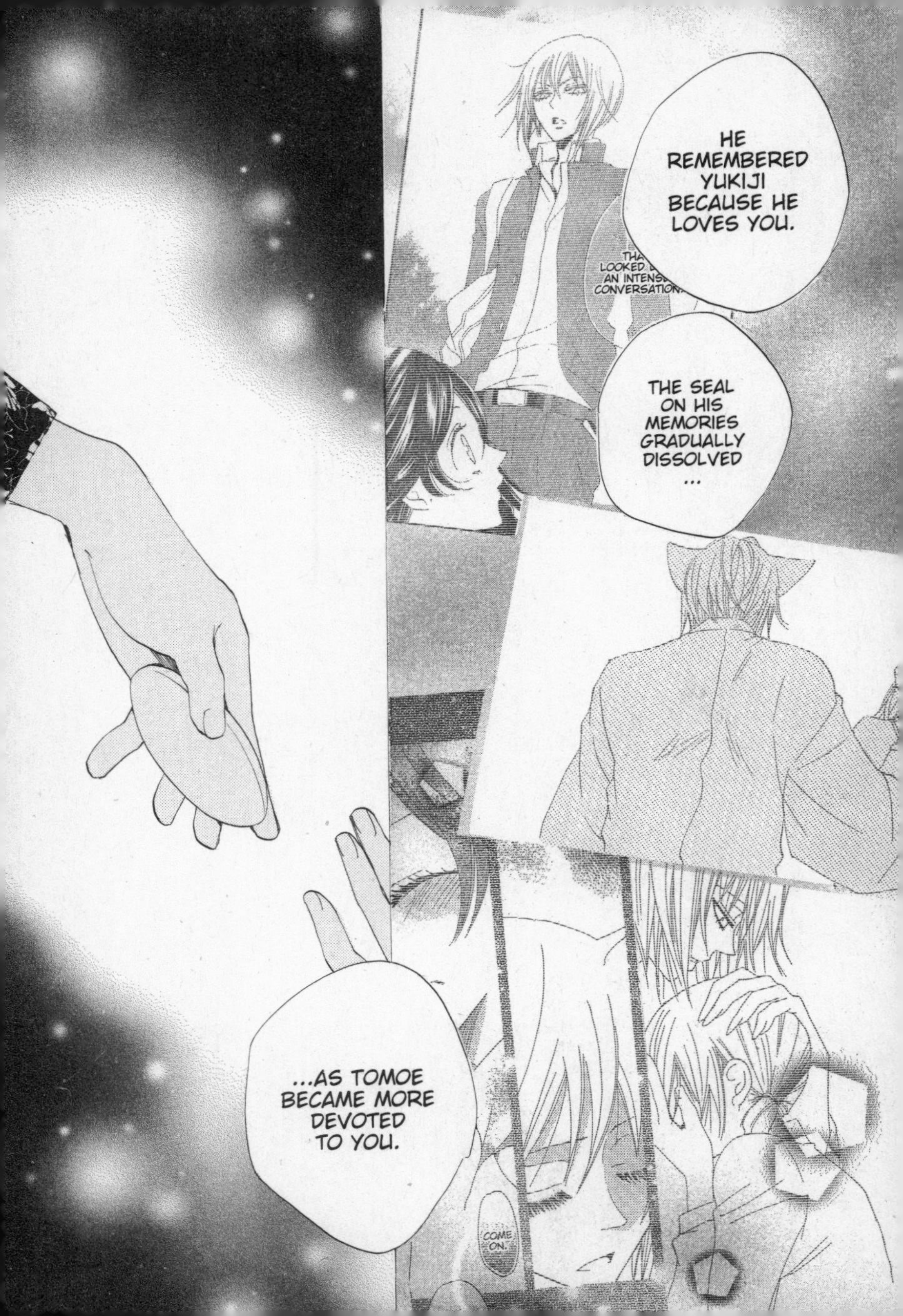
HE REMEMBERED YUKIJI BECAUSE HE LOVES YOU.
THE SEAL ON HIS MEMORIES GRADUALLY DISSOLVED ...
COME ON.
...AS TOMOE BECAME MORE DEVOTED TO YOU.

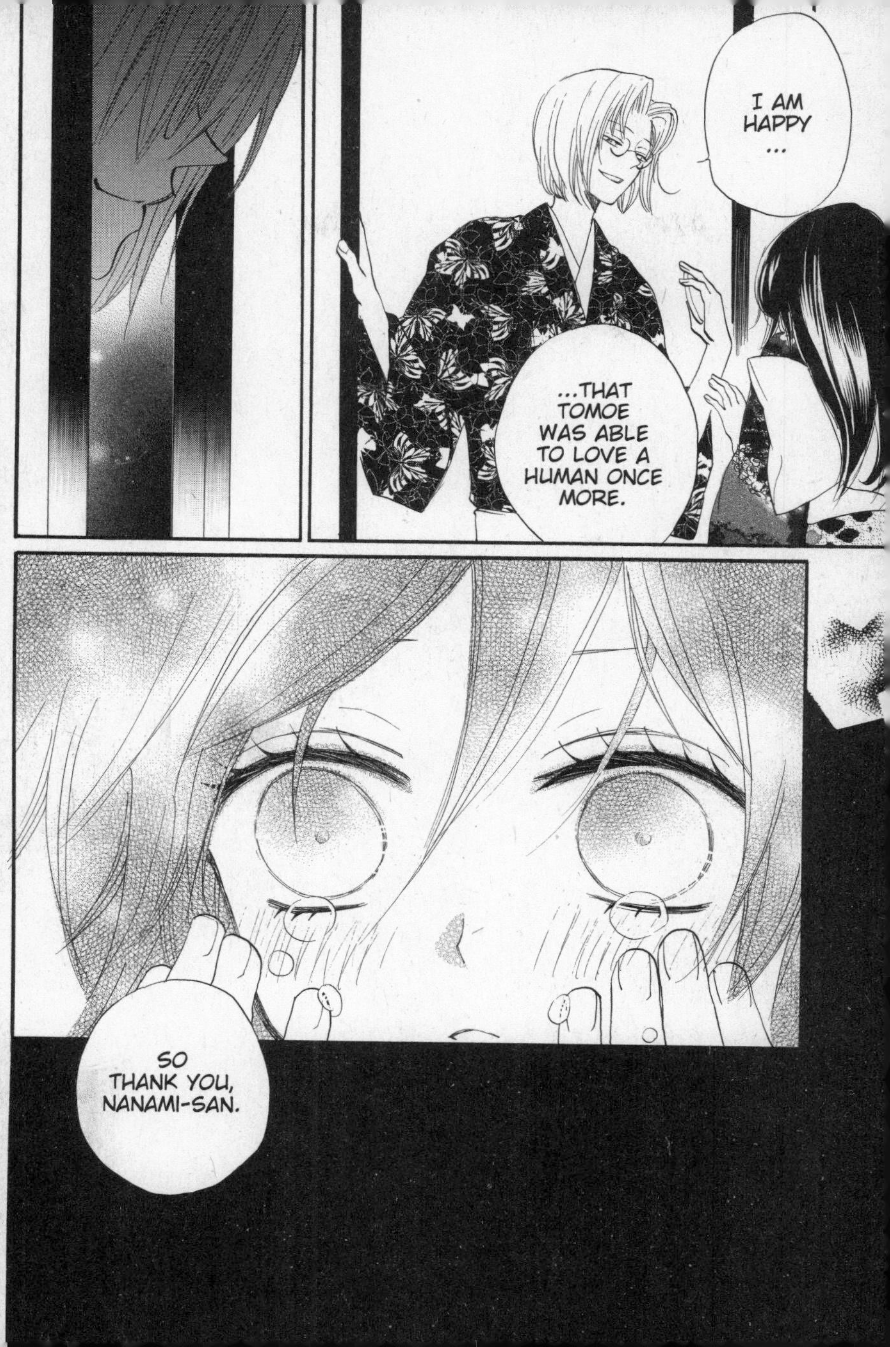
I AM HAPPY ...
...THAT TOMOE WAS ABLE TO LOVE A HUMAN ONCE MORE.
SO THANK YOU, NANAMI-SAN.

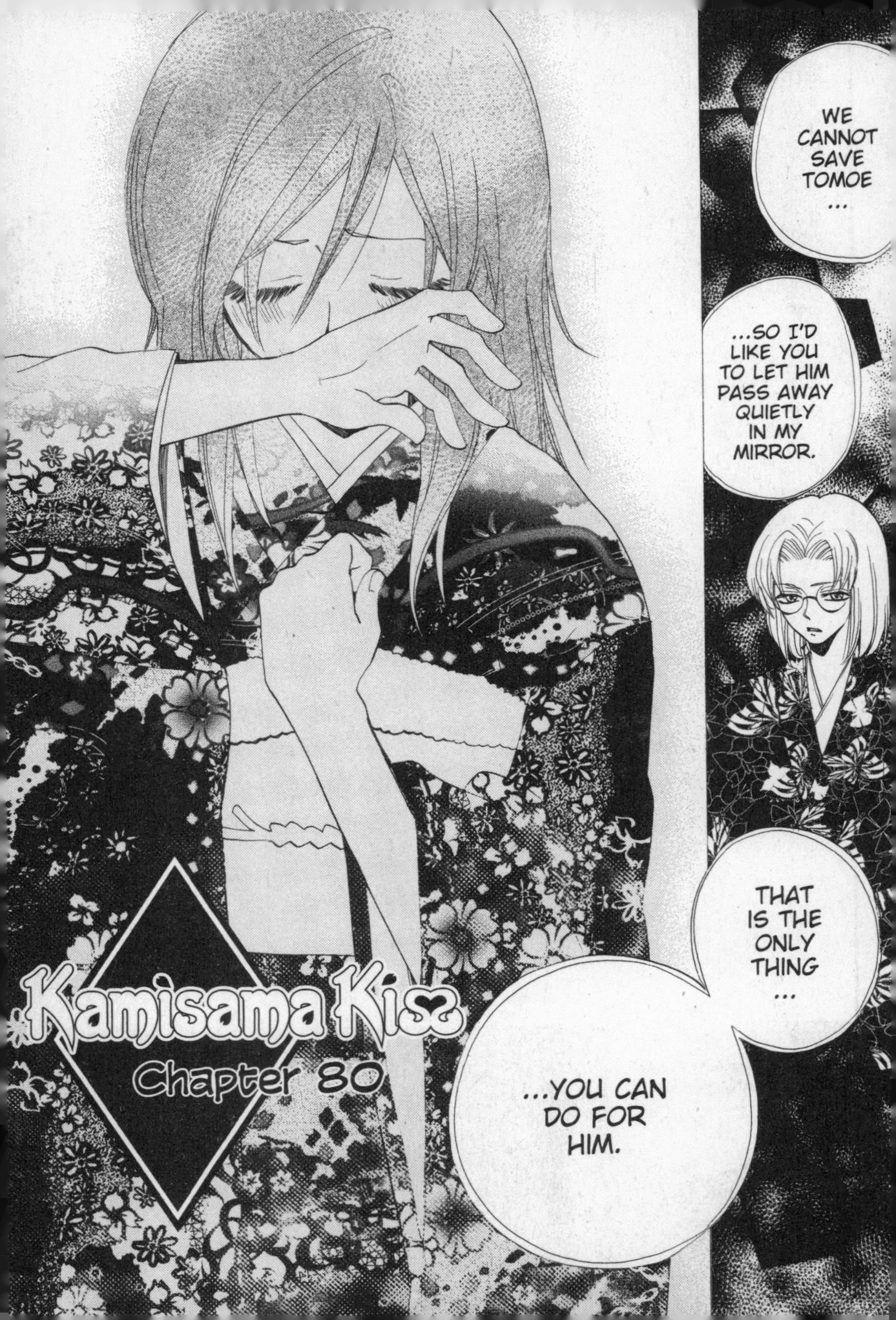
WE CANNOT SAVE TOMOE ...
...SO I'D LIKE YOU TO LET HIM PASS AWAY QUIETLY IN MY MIRROR.
THAT IS THE ONLY THING ...
...YOU CAN DO FOR HIM.
Kamisama Kiss
Chapter 80

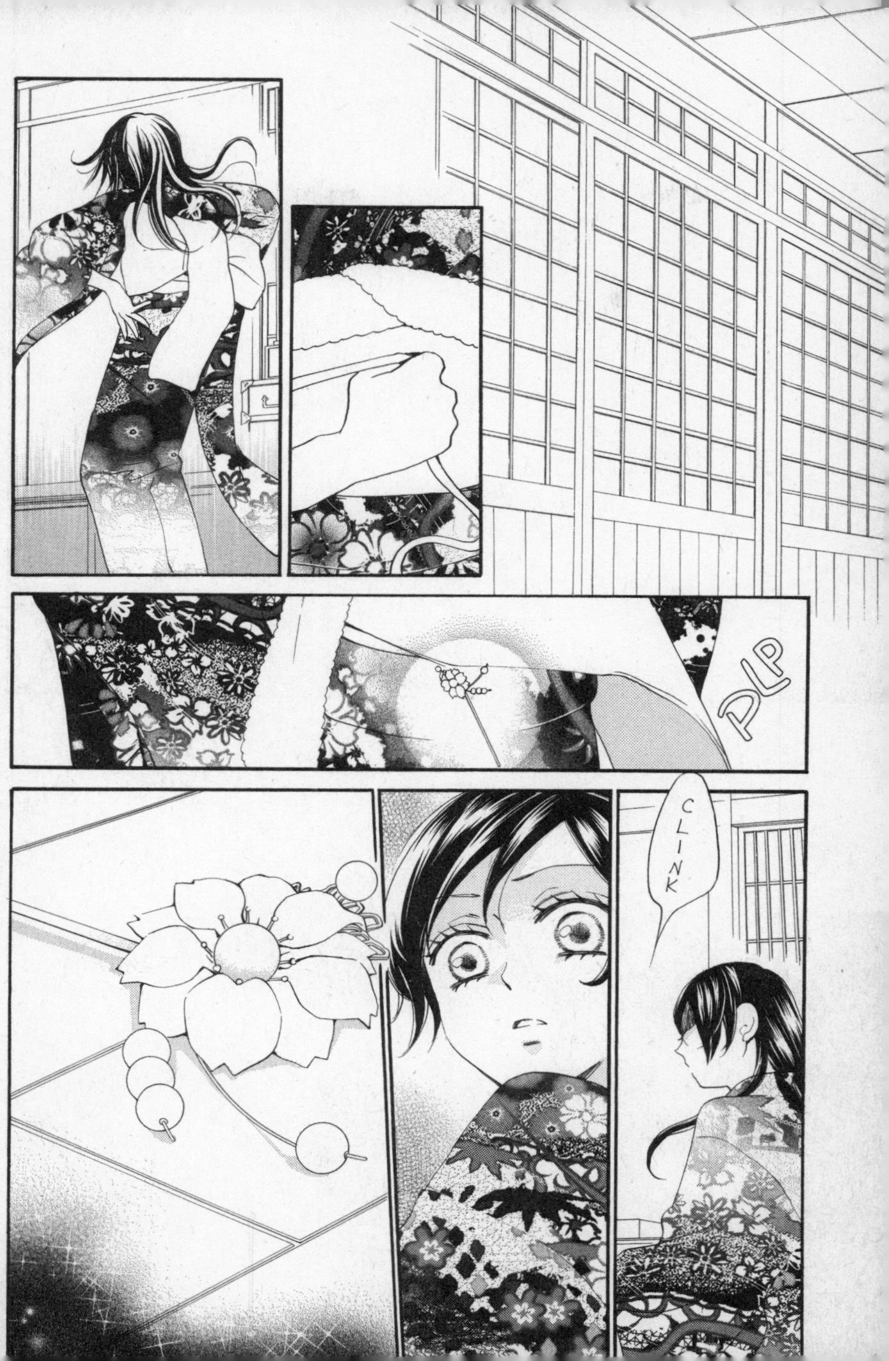
DLP
CLINK

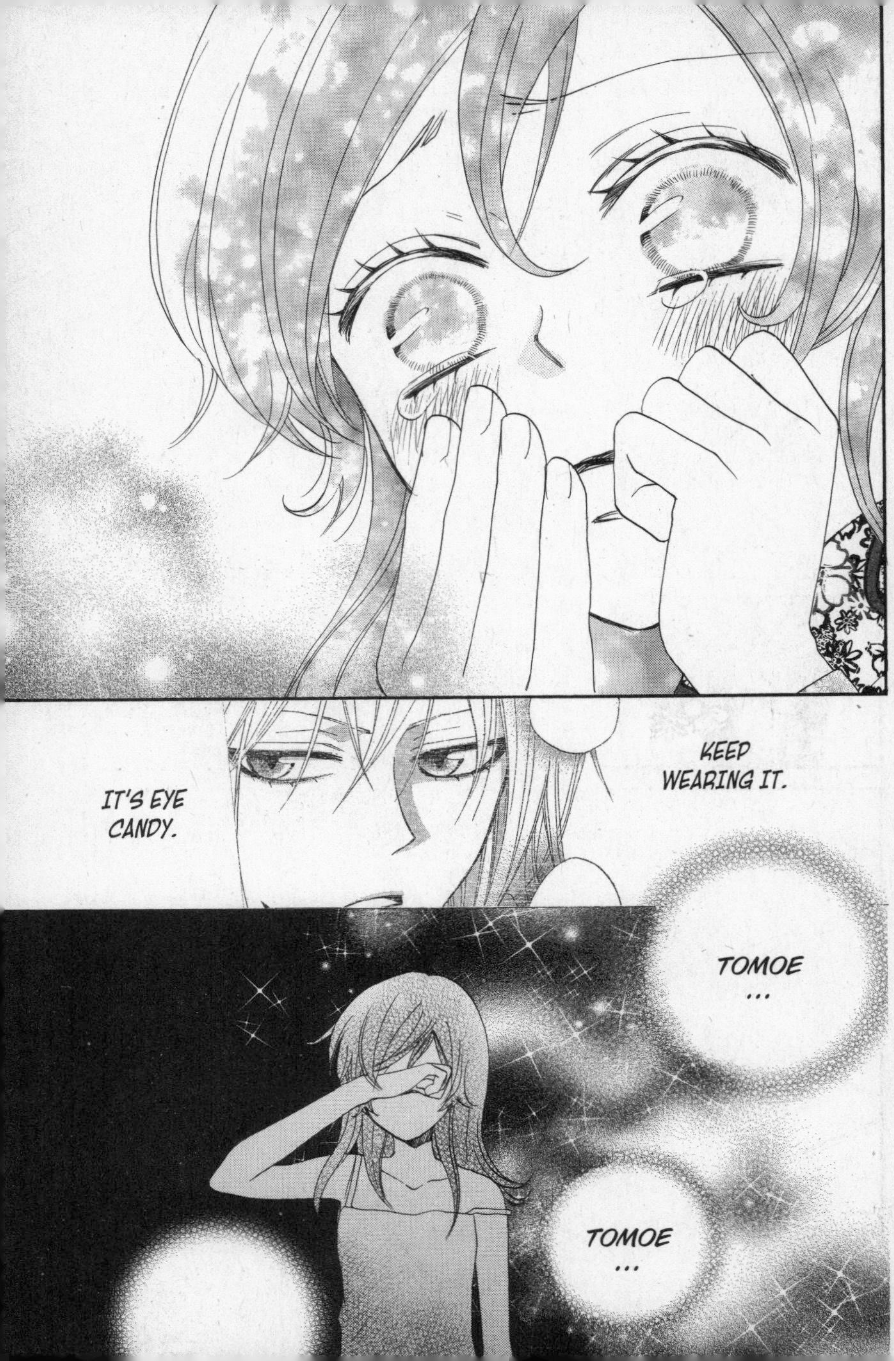
KEEP WEARING IT.
IT'S EYE CANDY.
TOMOE ...
TOMOE ...

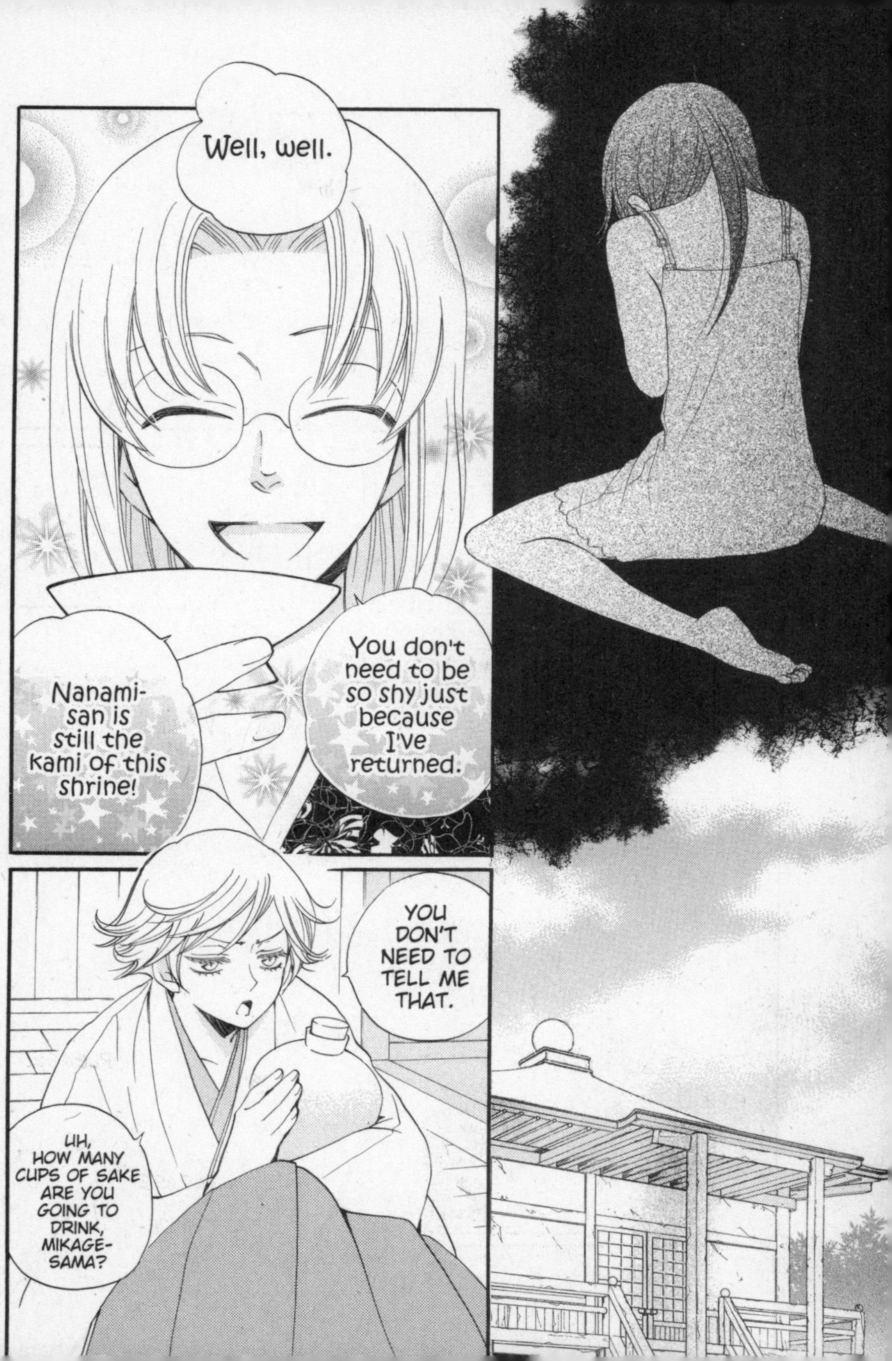
Well, well.
You don't need to be so shy just because I've returned.
Nanami-san is still the kami of this shrine!
YOU DON'T NEED TO TELL ME THAT.
UH, HOW MANY CUPS OF SAKE ARE YOU GOING TO DRINK, MIKAGE-SAMA?

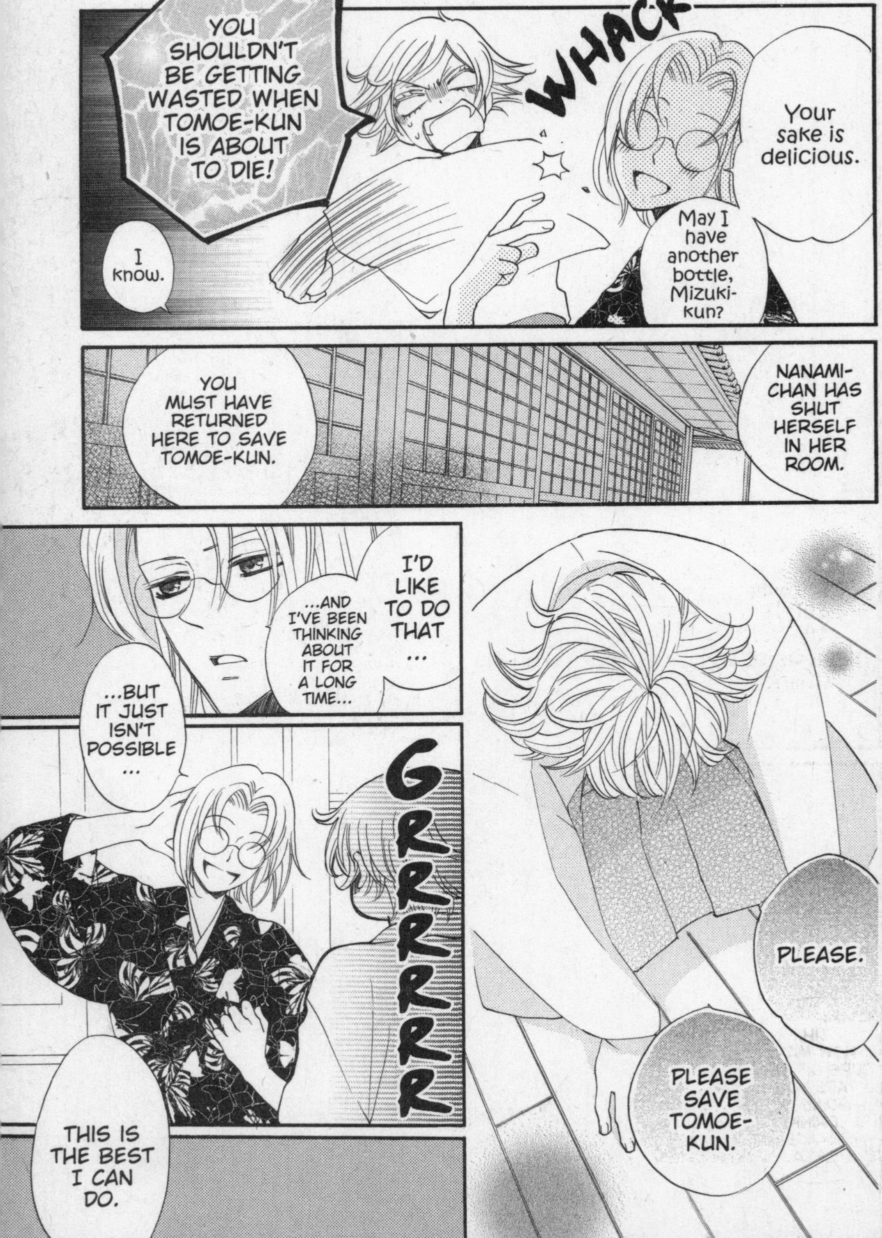
Your sake is delicious.
May I have another bottle, Mizuki-kun?
WHACK
YOU SHOULDN'T BE GETTING WASTED WHEN TOMOE-KUN IS ABOUT TO DIE!
I know.
NANAMI-CHAN HAS SHUT HERSELF IN HER ROOM.
YOU MUST HAVE RETURNED HERE TO SAVE TOMOE-KUN.
PLEASE.
PLEASE SAVE TOMOE-KUN.
I'D LIKE TO DO THAT...
...AND I'VE BEEN THINKING ABOUT IT FOR A LONG TIME...
...BUT IT JUST ISN'T POSSIBLE...
GRRRRRR
THIS IS THE BEST I CAN DO.

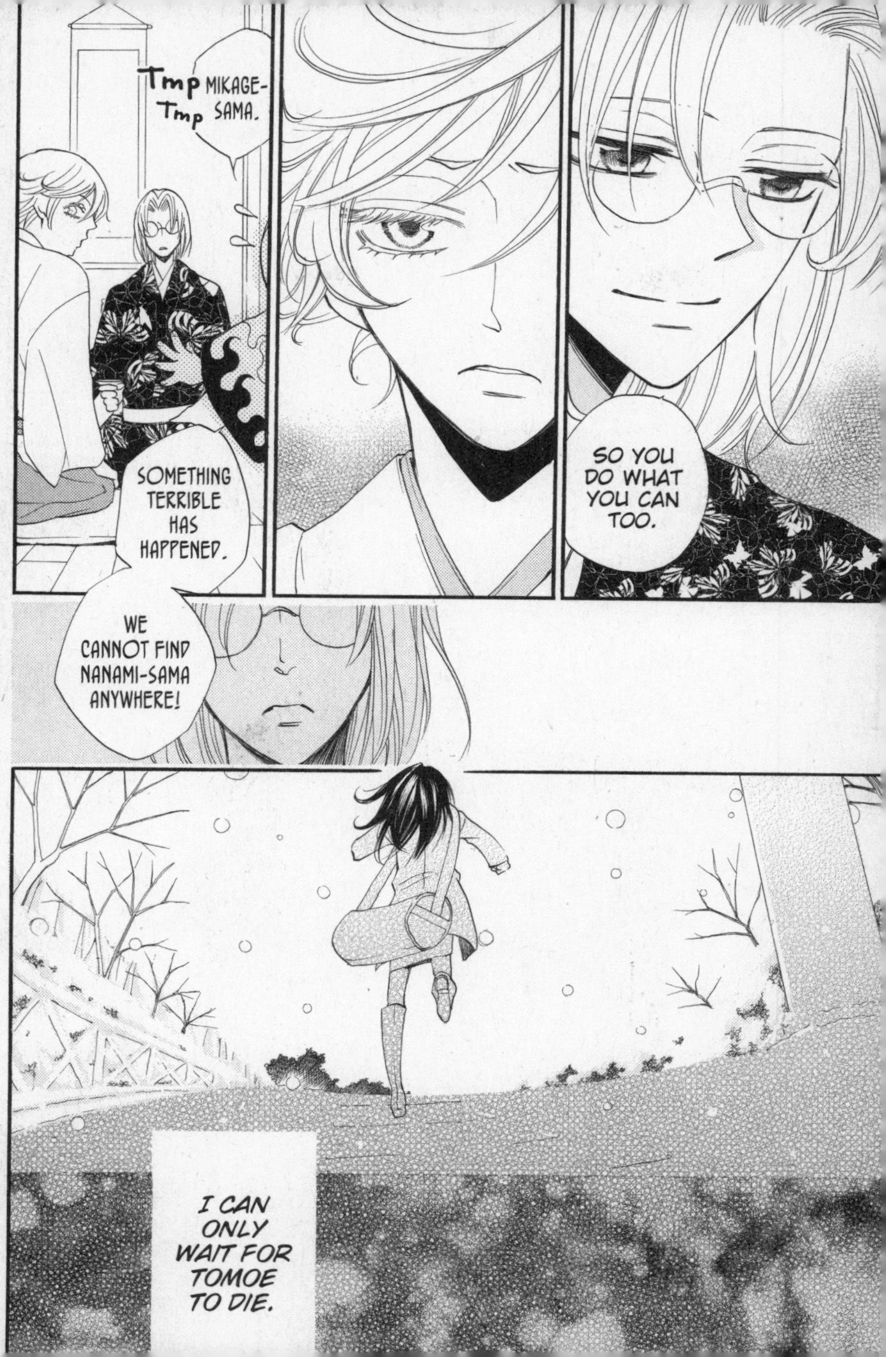
SO YOU DO WHAT YOU CAN TOO.
Tmp Tmp
MIKAGE-SAMA.
SOMETHING TERRIBLE HAS HAPPENED.
WE CANNOT FIND NANAMI-SAMA ANYWHERE!
I CAN ONLY WAIT FOR TOMOE TO DIE.

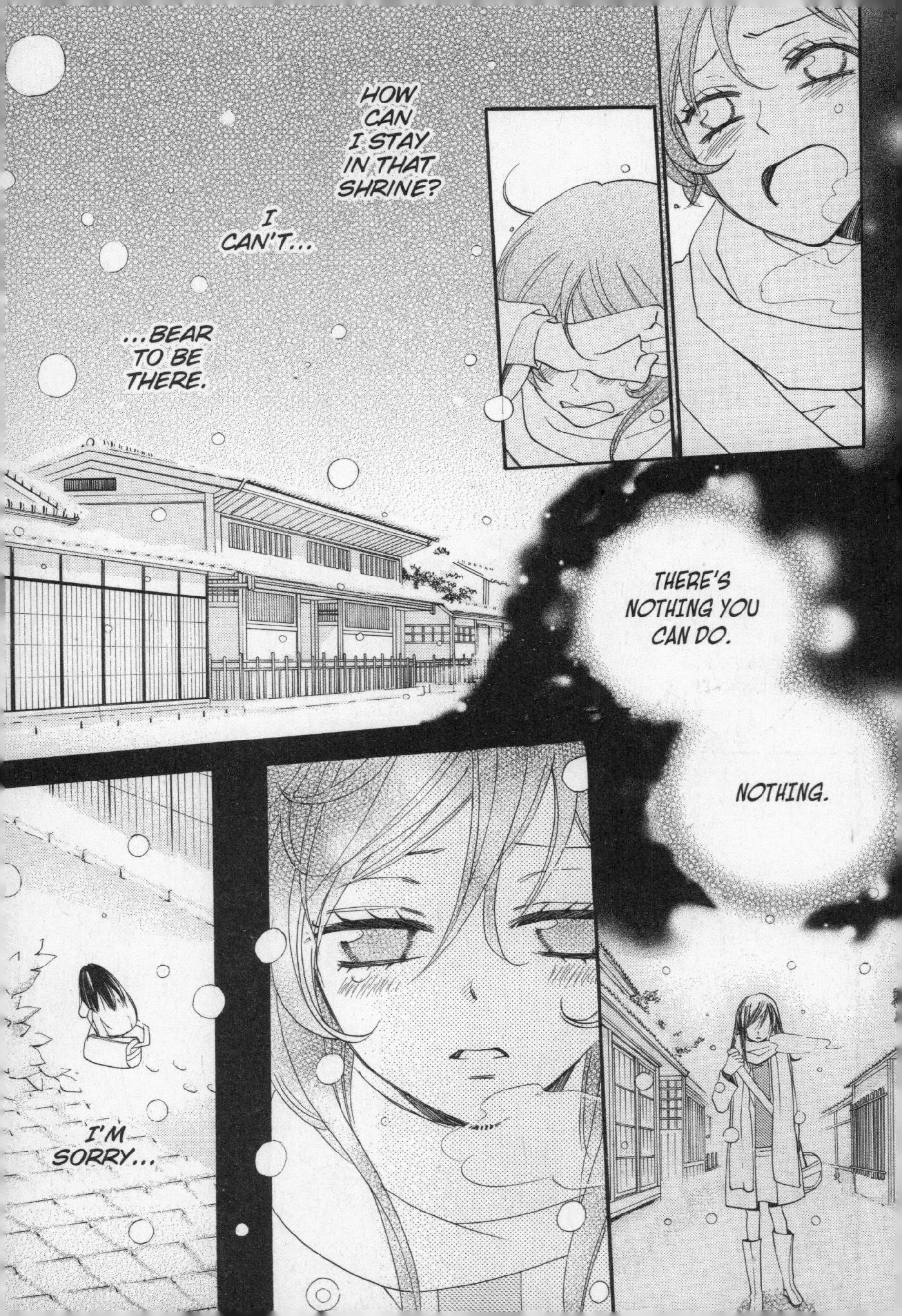
HOW CAN I STAY IN THAT SHRINE?
I CAN'T...
...BEAR TO BE THERE.
THERE'S NOTHING YOU CAN DO.
NOTHING.
I'M SORRY...

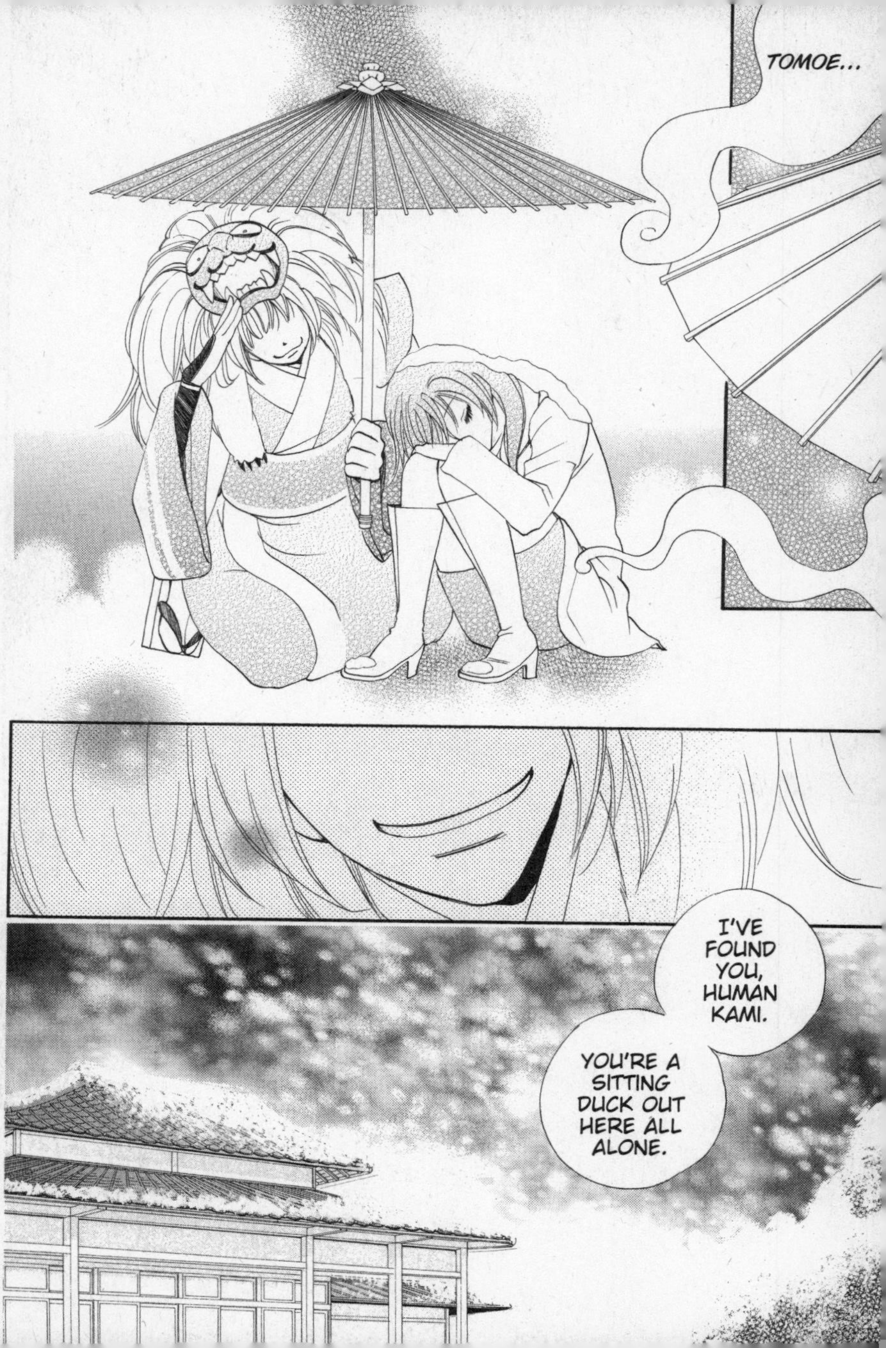
TOMOE...
I'VE FOUND YOU, HUMAN KAMI.
YOU'RE A SITTING DUCK OUT HERE ALL ALONE.

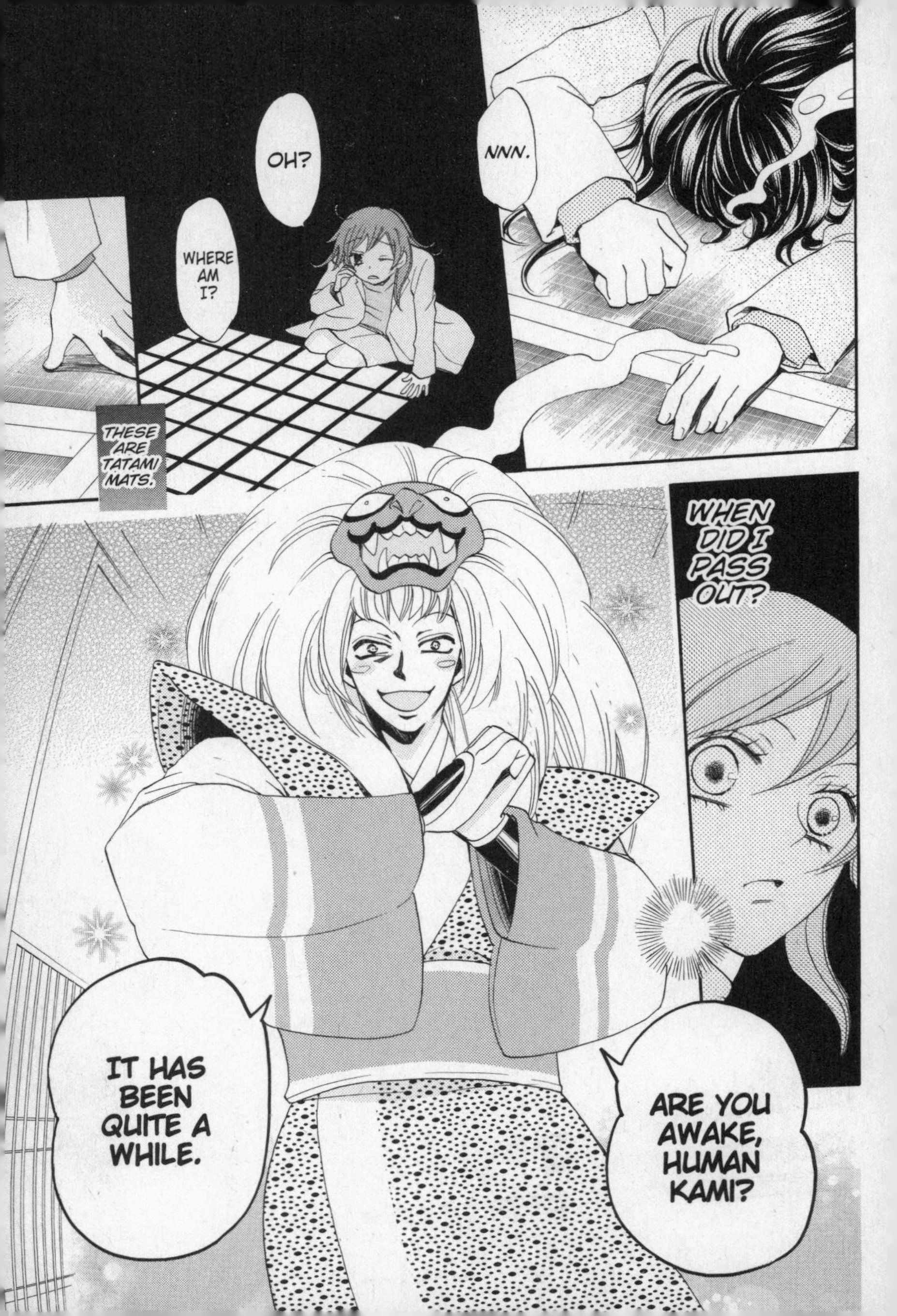
NNN.
OH?
WHERE AM I?
THESE ARE TATAMI MATS.
WHEN DID I PASS OUT?
ARE YOU AWAKE, HUMAN KAMI?
IT HAS BEEN QUITE A WHILE.

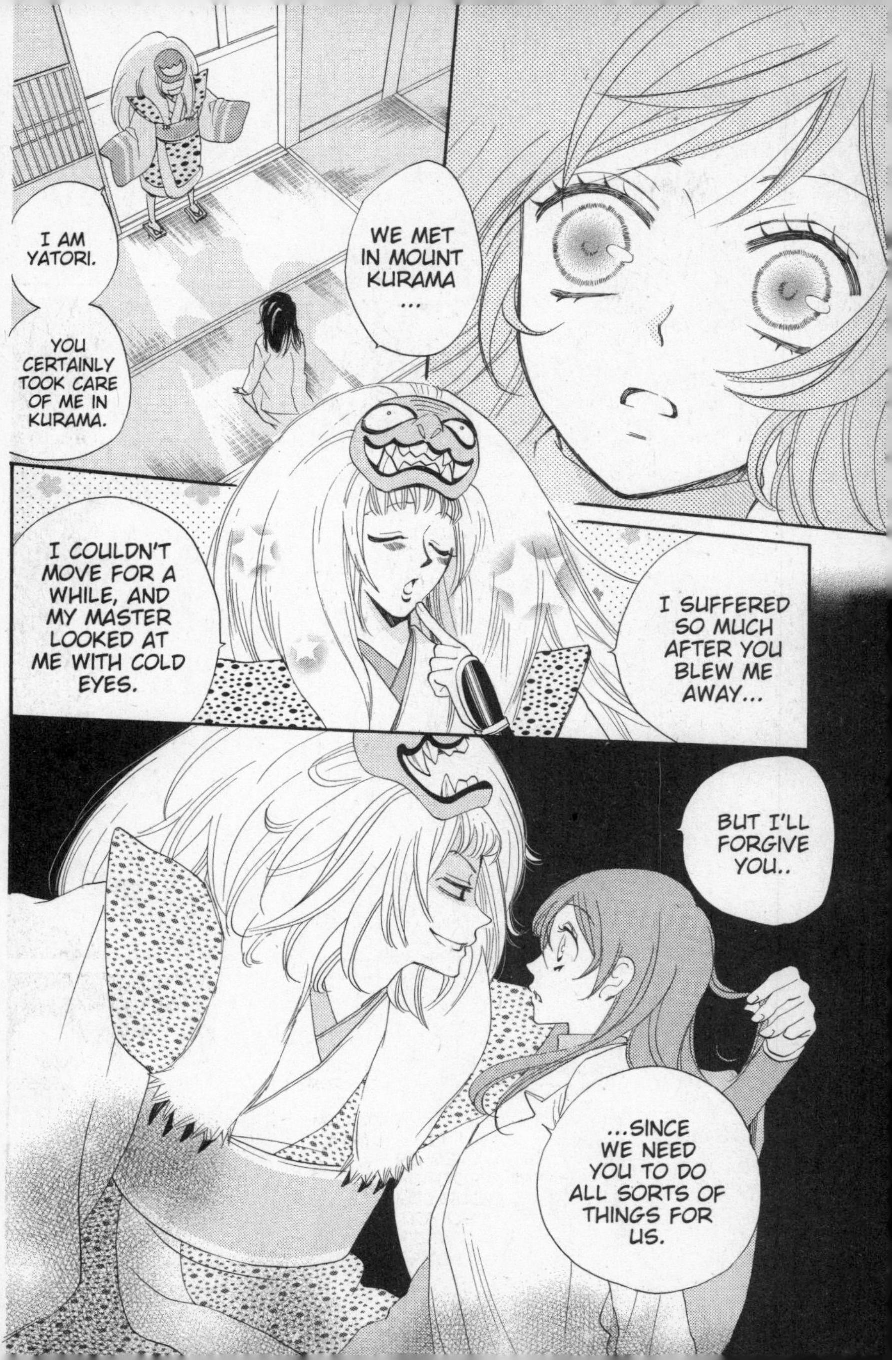
WE MET IN MOUNT KURAMA ...
I AM YATORI.
YOU CERTAINLY TOOK CARE OF ME IN KURAMA.
I SUFFERED SO MUCH AFTER YOU BLEW ME AWAY...
I COULDN'T MOVE FOR A WHILE, AND MY MASTER LOOKED AT ME WITH COLD EYES.
BUT I'LL FORGIVE YOU..
...SINCE WE NEED YOU TO DO ALL SORTS OF THINGS FOR US.

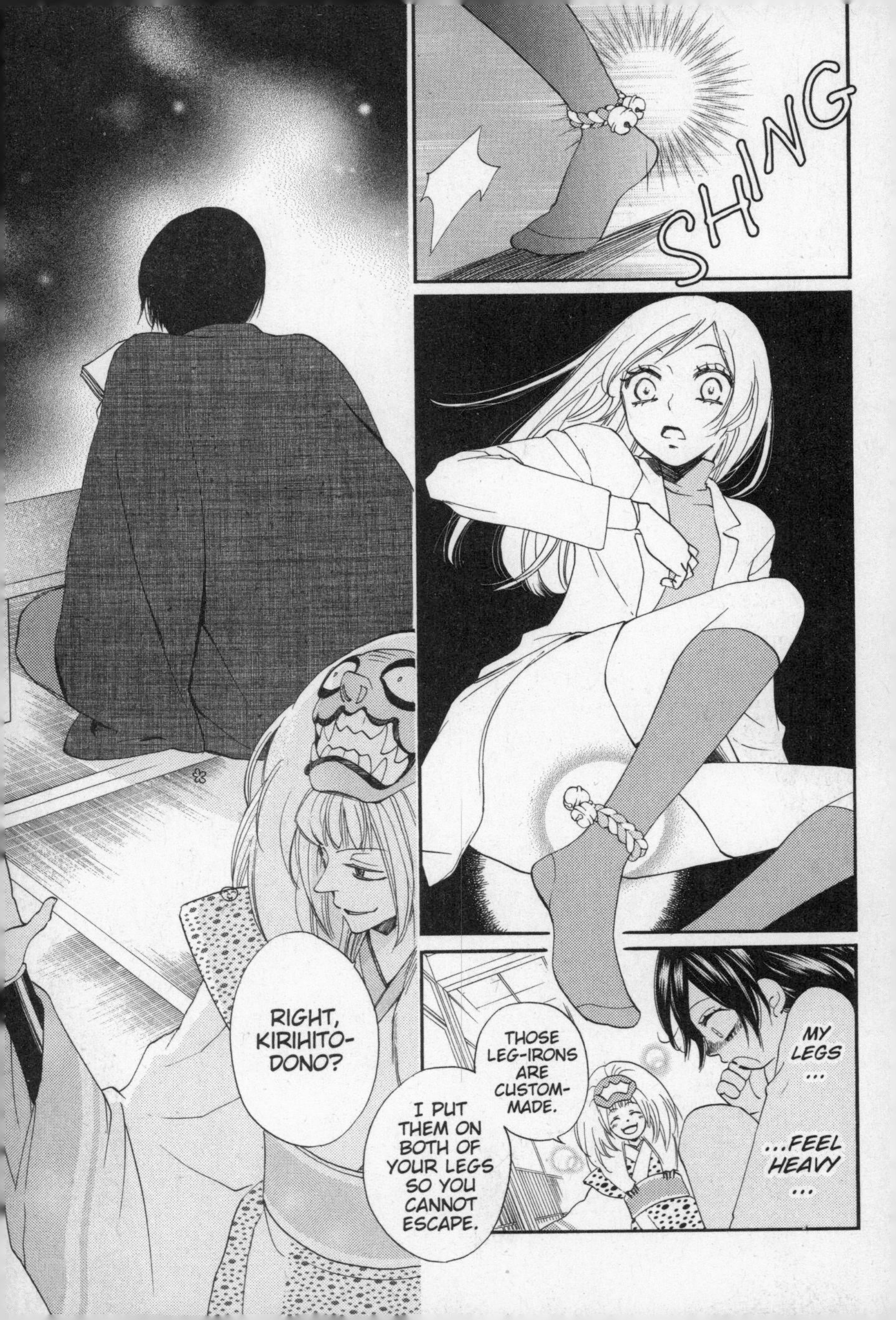
SHING
MY LEGS ...
...FEEL HEAVY ...
THOSE LEG-IRONS ARE CUSTOM-MADE.
I PUT THEM ON BOTH OF YOUR LEGS SO YOU CANNOT ESCAPE.
RIGHT, KIRIHITO-DONO?

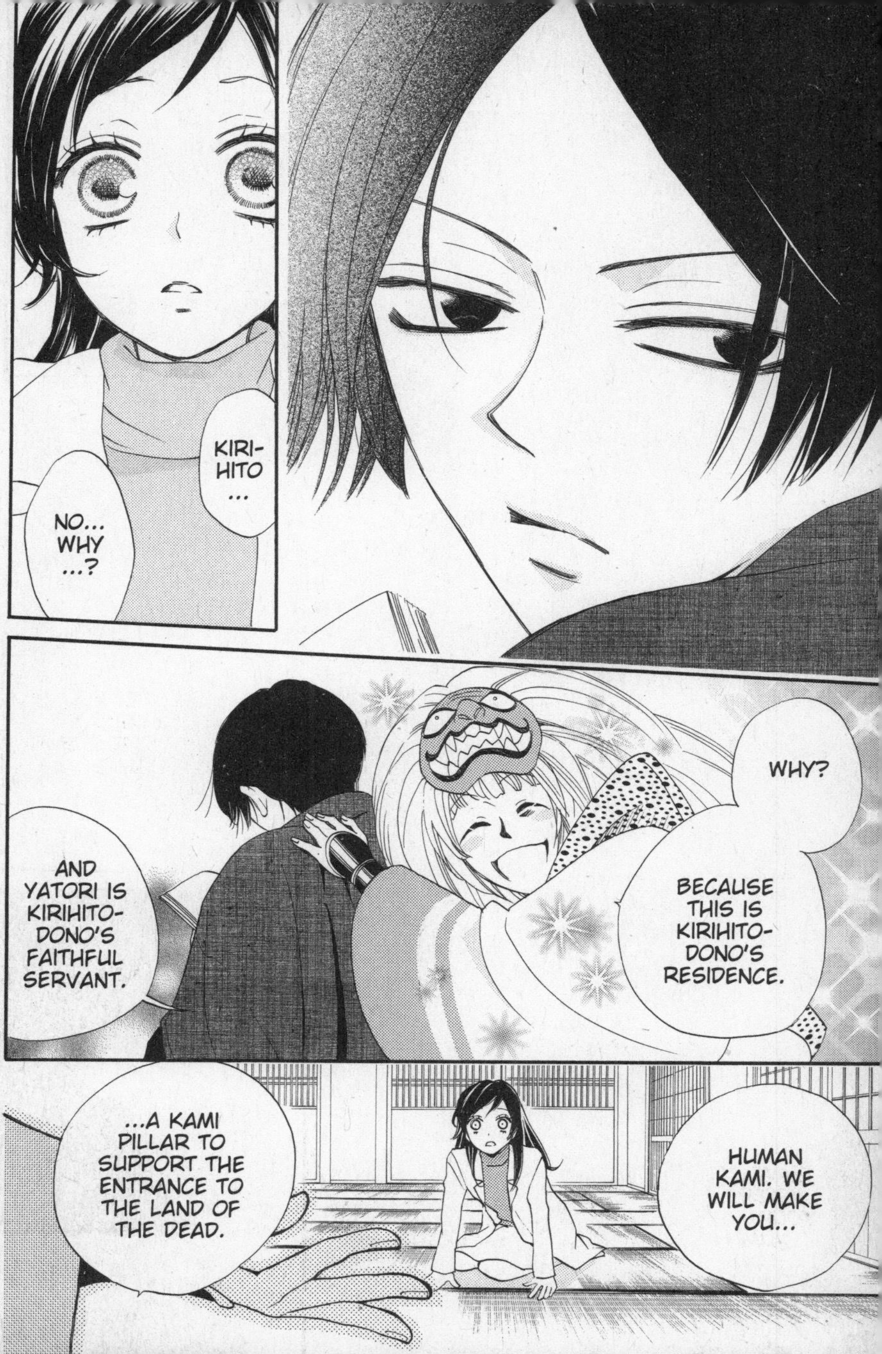
KIRI-HITO...
NO... WHY...?
WHY?
BECAUSE THIS IS KIRIHITO-DONO'S RESIDENCE.
AND YATORI IS KIRIHITO-DONO'S FAITHFUL SERVANT.
HUMAN KAMI. WE WILL MAKE YOU...
...A KAMI PILLAR TO SUPPORT THE ENTRANCE TO THE LAND OF THE DEAD.

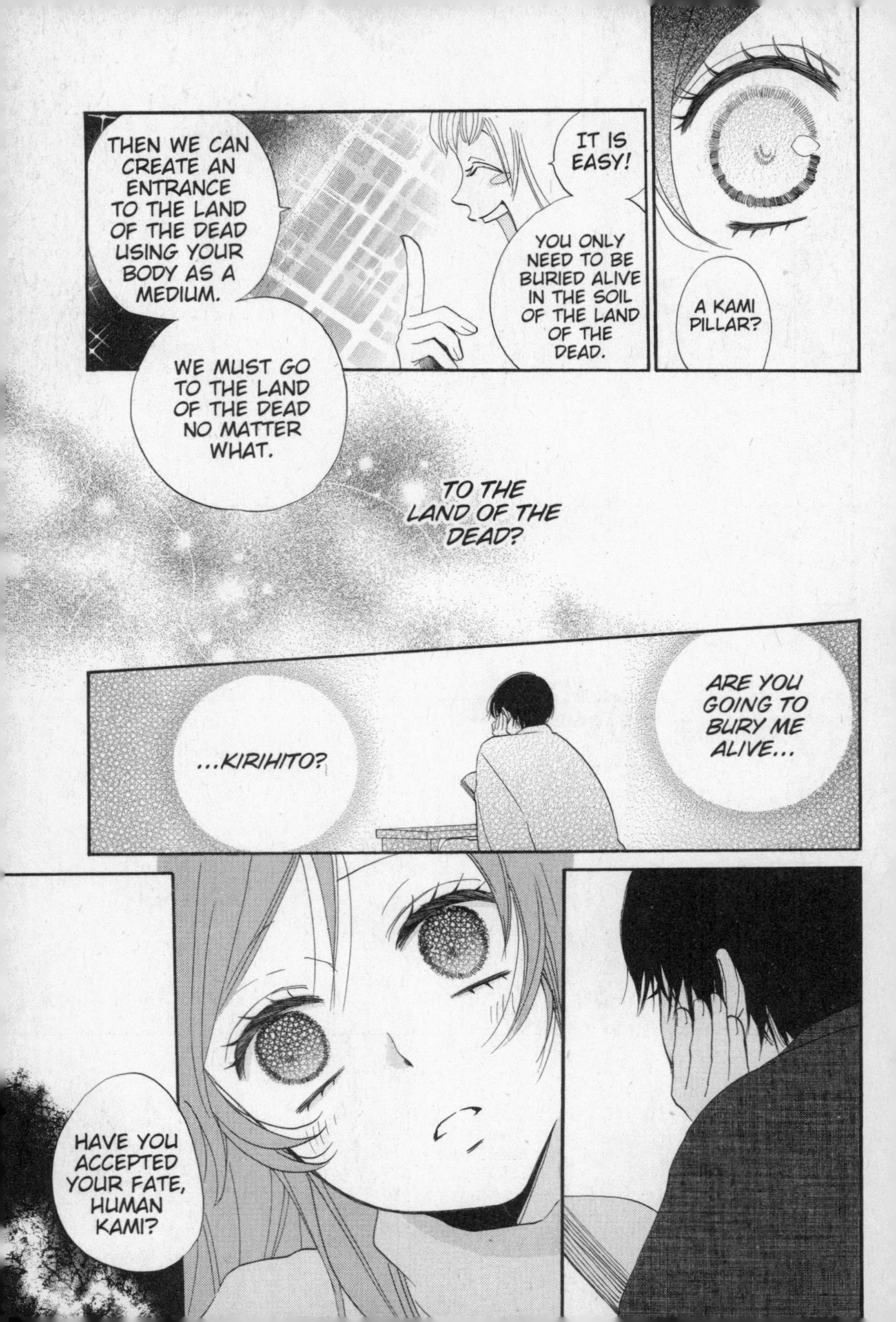
A KAMI PILLAR?
IT IS EASY!
YOU ONLY NEED TO BE BURIED ALIVE IN THE SOIL OF THE LAND OF THE DEAD.
THEN WE CAN CREATE AN ENTRANCE TO THE LAND OF THE DEAD USING YOUR BODY AS A MEDIUM.
WE MUST GO TO THE LAND OF THE DEAD NO MATTER WHAT.
TO THE LAND OF THE DEAD?
ARE YOU GOING TO BURY ME ALIVE...
...KIRIHITO?
HAVE YOU ACCEPTED YOUR FATE, HUMAN KAMI?

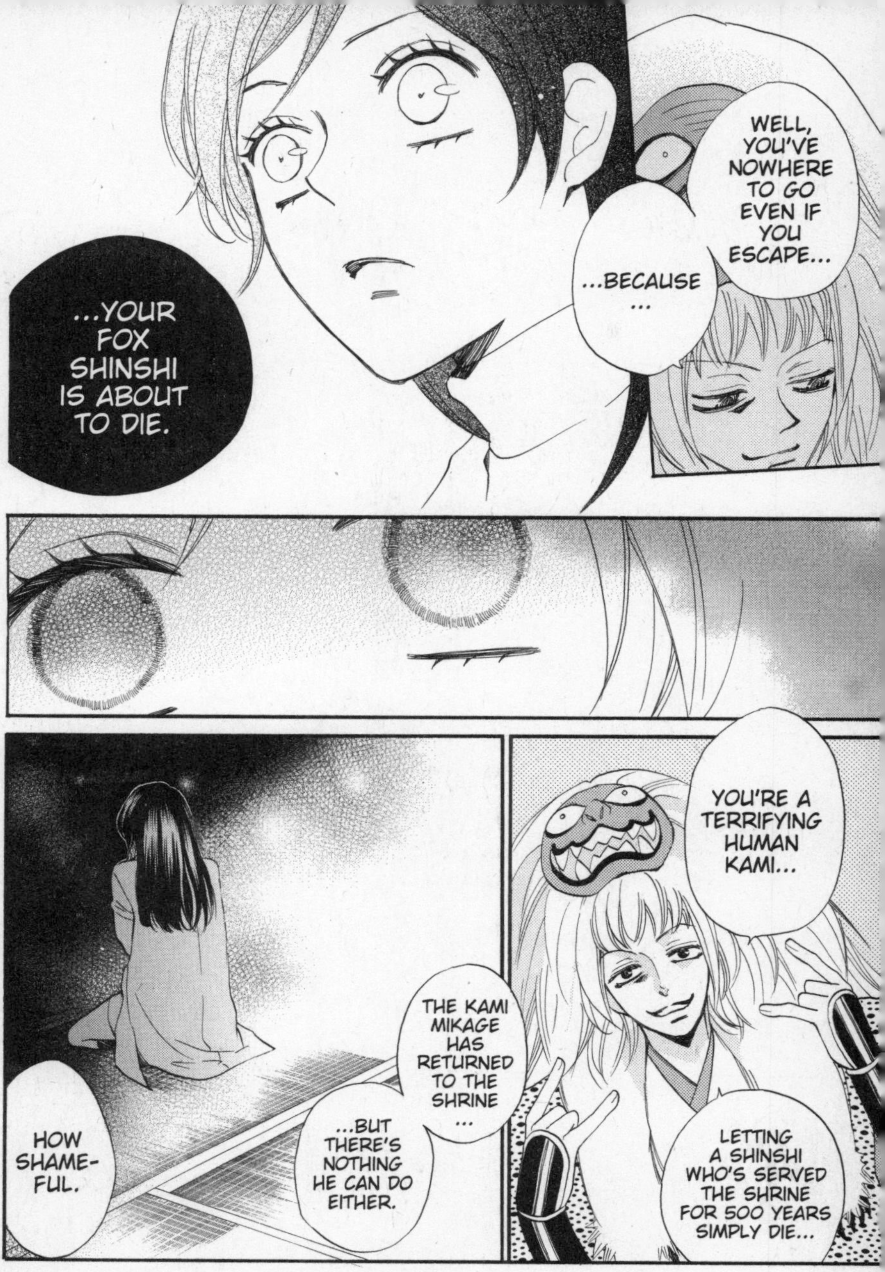
WELL, YOU'VE NOWHERE TO GO EVEN IF YOU ESCAPE...
...BECAUSE ...
...YOUR FOX SHINSHI IS ABOUT TO DIE.
YOU'RE A TERRIFYING HUMAN KAMI...
LETTING A SHINSHI WHO'S SERVED THE SHRINE FOR 500 YEARS SIMPLY DIE...
THE KAMI MIKAGE HAS RETURNED TO THE SHRINE ...
...BUT THERE'S NOTHING HE CAN DO EITHER.
HOW SHAME-FUL.

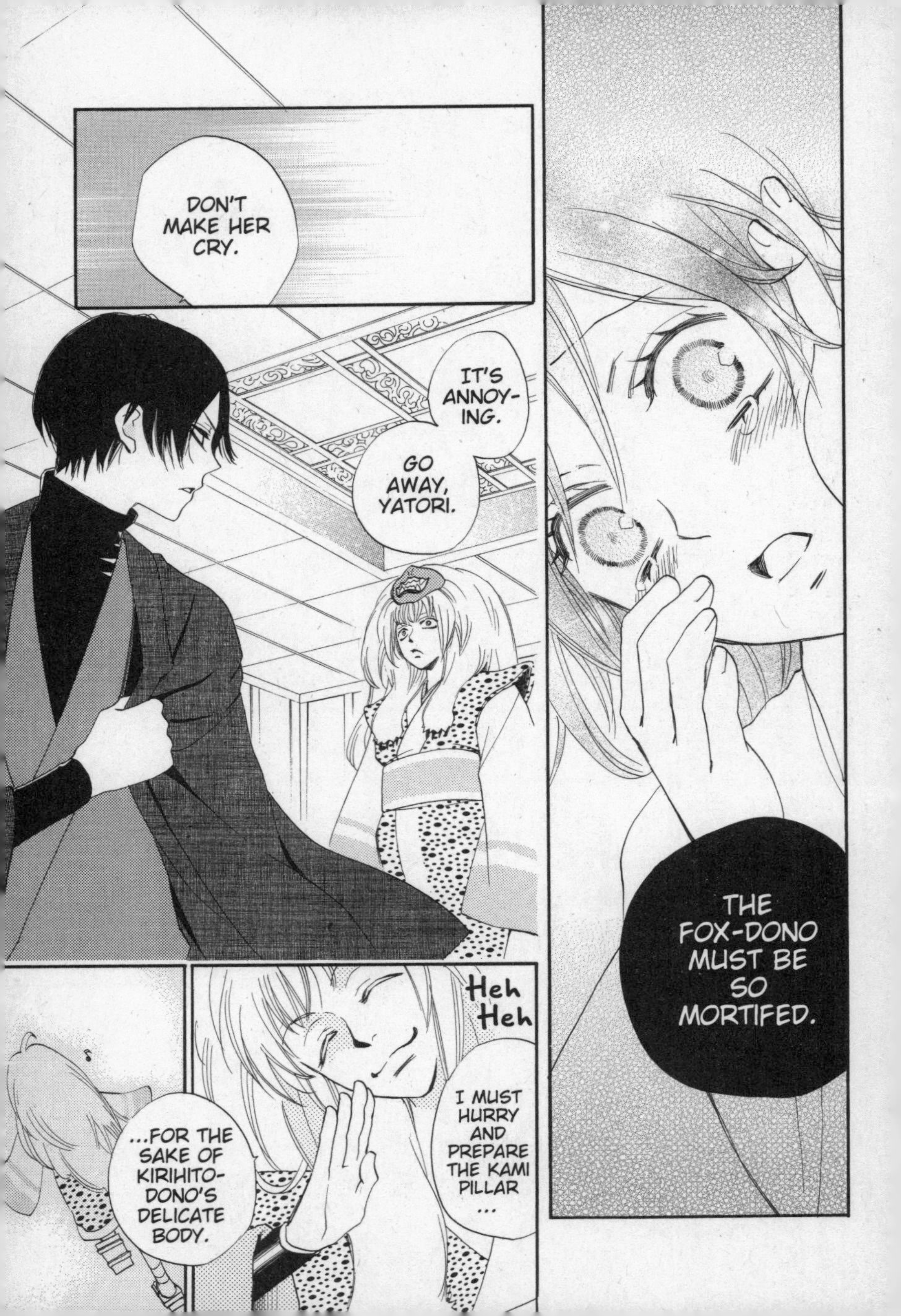
THE FOX-DONO MUST BE SO MORTIFED.
DON'T MAKE HER CRY.
IT'S ANNOYING.
GO AWAY, YATORI.
Heh Heh
I MUST HURRY AND PREPARE THE KAMI PILLAR ...
...FOR THE SAKE OF KIRIHITO-DONO'S DELICATE BODY.

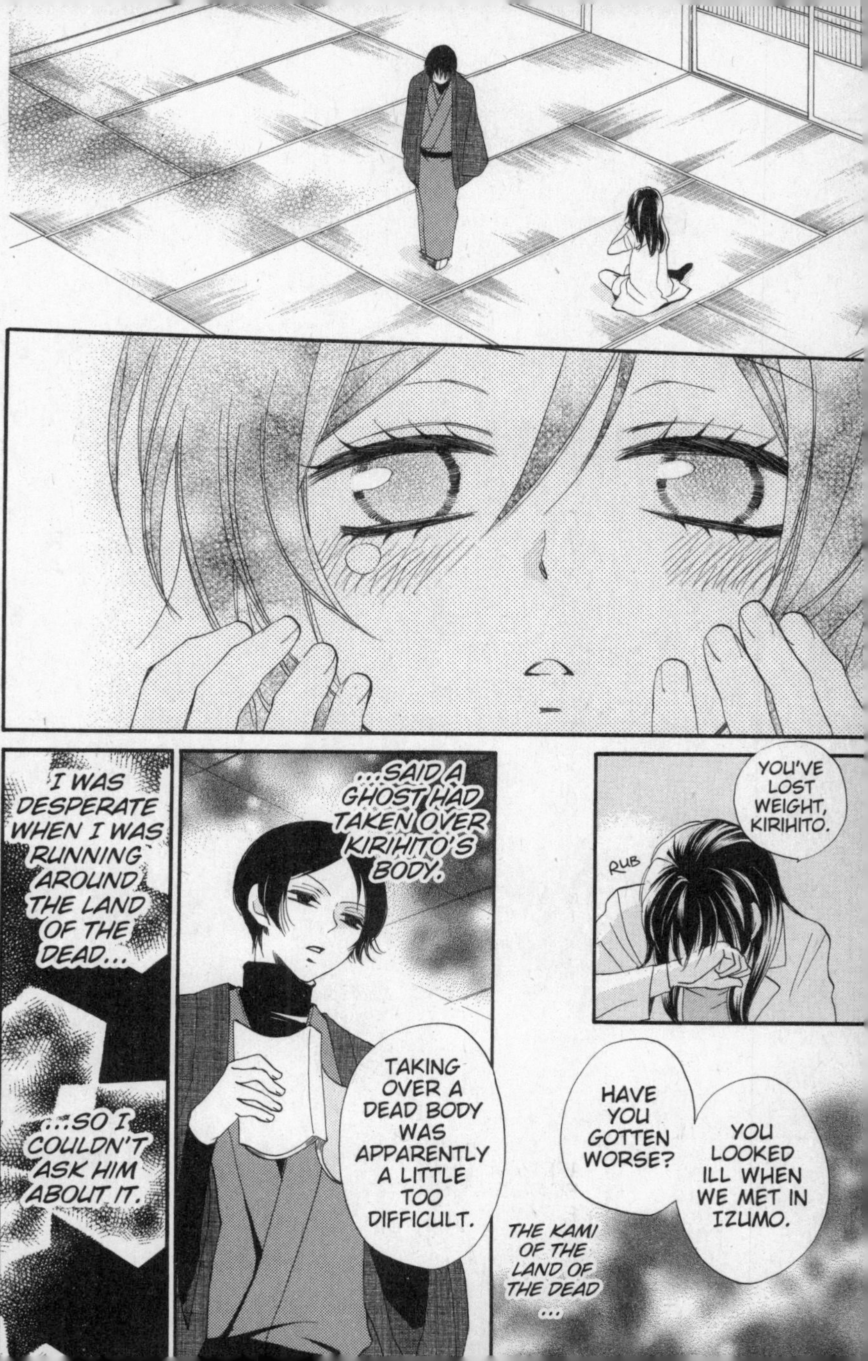
YOU'VE LOST WEIGHT, KIRIHITO.
RUB
YOU LOOKED ILL WHEN WE MET IN IZUMO.
HAVE YOU GOTTEN WORSE?
THE KAMI OF THE LAND OF THE DEAD ...
...SAID A GHOST HAD TAKEN OVER KIRIHITO'S BODY.
TAKING OVER A DEAD BODY WAS APPARENTLY A LITTLE TOO DIFFICULT.
I WAS DESPERATE WHEN I WAS RUNNING AROUND THE LAND OF THE DEAD...
...SO I COULDN'T ASK HIM ABOUT IT.

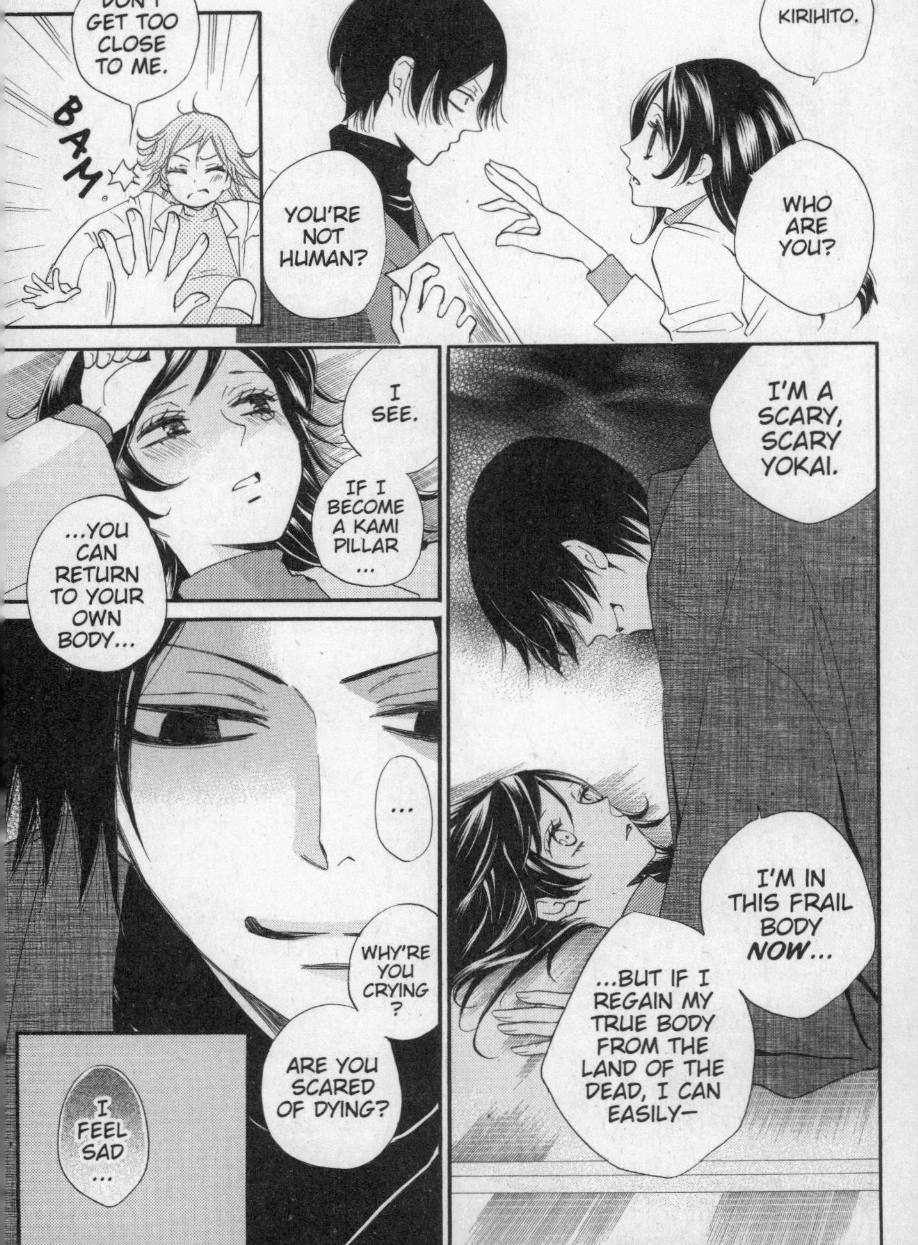
KIRIHITO.
WHO ARE YOU?
YOU'RE NOT HUMAN?
DON'T GET TOO CLOSE TO ME.
BAM
I'M A SCARY, SCARY YOKAI.
I'M IN THIS FRAIL BODY NOW...
...BUT IF I REGAIN MY TRUE BODY FROM THE LAND OF THE DEAD, I CAN EASILY—
I SEE.
IF I BECOME A KAMI PILLAR ...
...YOU CAN RETURN TO YOUR OWN BODY...
...
WHY'RE YOU CRYING ?
ARE YOU SCARED OF DYING?
I FEEL SAD ...

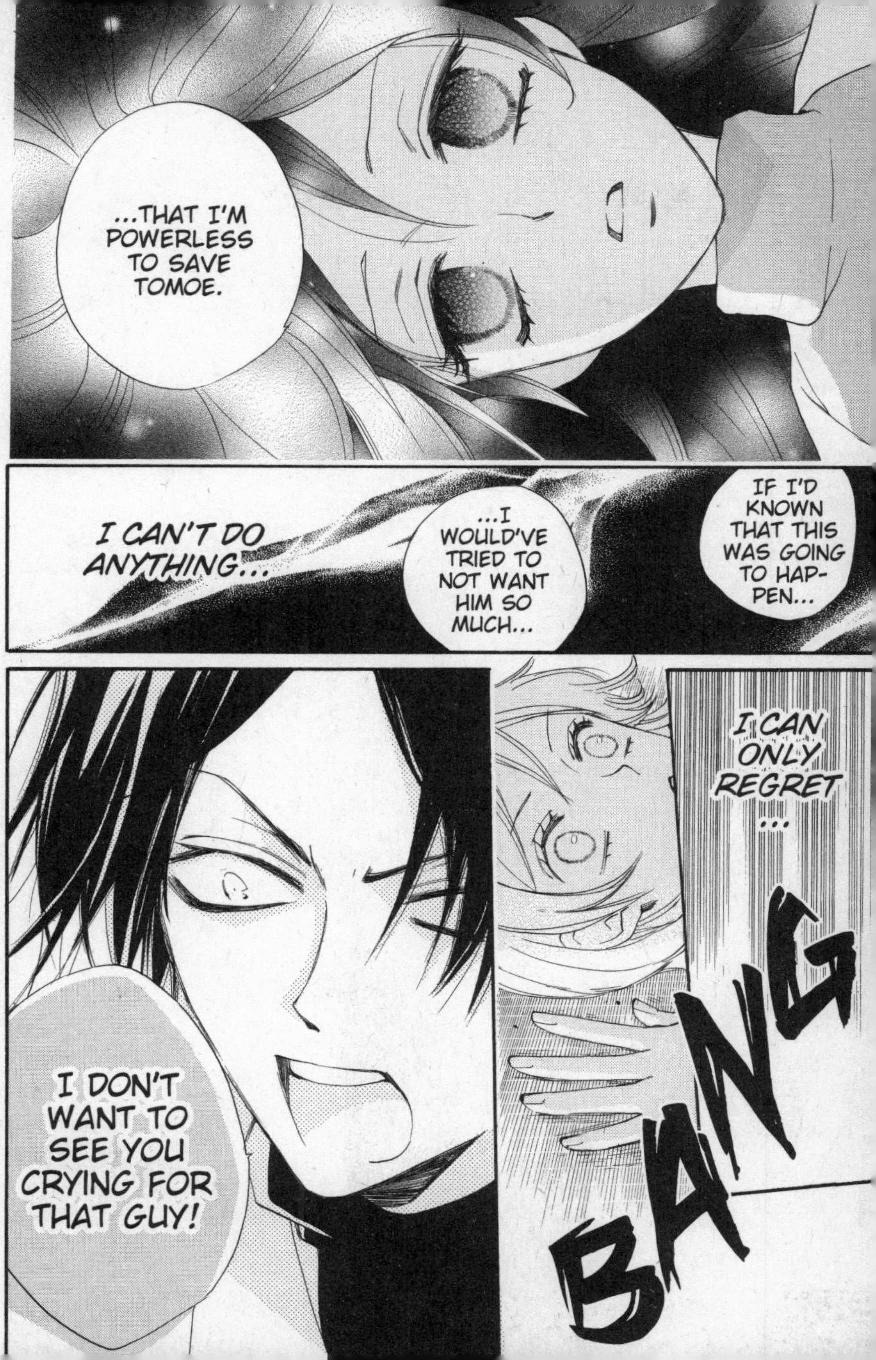
...THAT I'M POWERLESS TO SAVE TOMOE.
IF I'D KNOWN THAT THIS WAS GOING TO HAP-PEN...
...I WOULD'VE TRIED TO NOT WANT HIM SO MUCH...
I CAN'T DO ANYTHING...
I CAN ONLY REGRET...
BANG
I DON'T WANT TO SEE YOU CRYING FOR THAT GUY!

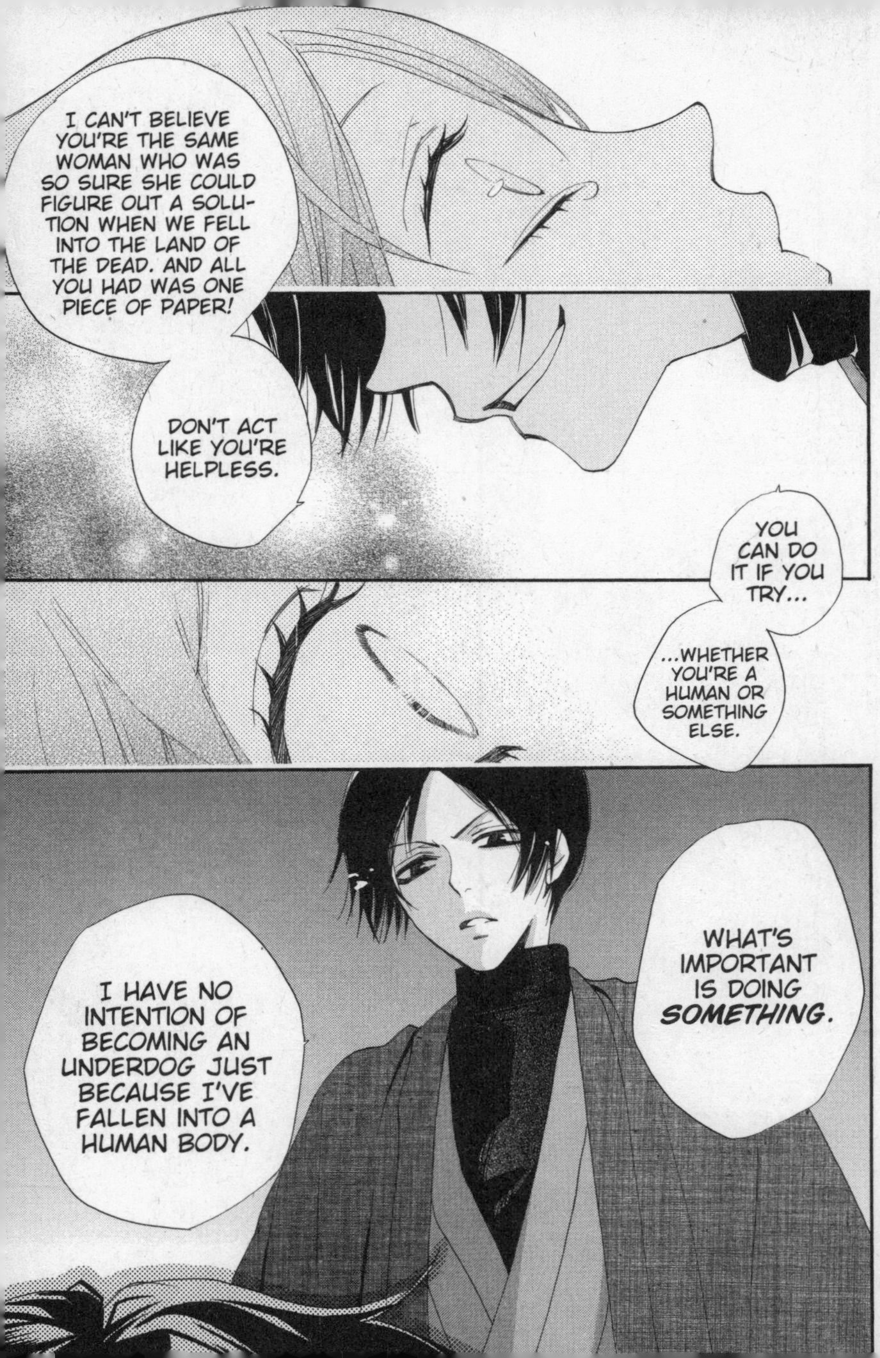
I CAN'T BELIEVE YOU'RE THE SAME WOMAN WHO WAS SO SURE SHE COULD FIGURE OUT A SOLUTION WHEN WE FELL INTO THE LAND OF THE DEAD. AND ALL YOU HAD WAS ONE PIECE OF PAPER!
DON'T ACT LIKE YOU'RE HELPLESS.
YOU CAN DO IT IF YOU TRY...
...WHETHER YOU'RE A HUMAN OR SOMETHING ELSE.
WHAT'S IMPORTANT IS DOING *SOMETHING*.
I HAVE NO INTENTION OF BECOMING AN UNDERDOG JUST BECAUSE I'VE FALLEN INTO A HUMAN BODY.

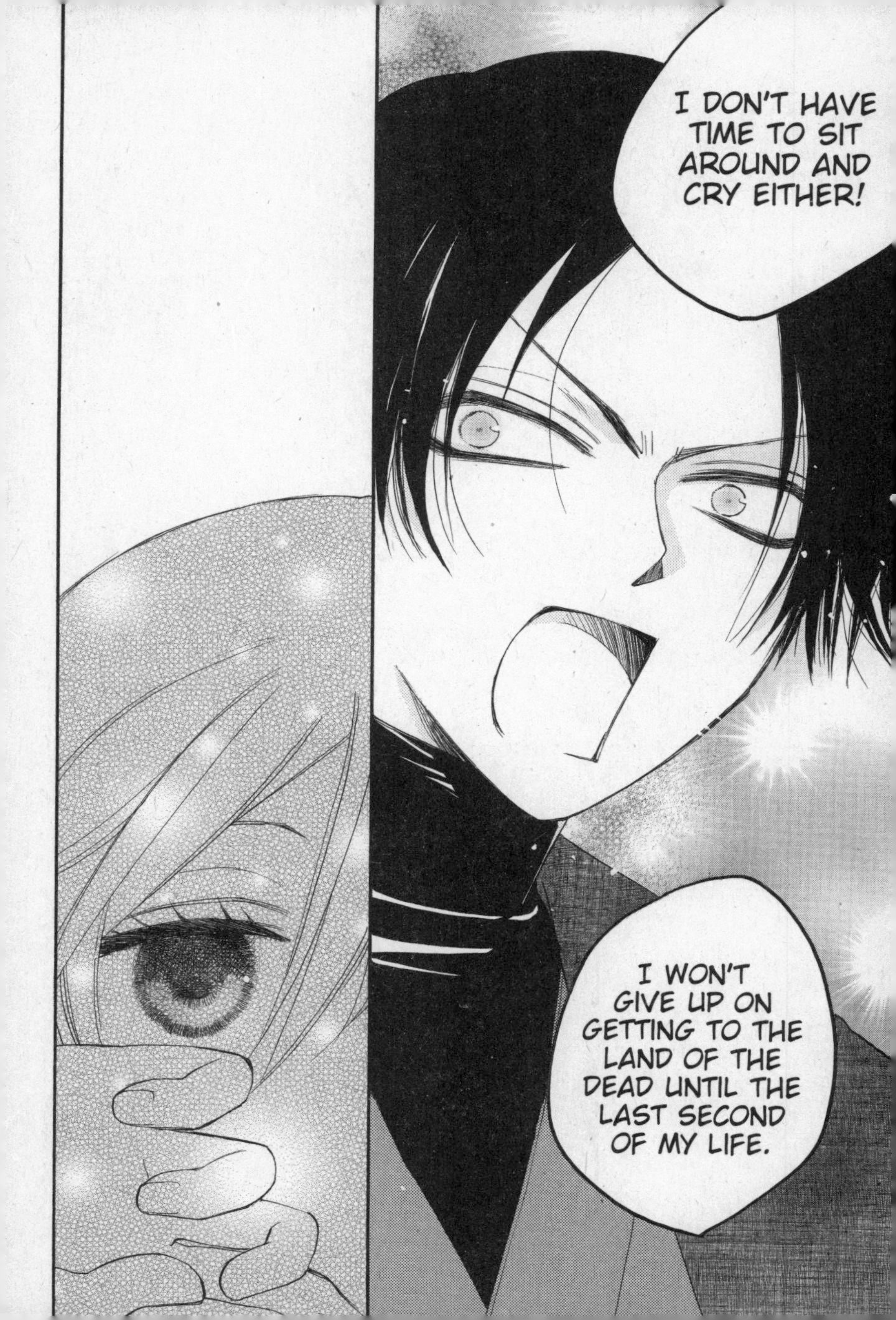
I DON'T HAVE TIME TO SIT AROUND AND CRY EITHER!
I WON'T GIVE UP ON GETTING TO THE LAND OF THE DEAD UNTIL THE LAST SECOND OF MY LIFE.

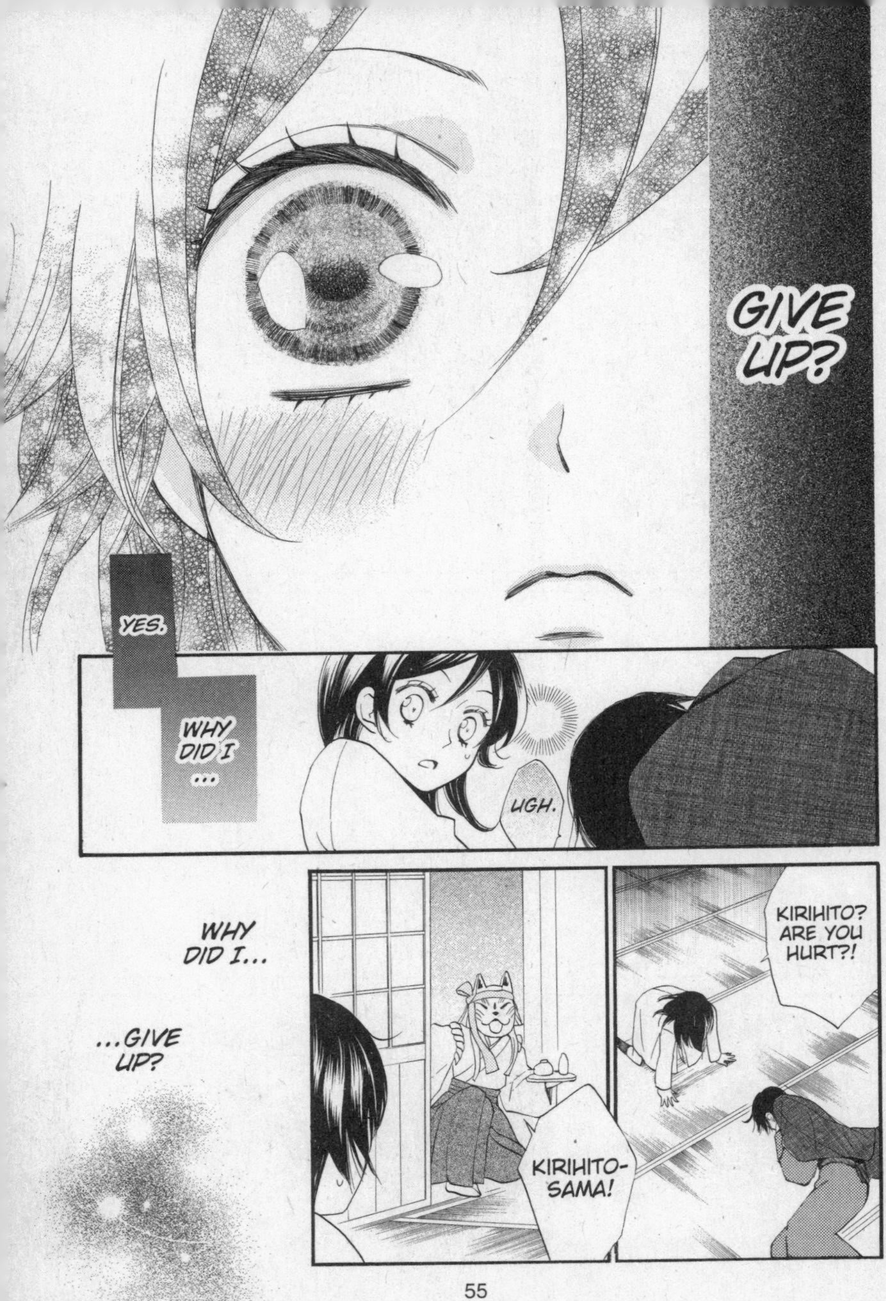
GIVE UP?
YES.
WHY DID I ...
UGH.
KIRIHITO? ARE YOU HURT?!
KIRIHITO-SAMA!
WHY DID I...
...GIVE UP?

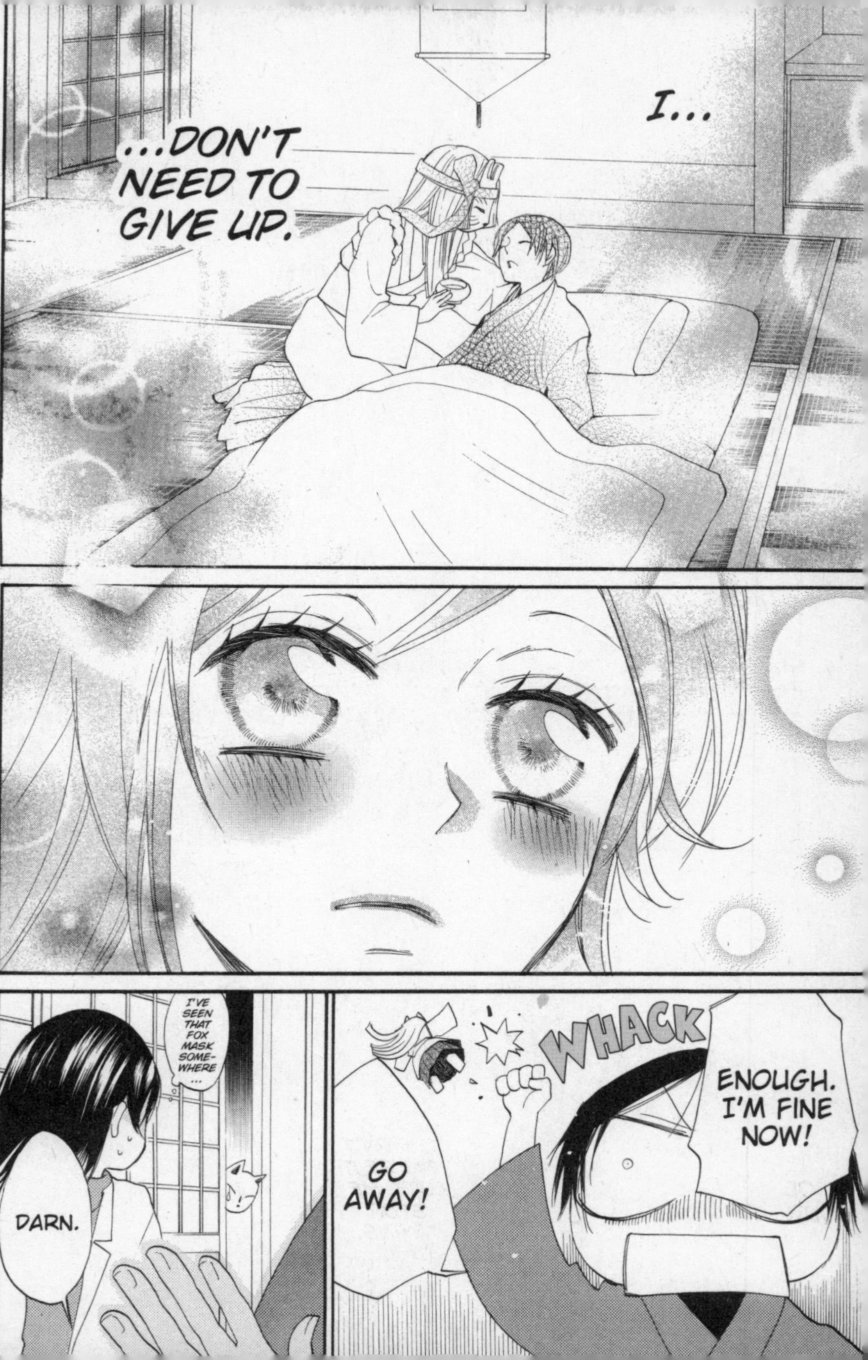
I...
...DON'T NEED TO GIVE UP.
ENOUGH. I'M FINE NOW!
WHACK
GO AWAY!
I'VE SEEN THAT FOX MASK SOMEWHERE...
DARN.

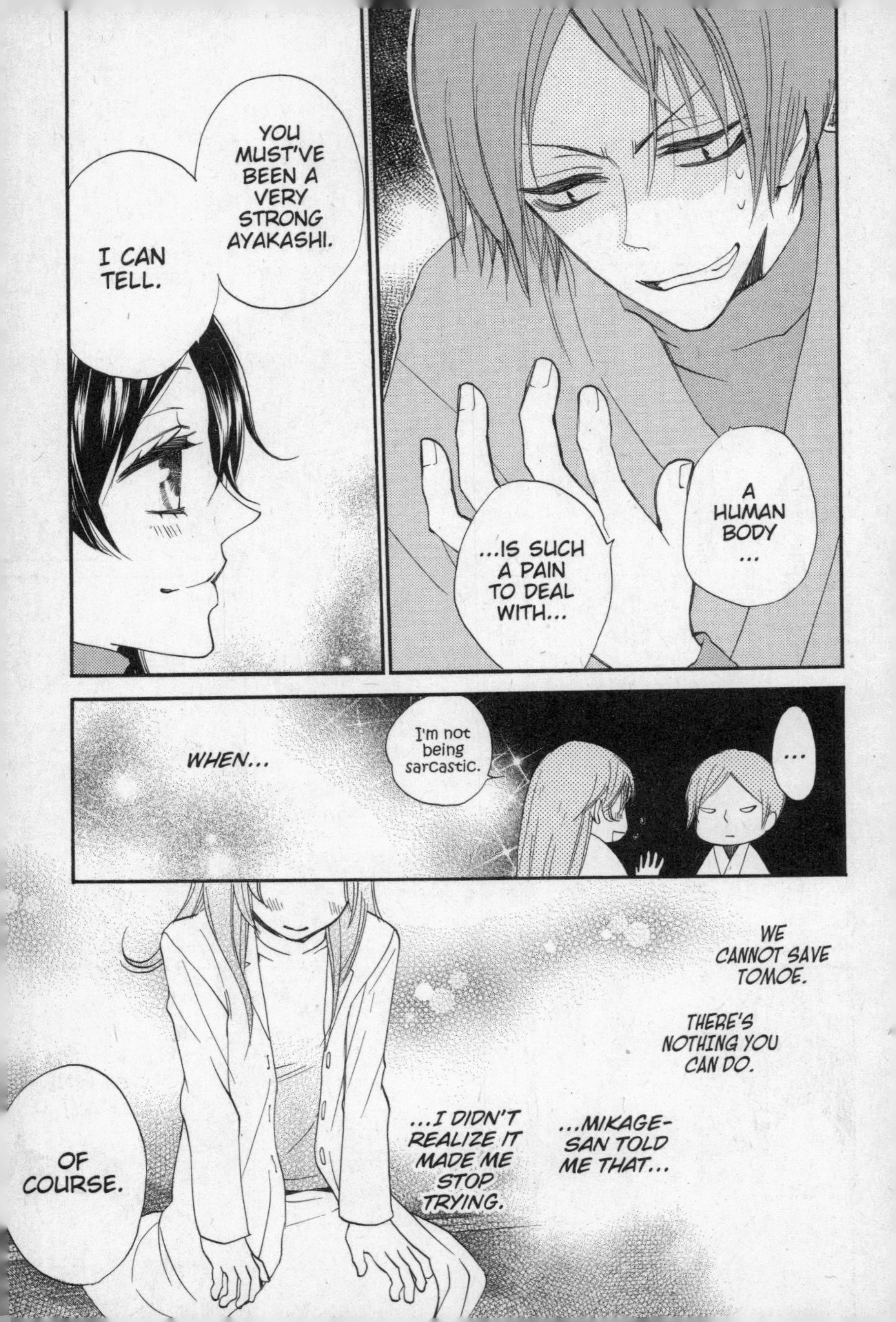
A HUMAN BODY...
...IS SUCH A PAIN TO DEAL WITH...
YOU MUST'VE BEEN A VERY STRONG AYAKASHI.
I CAN TELL.
...
I'm not being sarcastic.
WHEN...
WE CANNOT SAVE TOMOE.
THERE'S NOTHING YOU CAN DO.
...MIKAGE-SAN TOLD ME THAT...
...I DIDN'T REALIZE IT MADE ME STOP TRYING.
OF COURSE.

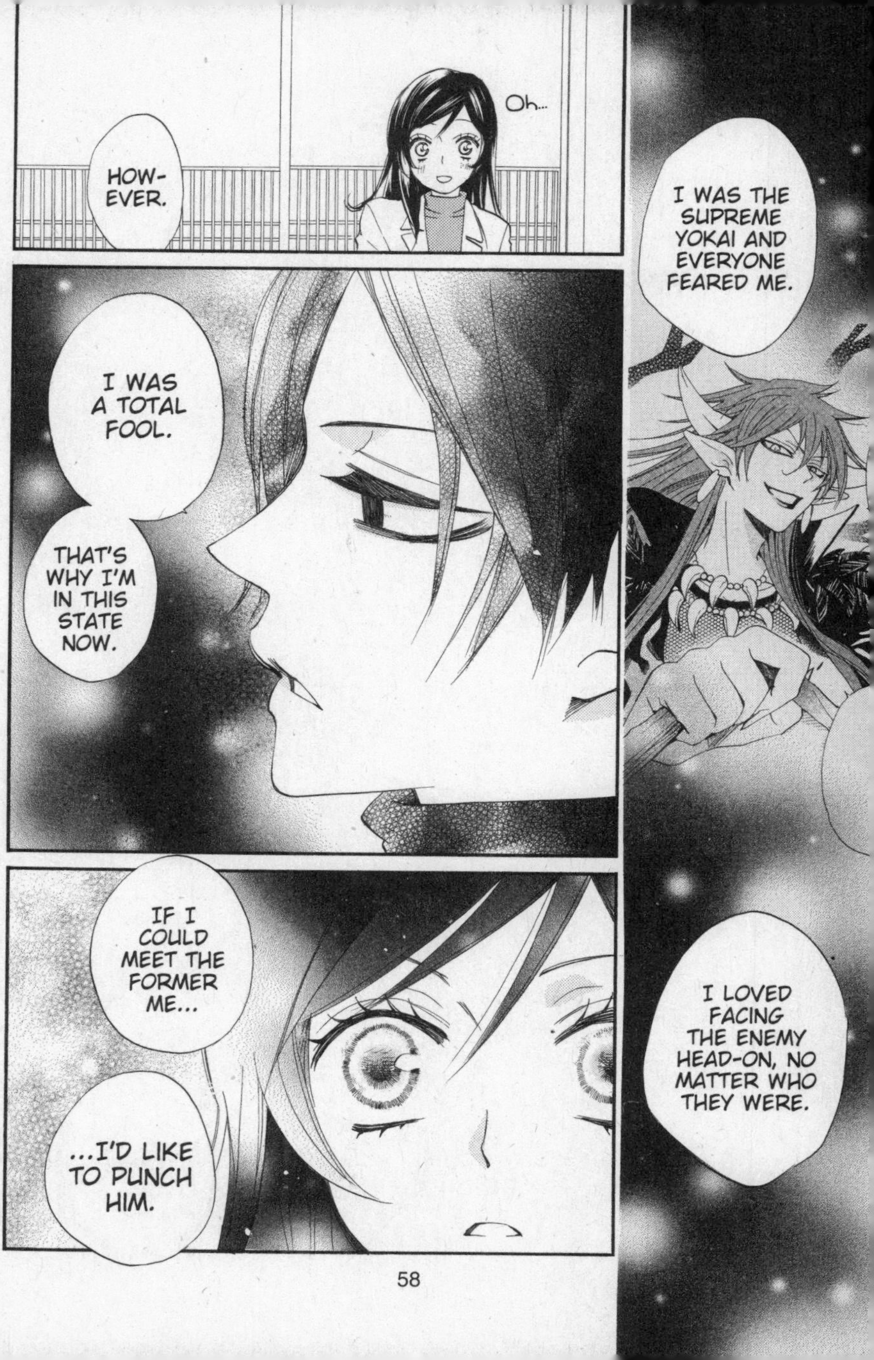
I WAS THE SUPREME YOKAI AND EVERYONE FEARED ME.
I LOVED FACING THE ENEMY HEAD-ON, NO MATTER WHO THEY WERE.
Oh...
HOW-EVER.
I WAS A TOTAL FOOL.
THAT'S WHY I'M IN THIS STATE NOW.
IF I COULD MEET THE FORMER ME...
...I'D LIKE TO PUNCH HIM.

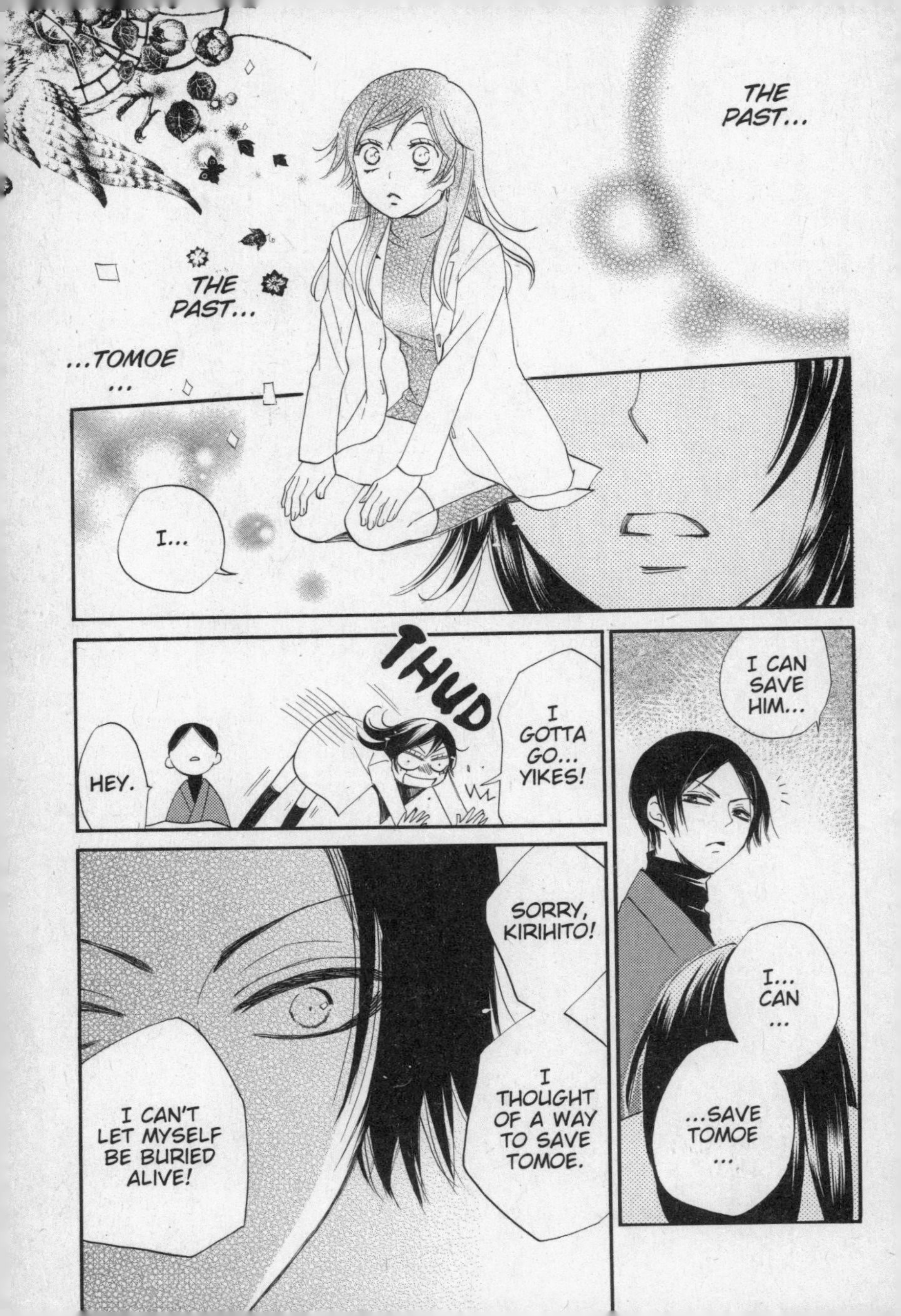
THE PAST...
THE PAST...
...TOMOE ...
I...
I CAN SAVE HIM...
I... CAN ...
...SAVE TOMOE ...
THUD
I GOTTA GO... YIKES!
HEY.
SORRY, KIRIHITO!
I THOUGHT OF A WAY TO SAVE TOMOE.
I CAN'T LET MYSELF BE BURIED ALIVE!

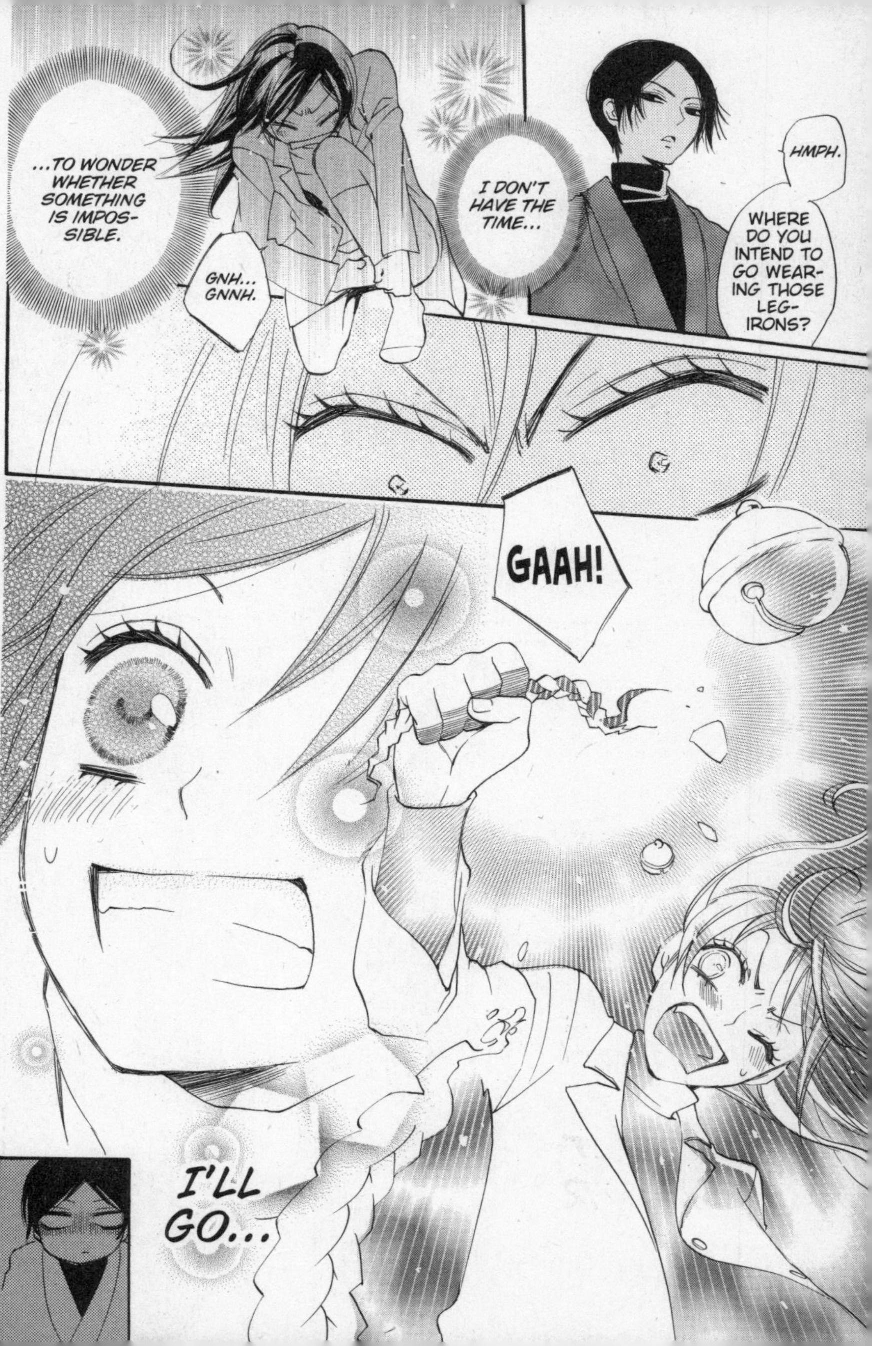
HMPH.
I DON'T HAVE THE TIME...
WHERE DO YOU INTEND TO GO WEARING THOSE LEG-IRONS?
...TO WONDER WHETHER SOMETHING IS IMPOSSIBLE.
GNH... GNNH.
GAAH!
I'LL GO...

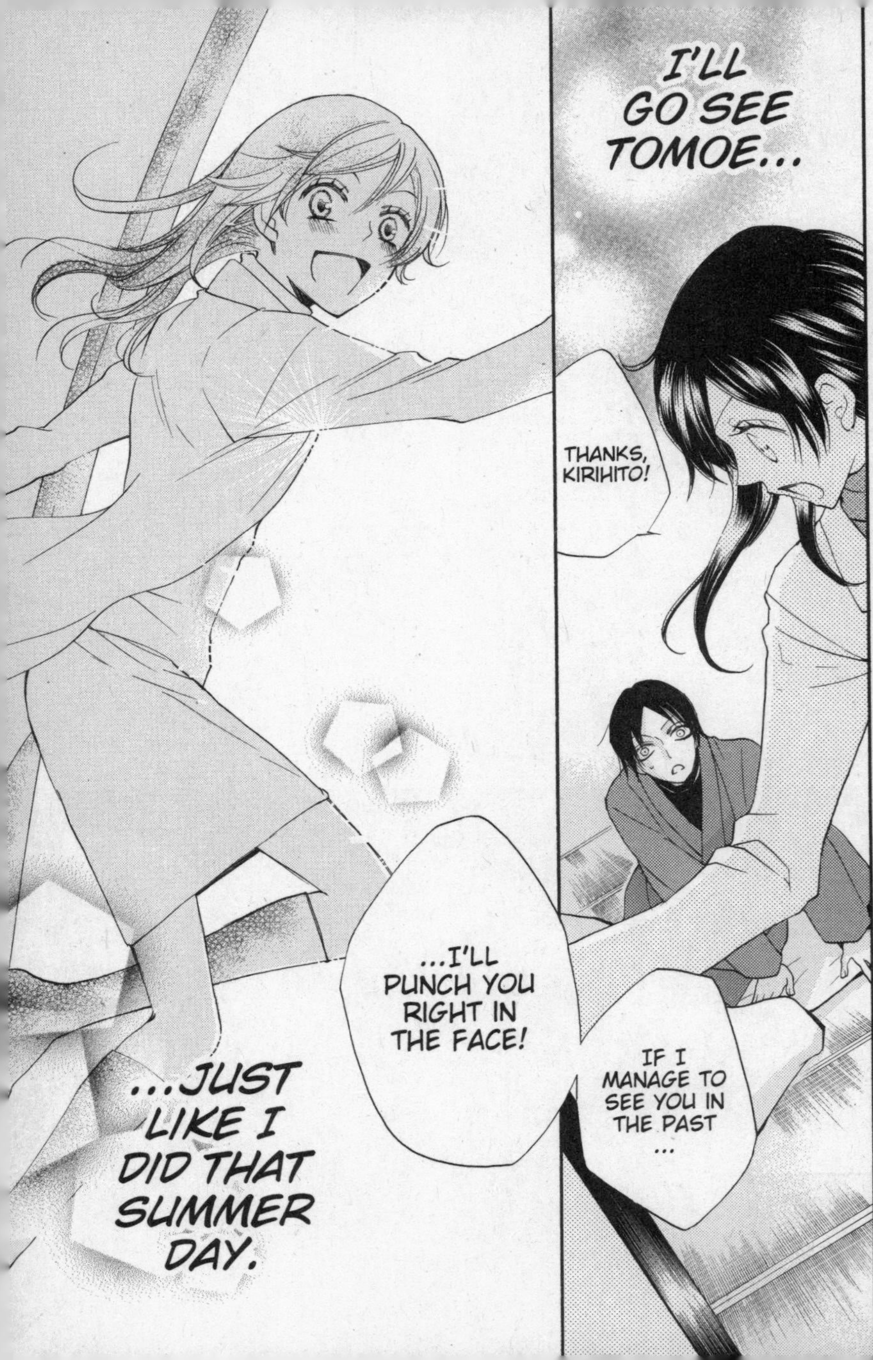
I'LL GO SEE TOMOE...
THANKS, KIRIHITO!
IF I MANAGE TO SEE YOU IN THE PAST ...
...I'LL PUNCH YOU RIGHT IN THE FACE!
...JUST LIKE I DID THAT SUMMER DAY.

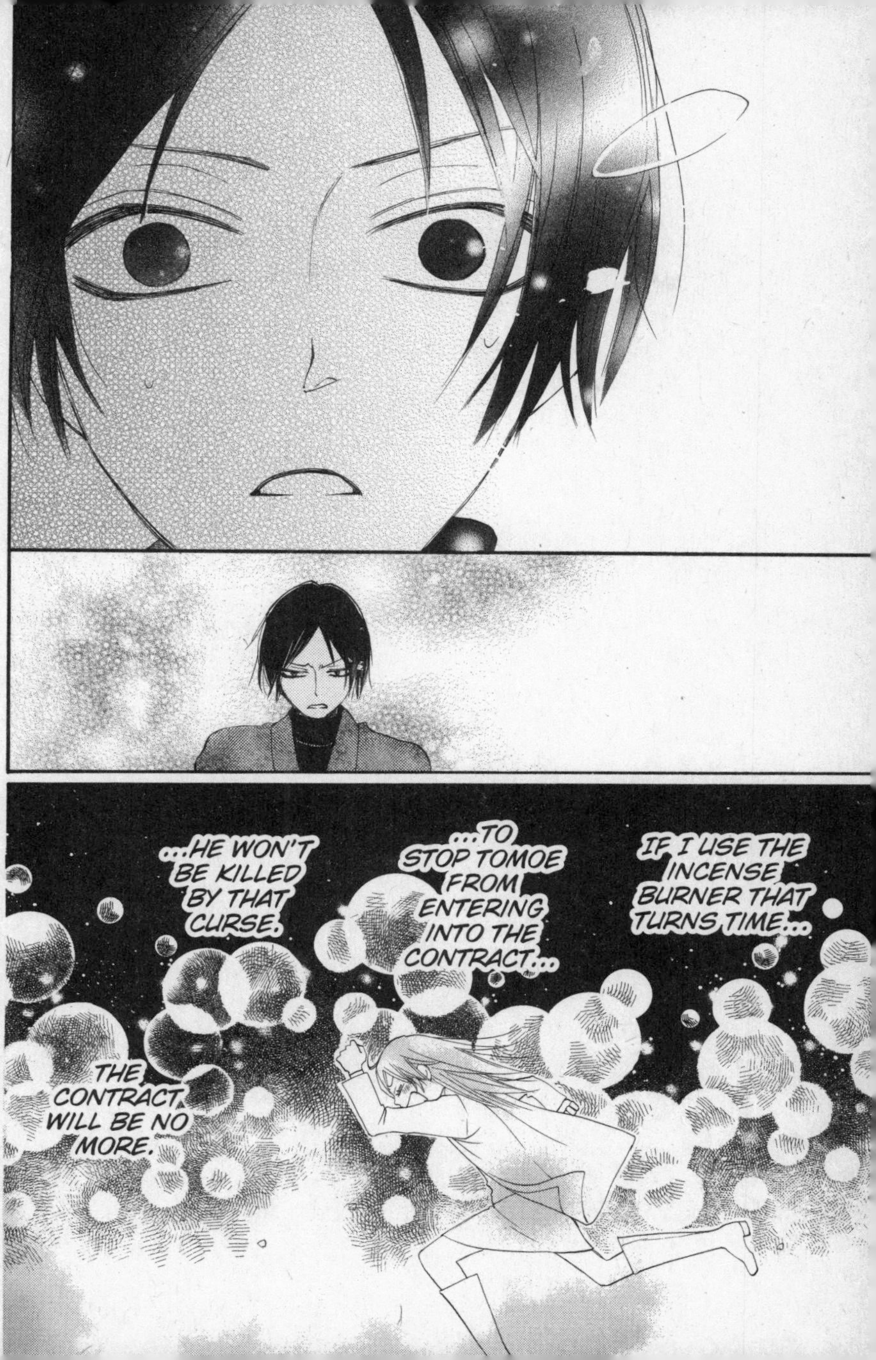
IF I USE THE INCENSE BURNER THAT TURNS TIME...
...TO STOP TOMOE FROM ENTERING INTO THE CONTRACT...
...HE WON'T BE KILLED BY THAT CURSE.
THE CONTRACT WILL BE NO MORE.

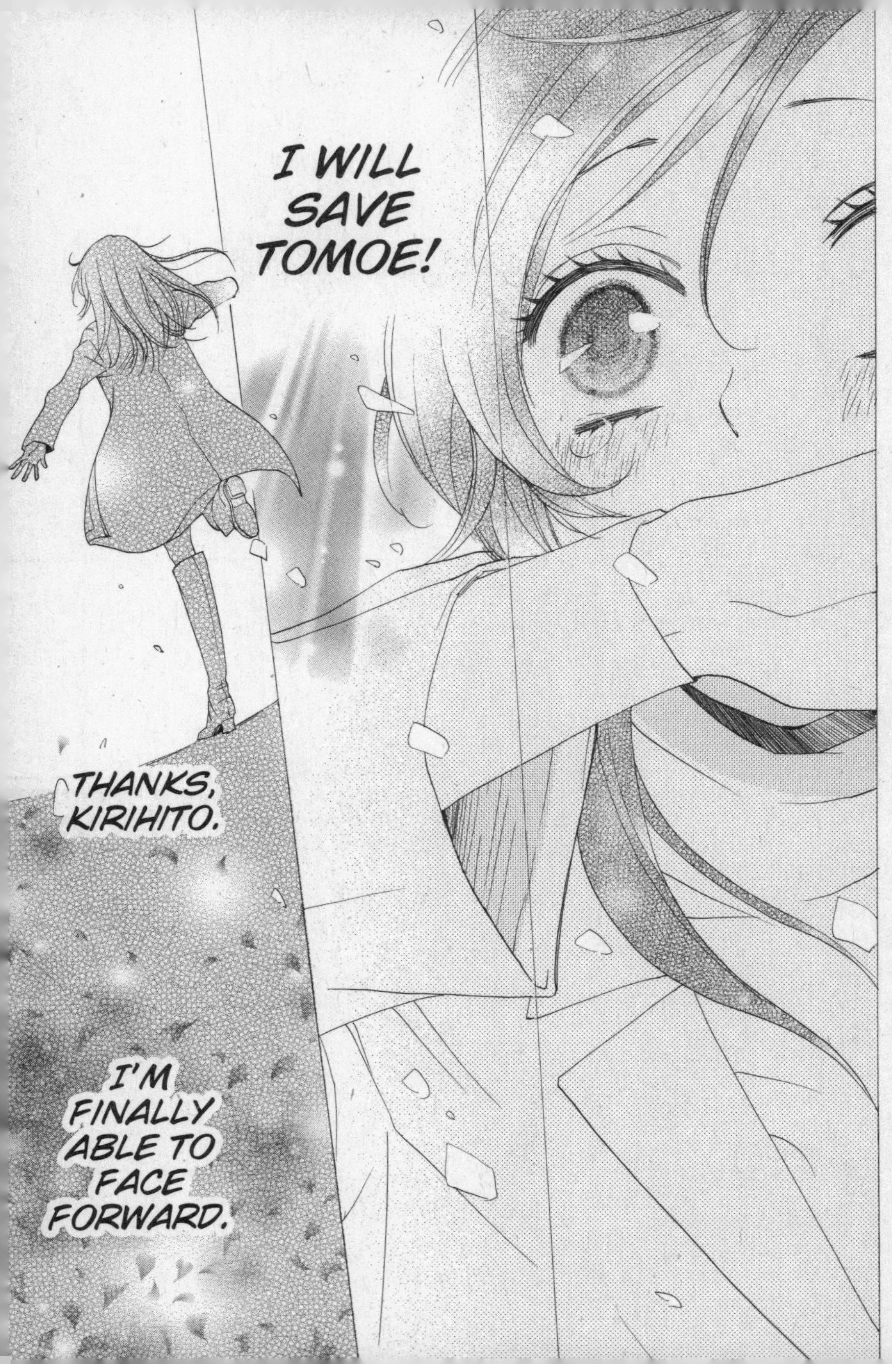
I WILL SAVE TOMOE!
THANKS, KIRIHITO.
I'M FINALLY ABLE TO FACE FORWARD.

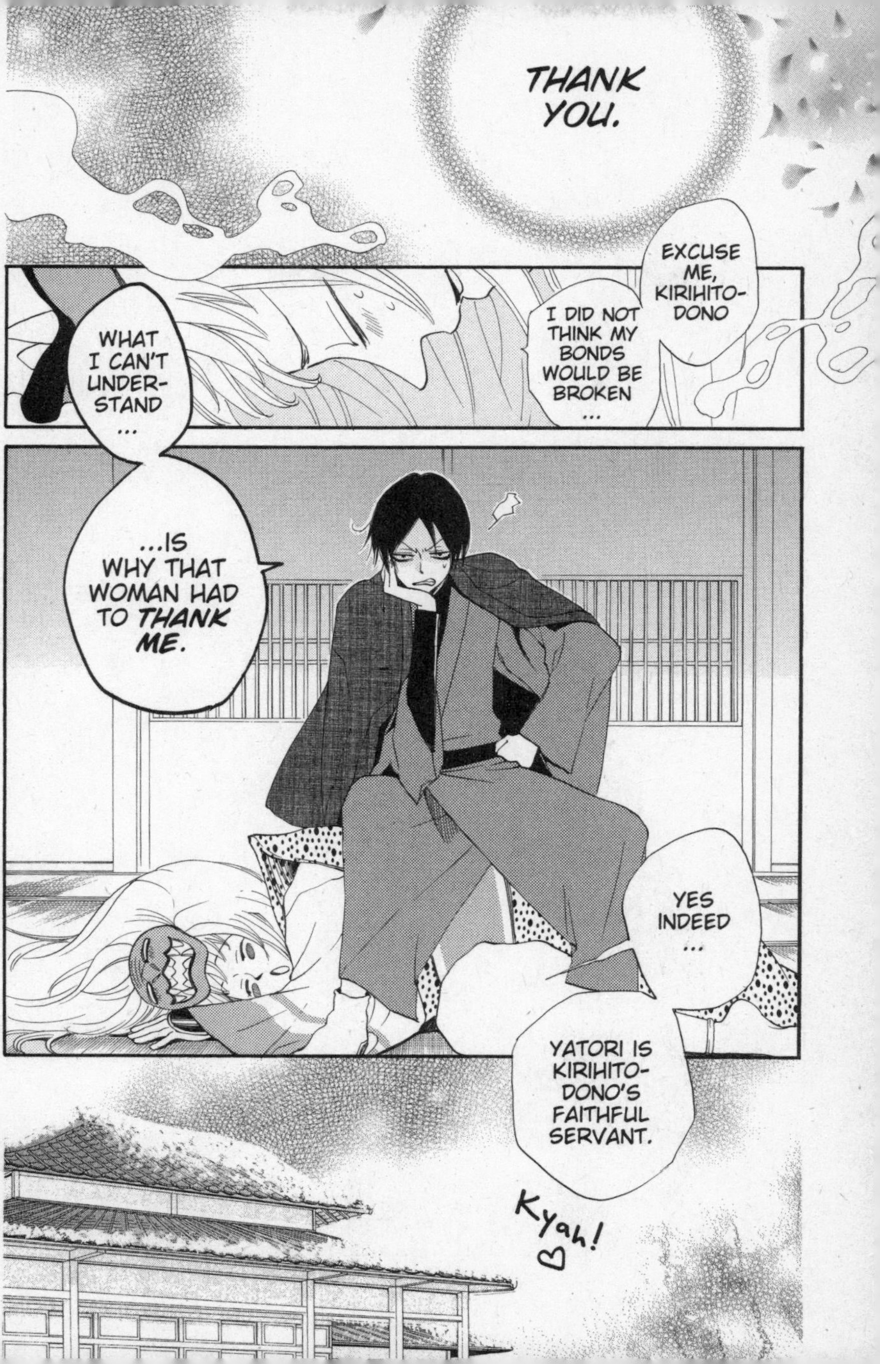
THANK YOU.
EXCUSE ME, KIRIHITO-DONO
I DID NOT THINK MY BONDS WOULD BE BROKEN ...
WHAT I CAN'T UNDER-STAND ...
...IS WHY THAT WOMAN HAD TO *THANK ME*.
YES INDEED ...
YATORI IS KIRIHITO-DONO'S FAITHFUL SERVANT.
Kyah! ♡

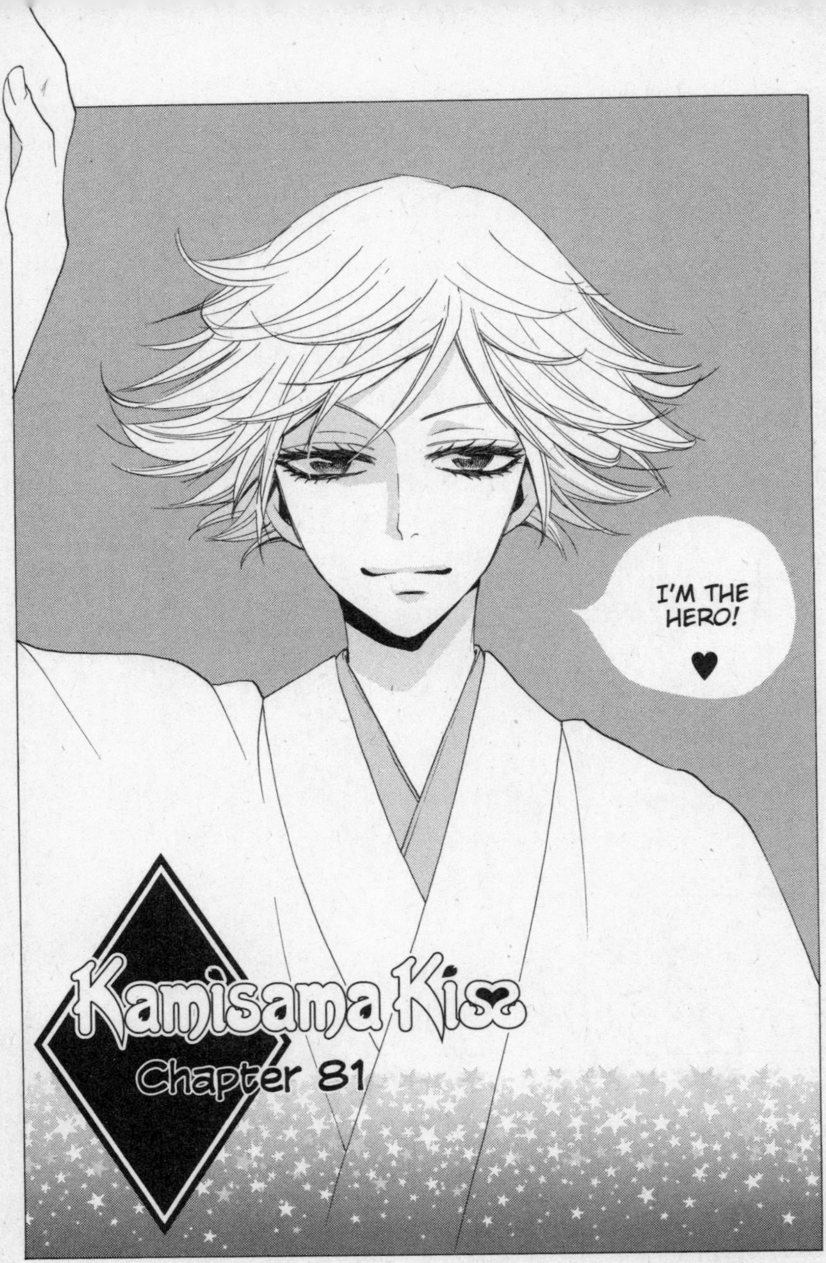
I'M THE HERO! ♥
Kamisama Kiss
Chapter 81

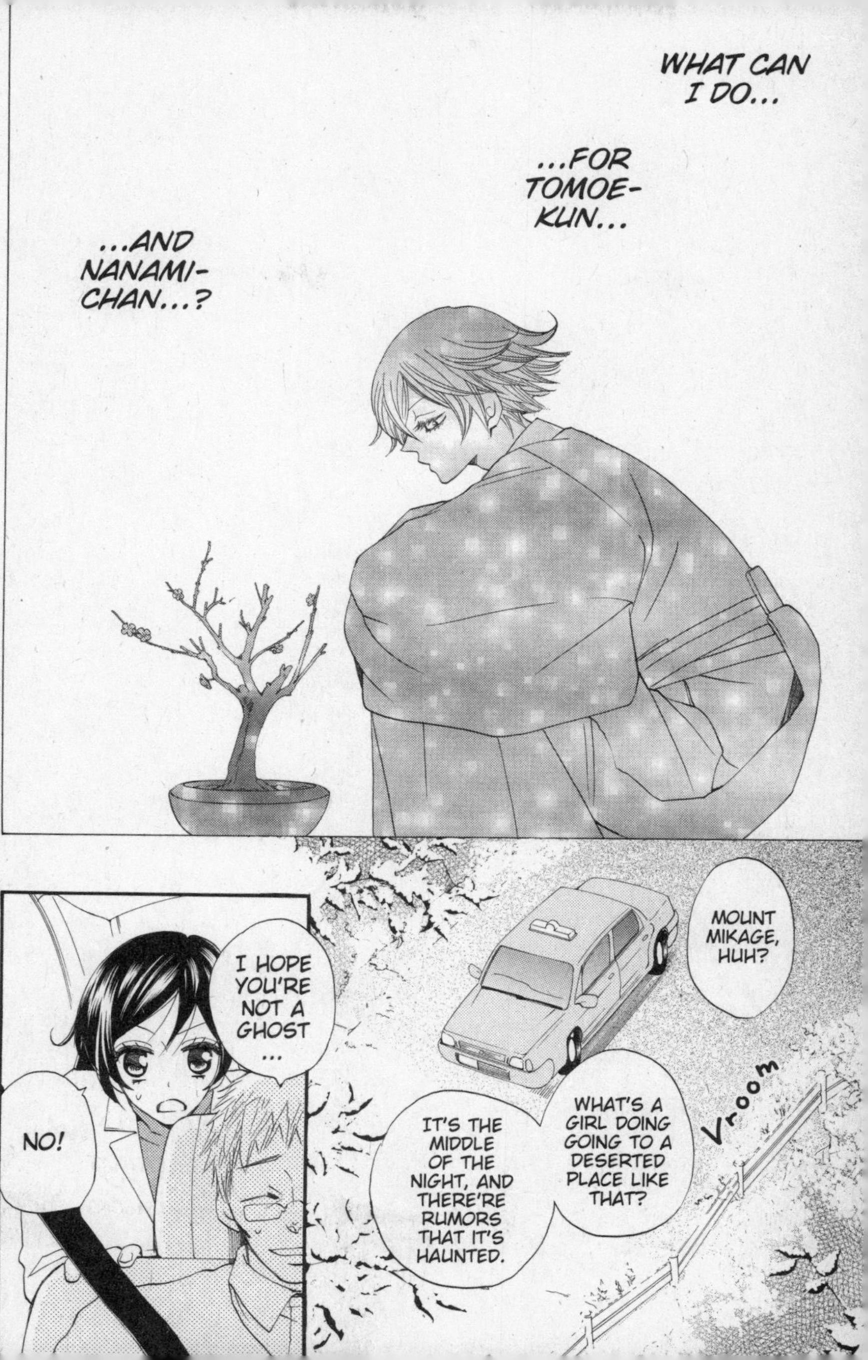
WHAT CAN I DO...
...FOR TOMOE-KUN...
...AND NANAMI-CHAN...?
MOUNT MIKAGE, HUH?
Vroom
WHAT'S A GIRL DOING GOING TO A DESERTED PLACE LIKE THAT?
IT'S THE MIDDLE OF THE NIGHT, AND THERE'RE RUMORS THAT IT'S HAUNTED.
I HOPE YOU'RE NOT A GHOST...
NO!

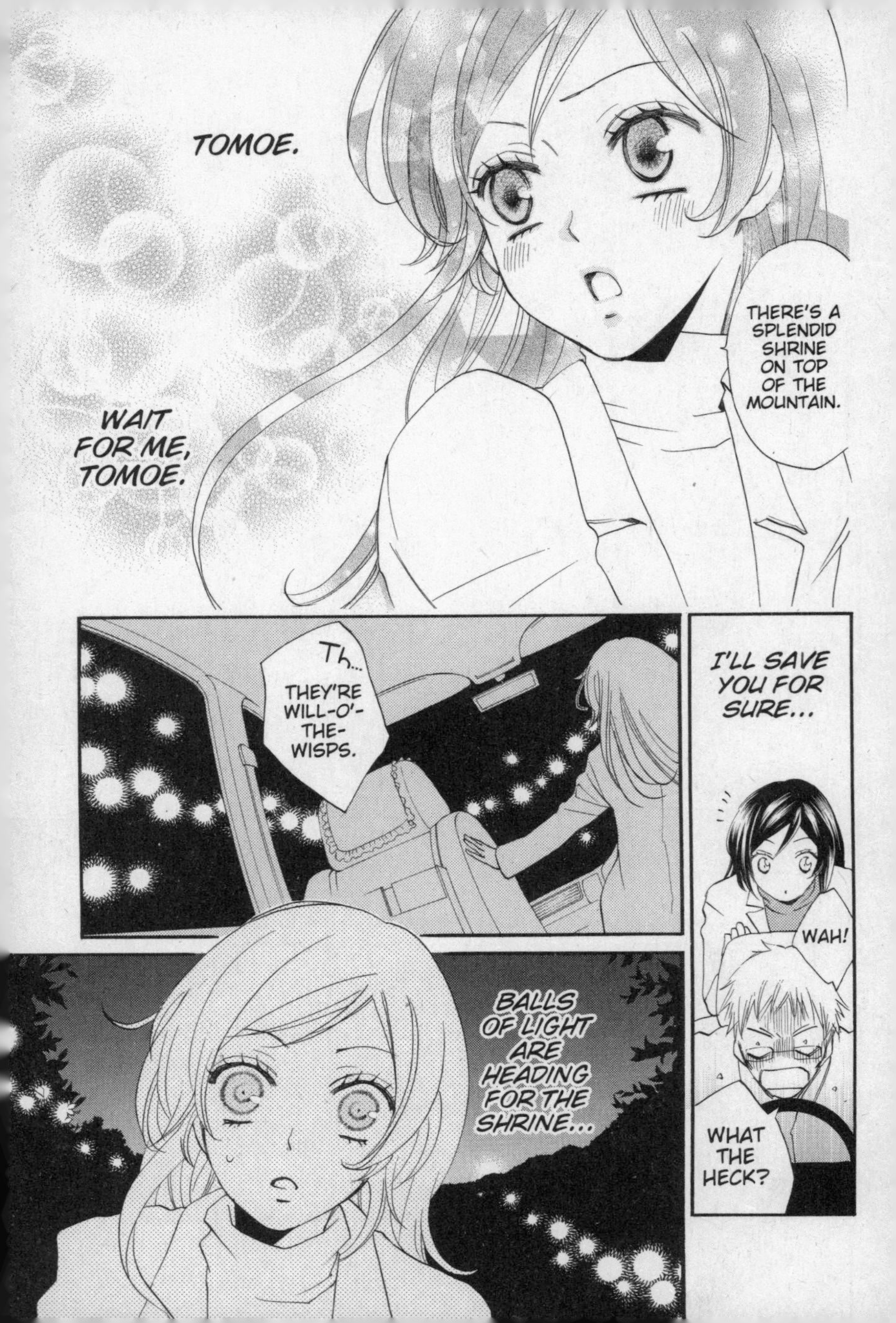
THERE'S A SPLENDID SHRINE ON TOP OF THE MOUNTAIN.
TOMOE.
WAIT FOR ME, TOMOE.
I'LL SAVE YOU FOR SURE...
WAH!
WHAT THE HECK?
Th... THEY'RE WILL-O'-THE-WISPS.
BALLS OF LIGHT ARE HEADING FOR THE SHRINE...

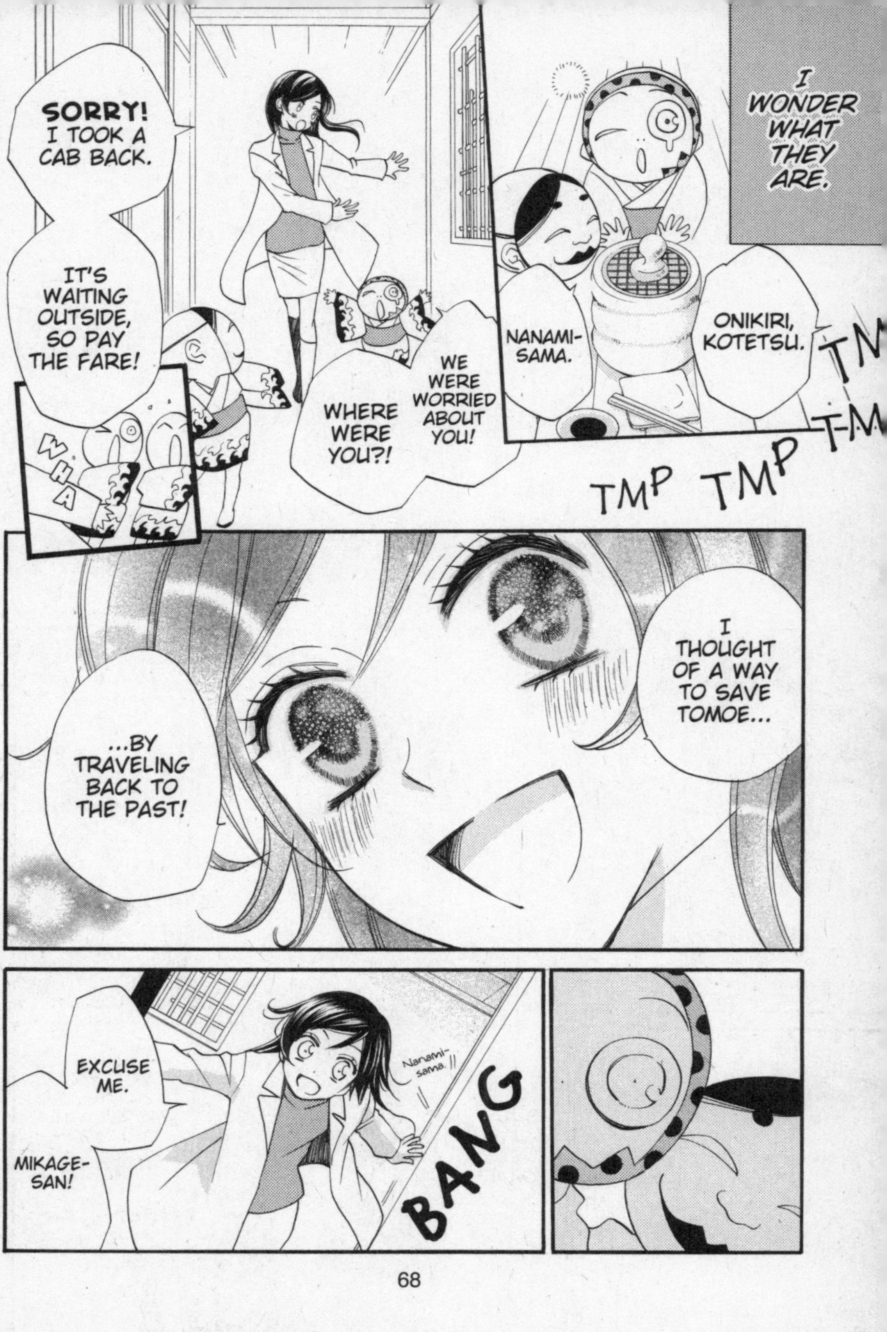
I WONDER WHAT THEY ARE.
ONIKIRI, KOTETSU.
NANAMI-SAMA.
TMP TMP
WE WERE WORRIED ABOUT YOU!
WHERE WERE YOU?!
SORRY! I TOOK A CAB BACK.
IT'S WAITING OUTSIDE, SO PAY THE FARE!
WHA
I THOUGHT OF A WAY TO SAVE TOMOE...
...BY TRAVELING BACK TO THE PAST!
Nanami-sama!!
BANG
EXCUSE ME.
MIKAGE-SAN!

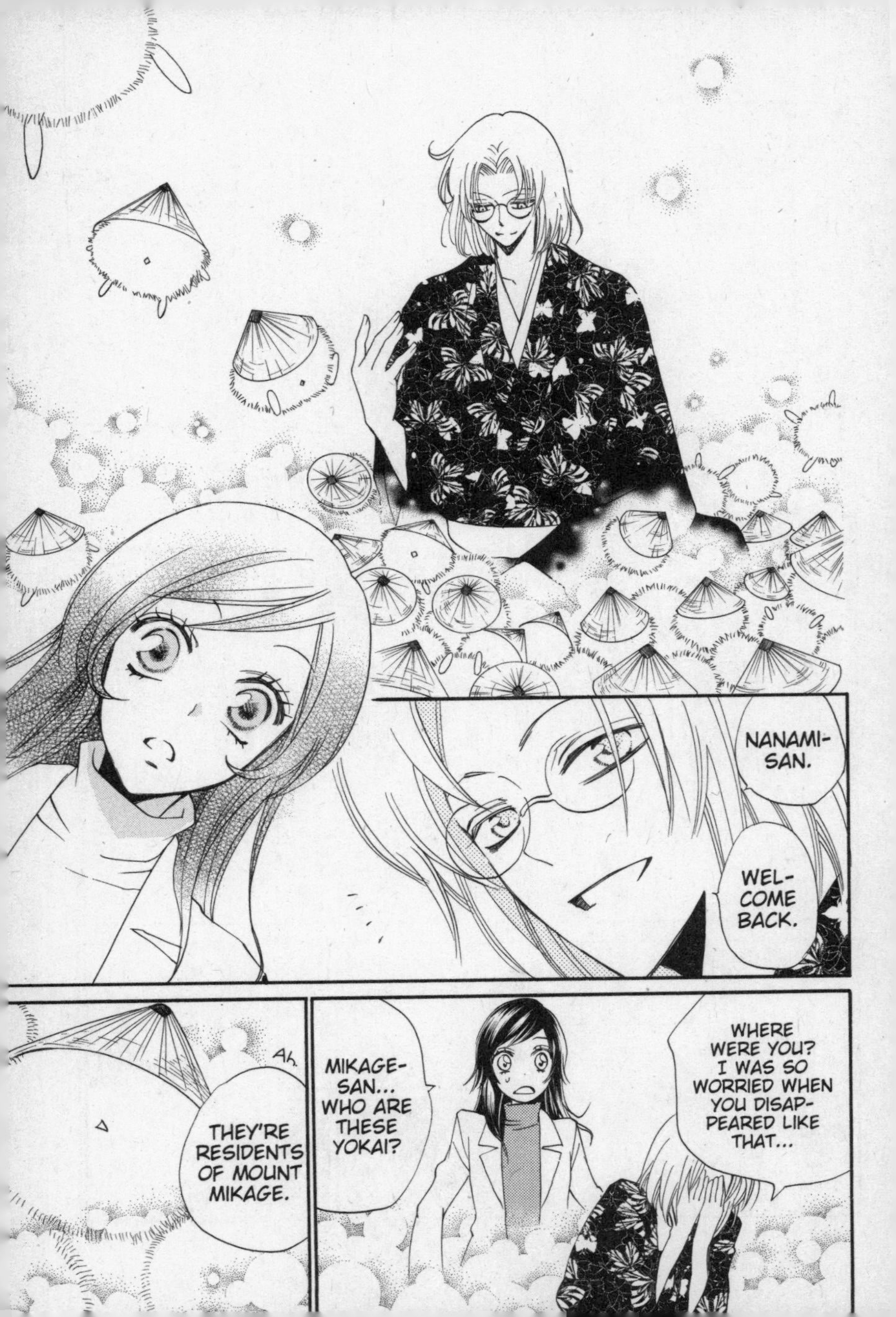
NANAMI-SAN.
WEL-COME BACK.
WHERE WERE YOU? I WAS SO WORRIED WHEN YOU DISAP-PEARED LIKE THAT...
MIKAGE-SAN... WHO ARE THESE YOKAI?
Ah.
THEY'RE RESIDENTS OF MOUNT MIKAGE.

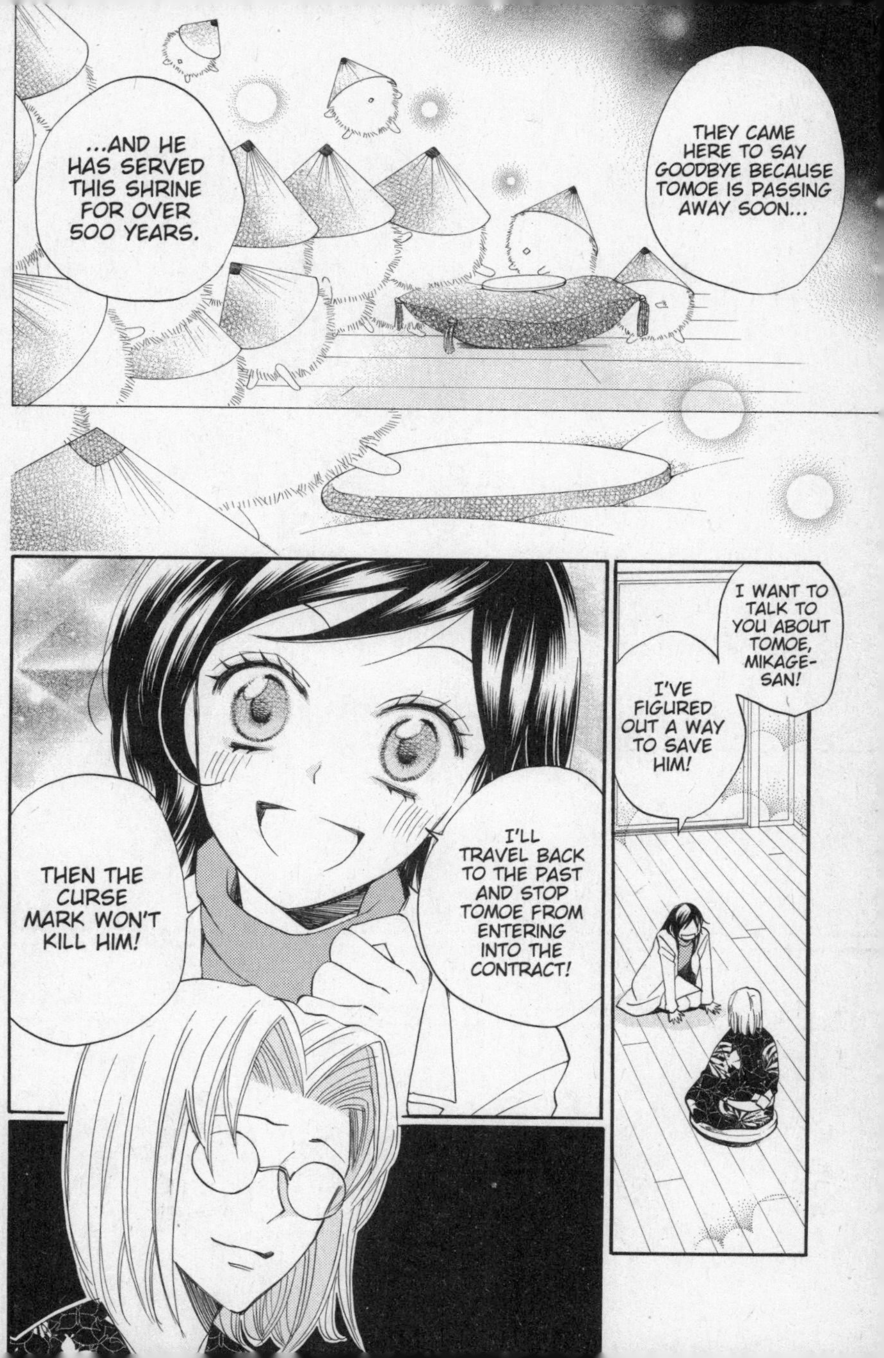
THEY CAME HERE TO SAY GOODBYE BECAUSE TOMOE IS PASSING AWAY SOON...
...AND HE HAS SERVED THIS SHRINE FOR OVER 500 YEARS.
I WANT TO TALK TO YOU ABOUT TOMOE, MIKAGE-SAN!
I'VE FIGURED OUT A WAY TO SAVE HIM!
I'LL TRAVEL BACK TO THE PAST AND STOP TOMOE FROM ENTERING INTO THE CONTRACT!
THEN THE CURSE MARK WON'T KILL HIM!

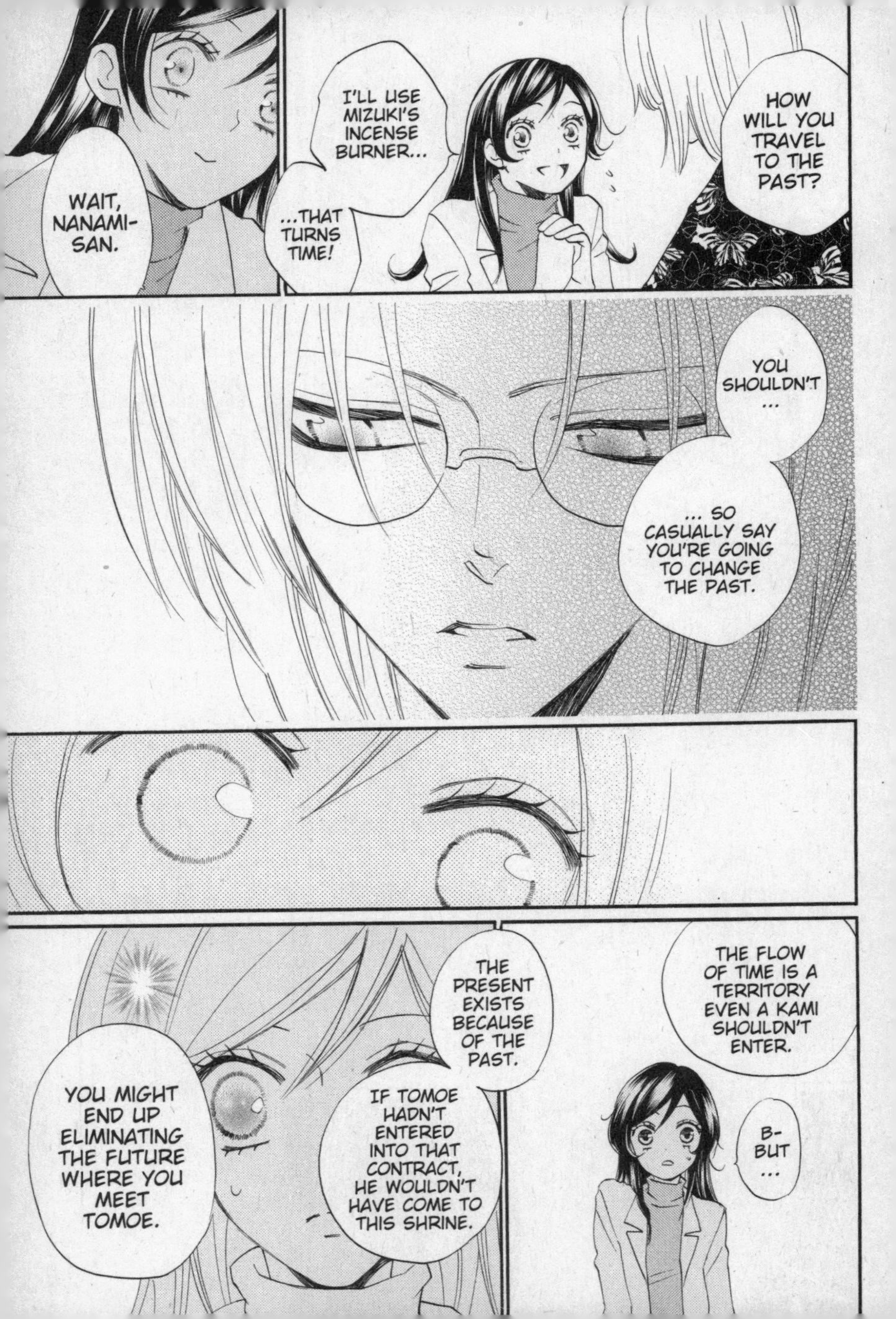
HOW WILL YOU TRAVEL TO THE PAST?
I'LL USE MIZUKI'S INCENSE BURNER...
...THAT TURNS TIME!
WAIT, NANAMI-SAN.
YOU SHOULDN'T ...
... SO CASUALLY SAY YOU'RE GOING TO CHANGE THE PAST.
THE FLOW OF TIME IS A TERRITORY EVEN A KAMI SHOULDN'T ENTER.
B-BUT ...
THE PRESENT EXISTS BECAUSE OF THE PAST.
IF TOMOE HADN'T ENTERED INTO THAT CONTRACT, HE WOULDN'T HAVE COME TO THIS SHRINE.
YOU MIGHT END UP ELIMINATING THE FUTURE WHERE YOU MEET TOMOE.

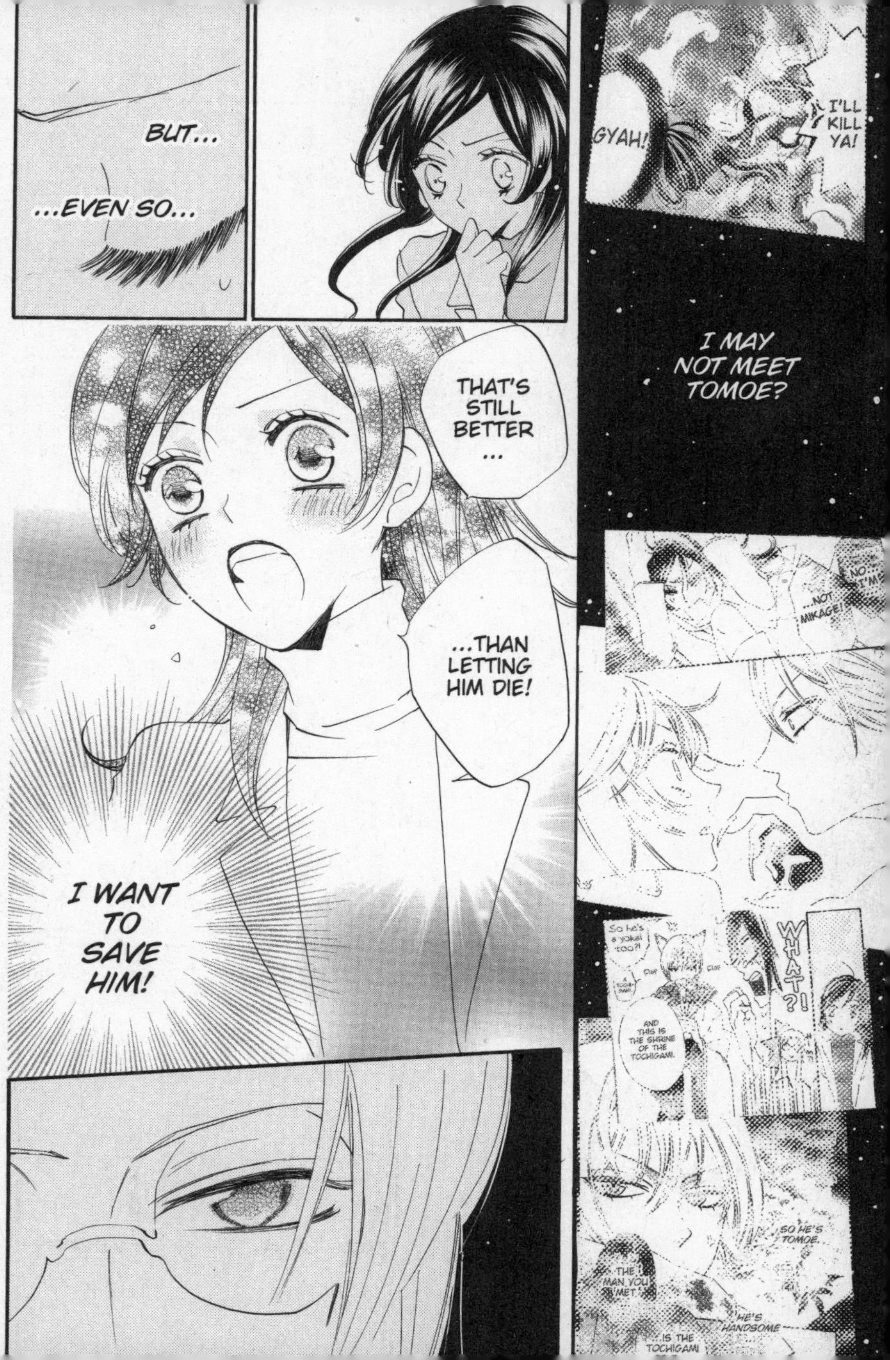
I'LL KILL YA!
GYAH!
I MAY NOT MEET TOMOE?
NO... I'M
...NOT MIKAGE!
WHAT?!
So he's a yokai too?!
A TOCHIGAMI
AND THIS IS THE SHRINE OF THE TOCHIGAMI.
SO HE'S TOMOE.
HE'S HANDSOME
THE MAN YOU MET
...IS THE TOCHIGAMI
BUT...
...EVEN SO...
THAT'S STILL BETTER...
...THAN LETTING HIM DIE!
I WANT TO SAVE HIM!

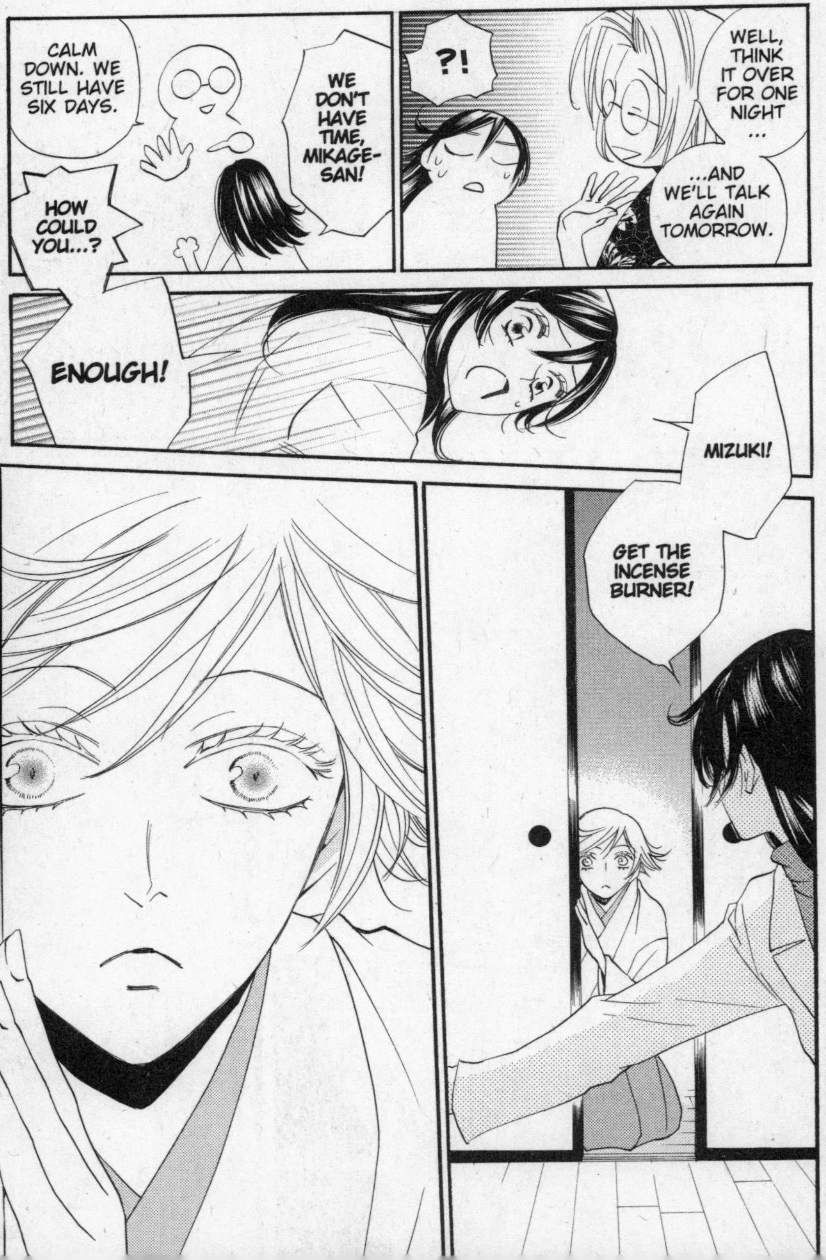
WELL, THINK IT OVER FOR ONE NIGHT ...
...AND WE'LL TALK AGAIN TOMORROW.
?!
WE DON'T HAVE TIME, MIKAGE-SAN!
CALM DOWN. WE STILL HAVE SIX DAYS.
HOW COULD YOU...?
ENOUGH!
MIZUKI!
GET THE INCENSE BURNER!

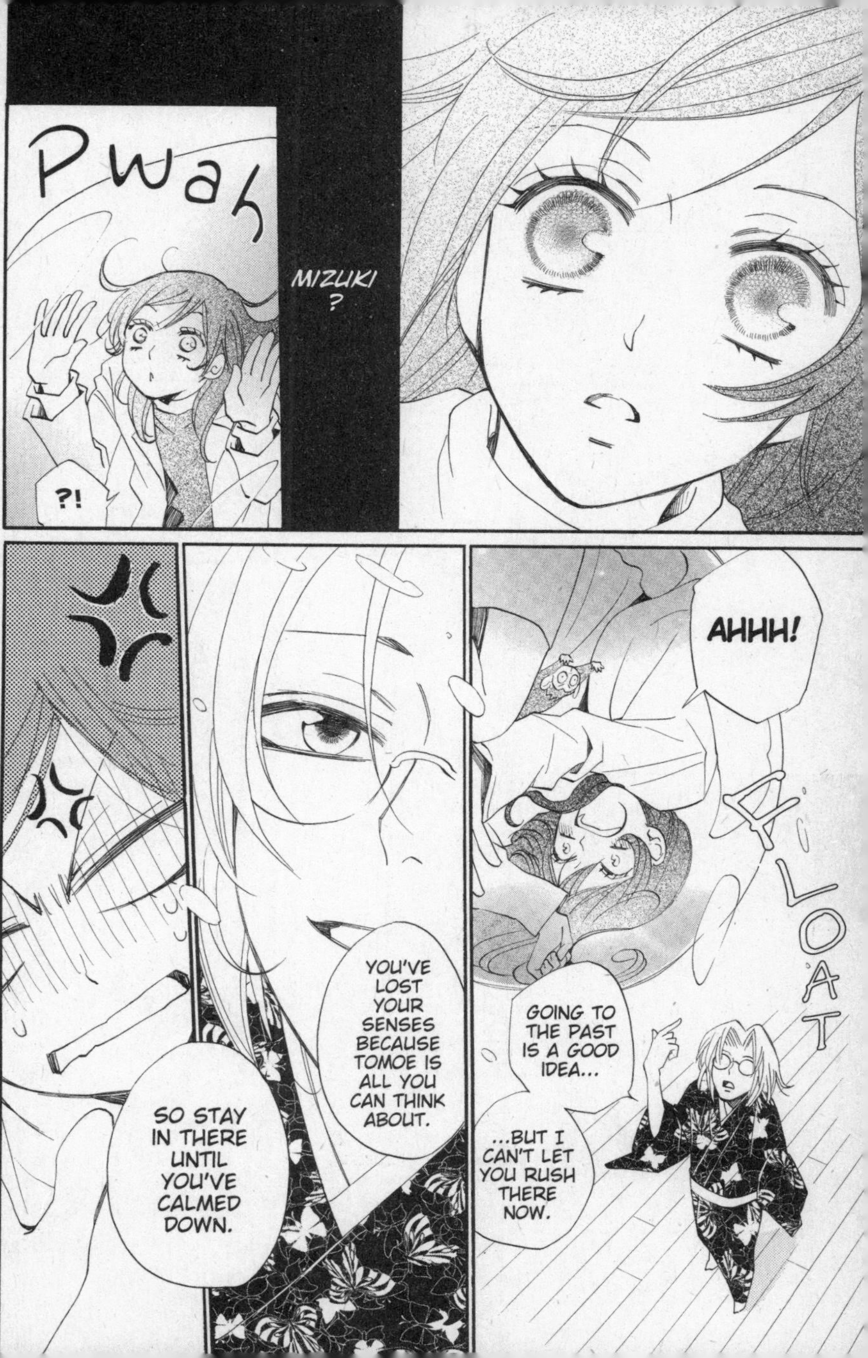
MIZUKI ?
Pwah
?!
AHHH!
FLOAT
GOING TO THE PAST IS A GOOD IDEA...
...BUT I CAN'T LET YOU RUSH THERE NOW.
YOU'VE LOST YOUR SENSES BECAUSE TOMOE IS ALL YOU CAN THINK ABOUT.
SO STAY IN THERE UNTIL YOU'VE CALMED DOWN.

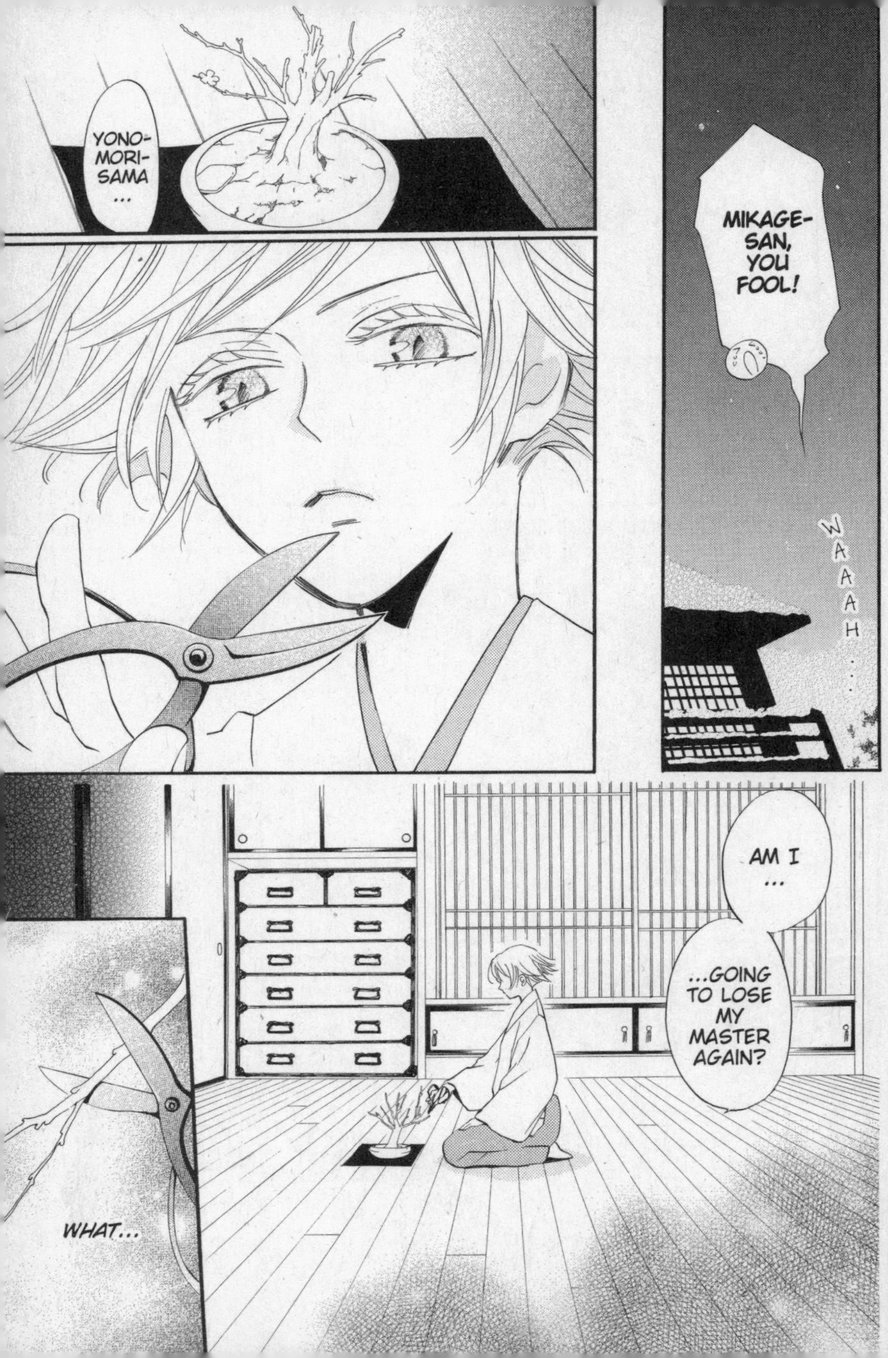
MIKAGE-SAN, YOU FOOL!
WAAAH...
YONO-MORI-SAMA...
AM I...
...GOING TO LOSE MY MASTER AGAIN?
WHAT...

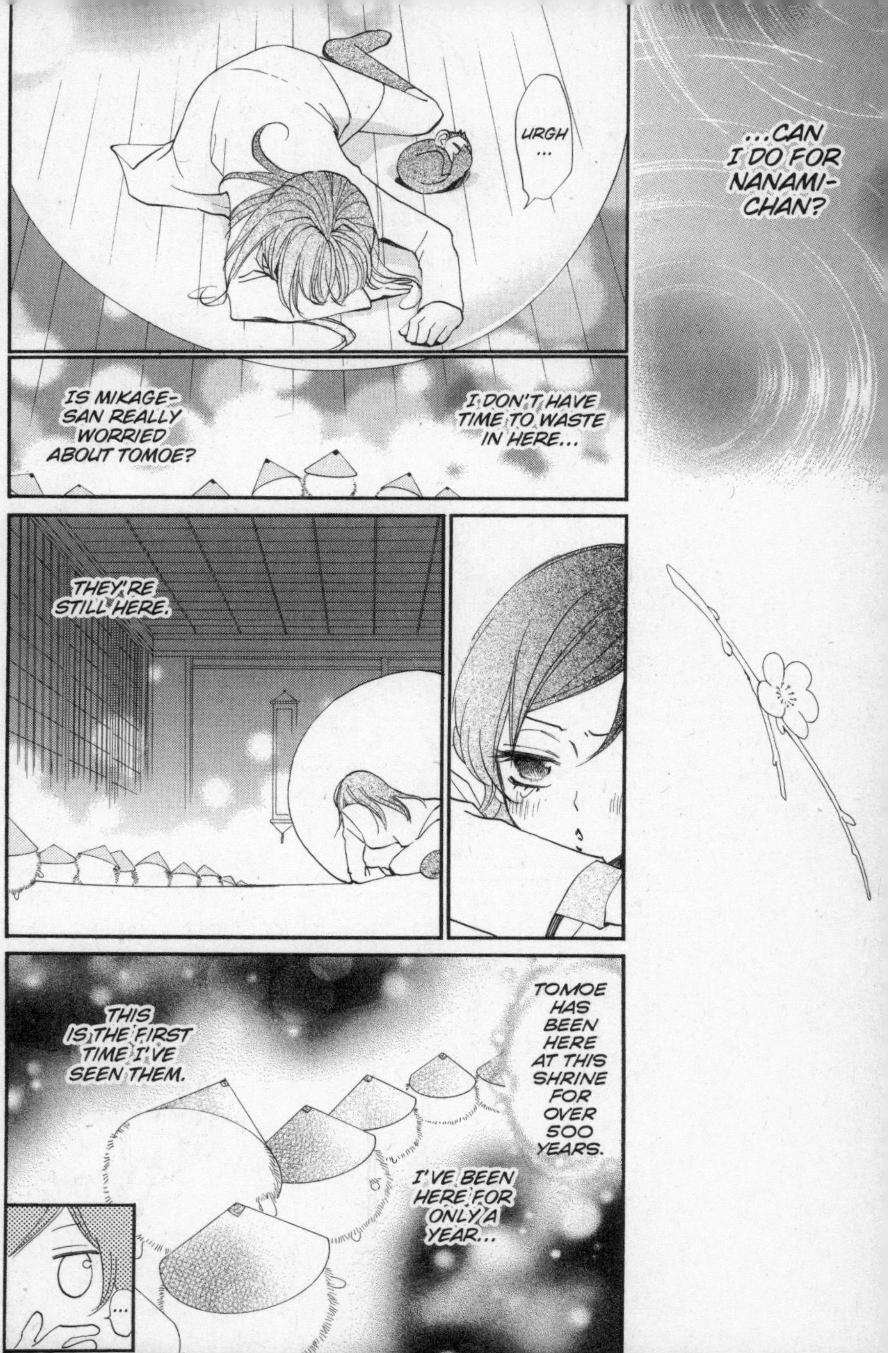
...CAN I DO FOR NANAMI-CHAN?
URGH ...
I DON'T HAVE TIME TO WASTE IN HERE...
IS MIKAGE-SAN REALLY WORRIED ABOUT TOMOE?
THEY'RE STILL HERE.
TOMOE HAS BEEN HERE AT THIS SHRINE FOR OVER 500 YEARS.
THIS IS THE FIRST TIME I'VE SEEN THEM.
I'VE BEEN HERE FOR ONLY A YEAR...
...

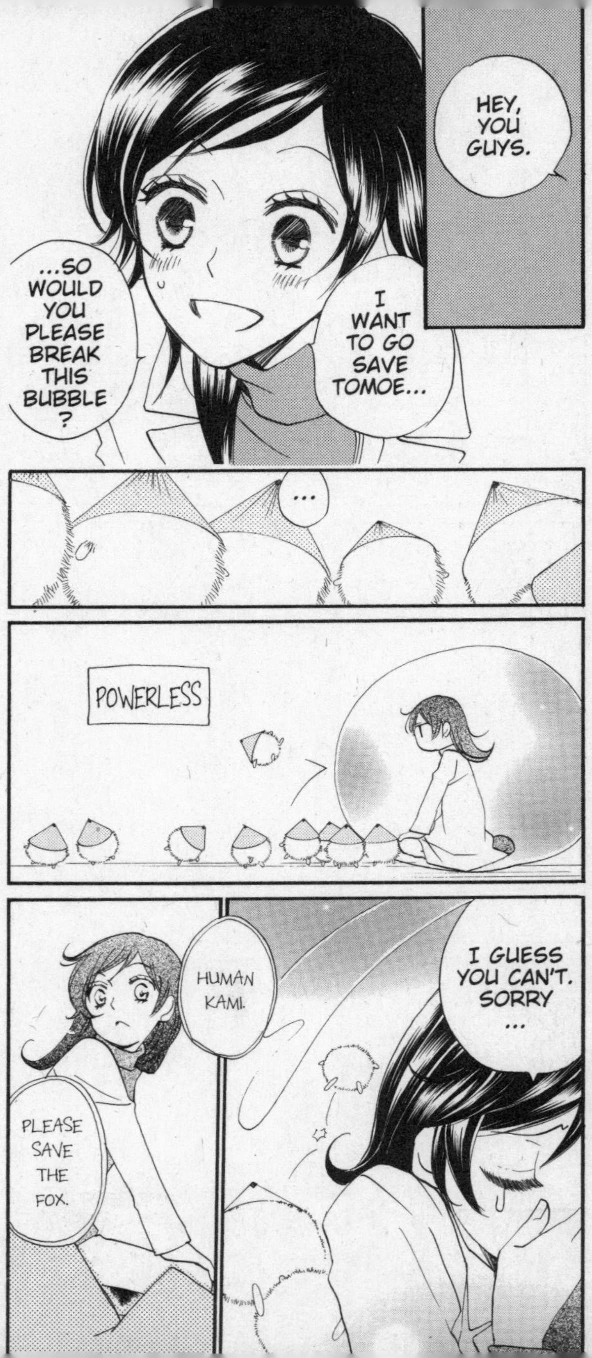
HEY, YOU GUYS.
I WANT TO GO SAVE TOMOE...
...SO WOULD YOU PLEASE BREAK THIS BUBBLE?
...
POWERLESS
I GUESS YOU CAN'T. SORRY...
HUMAN KAMI.
PLEASE SAVE THE FOX.

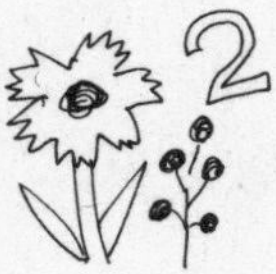
2

These days I want to eat tasty things, so I hunt for delicious treats and eat them!

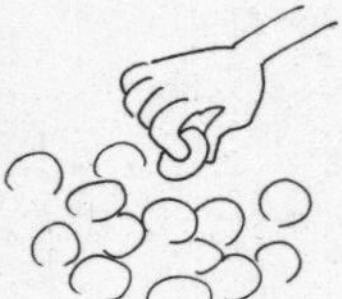

Sometimes they're very good cookies and I think "Wah, I want to see them again!" But I don't remember where I got them, or the shop is far away.

I'll go search for new encounters.

I should bake some and eat them fresh out of the oven!

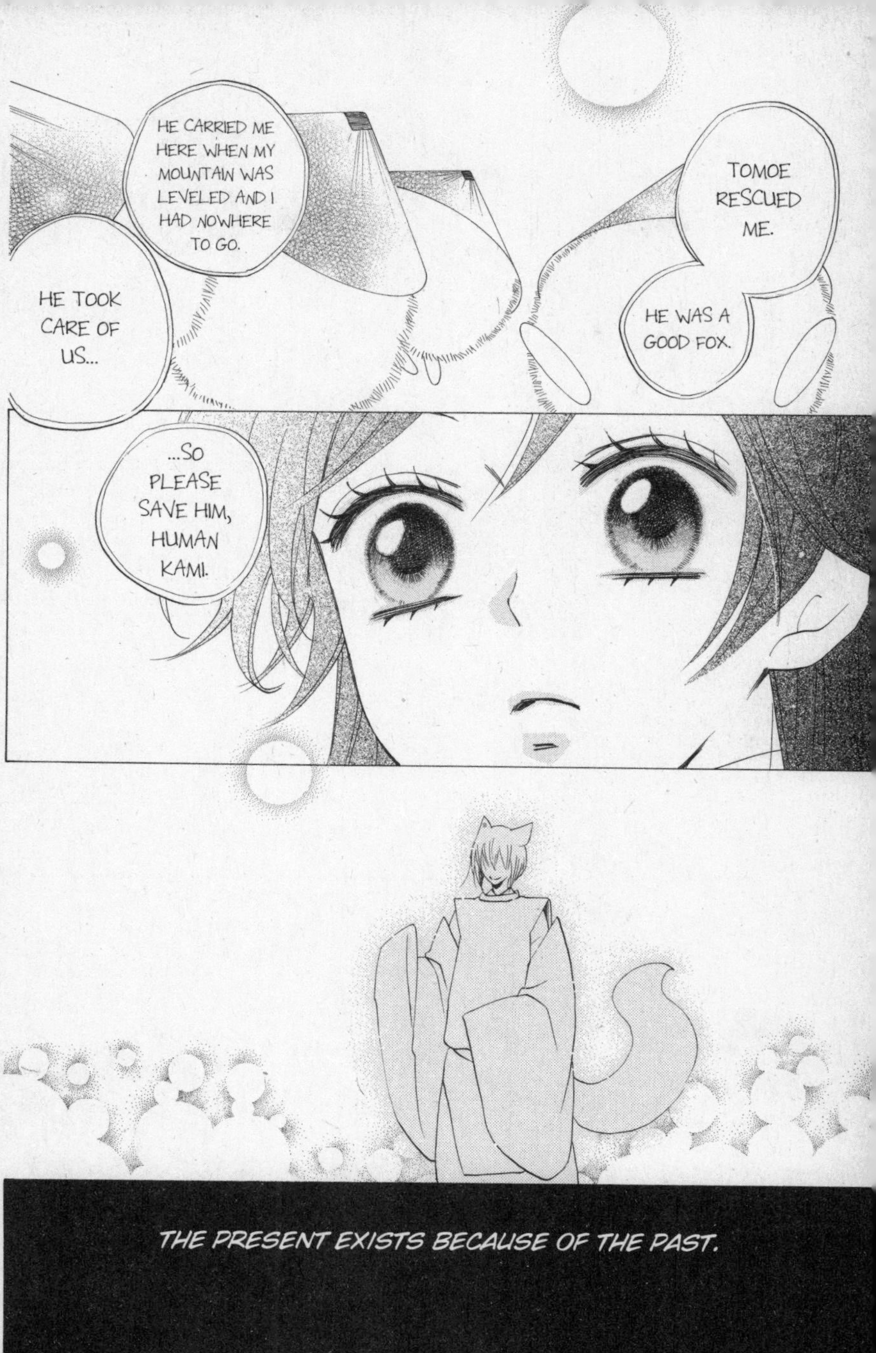
TOMOE RESCUED ME.
HE WAS A GOOD FOX.
HE CARRIED ME HERE WHEN MY MOUNTAIN WAS LEVELED AND I HAD NOWHERE TO GO.
HE TOOK CARE OF US...
...SO PLEASE SAVE HIM, HUMAN KAMI.
THE PRESENT EXISTS BECAUSE OF THE PAST.

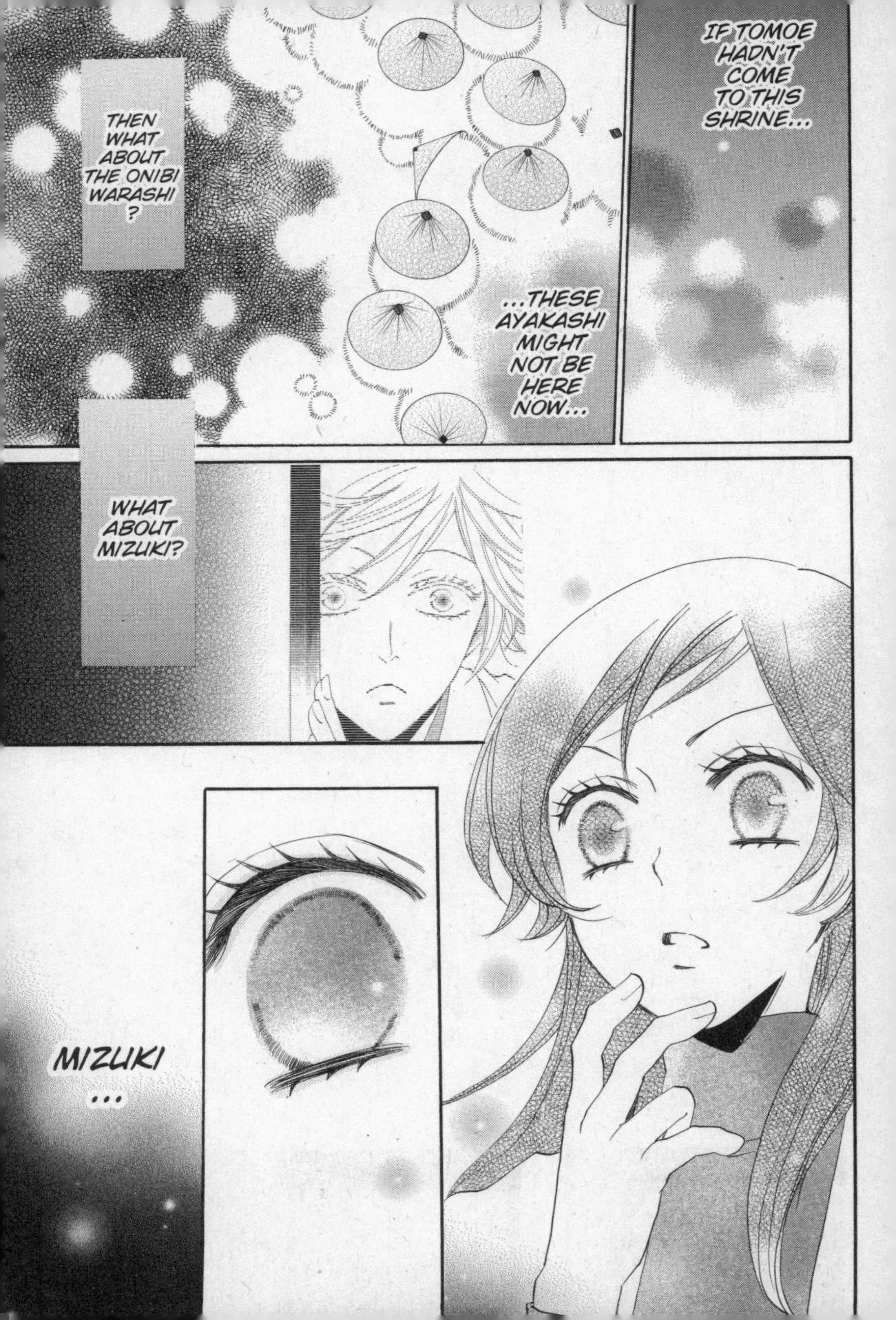
IF TOMOE HADN'T COME TO THIS SHRINE...
...THESE AYAKASHI MIGHT NOT BE HERE NOW...
THEN WHAT ABOUT THE ONIBI WARASHI?
WHAT ABOUT MIZUKI?
MIZUKI...

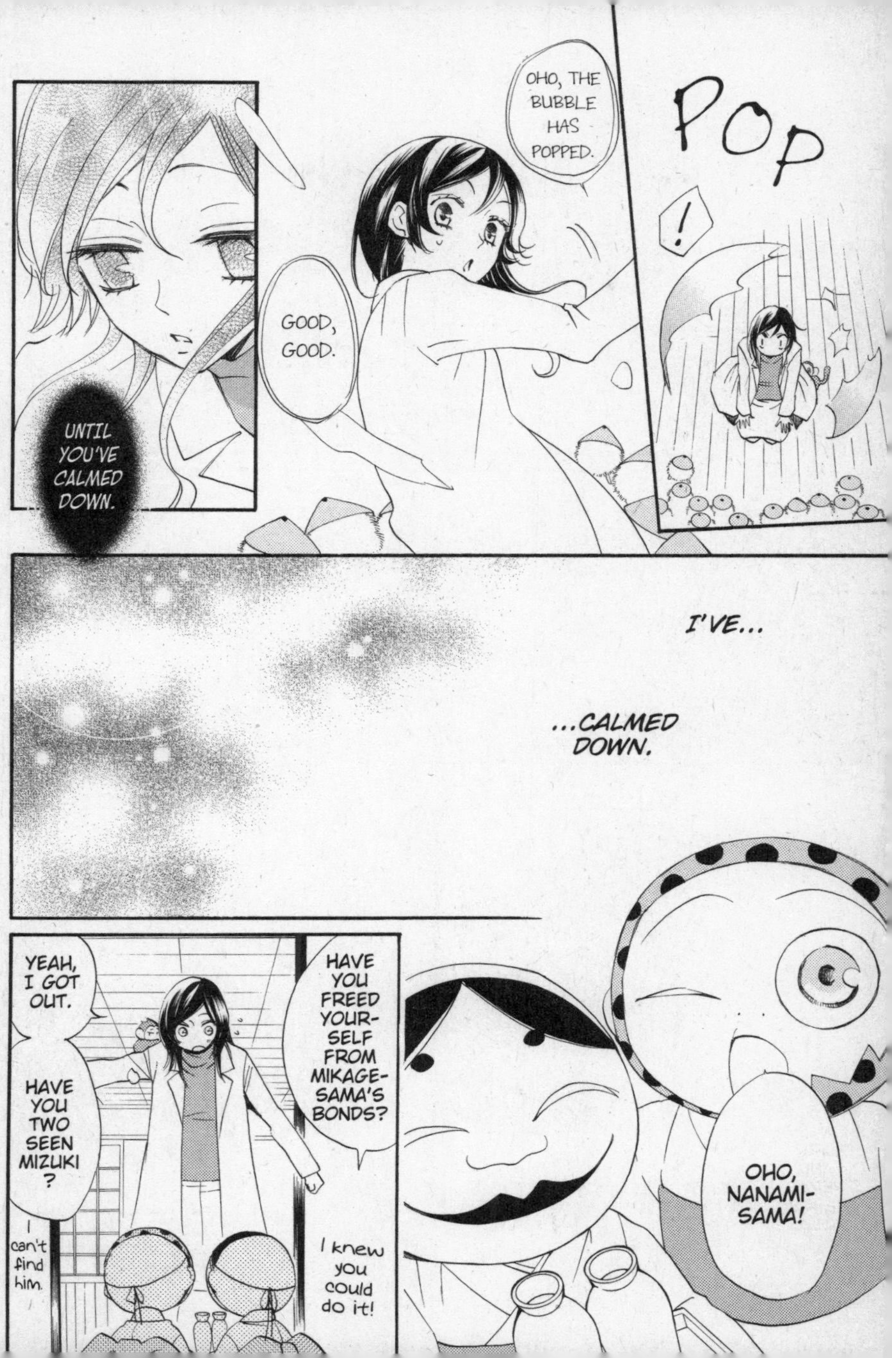
POP
!
OHO, THE BUBBLE HAS POPPED.
GOOD, GOOD.
UNTIL YOU'VE CALMED DOWN.
I'VE...
...CALMED DOWN.
OHO, NANAMI-SAMA!
HAVE YOU FREED YOURSELF FROM MIKAGE-SAMA'S BONDS?
I knew you could do it!
YEAH, I GOT OUT.
HAVE YOU TWO SEEN MIZUKI?
I can't find him.

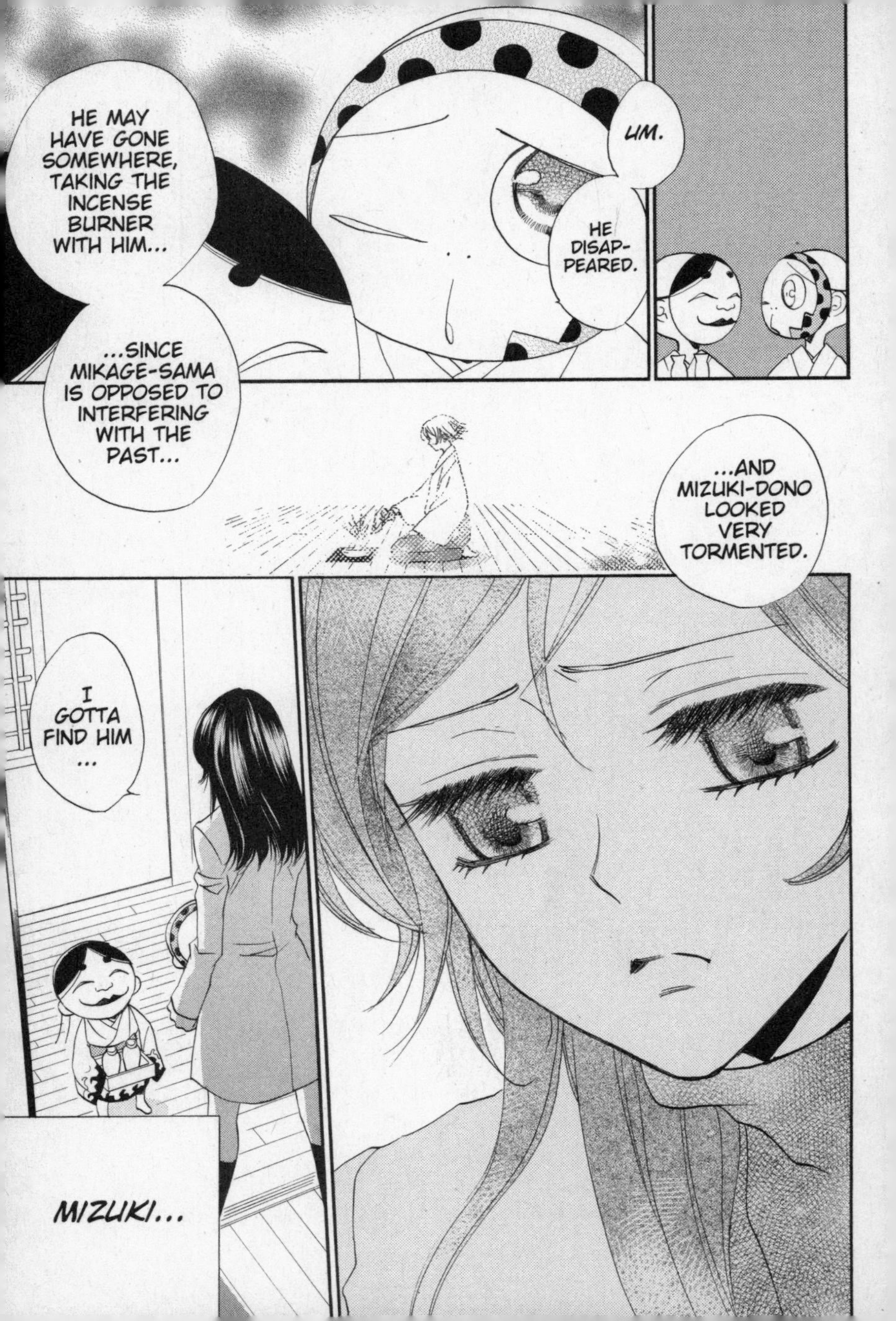
UM.
HE DISAPPEARED.
HE MAY HAVE GONE SOMEWHERE, TAKING THE INCENSE BURNER WITH HIM...
...SINCE MIKAGE-SAMA IS OPPOSED TO INTERFERING WITH THE PAST...
...AND MIZUKI-DONO LOOKED VERY TORMENTED.
I GOTTA FIND HIM ...
MIZUKI...

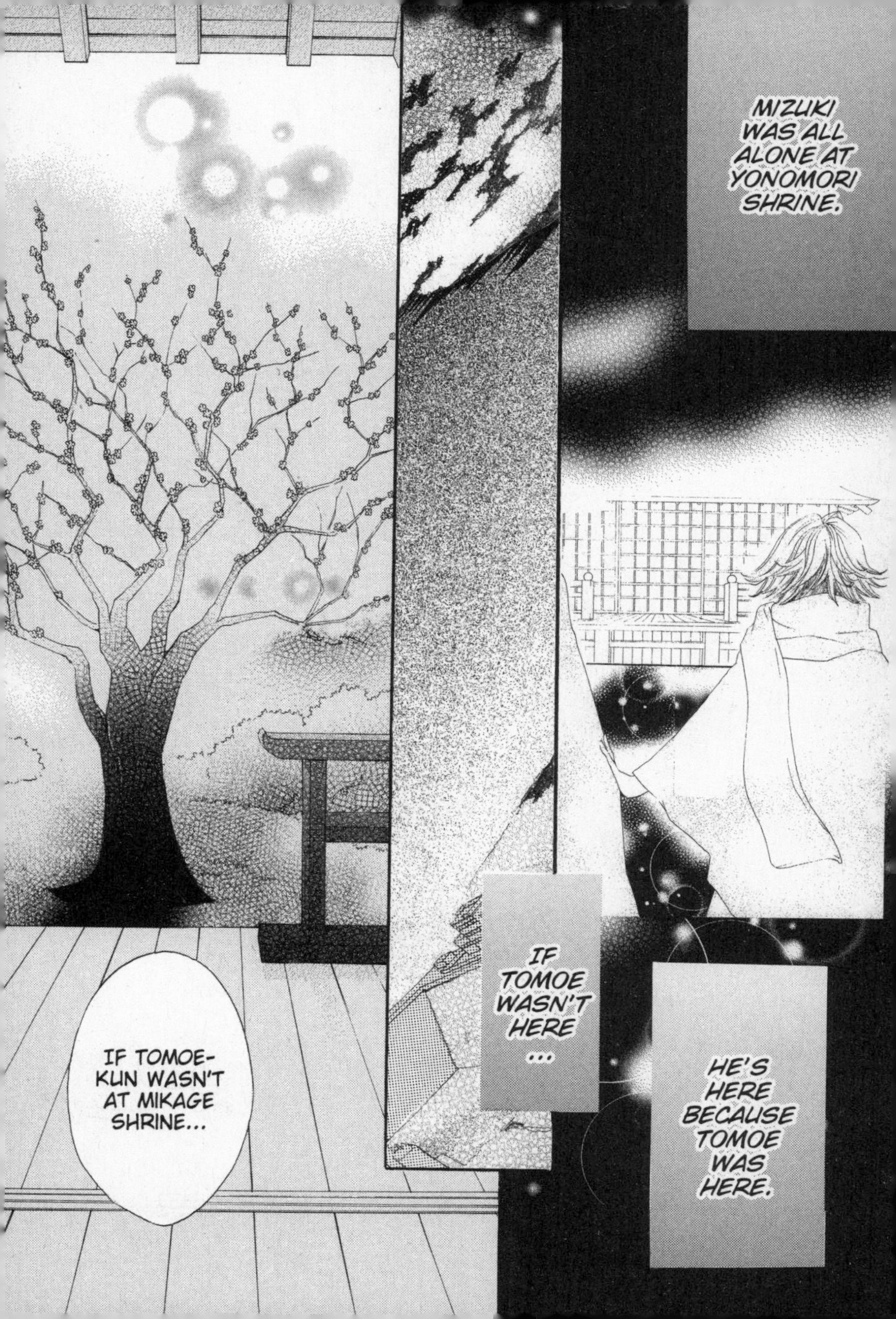
MIZUKI WAS ALL ALONE AT YONOMORI SHRINE.
IF TOMOE WASN'T HERE...
HE'S HERE BECAUSE TOMOE WAS HERE.
IF TOMOE-KUN WASN'T AT MIKAGE SHRINE...

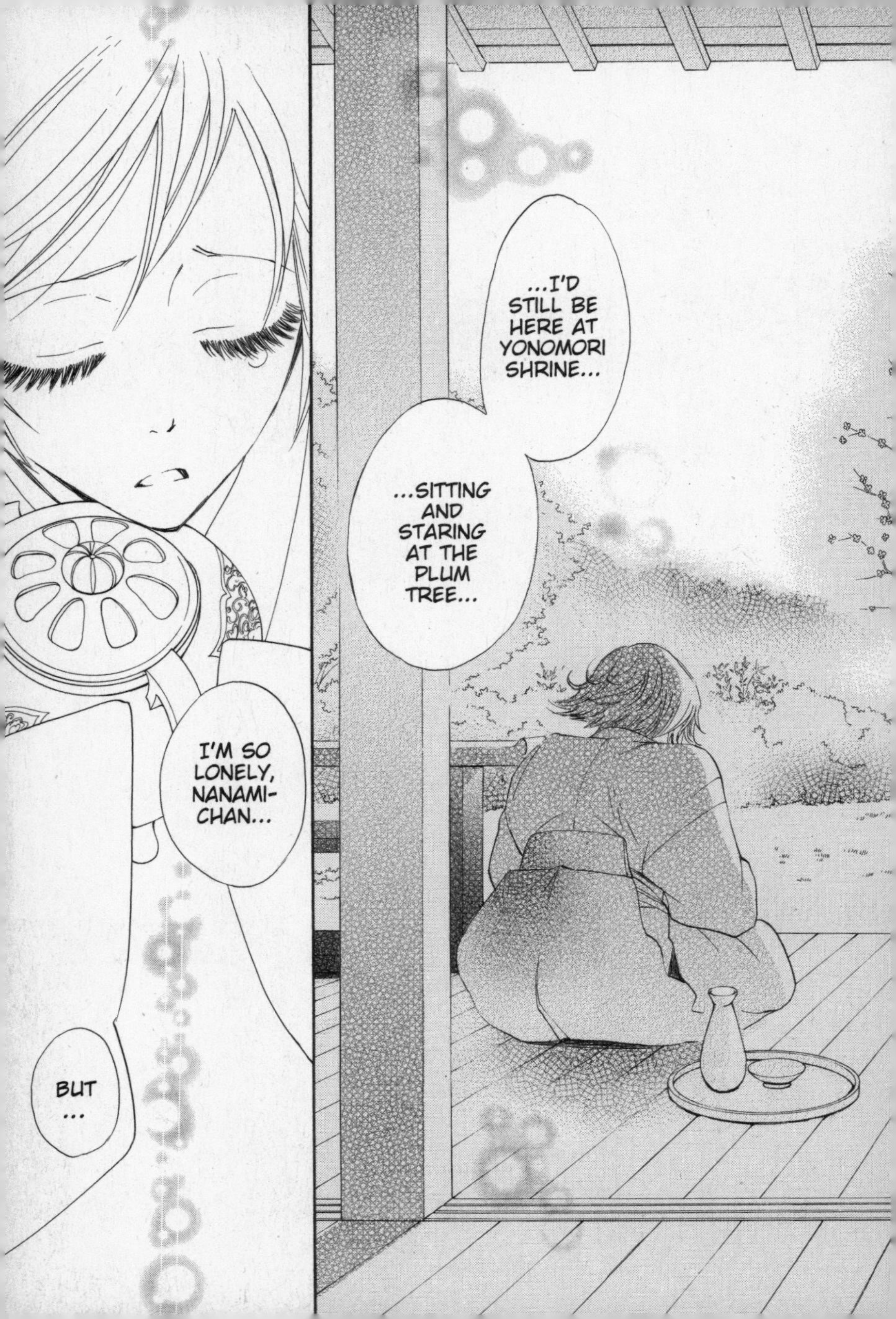
...I'D STILL BE HERE AT YONOMORI SHRINE...
...SITTING AND STARING AT THE PLUM TREE...
I'M SO LONELY, NANAMI-CHAN...
BUT ...

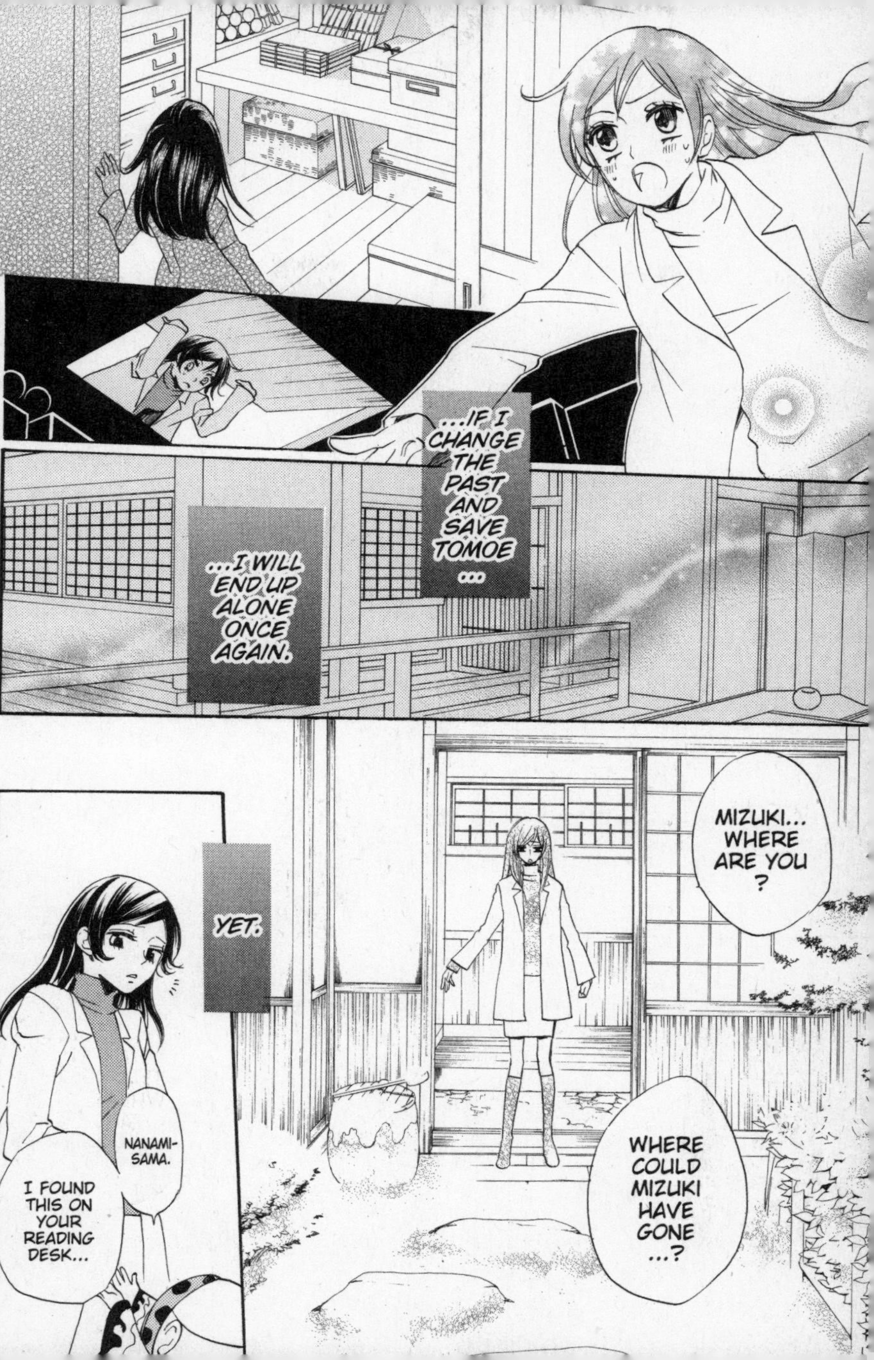
...IF I CHANGE THE PAST AND SAVE TOMOE ...
...I WILL END UP ALONE ONCE AGAIN.
MIZUKI... WHERE ARE YOU ?
WHERE COULD MIZUKI HAVE GONE ...?
YET.
NANAMI-SAMA.
I FOUND THIS ON YOUR READING DESK...

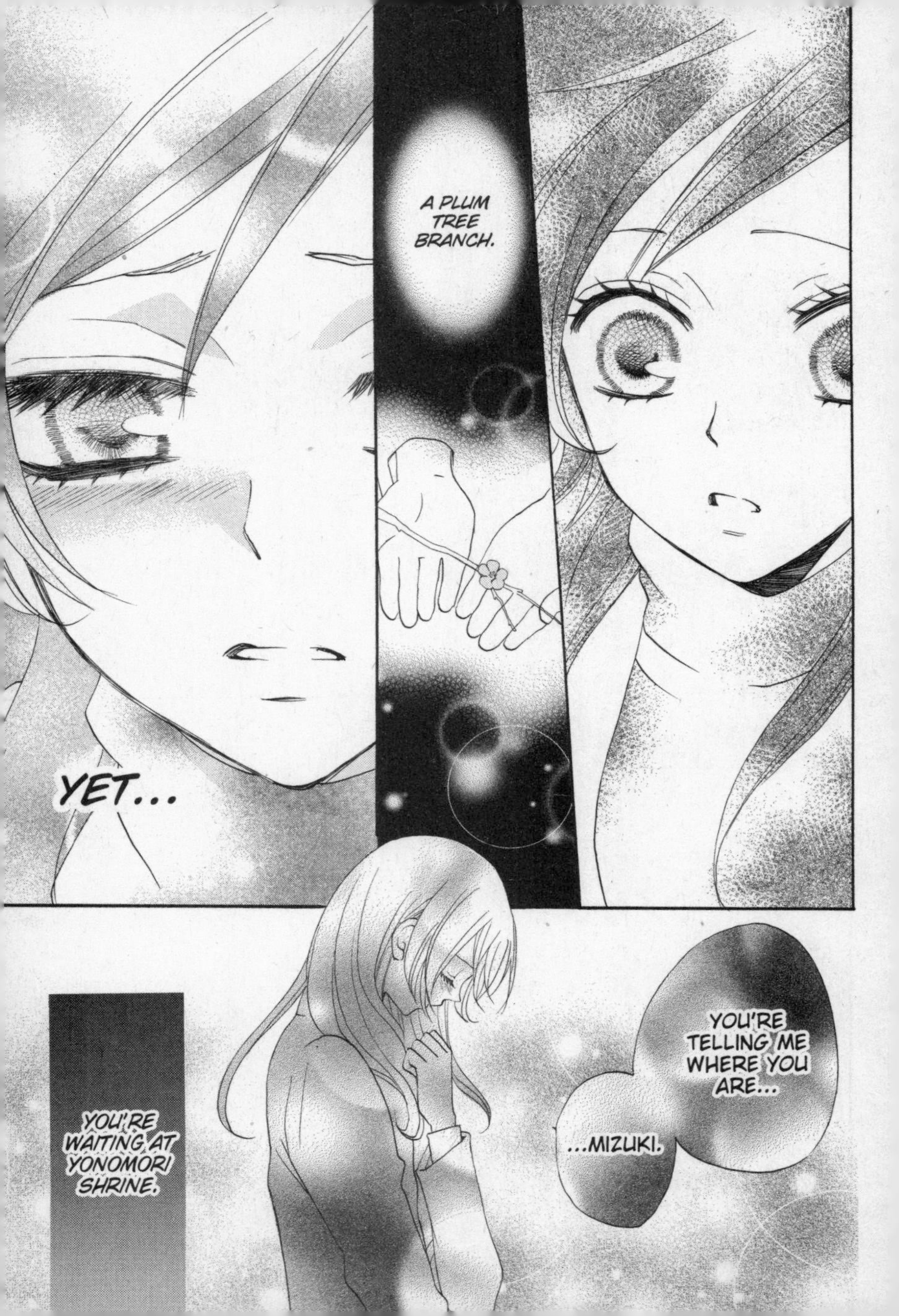
A PLUM TREE BRANCH.
YET...
YOU'RE TELLING ME WHERE YOU ARE...
...MIZUKI.
YOU'RE WAITING AT YONOMORI SHRINE.

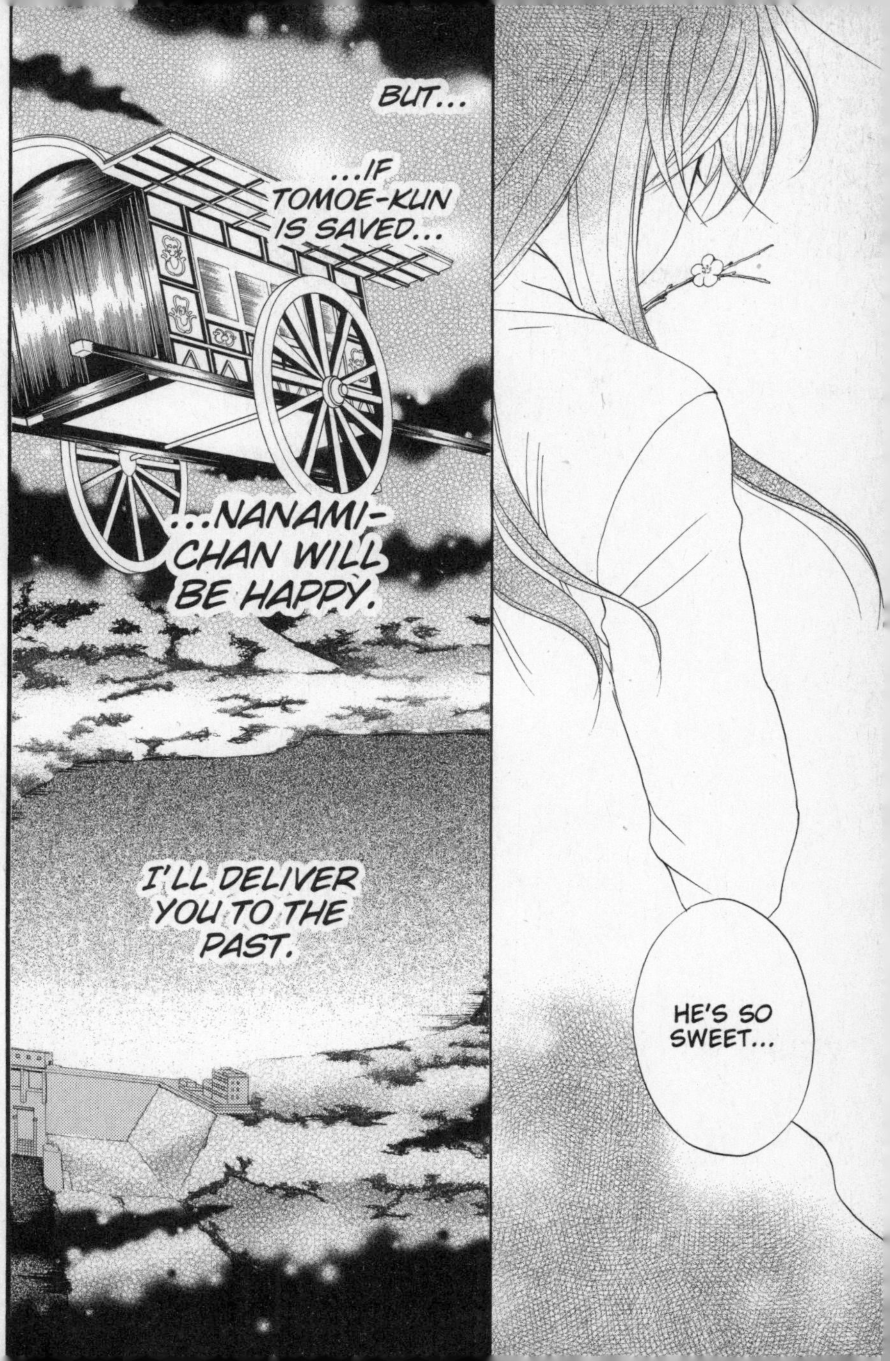
HE'S SO SWEET...
BUT...
...IF TOMOE-KUN IS SAVED...
...NANAMI-CHAN WILL BE HAPPY.
I'LL DELIVER YOU TO THE PAST.

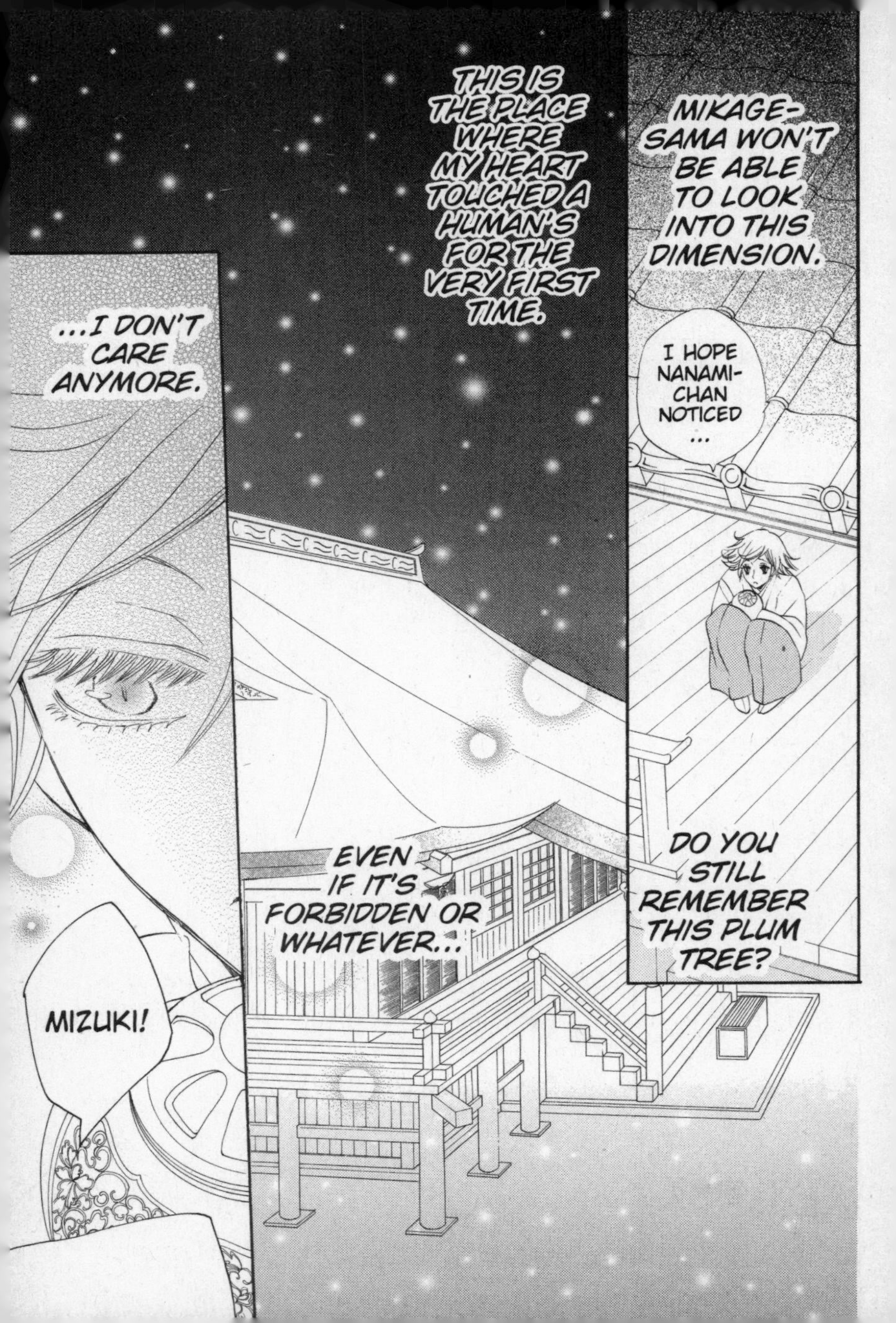
MIKAGE-SAMA WON'T BE ABLE TO LOOK INTO THIS DIMENSION.
I HOPE NANAMI-CHAN NOTICED...
DO YOU STILL REMEMBER THIS PLUM TREE?
THIS IS THE PLACE WHERE MY HEART TOUCHED A HUMAN'S FOR THE VERY FIRST TIME.
EVEN IF IT'S FORBIDDEN OR WHATEVER...
...I DON'T CARE ANYMORE.
MIZUKI!

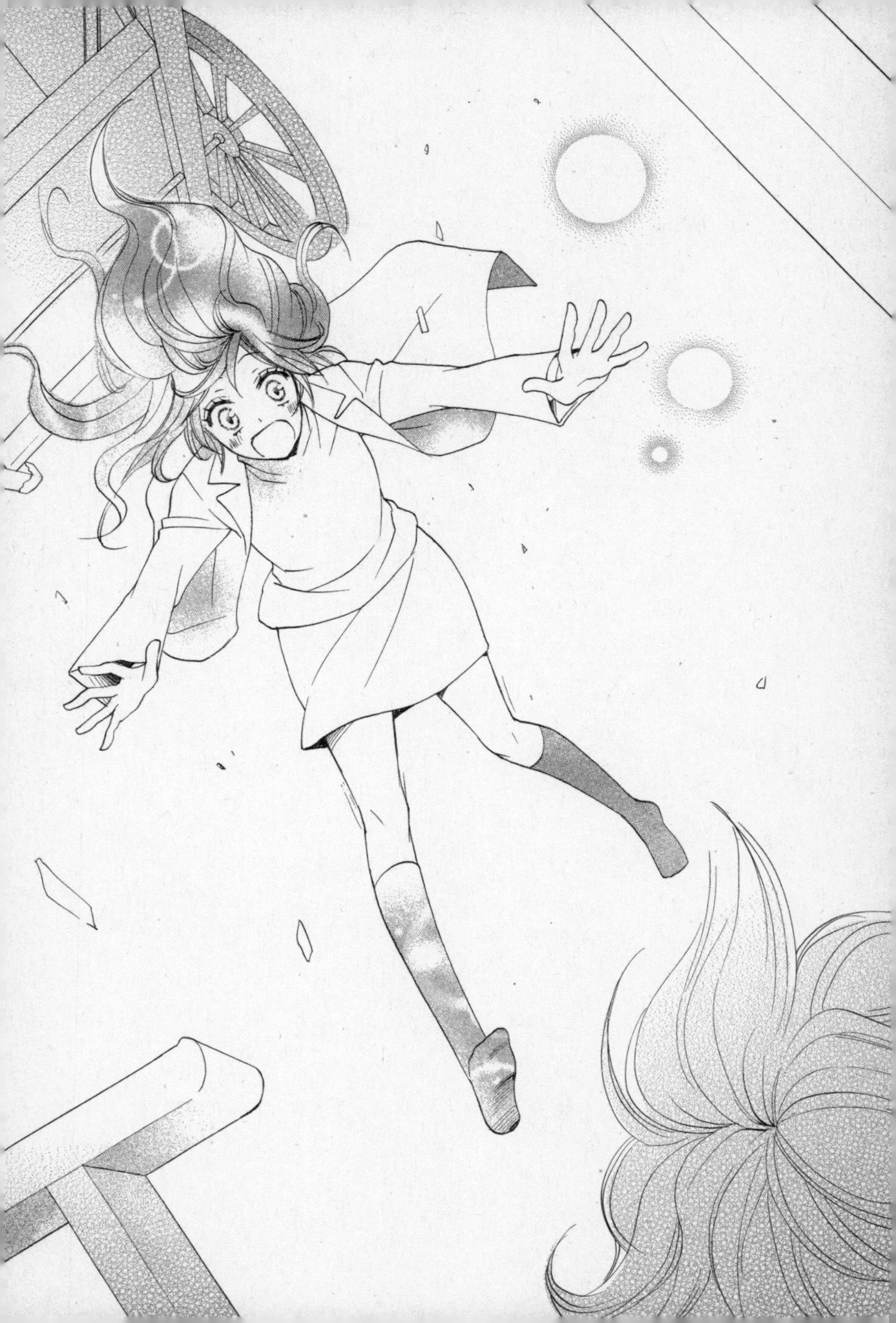

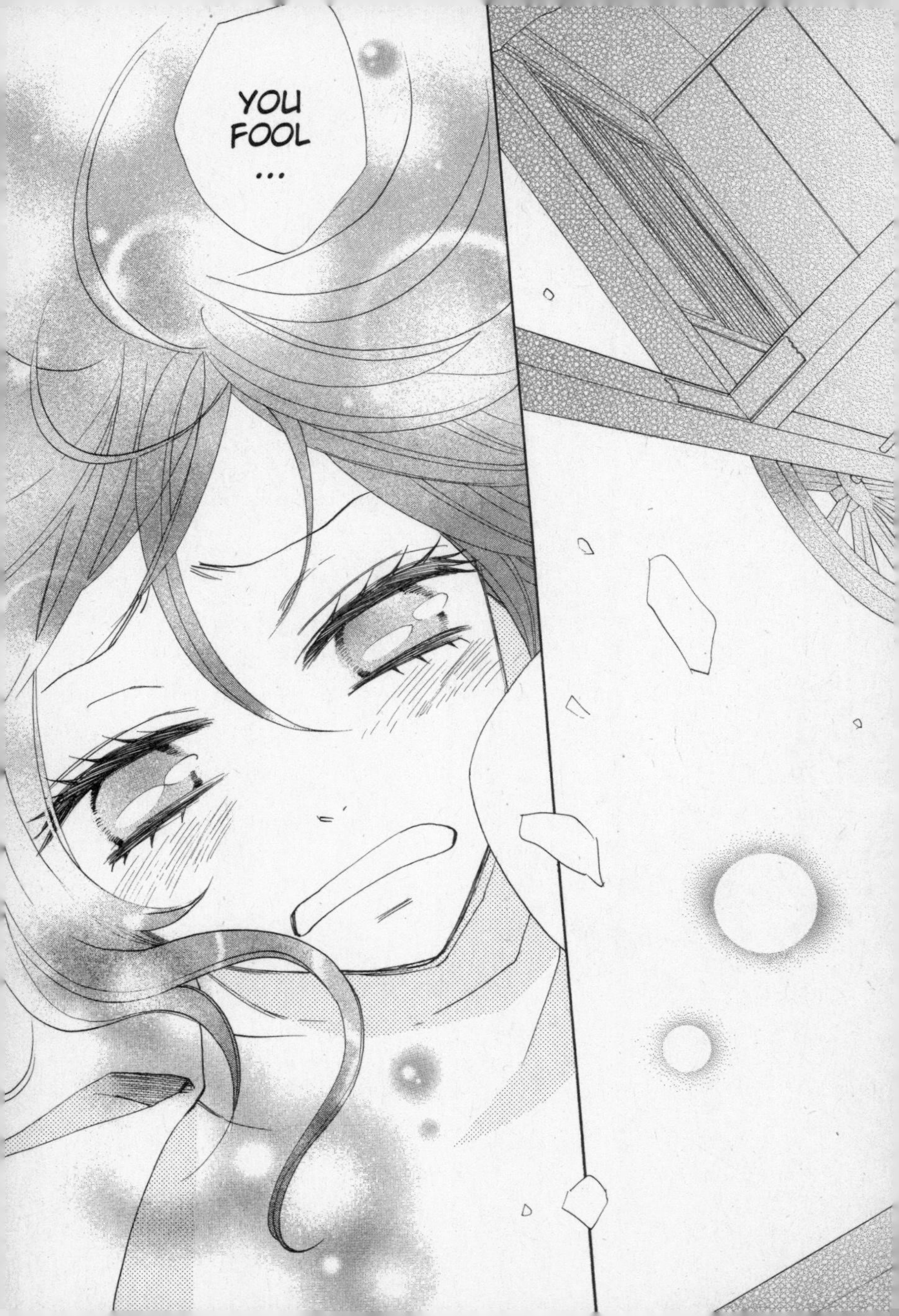
YOU FOOL ...

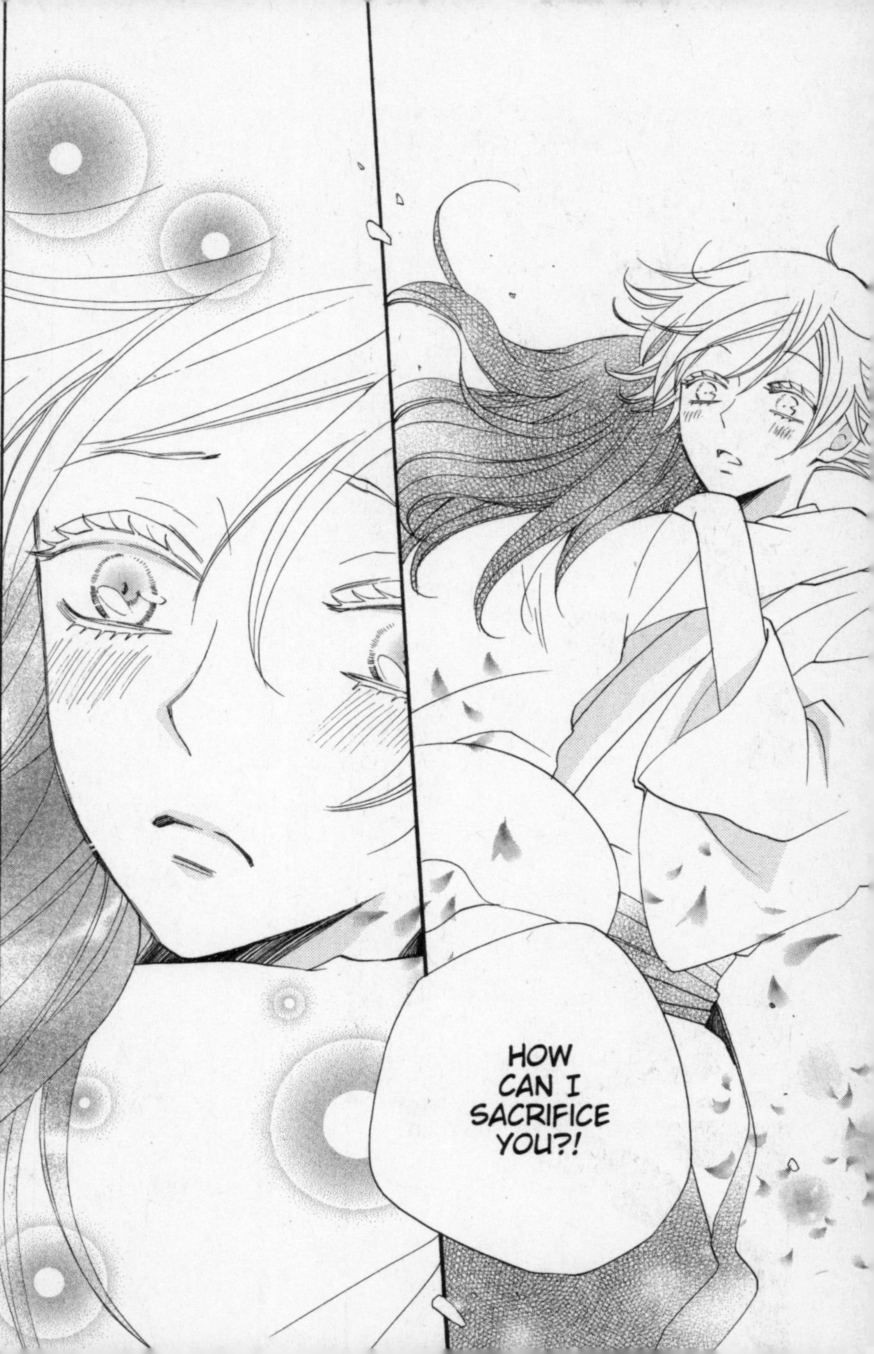
HOW CAN I SACRIFICE YOU?!

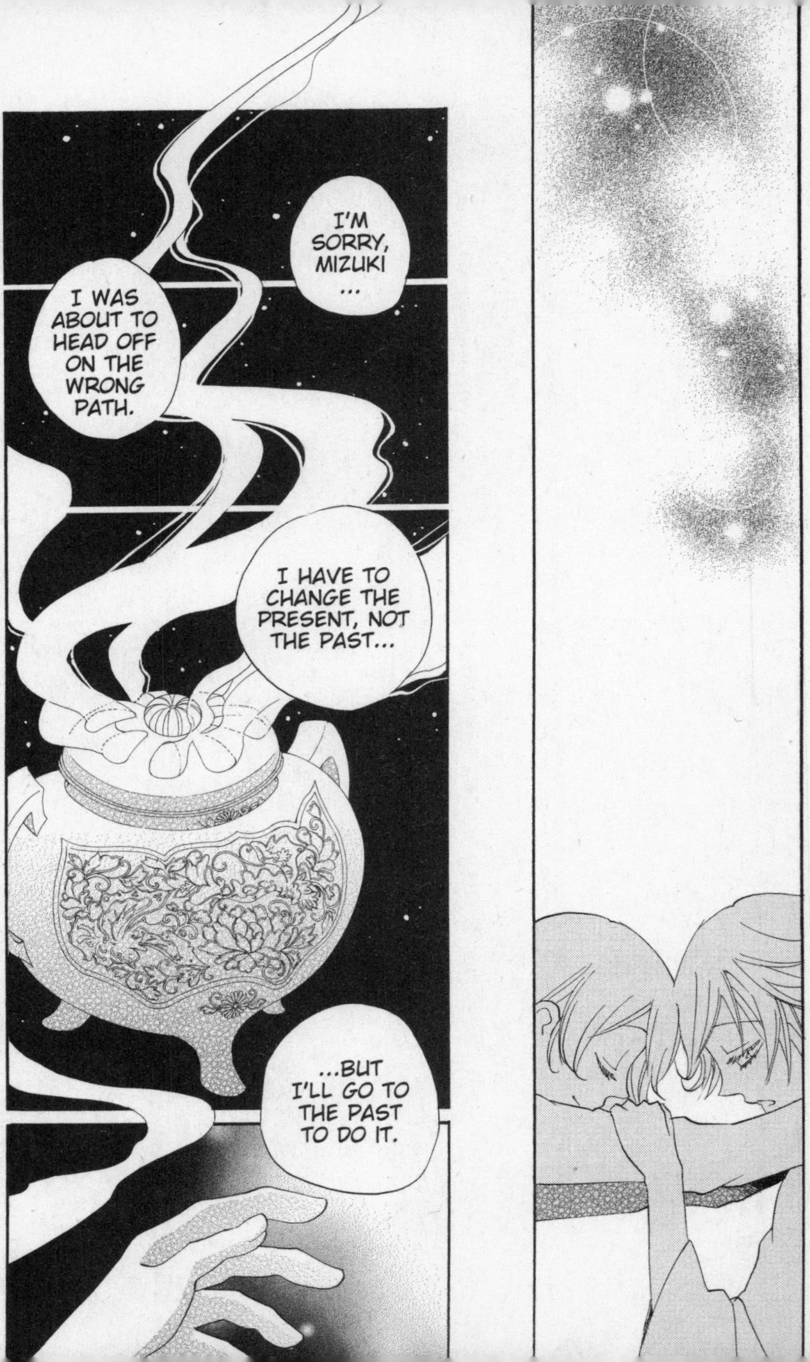
I'M SORRY, MIZUKI ...
I WAS ABOUT TO HEAD OFF ON THE WRONG PATH.
I HAVE TO CHANGE THE PRESENT, NOT THE PAST...
...BUT I'LL GO TO THE PAST TO DO IT.

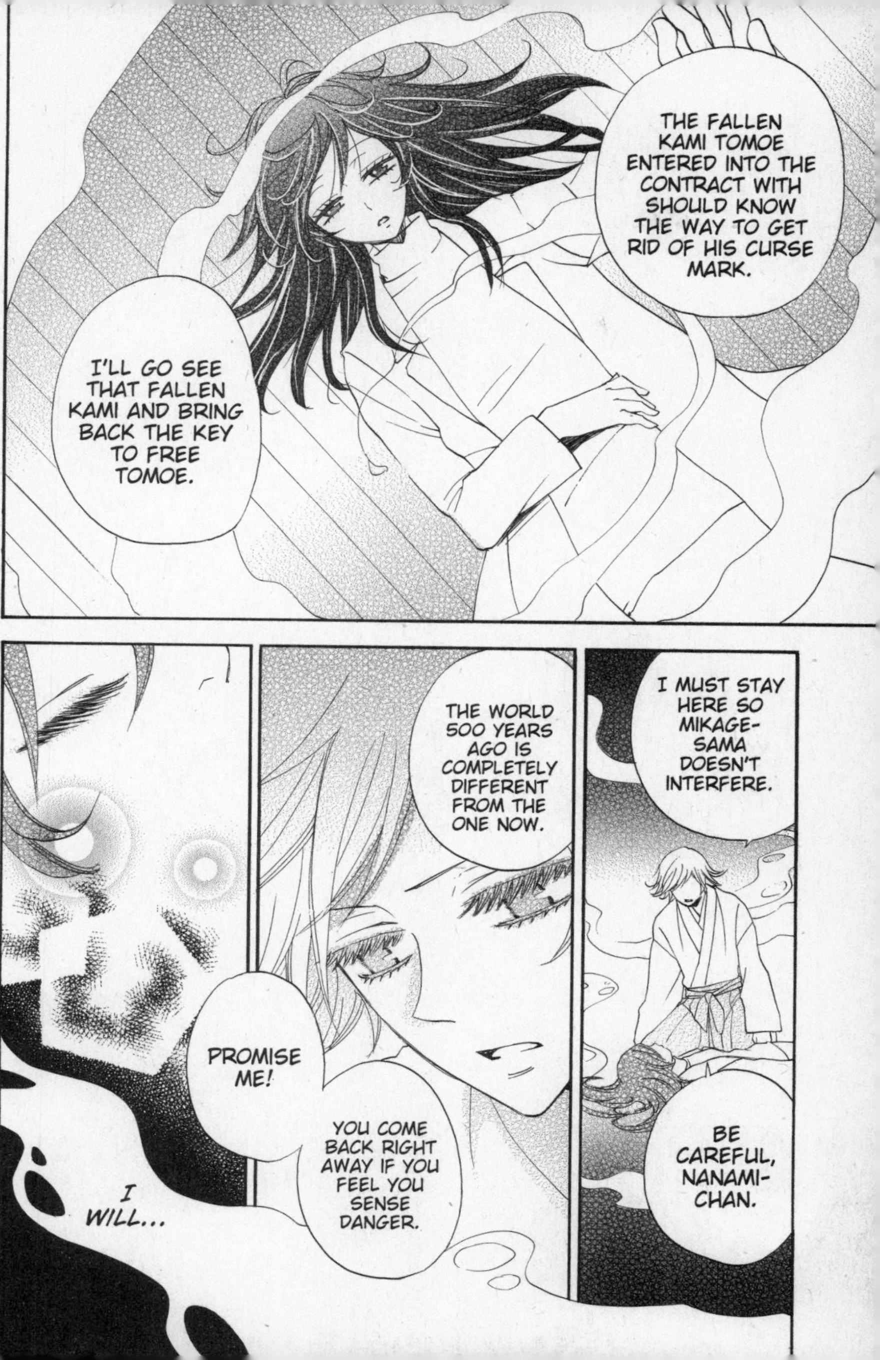
THE FALLEN KAMI TOMOE ENTERED INTO THE CONTRACT WITH SHOULD KNOW THE WAY TO GET RID OF HIS CURSE MARK.
I'LL GO SEE THAT FALLEN KAMI AND BRING BACK THE KEY TO FREE TOMOE.
I MUST STAY HERE SO MIKAGE-SAMA DOESN'T INTERFERE.
BE CAREFUL, NANAMI-CHAN.
THE WORLD 500 YEARS AGO IS COMPLETELY DIFFERENT FROM THE ONE NOW.
YOU COME BACK RIGHT AWAY IF YOU FEEL YOU SENSE DANGER.
PROMISE ME!
I WILL...

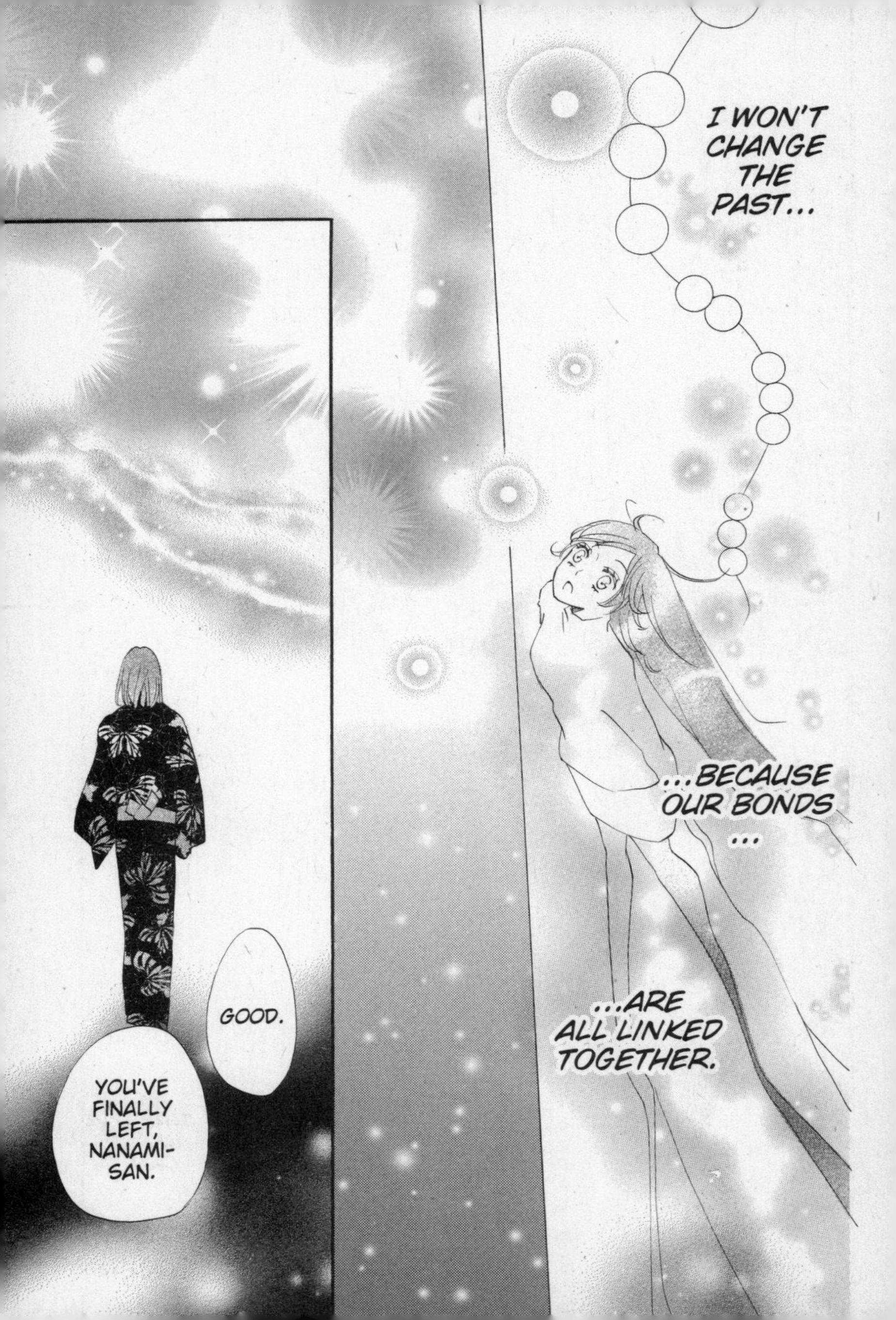
I WON'T CHANGE THE PAST...
...BECAUSE OUR BONDS ...
...ARE ALL LINKED TOGETHER.
GOOD.
YOU'VE FINALLY LEFT, NANAMI-SAN.

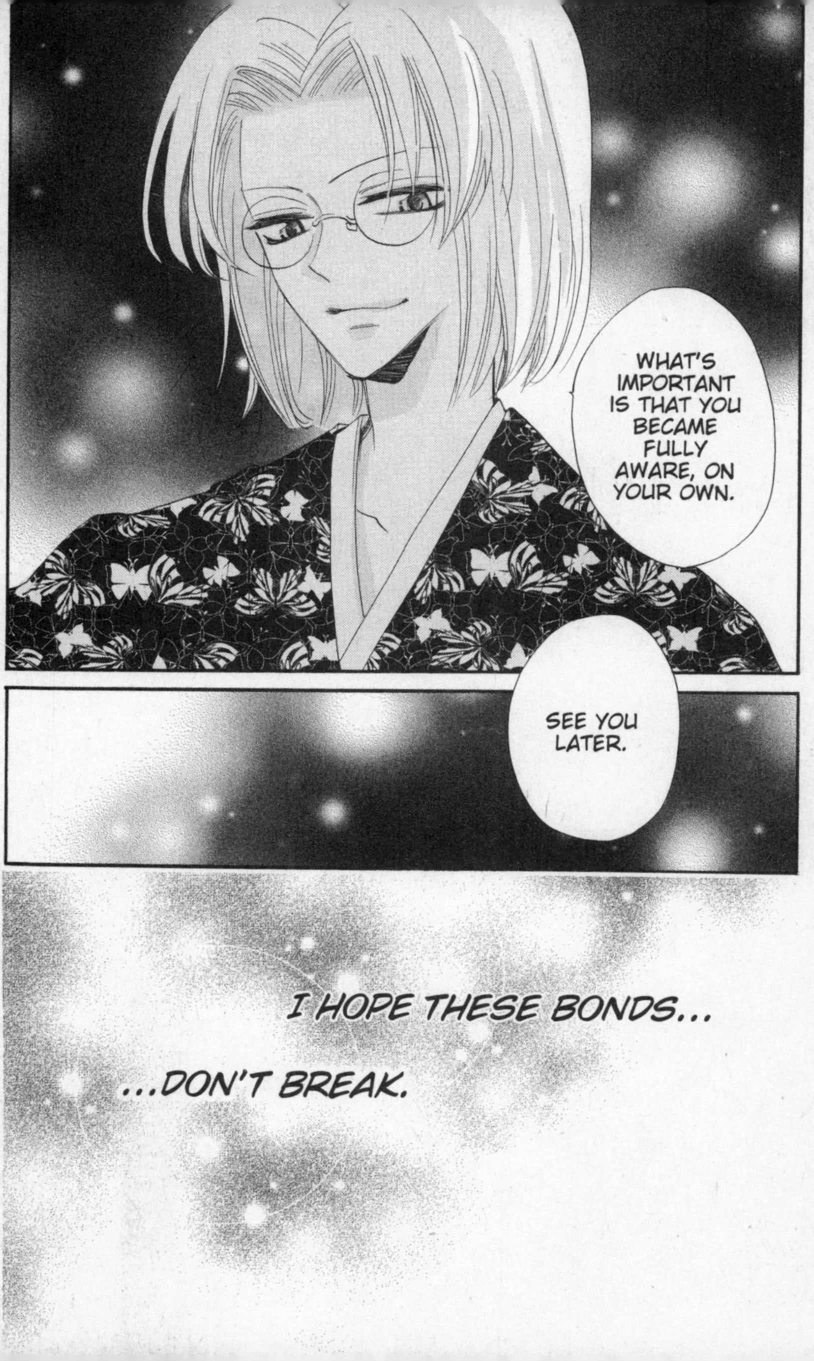
WHAT'S IMPORTANT IS THAT YOU BECAME FULLY AWARE, ON YOUR OWN.
SEE YOU LATER.
I HOPE THESE BONDS...
...DON'T BREAK.

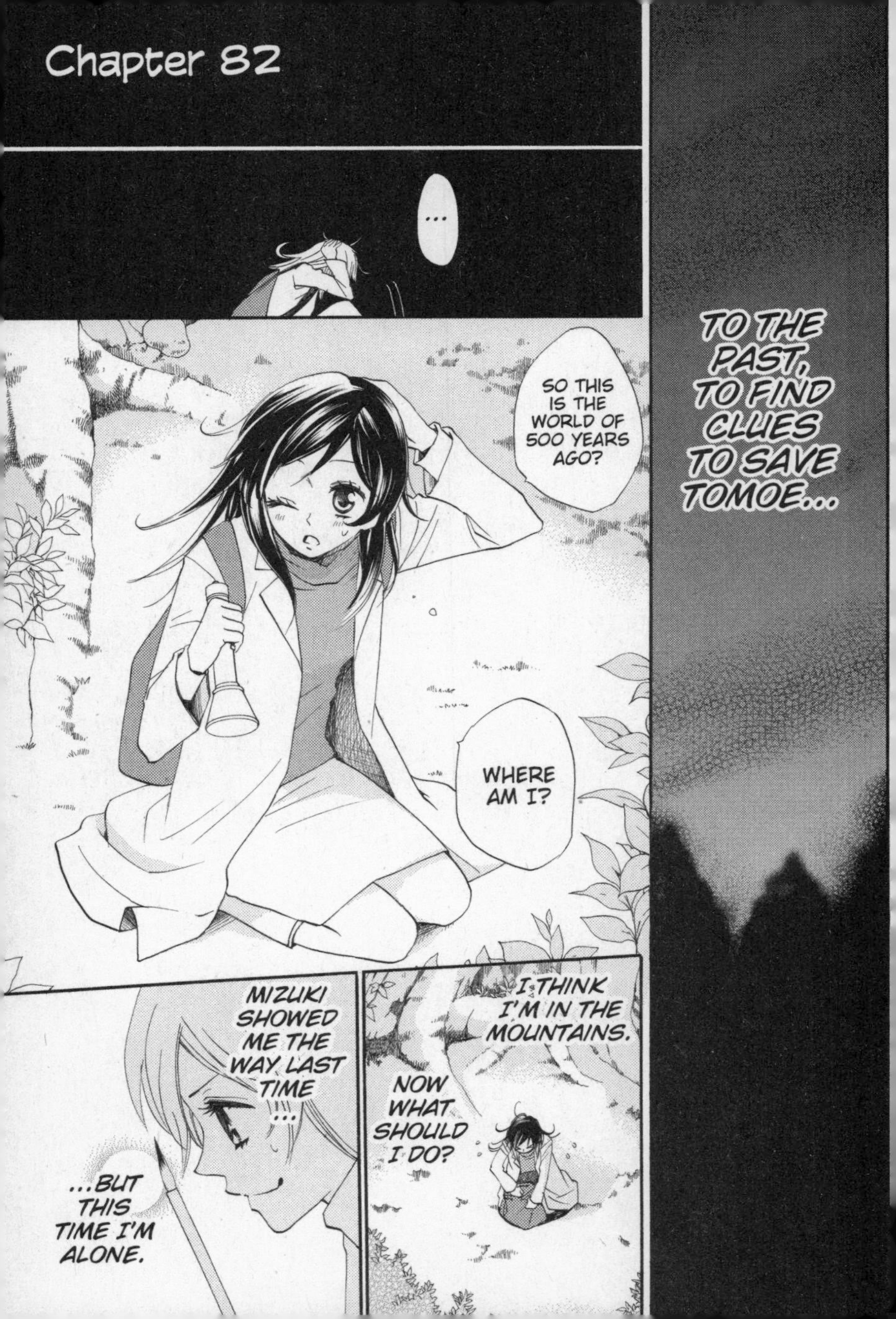
TO THE PAST, TO FIND CLUES TO SAVE TOMOE...
Chapter 82
...
SO THIS IS THE WORLD OF 500 YEARS AGO?
WHERE AM I?
I THINK I'M IN THE MOUNTAINS.
NOW WHAT SHOULD I DO?
MIZUKI SHOWED ME THE WAY LAST TIME ...
...BUT THIS TIME I'M ALONE.

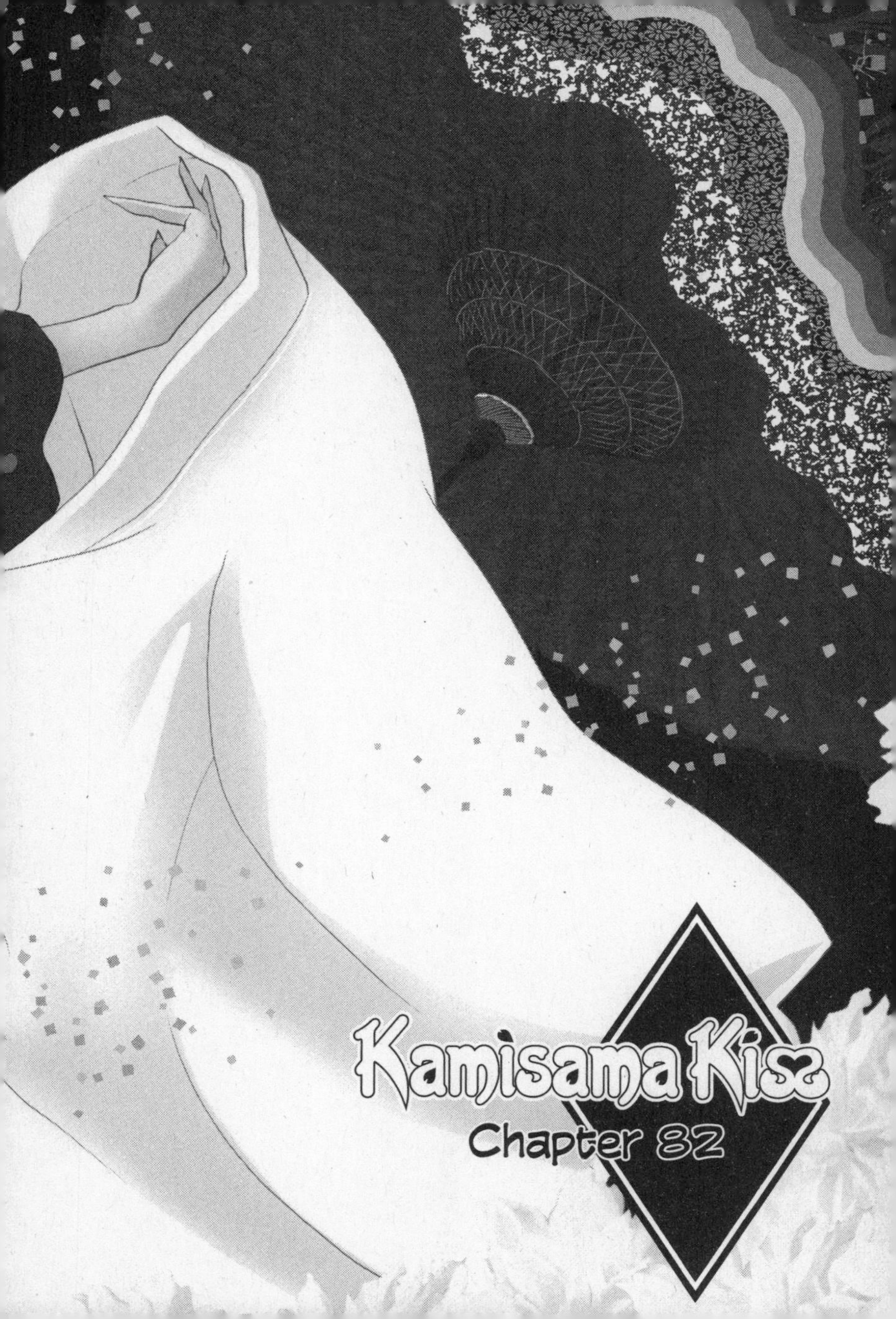
Kamisama Kiss
Chapter 82

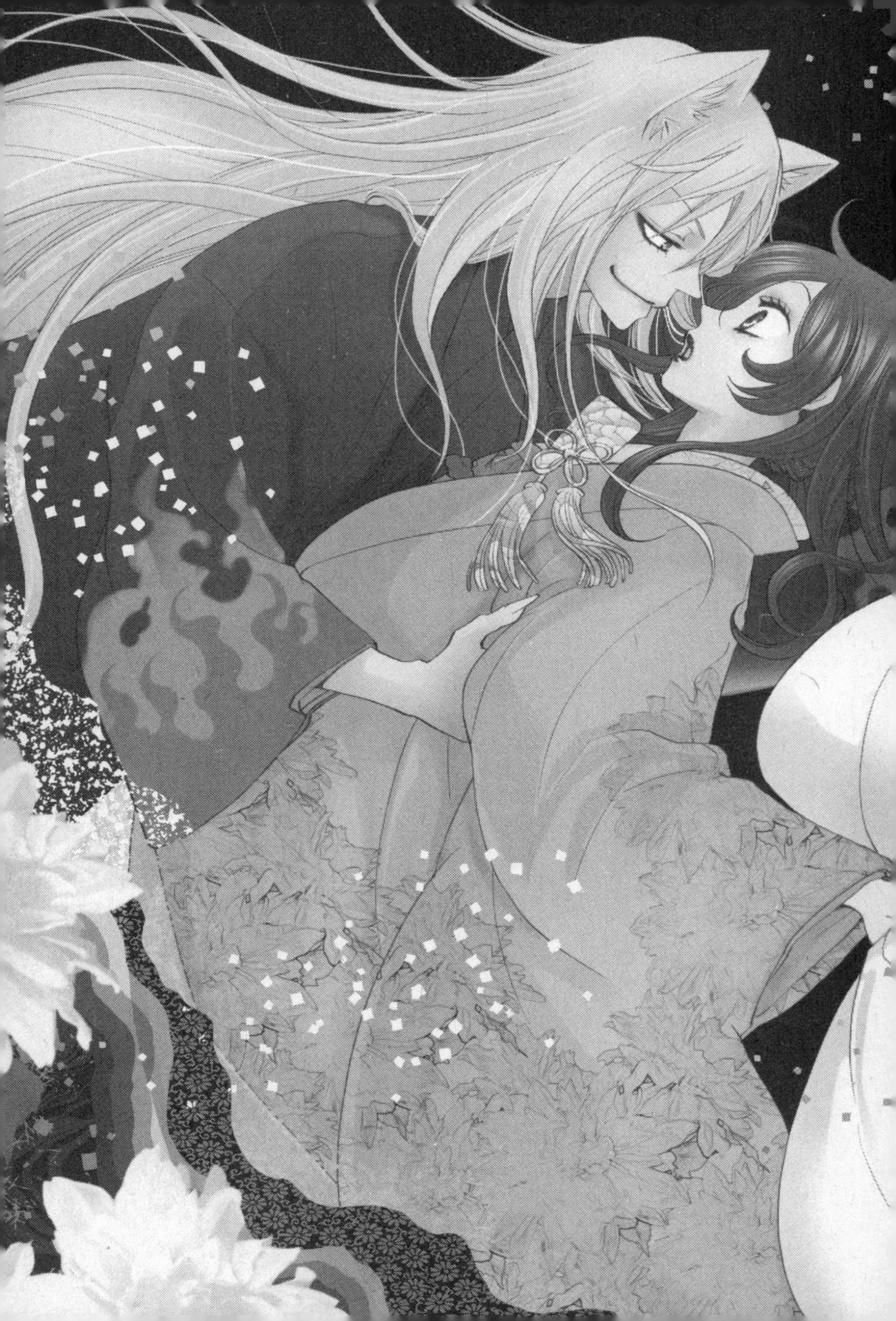

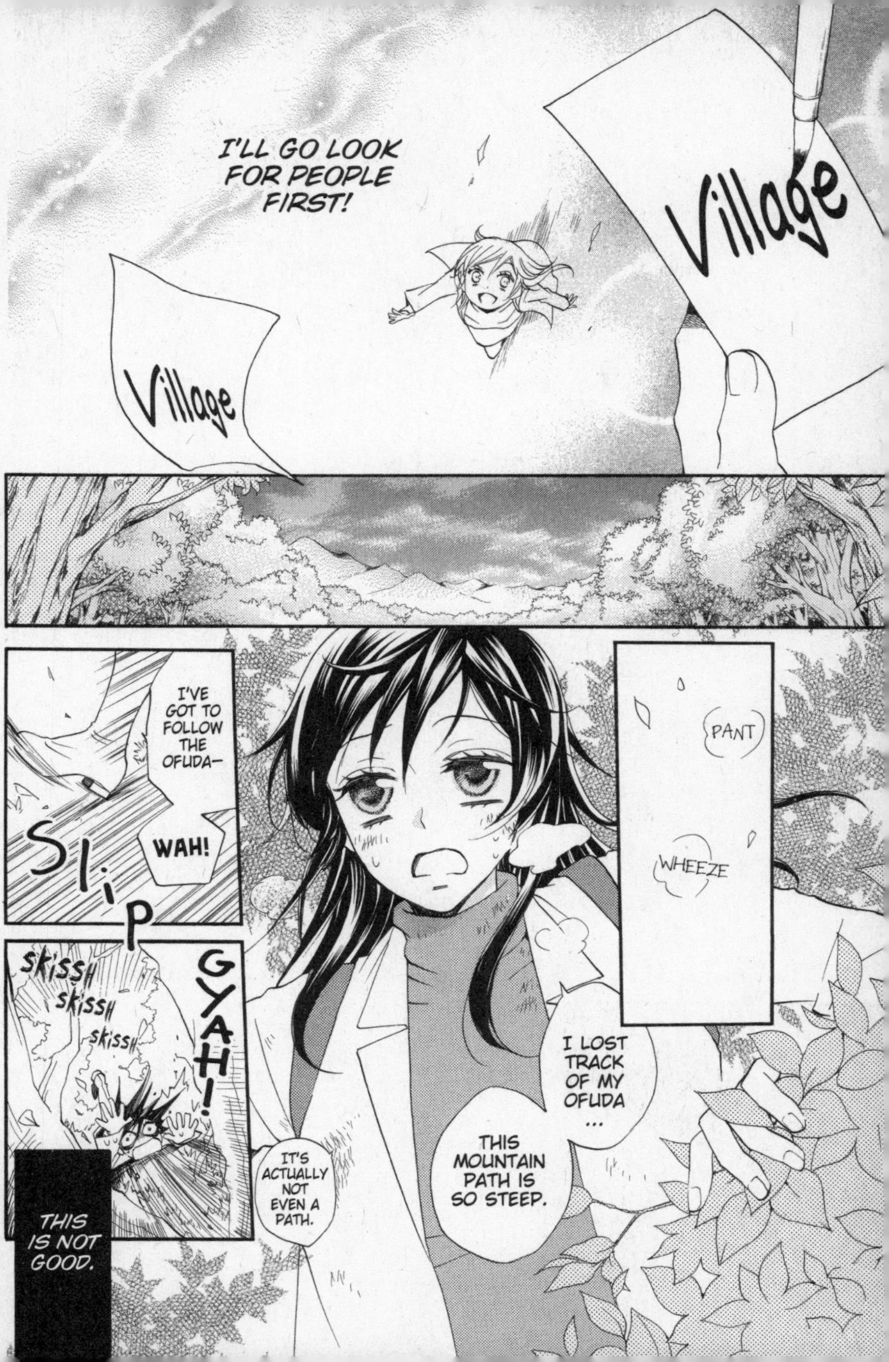
Village
I'LL GO LOOK FOR PEOPLE FIRST!
Village
PANT
WHEEZE
I LOST TRACK OF MY OFUDA ...
THIS MOUNTAIN PATH IS SO STEEP.
IT'S ACTUALLY NOT EVEN A PATH.
I'VE GOT TO FOLLOW THE OFUDA—
WAH!
SLIP
SKISSH
SKISSH
SKISSH
GYAH!
THIS IS NOT GOOD.

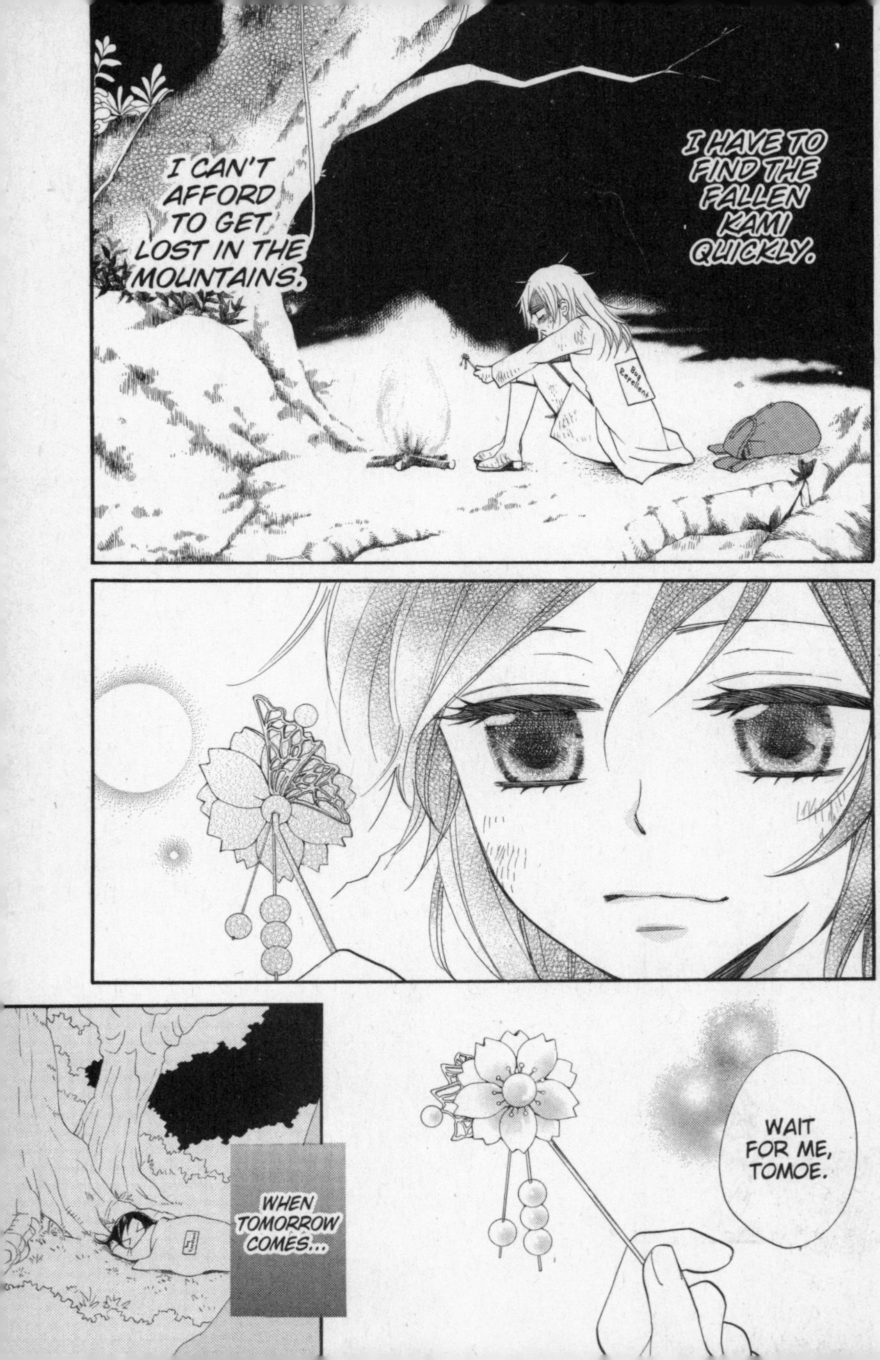
I HAVE TO FIND THE FALLEN KAMI QUICKLY.
I CAN'T AFFORD TO GET LOST IN THE MOUNTAINS.
Bug Repellent
WAIT FOR ME, TOMOE.
WHEN TOMORROW COMES...

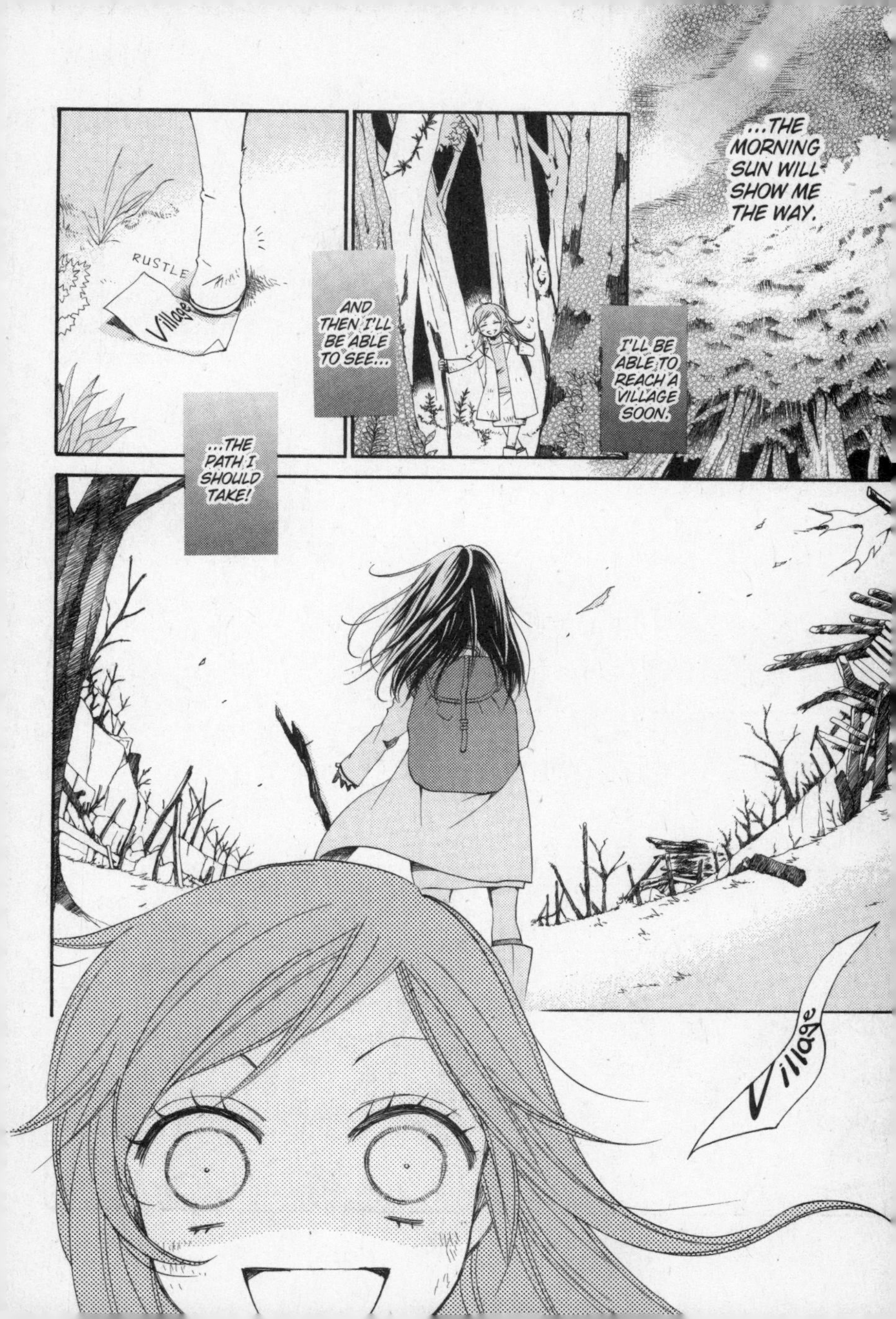
...THE MORNING SUN WILL SHOW ME THE WAY.
I'LL BE ABLE TO REACH A VILLAGE SOON.
AND THEN I'LL BE ABLE TO SEE...
RUSTLE
Village
...THE PATH I SHOULD TAKE!
Village

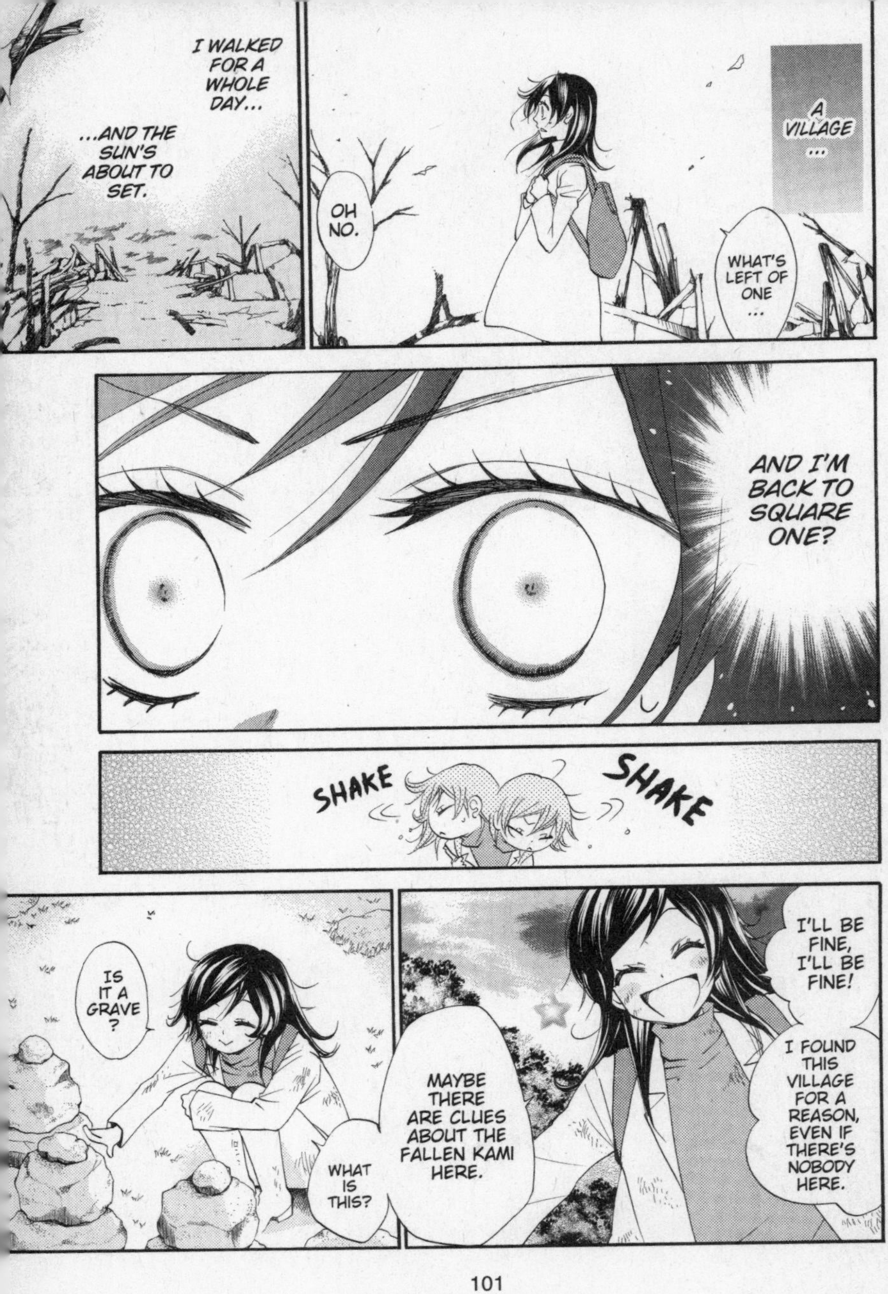

A VILLAGE ...
WHAT'S LEFT OF ONE ...
OH NO.
I WALKED FOR A WHOLE DAY...
...AND THE SUN'S ABOUT TO SET.
AND I'M BACK TO SQUARE ONE?
SHAKE
SHAKE
I'LL BE FINE, I'LL BE FINE!
I FOUND THIS VILLAGE FOR A REASON, EVEN IF THERE'S NOBODY HERE.
MAYBE THERE ARE CLUES ABOUT THE FALLEN KAMI HERE.
WHAT IS THIS?
IS IT A GRAVE?

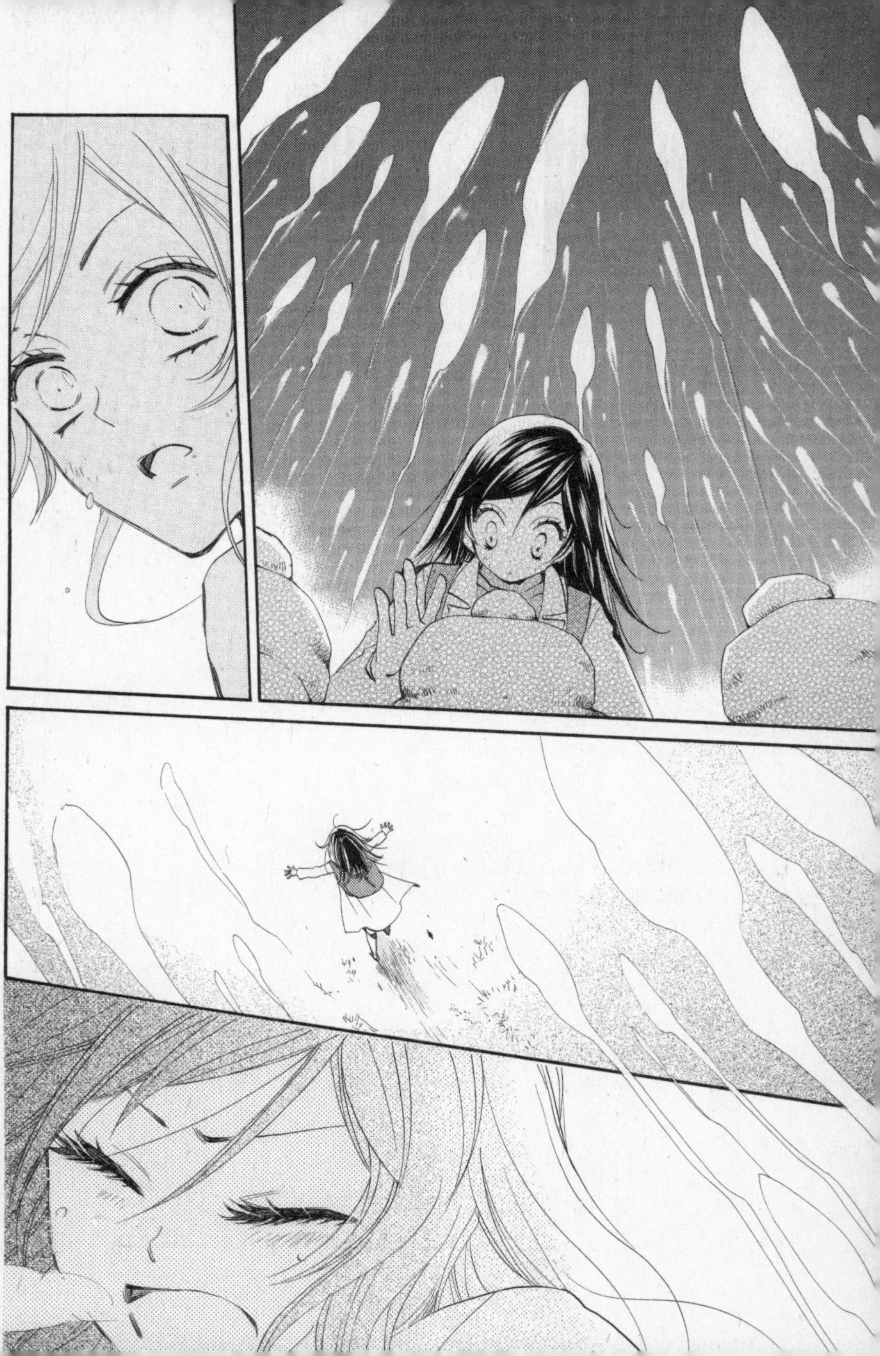

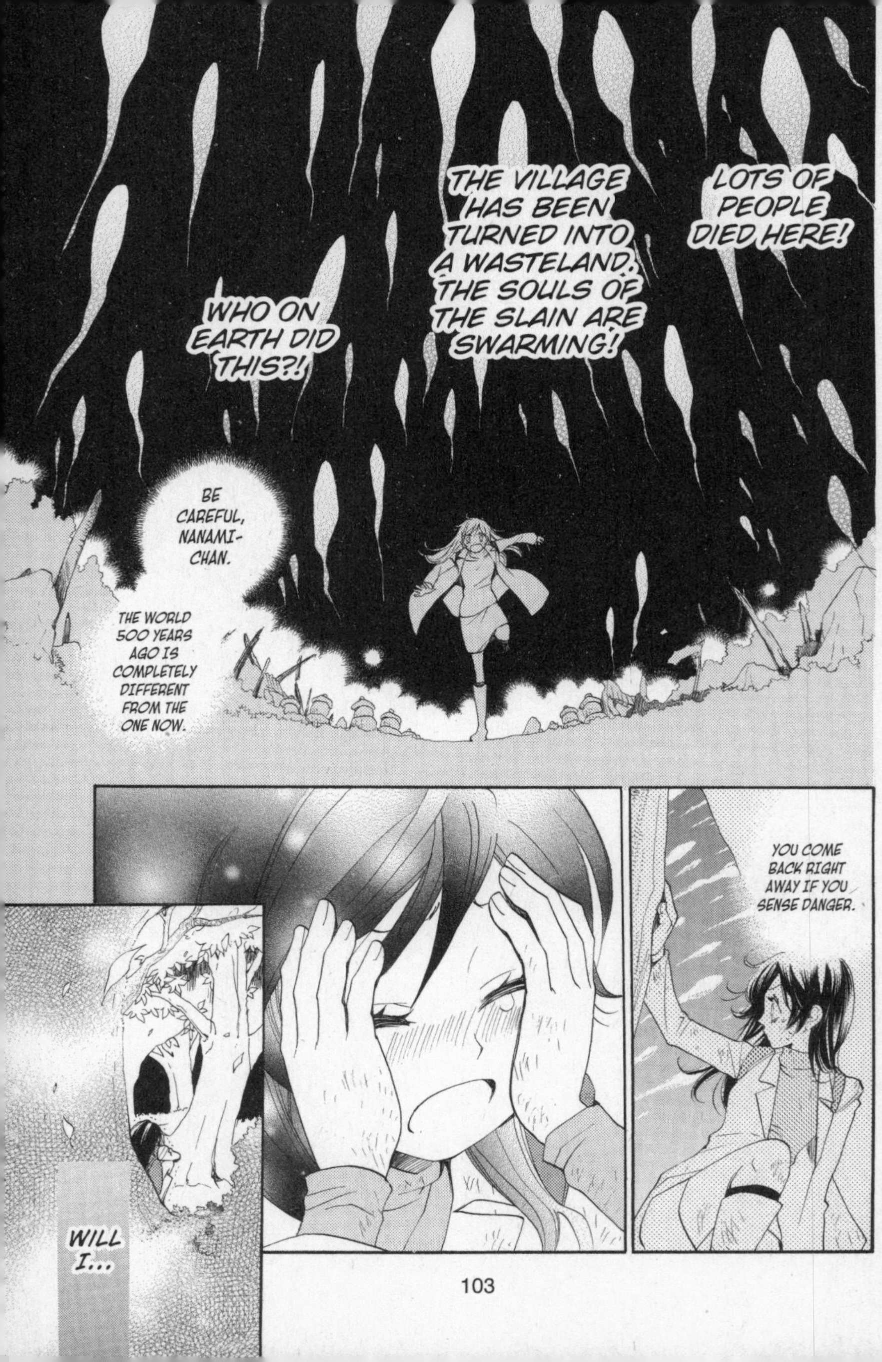
LOTS OF PEOPLE DIED HERE!
THE VILLAGE HAS BEEN TURNED INTO A WASTELAND. THE SOULS OF THE SLAIN ARE SWARMING!
WHO ON EARTH DID THIS?!
BE CAREFUL, NANAMI-CHAN.
THE WORLD 500 YEARS AGO IS COMPLETELY DIFFERENT FROM THE ONE NOW.
YOU COME BACK RIGHT AWAY IF YOU SENSE DANGER.
WILL I...

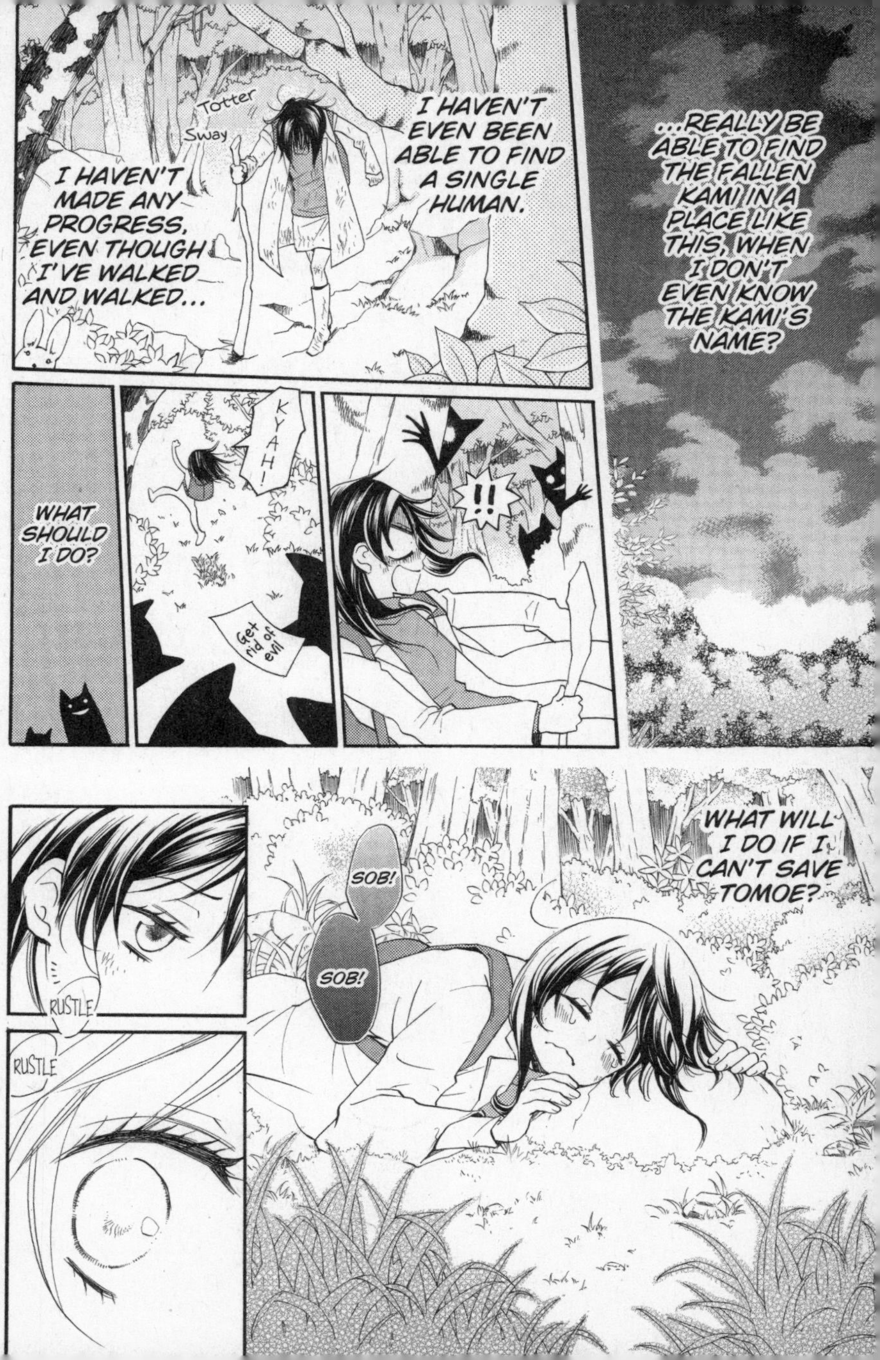
...REALLY BE ABLE TO FIND THE FALLEN KAMI IN A PLACE LIKE THIS, WHEN I DON'T EVEN KNOW THE KAMI'S NAME?
Totter
Sway
I HAVEN'T EVEN BEEN ABLE TO FIND A SINGLE HUMAN.
I HAVEN'T MADE ANY PROGRESS, EVEN THOUGH I'VE WALKED AND WALKED...
!!
KYAH!
Get rid of evil
WHAT SHOULD I DO?
WHAT WILL I DO IF I CAN'T SAVE TOMOE?
SOB!
SOB!
RUSTLE
RUSTLE

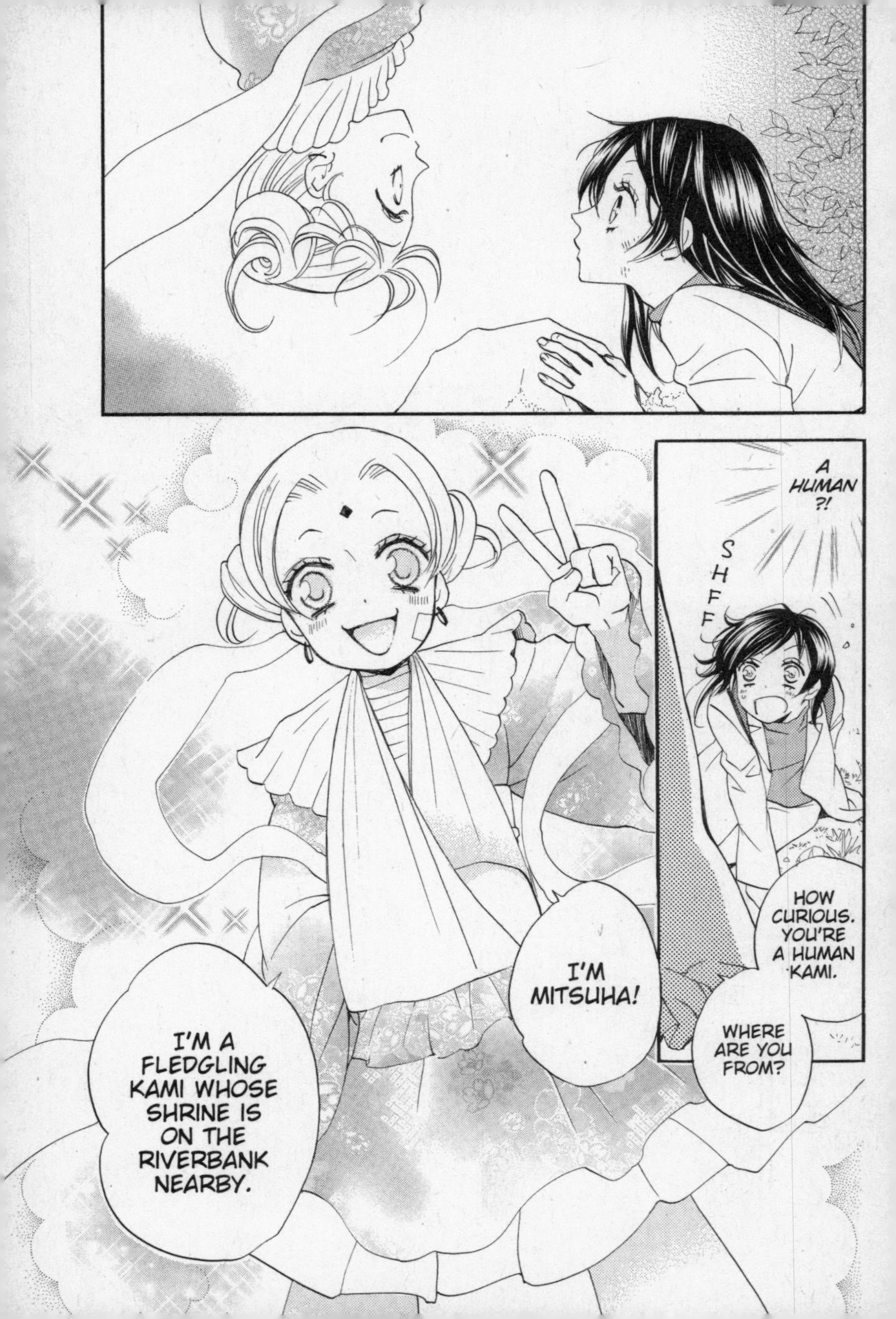
A HUMAN ?!
SHFF
HOW CURIOUS. YOU'RE A HUMAN KAMI.
WHERE ARE YOU FROM?
I'M MITSUHA!
I'M A FLEDGLING KAMI WHOSE SHRINE IS ON THE RIVERBANK NEARBY.

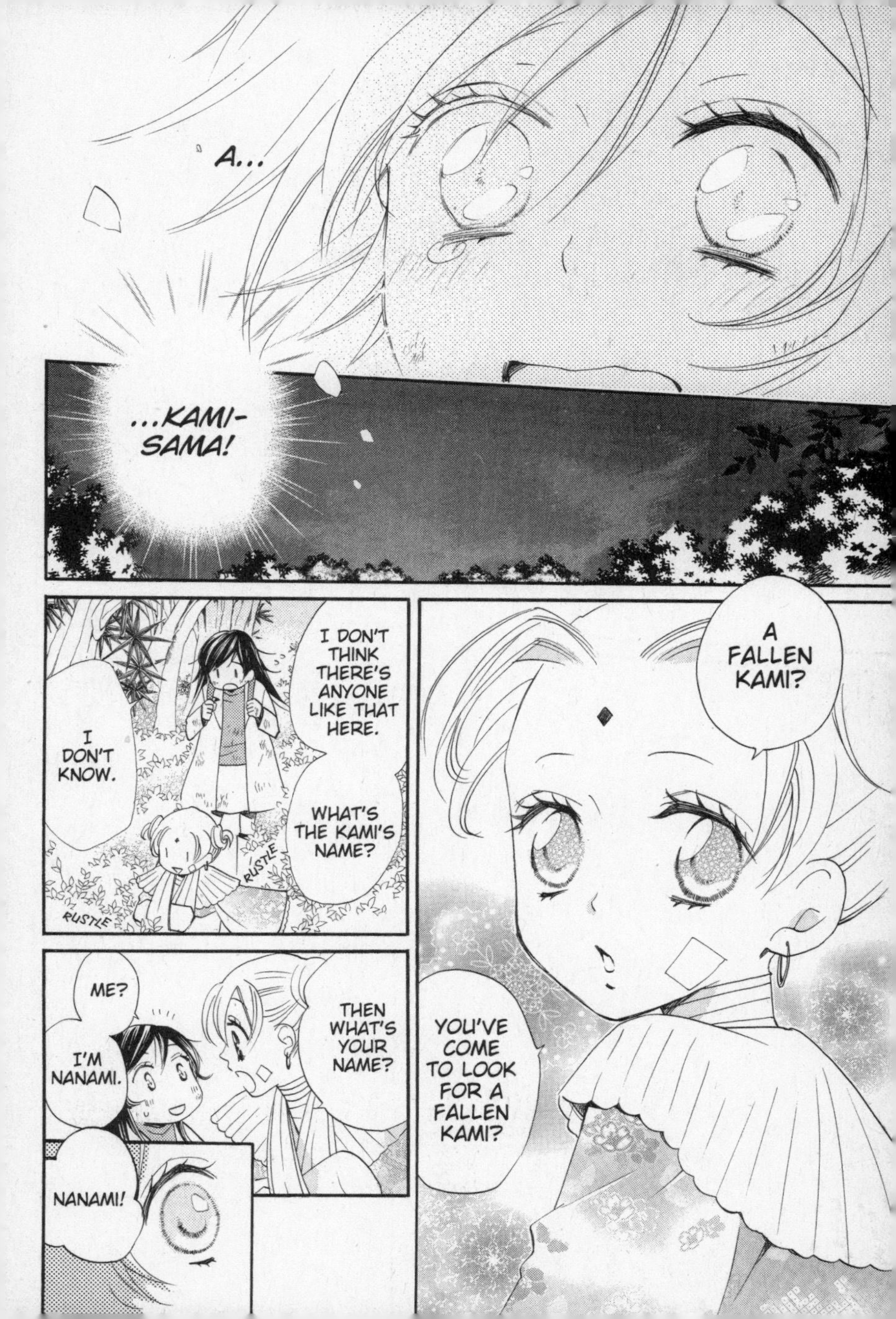
A...
...KAMI-SAMA!
A FALLEN KAMI?
YOU'VE COME TO LOOK FOR A FALLEN KAMI?
I DON'T THINK THERE'S ANYONE LIKE THAT HERE.
WHAT'S THE KAMI'S NAME?
I DON'T KNOW.
RUSTLE
RUSTLE
THEN WHAT'S YOUR NAME?
ME?
I'M NANAMI.
NANAMI!

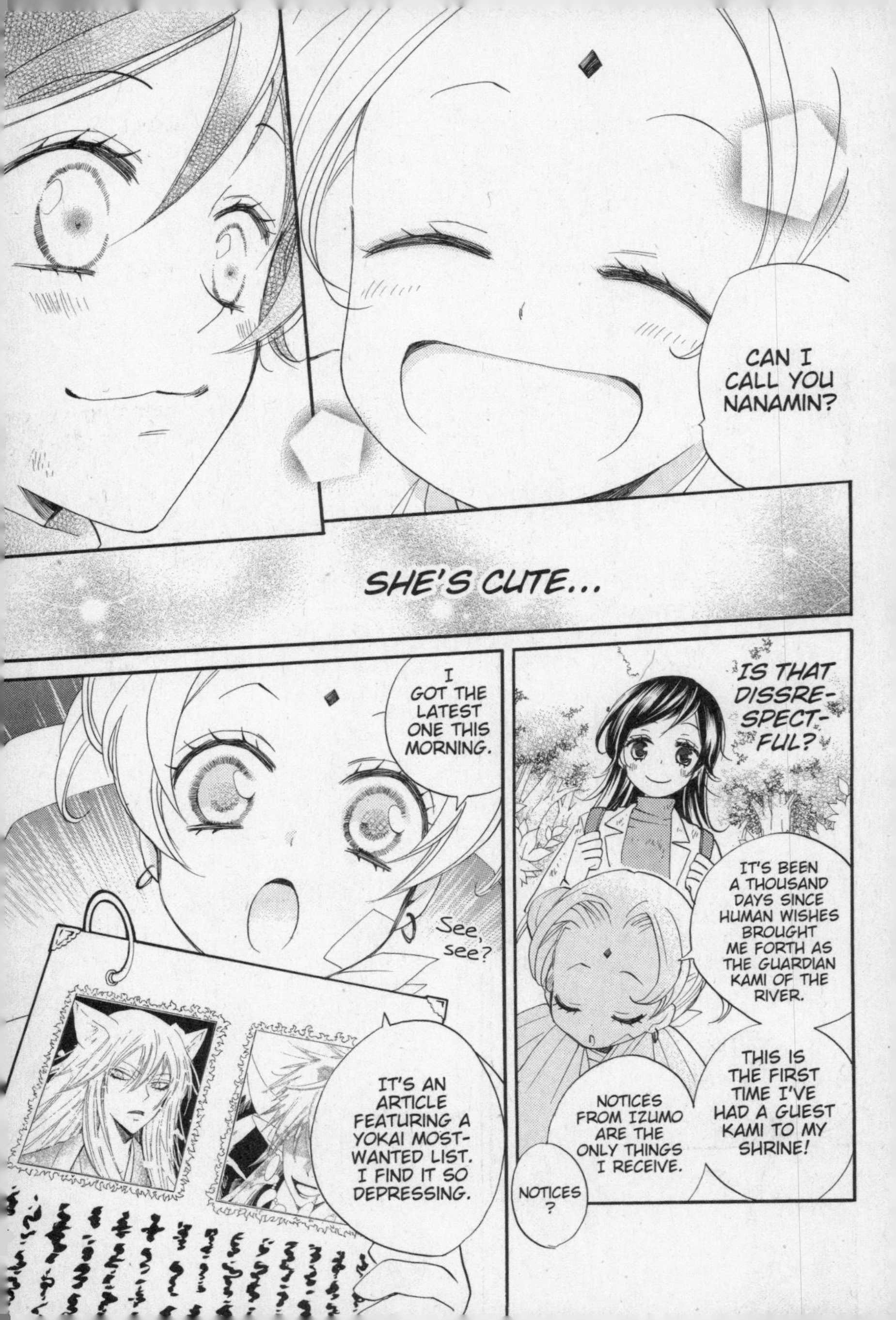

CAN I CALL YOU NANAMIN?
SHE'S CUTE...
IS THAT DISSRESPECTFUL?
IT'S BEEN A THOUSAND DAYS SINCE HUMAN WISHES BROUGHT ME FORTH AS THE GUARDIAN KAMI OF THE RIVER.
THIS IS THE FIRST TIME I'VE HAD A GUEST KAMI TO MY SHRINE!
NOTICES FROM IZUMO ARE THE ONLY THINGS I RECEIVE.
NOTICES?
I GOT THE LATEST ONE THIS MORNING.
See, see?
IT'S AN ARTICLE FEATURING A YOKAI MOST-WANTED LIST. I FIND IT SO DEPRESSING.

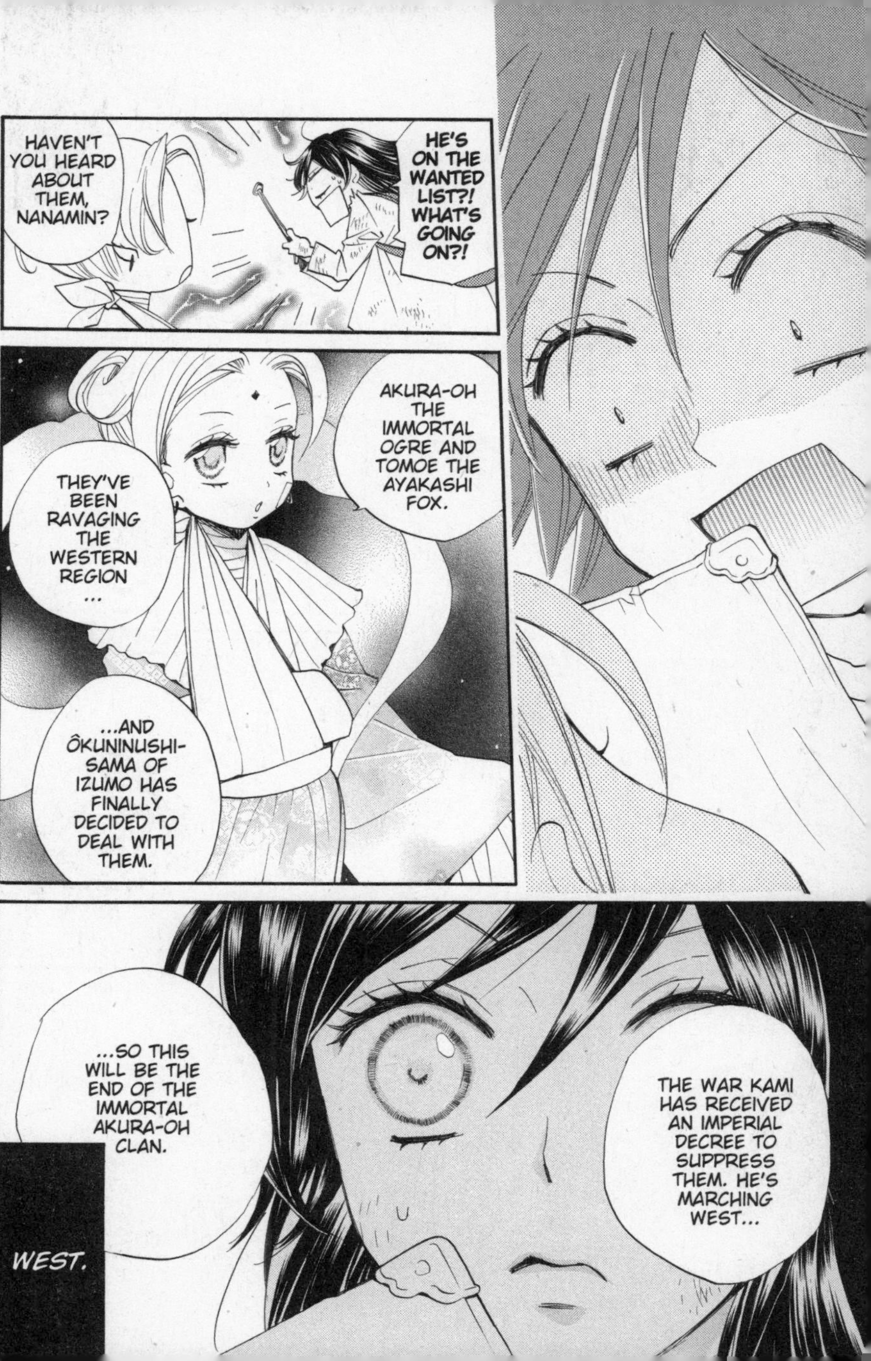
HE'S ON THE WANTED LIST?! WHAT'S GOING ON?!
HAVEN'T YOU HEARD ABOUT THEM, NANAMIN?
AKURA-OH THE IMMORTAL OGRE AND TOMOE THE AYAKASHI FOX.
THEY'VE BEEN RAVAGING THE WESTERN REGION ...
...AND ÔKUNINUSHI-SAMA OF IZUMO HAS FINALLY DECIDED TO DEAL WITH THEM.
THE WAR KAMI HAS RECEIVED AN IMPERIAL DECREE TO SUPPRESS THEM. HE'S MARCHING WEST...
...SO THIS WILL BE THE END OF THE IMMORTAL AKURA-OH CLAN.
WEST.

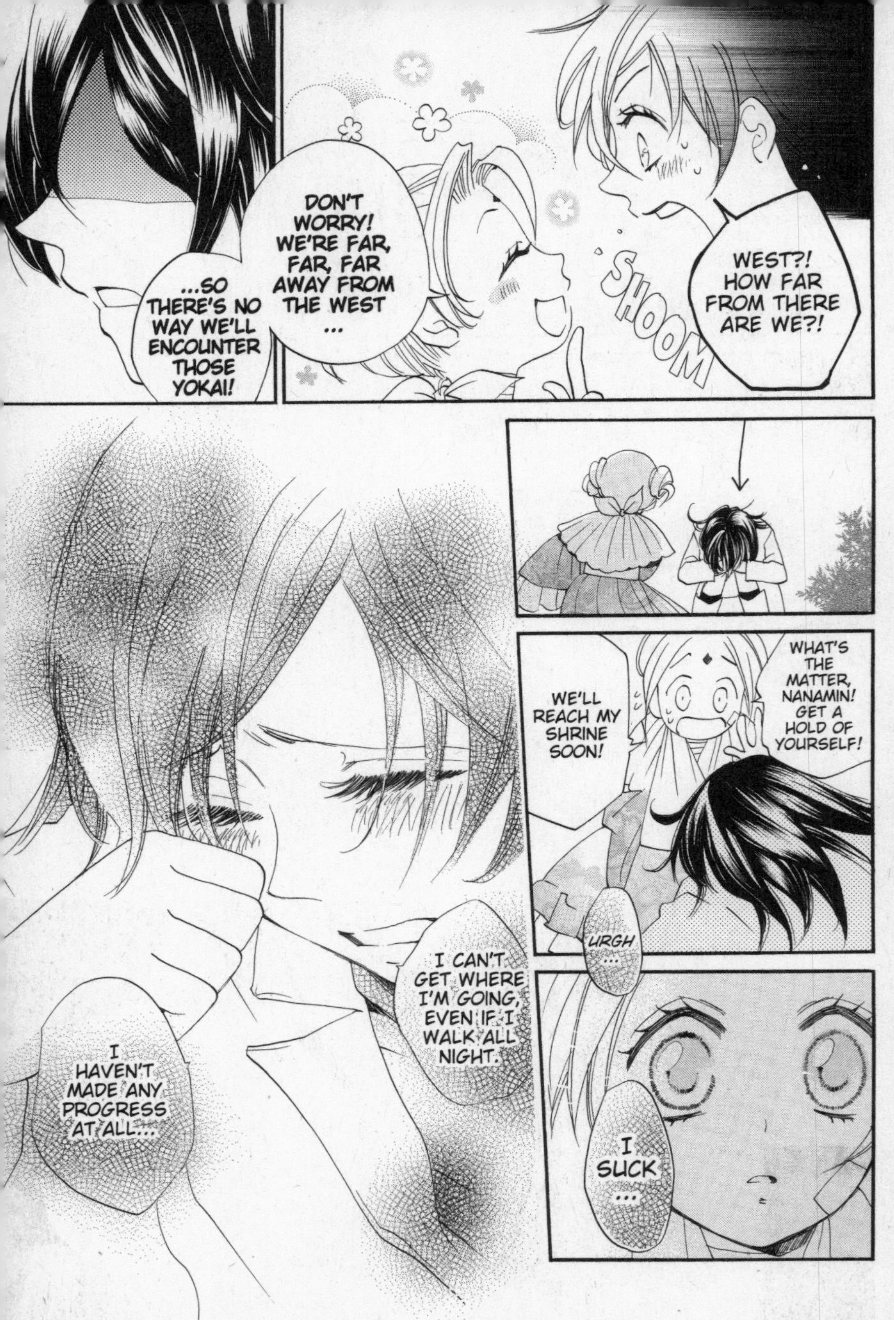
WEST?! HOW FAR FROM THERE ARE WE?!
SHOOM
DON'T WORRY! WE'RE FAR, FAR, FAR AWAY FROM THE WEST ...
...SO THERE'S NO WAY WE'LL ENCOUNTER THOSE YOKAI!
WHAT'S THE MATTER, NANAMIN! GET A HOLD OF YOURSELF!
WE'LL REACH MY SHRINE SOON!
URGH ...
I SUCK ...
I CAN'T GET WHERE I'M GOING, EVEN IF I WALK ALL NIGHT.
I HAVEN'T MADE ANY PROGRESS AT ALL...

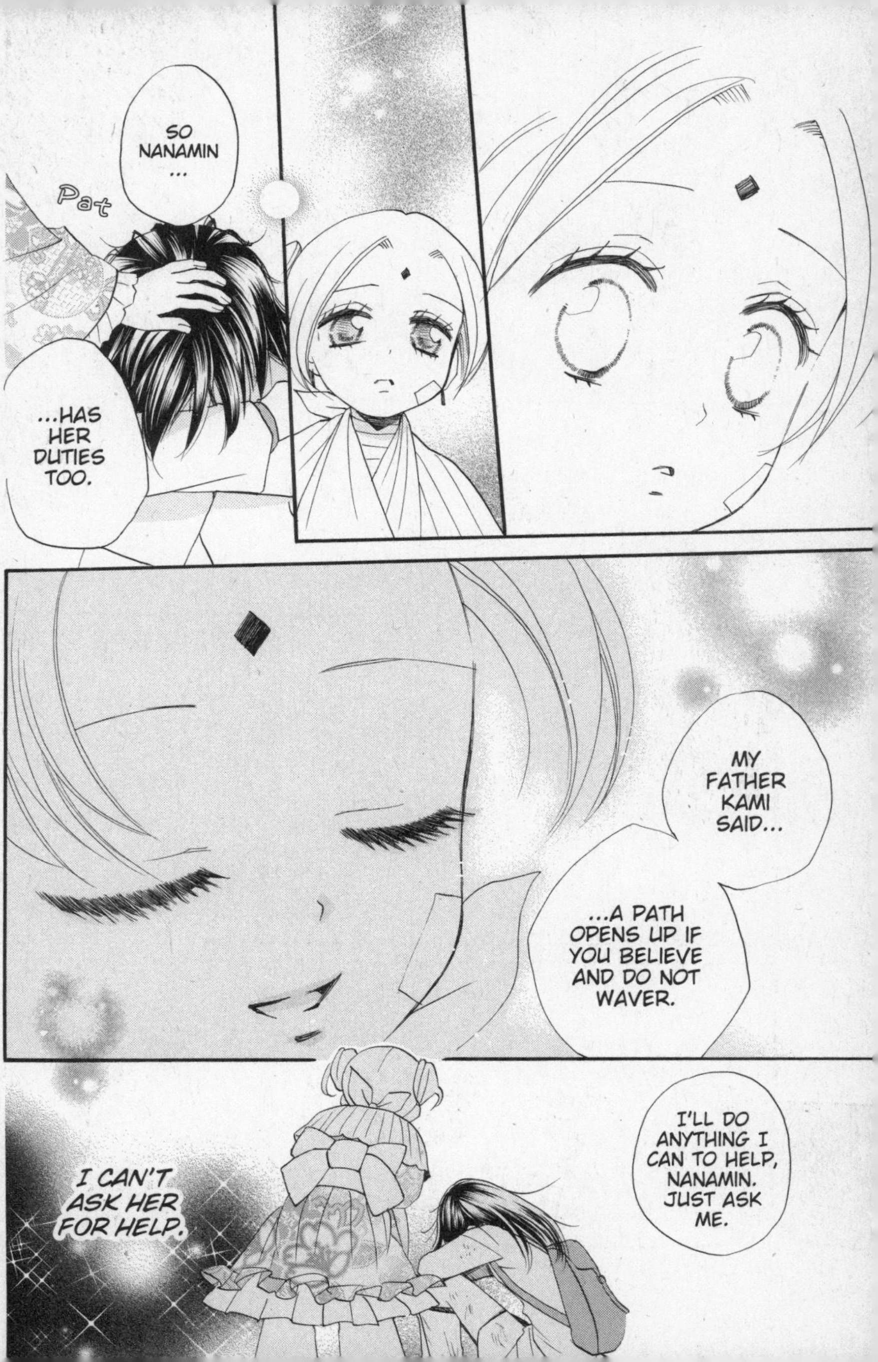
SO NANAMIN ...
Pat
...HAS HER DUTIES TOO.
MY FATHER KAMI SAID...
...A PATH OPENS UP IF YOU BELIEVE AND DO NOT WAVER.
I'LL DO ANYTHING I CAN TO HELP, NANAMIN. JUST ASK ME.
I CAN'T ASK HER FOR HELP.

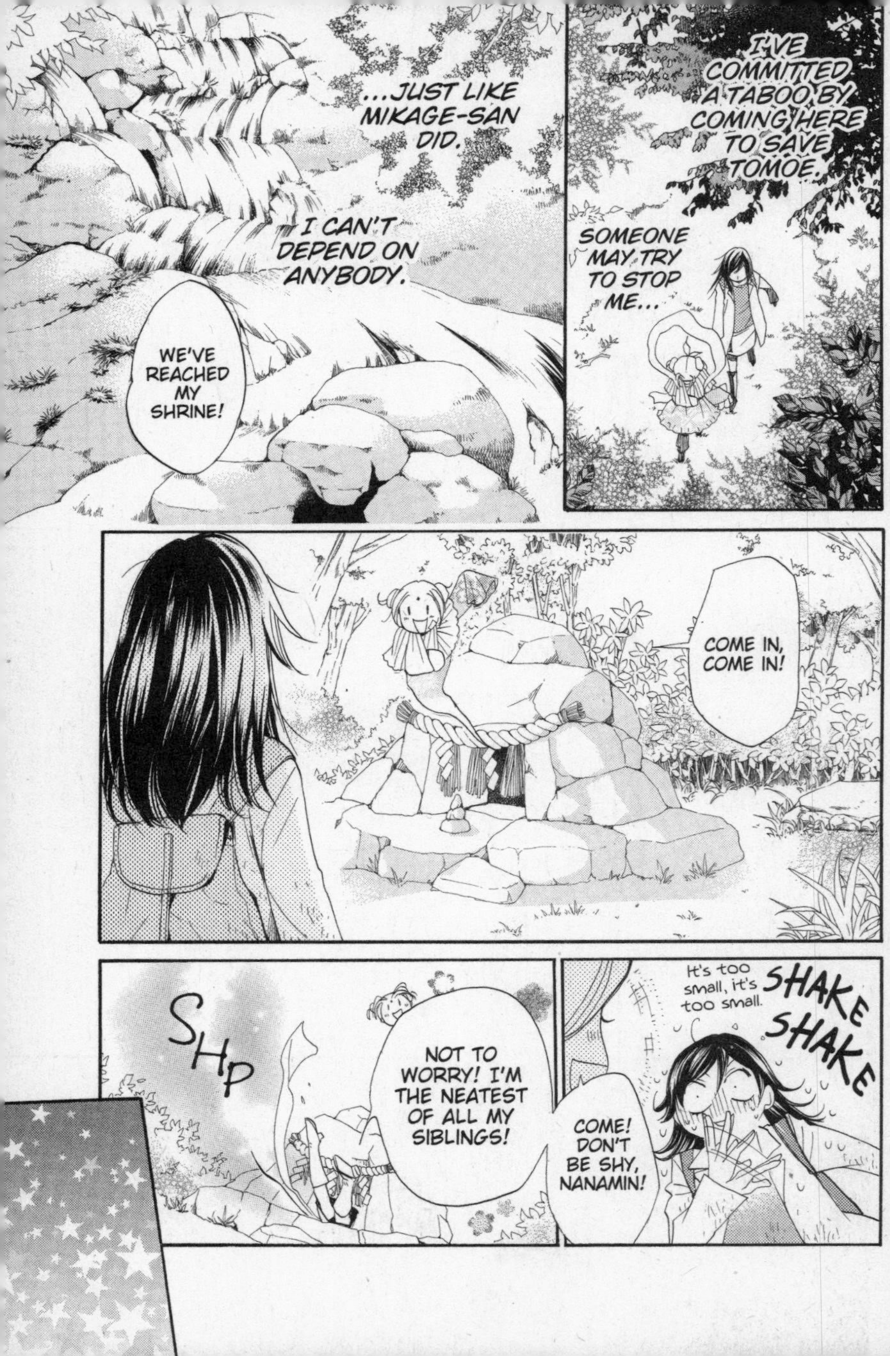
I'VE COMMITTED A TABOO BY COMING HERE TO SAVE TOMOE.
SOMEONE MAY TRY TO STOP ME...
...JUST LIKE MIKAGE-SAN DID.
I CAN'T DEPEND ON ANYBODY.
WE'VE REACHED MY SHRINE!
COME IN, COME IN!
SHAKE SHAKE
It's too small, it's too small.
COME! DON'T BE SHY, NANAMIN!
NOT TO WORRY! I'M THE NEATEST OF ALL MY SIBLINGS!
SHP

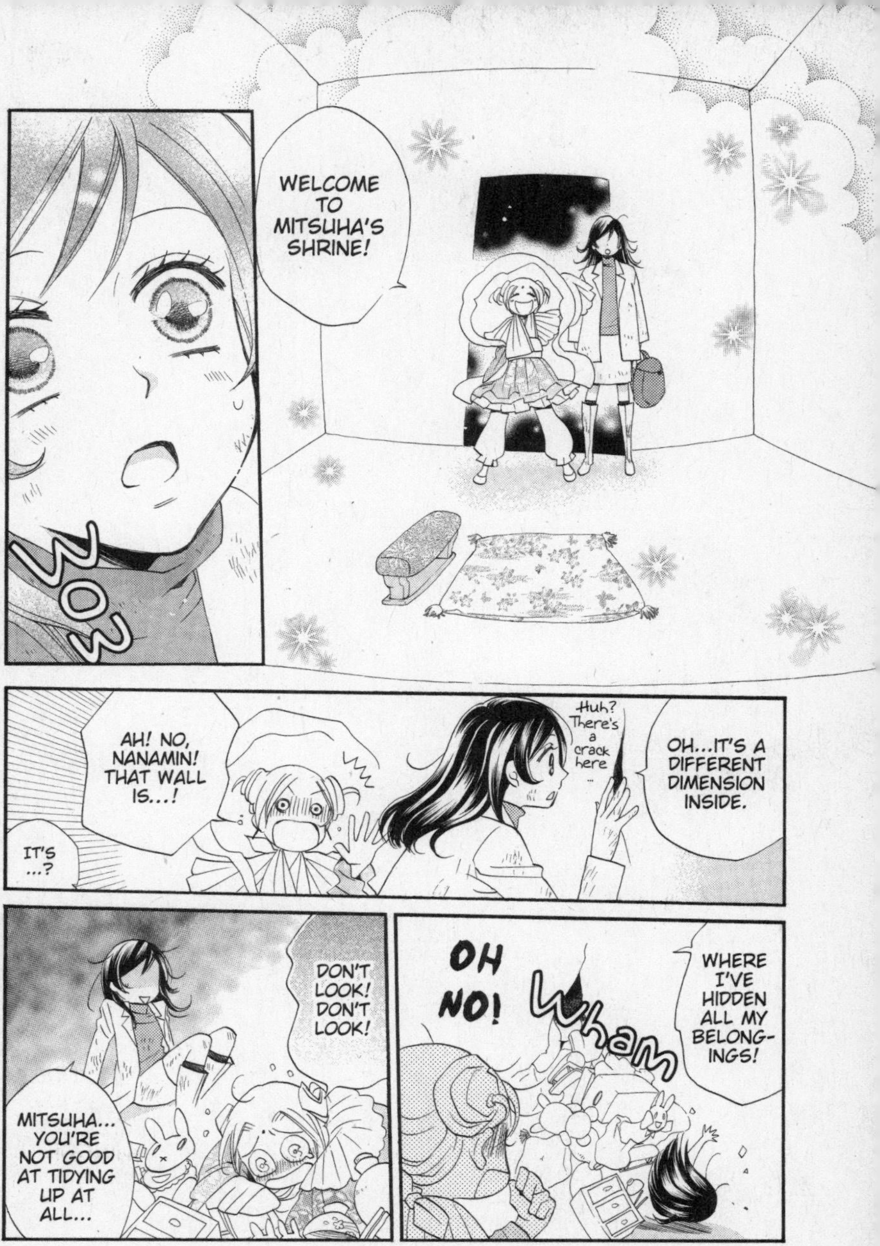
WELCOME TO MITSUHA'S SHRINE!
WOW
OH...IT'S A DIFFERENT DIMENSION INSIDE.
Huh? There's a crack here ...
AH! NO, NANAMIN! THAT WALL IS...!
IT'S ...?
WHERE I'VE HIDDEN ALL MY BELONG-INGS!
OH NO!
Wham
DON'T LOOK! DON'T LOOK!
MITSUHA... YOU'RE NOT GOOD AT TIDYING UP AT ALL...

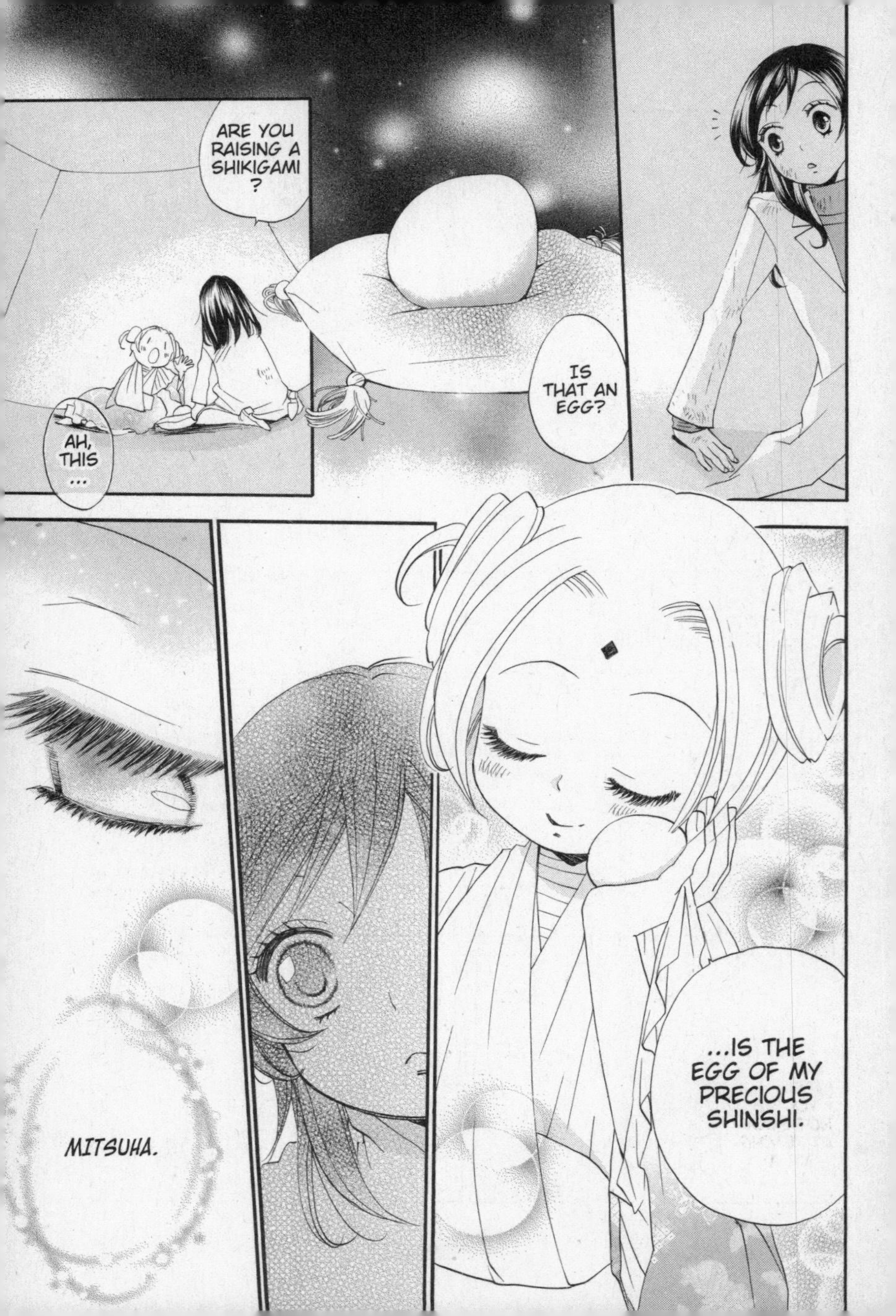
IS THAT AN EGG?
ARE YOU RAISING A SHIKIGAMI?
AH, THIS ...
...IS THE EGG OF MY PRECIOUS SHINSHI.
MITSUHA.

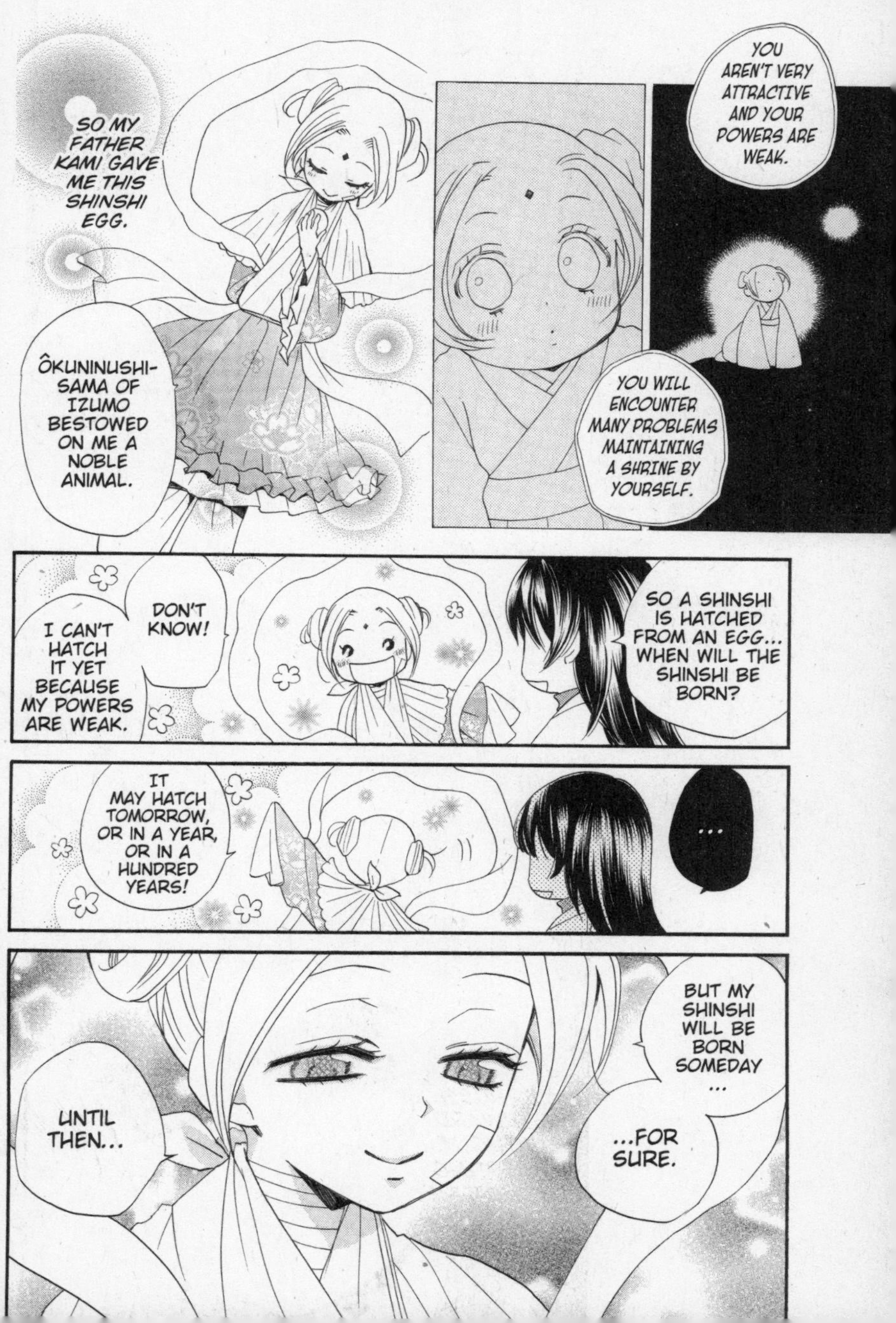
YOU AREN'T VERY ATTRACTIVE AND YOUR POWERS ARE WEAK.
YOU WILL ENCOUNTER MANY PROBLEMS MAINTAINING A SHRINE BY YOURSELF.
SO MY FATHER KAMI GAVE ME THIS SHINSHI EGG.
ÔKUNINUSHI-SAMA OF IZUMO BESTOWED ON ME A NOBLE ANIMAL.
SO A SHINSHI IS HATCHED FROM AN EGG... WHEN WILL THE SHINSHI BE BORN?
DON'T KNOW!
I CAN'T HATCH IT YET BECAUSE MY POWERS ARE WEAK.
...
IT MAY HATCH TOMORROW, OR IN A YEAR, OR IN A HUNDRED YEARS!
BUT MY SHINSHI WILL BE BORN SOMEDAY...
...FOR SURE.
UNTIL THEN...

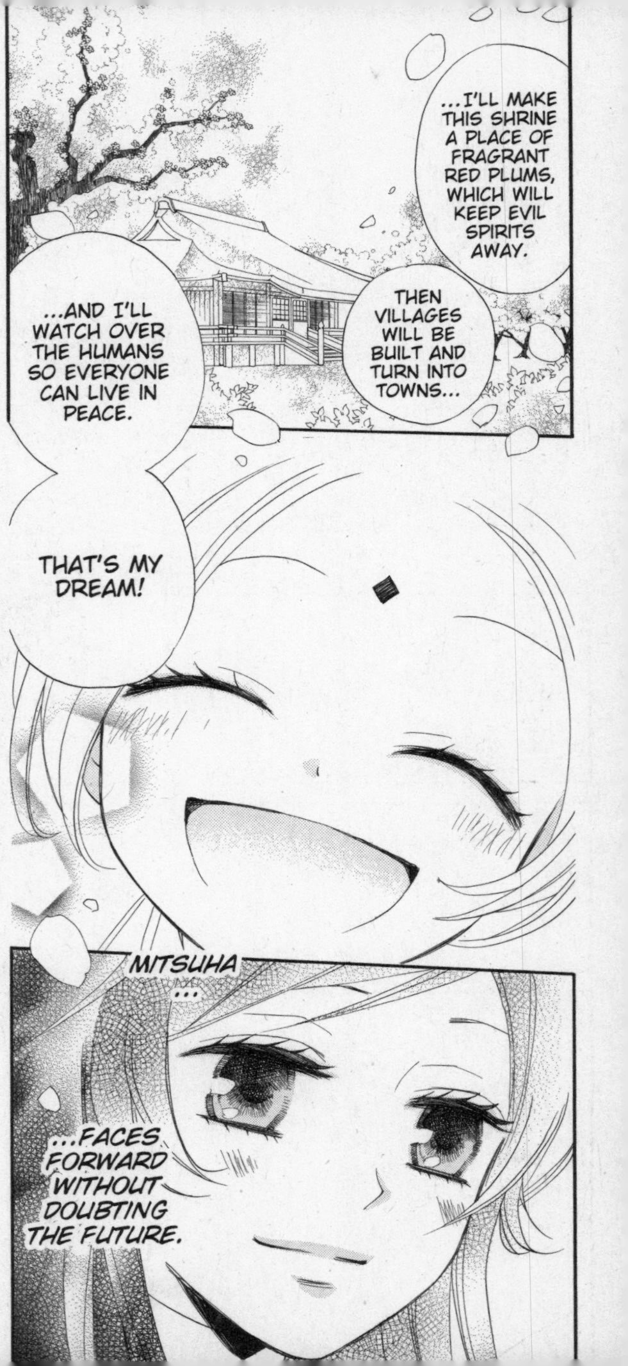
...I'LL MAKE THIS SHRINE A PLACE OF FRAGRANT RED PLUMS, WHICH WILL KEEP EVIL SPIRITS AWAY.
THEN VILLAGES WILL BE BUILT AND TURN INTO TOWNS...
...AND I'LL WATCH OVER THE HUMANS SO EVERYONE CAN LIVE IN PEACE.
THAT'S MY DREAM!
MITSUHA...
...FACES FORWARD WITHOUT DOUBTING THE FUTURE.

3

Summer is ending soon.

I didn't use to like summer because it's hot, but this year I've begun to love summer...! Therefore I'd like to be aggressive next summer and go to the sea and mountains, and go camping (I simply wanted to say this). And have barbecues (I simply wanted to say this too).

I'll go see some fireworks at the very least. I've never actually gone to see fireworks, not even once.

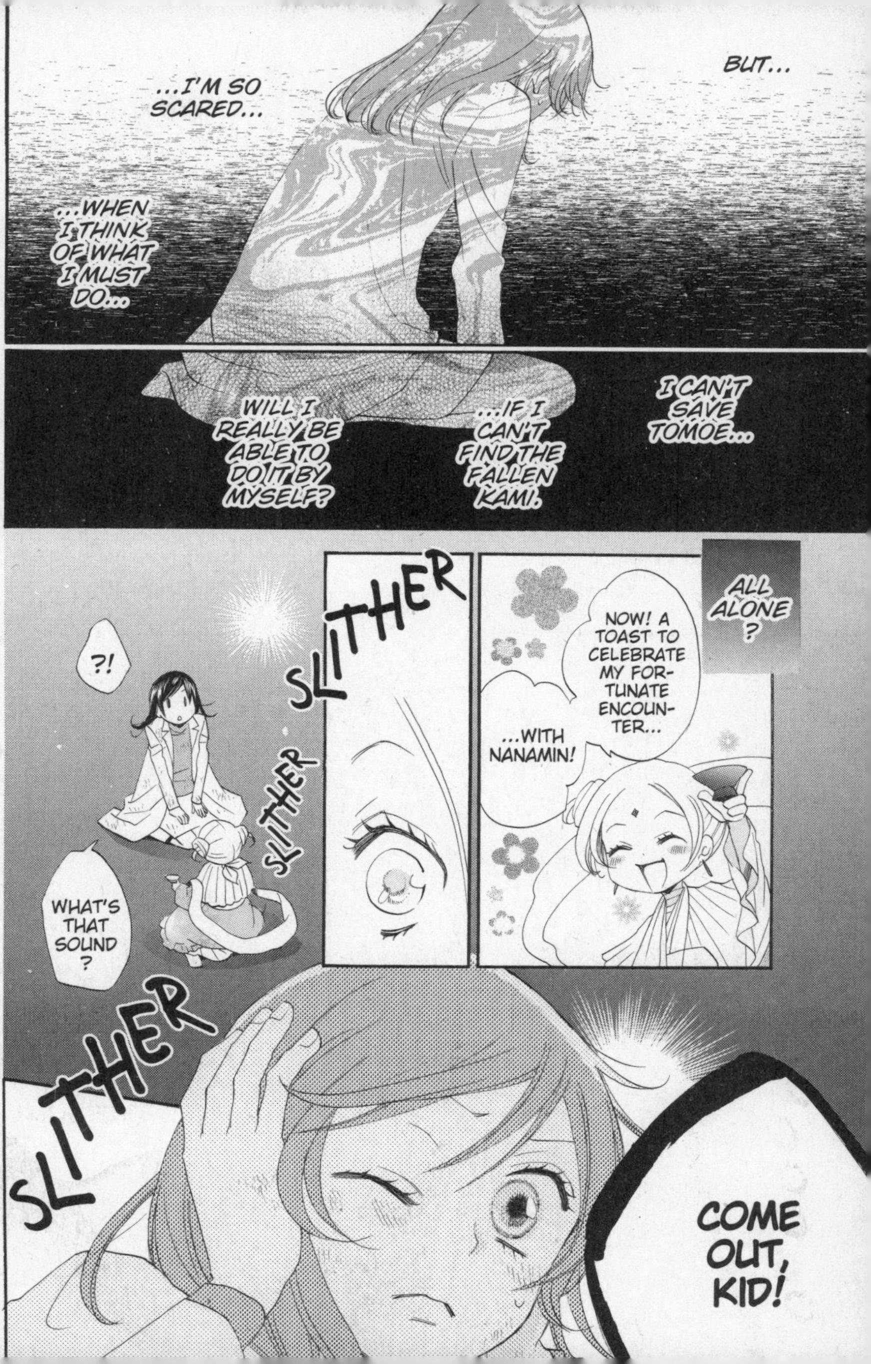
BUT...
...I'M SO SCARED...
...WHEN I THINK OF WHAT I MUST DO...
I CAN'T SAVE TOMOE...
...IF I CAN'T FIND THE FALLEN KAMI.
WILL I REALLY BE ABLE TO DO IT BY MYSELF?
ALL ALONE?
NOW! A TOAST TO CELEBRATE MY FORTUNATE ENCOUNTER...
...WITH NANAMIN!
SLITHER
?!
SLITHER
WHAT'S THAT SOUND?
COME OUT, KID!
SLITHER

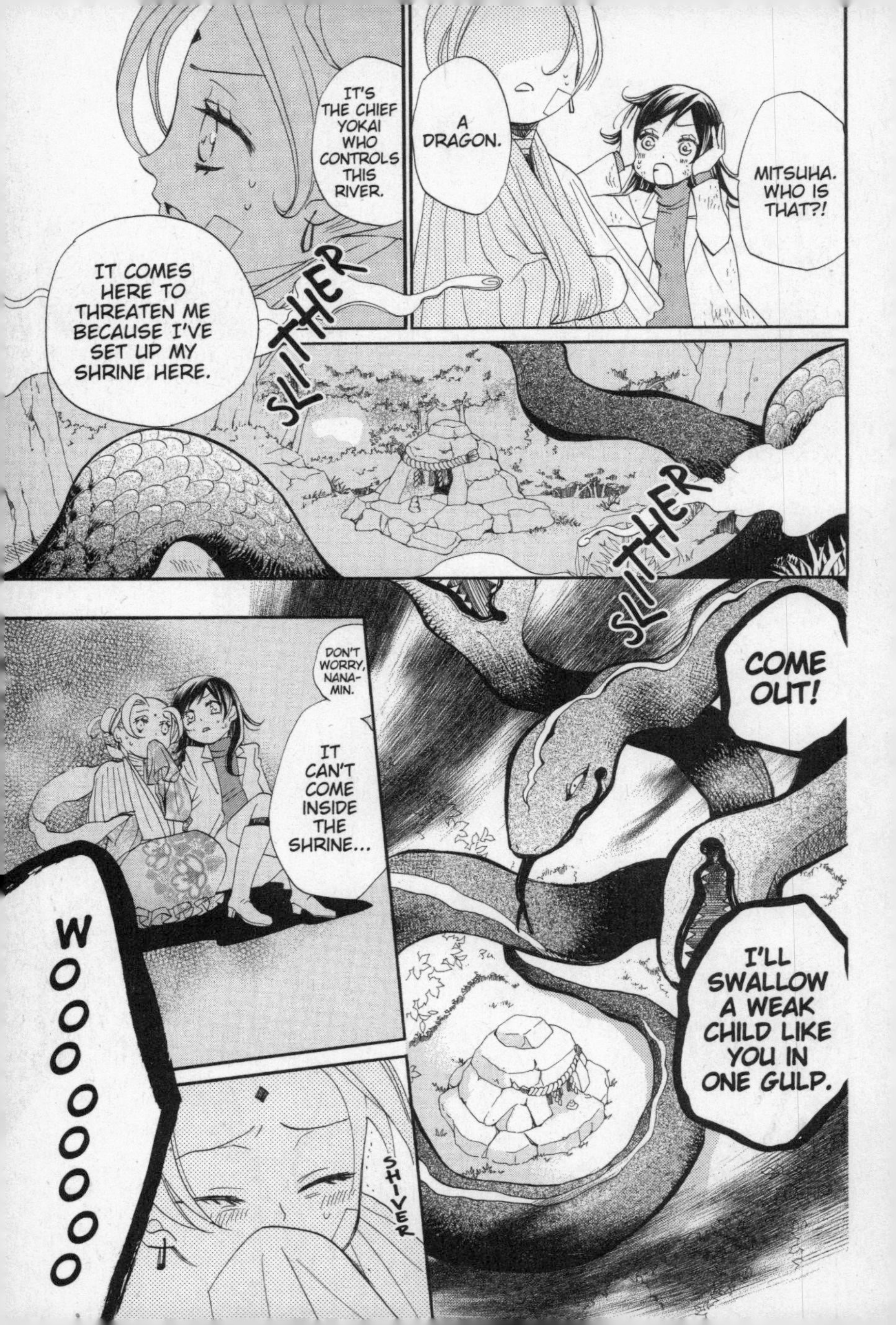
MITSUHA. WHO IS THAT?!
A DRAGON.
IT'S THE CHIEF YOKAI WHO CONTROLS THIS RIVER.
IT COMES HERE TO THREATEN ME BECAUSE I'VE SET UP MY SHRINE HERE.
SLITHER
SLITHER
COME OUT!
I'LL SWALLOW A WEAK CHILD LIKE YOU IN ONE GULP.
DON'T WORRY, NANA-MIN.
IT CAN'T COME INSIDE THE SHRINE...
WOOOOOOOO
SHIVER

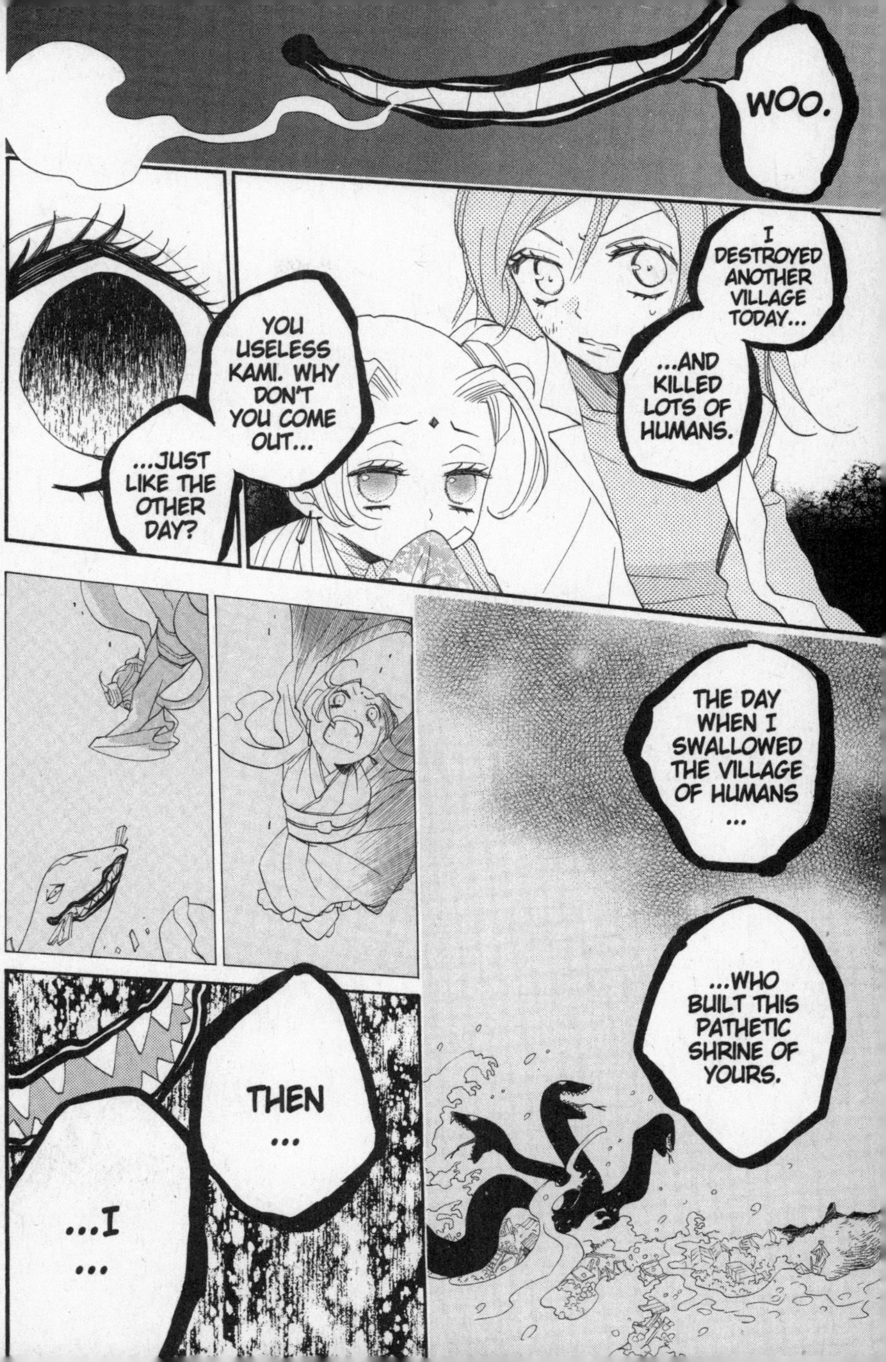
WOO.
I DESTROYED ANOTHER VILLAGE TODAY...
...AND KILLED LOTS OF HUMANS.
YOU USELESS KAMI. WHY DON'T YOU COME OUT...
...JUST LIKE THE OTHER DAY?
THE DAY WHEN I SWALLOWED THE VILLAGE OF HUMANS...
...WHO BUILT THIS PATHETIC SHRINE OF YOURS.
THEN...
...I...

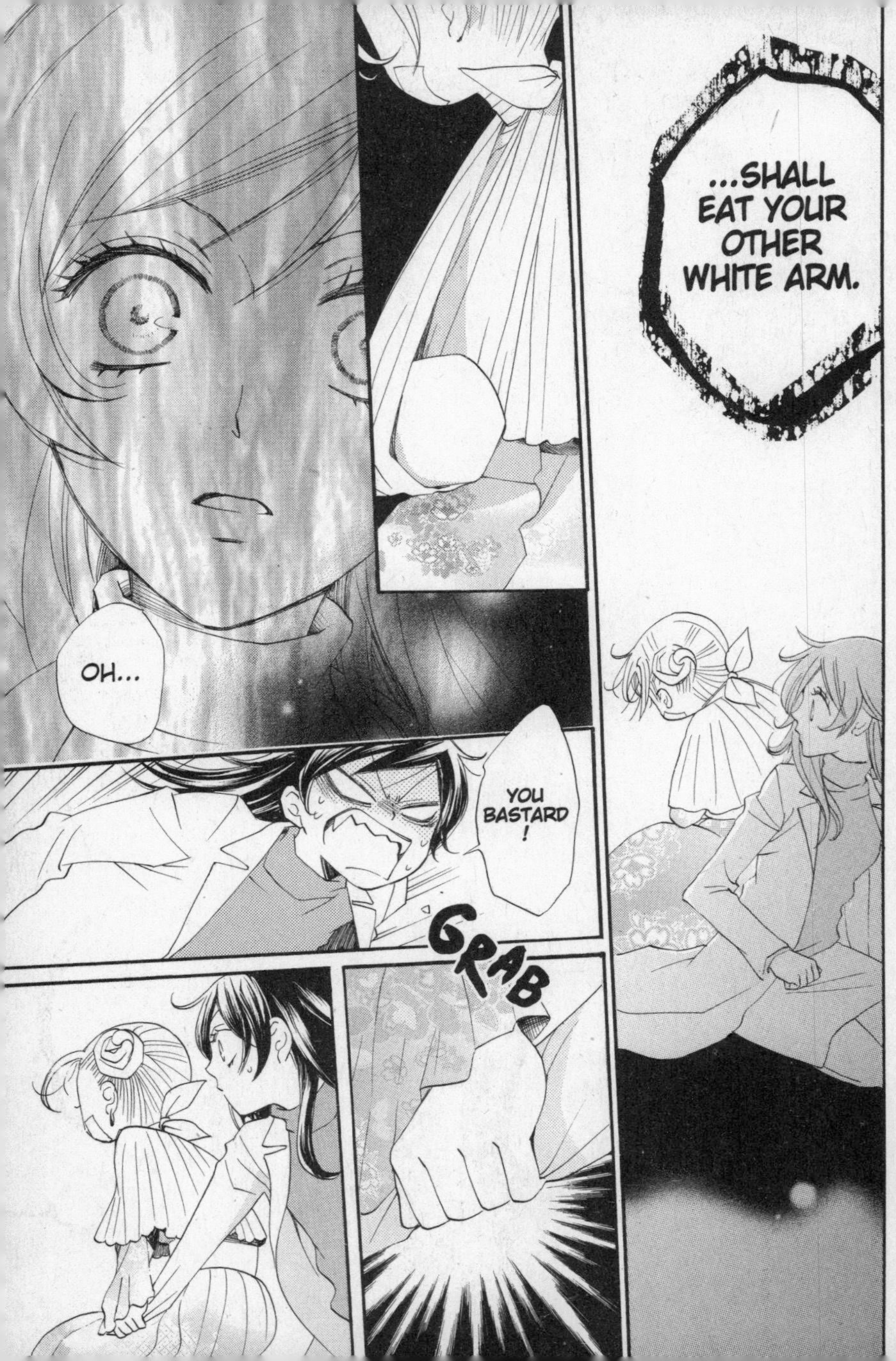
...SHALL EAT YOUR OTHER WHITE ARM.
OH...
YOU BASTARD!
GRAB

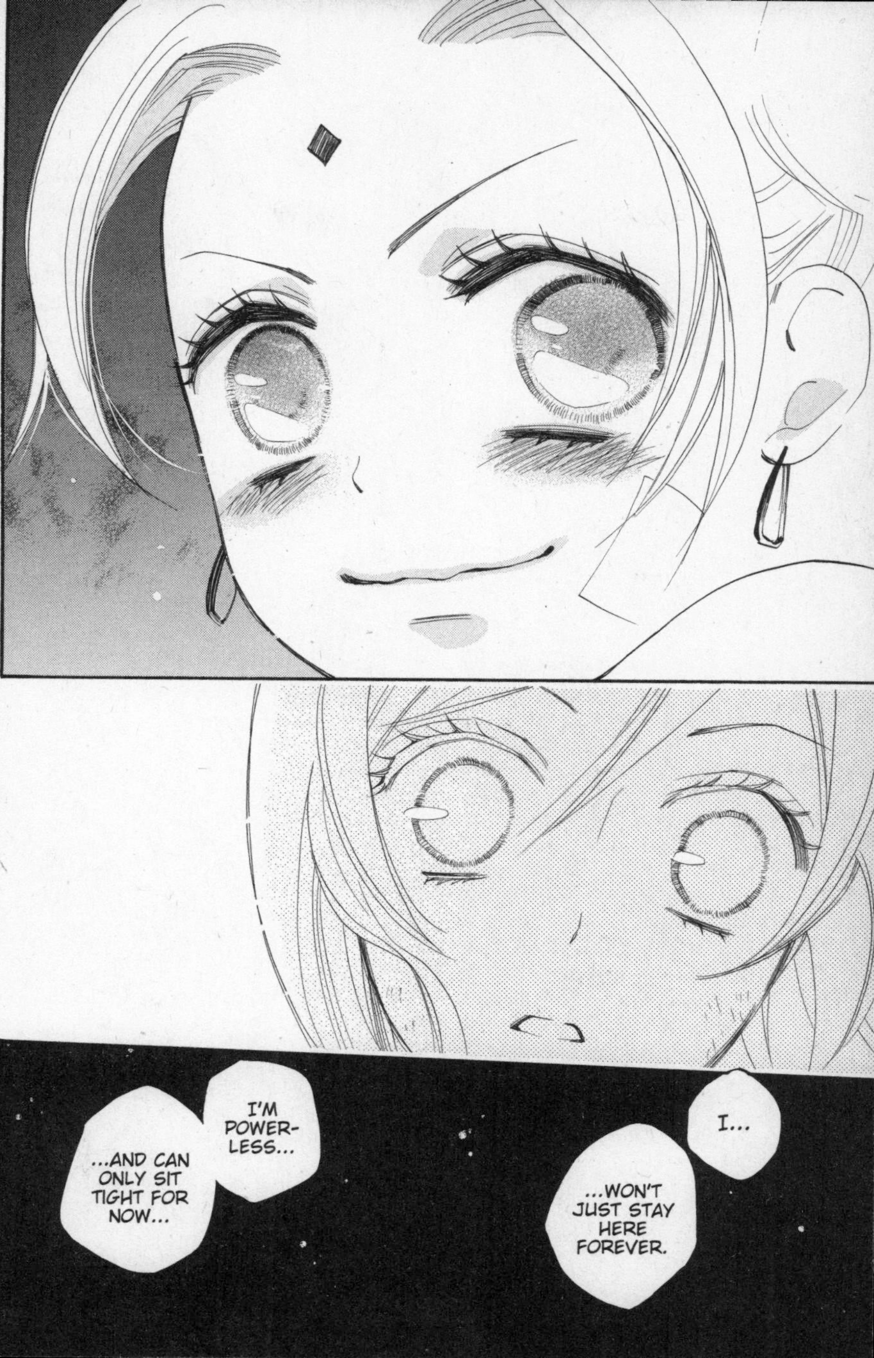
I...
...WON'T JUST STAY HERE FOREVER.
I'M POWER-LESS...
...AND CAN ONLY SIT TIGHT FOR NOW...

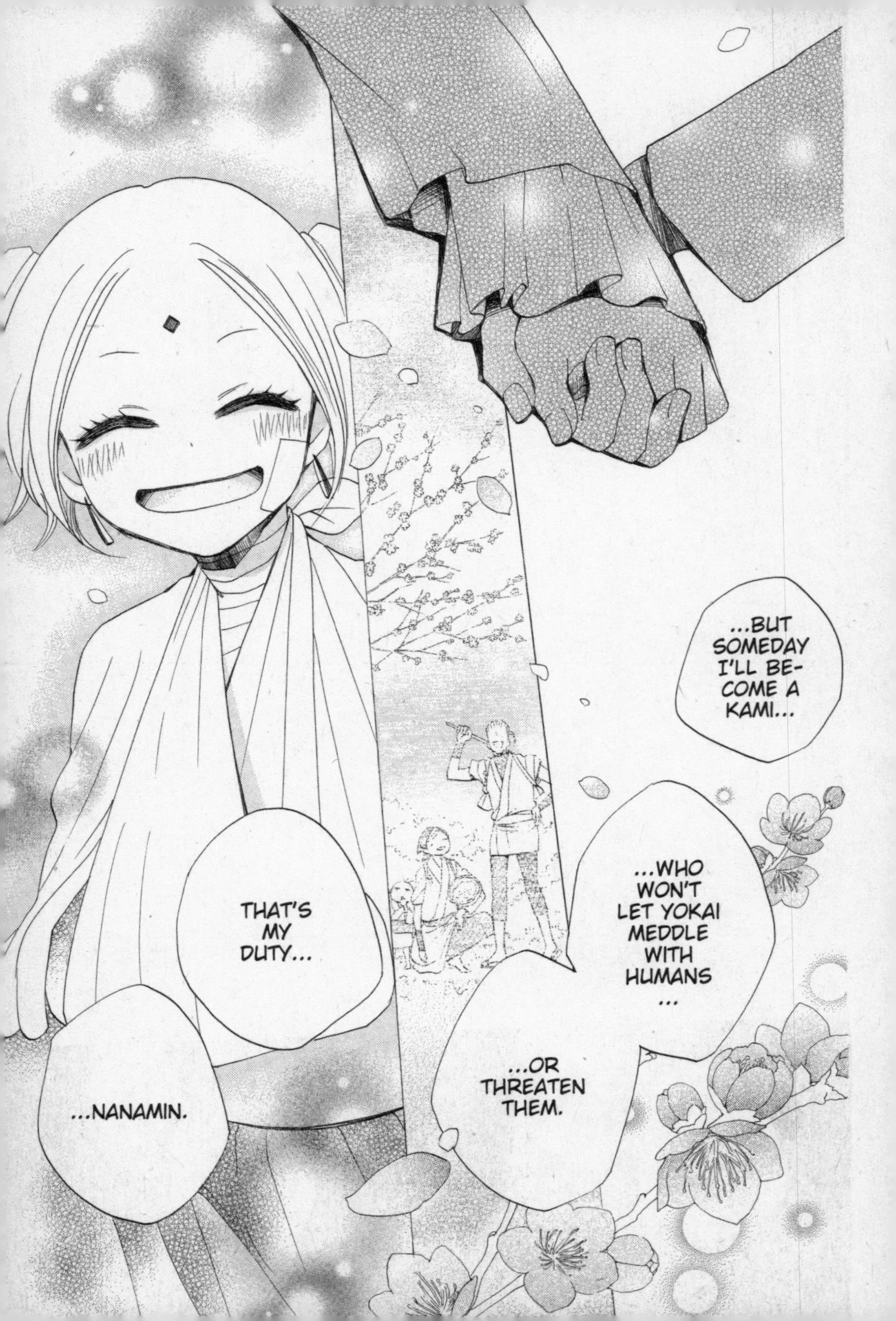
...BUT SOMEDAY I'LL BE-COME A KAMI...
...WHO WON'T LET YOKAI MEDDLE WITH HUMANS ...
...OR THREATEN THEM.
THAT'S MY DUTY...
...NANAMIN.

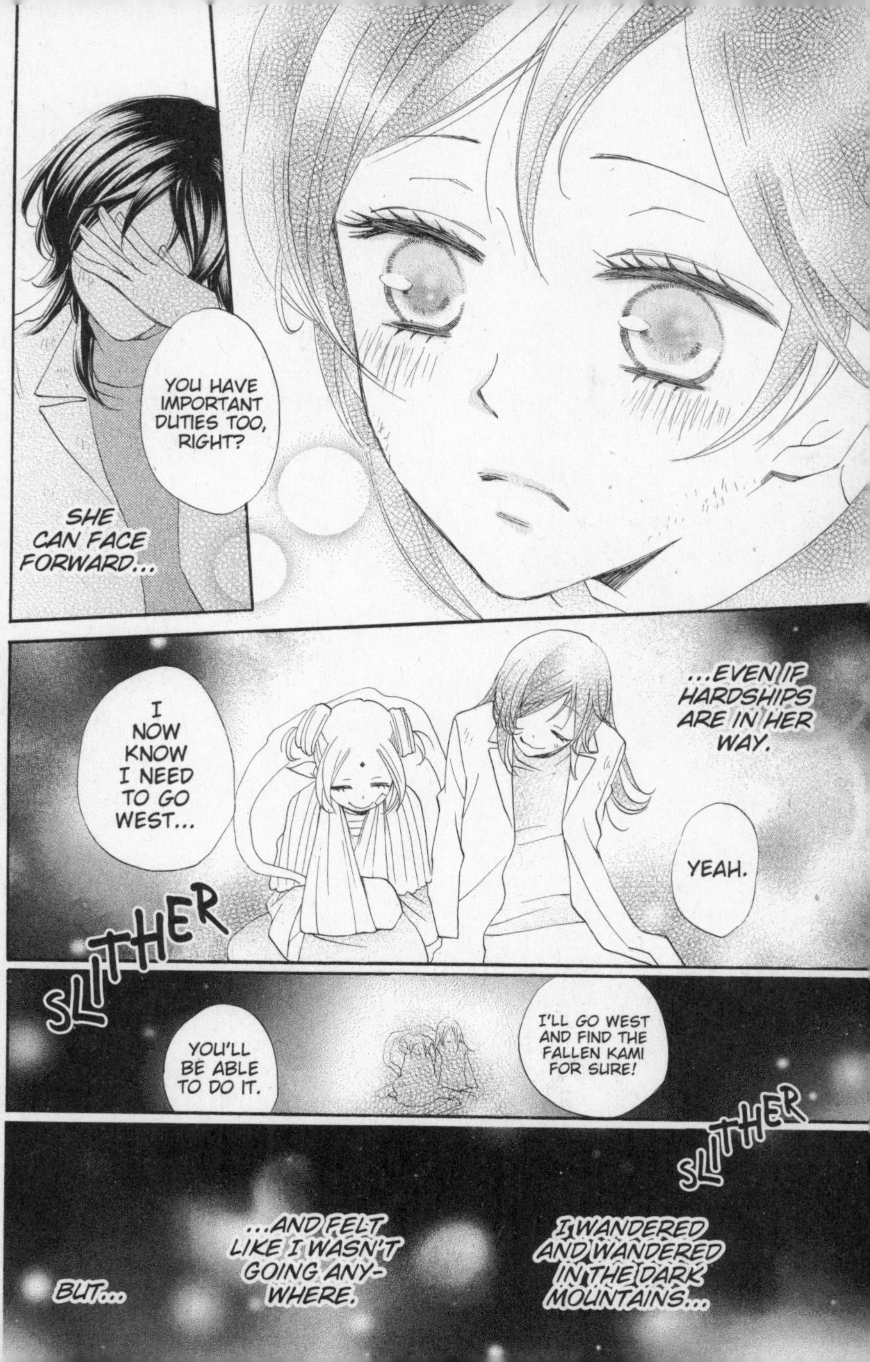
YOU HAVE IMPORTANT DUTIES TOO, RIGHT?
SHE CAN FACE FORWARD...
...EVEN IF HARDSHIPS ARE IN HER WAY.
I NOW KNOW I NEED TO GO WEST...
YEAH.
SLITHER
I'LL GO WEST AND FIND THE FALLEN KAMI FOR SURE!
YOU'LL BE ABLE TO DO IT.
SLITHER
I WANDERED AND WANDERED IN THE DARK MOUNTAINS...
...AND FELT LIKE I WASN'T GOING ANY-WHERE.
BUT...

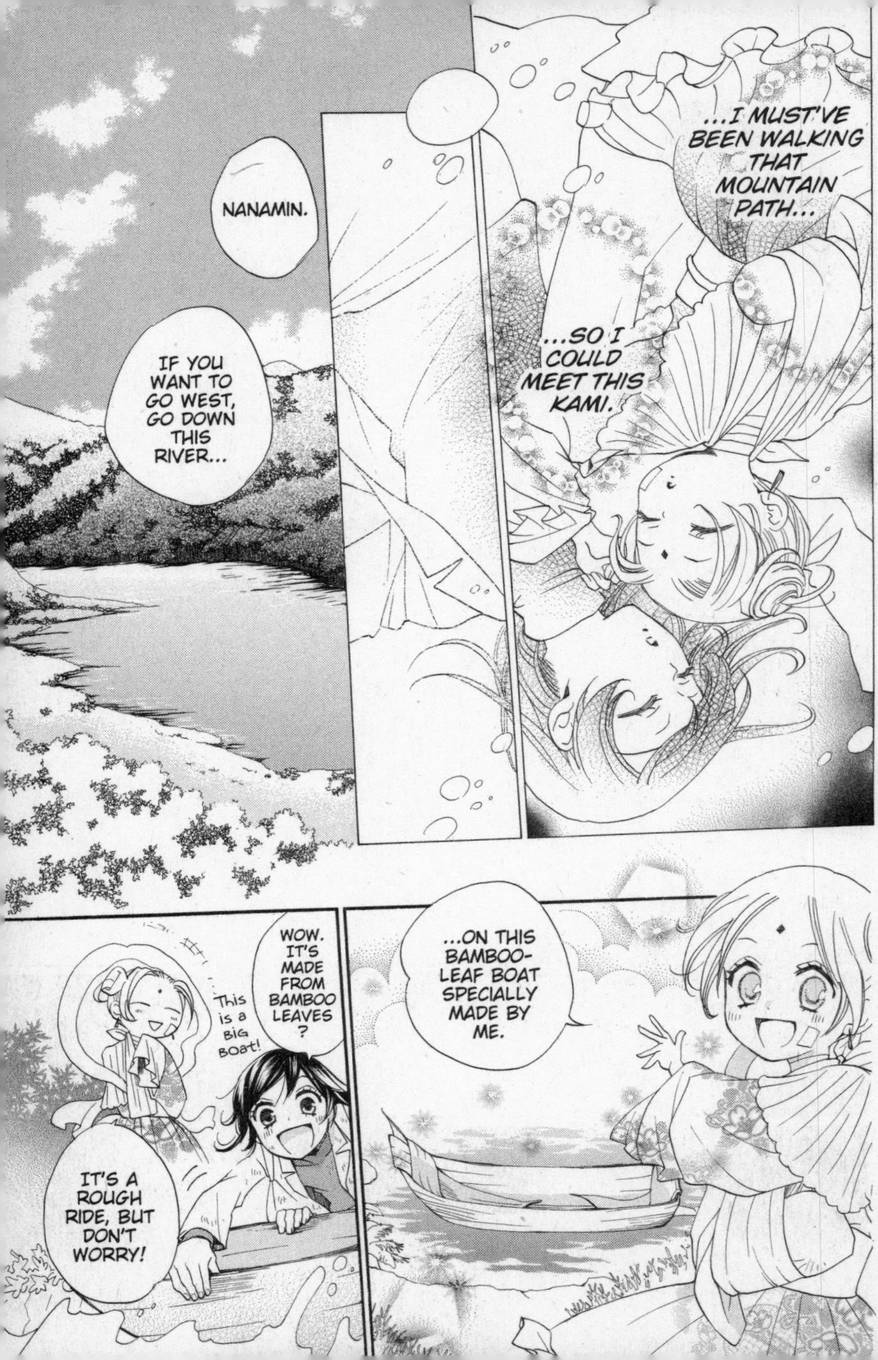

...I MUST'VE BEEN WALKING THAT MOUNTAIN PATH...
...SO I COULD MEET THIS KAMI.
NANAMIN.
IF YOU WANT TO GO WEST, GO DOWN THIS RIVER...
...ON THIS BAMBOO-LEAF BOAT SPECIALLY MADE BY ME.
WOW. IT'S MADE FROM BAMBOO LEAVES?
This is a big boat!
IT'S A ROUGH RIDE, BUT DON'T WORRY!

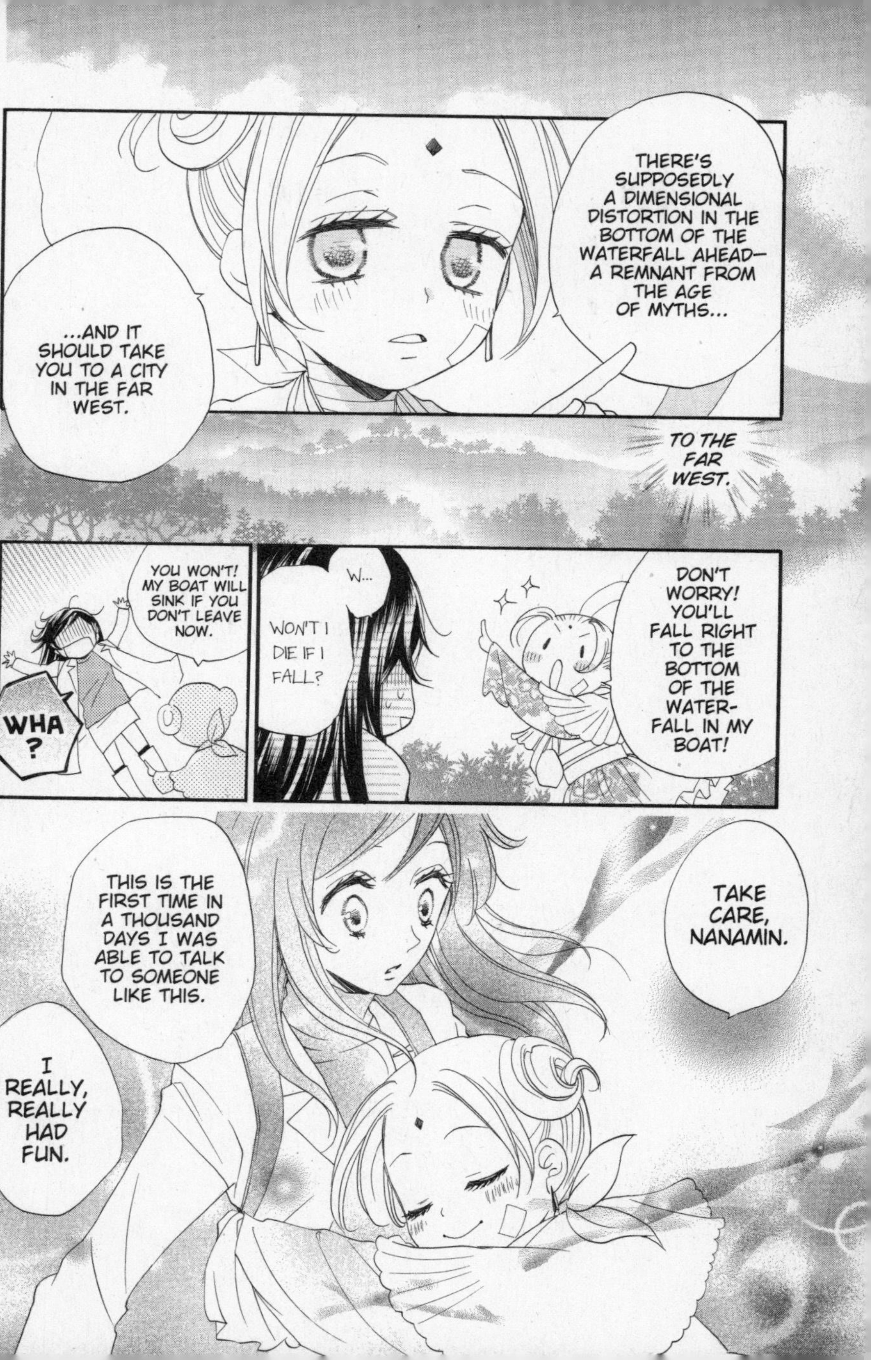
THERE'S SUPPOSEDLY A DIMENSIONAL DISTORTION IN THE BOTTOM OF THE WATERFALL AHEAD— A REMNANT FROM THE AGE OF MYTHS...
...AND IT SHOULD TAKE YOU TO A CITY IN THE FAR WEST.
TO THE FAR WEST.
DON'T WORRY! YOU'LL FALL RIGHT TO THE BOTTOM OF THE WATER-FALL IN MY BOAT!
W...
WON'T I DIE IF I FALL?
YOU WON'T! MY BOAT WILL SINK IF YOU DON'T LEAVE NOW.
WHA ?
TAKE CARE, NANAMIN.
THIS IS THE FIRST TIME IN A THOUSAND DAYS I WAS ABLE TO TALK TO SOMEONE LIKE THIS.
I REALLY, REALLY HAD FUN.

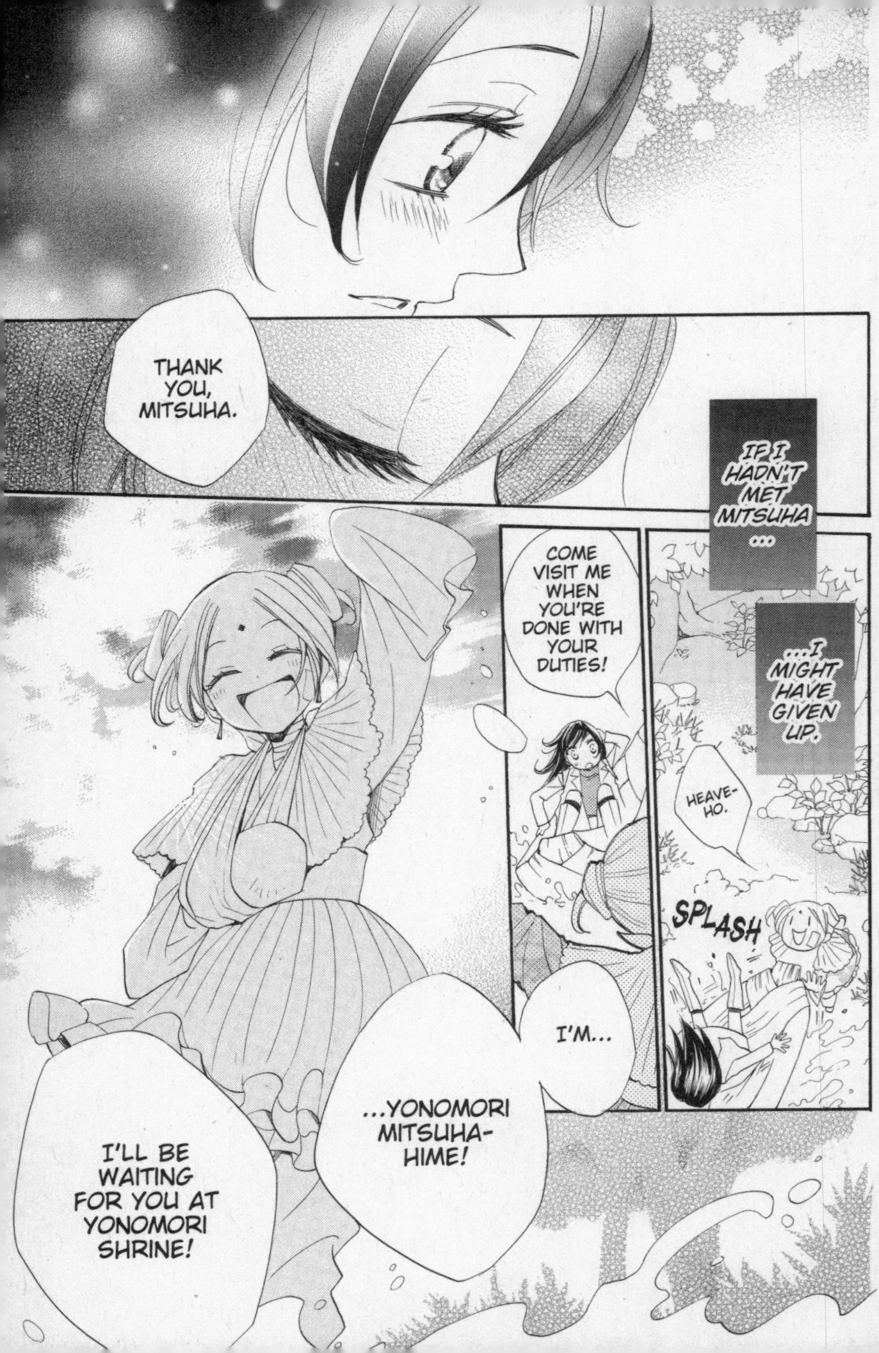
THANK YOU, MITSUHA.
IF I HADN'T MET MITSUHA...
...I MIGHT HAVE GIVEN UP.
HEAVE-HO.
SPLASH
COME VISIT ME WHEN YOU'RE DONE WITH YOUR DUTIES!
I'M...
...YONOMORI MITSUHA-HIME!
I'LL BE WAITING FOR YOU AT YONOMORI SHRINE!

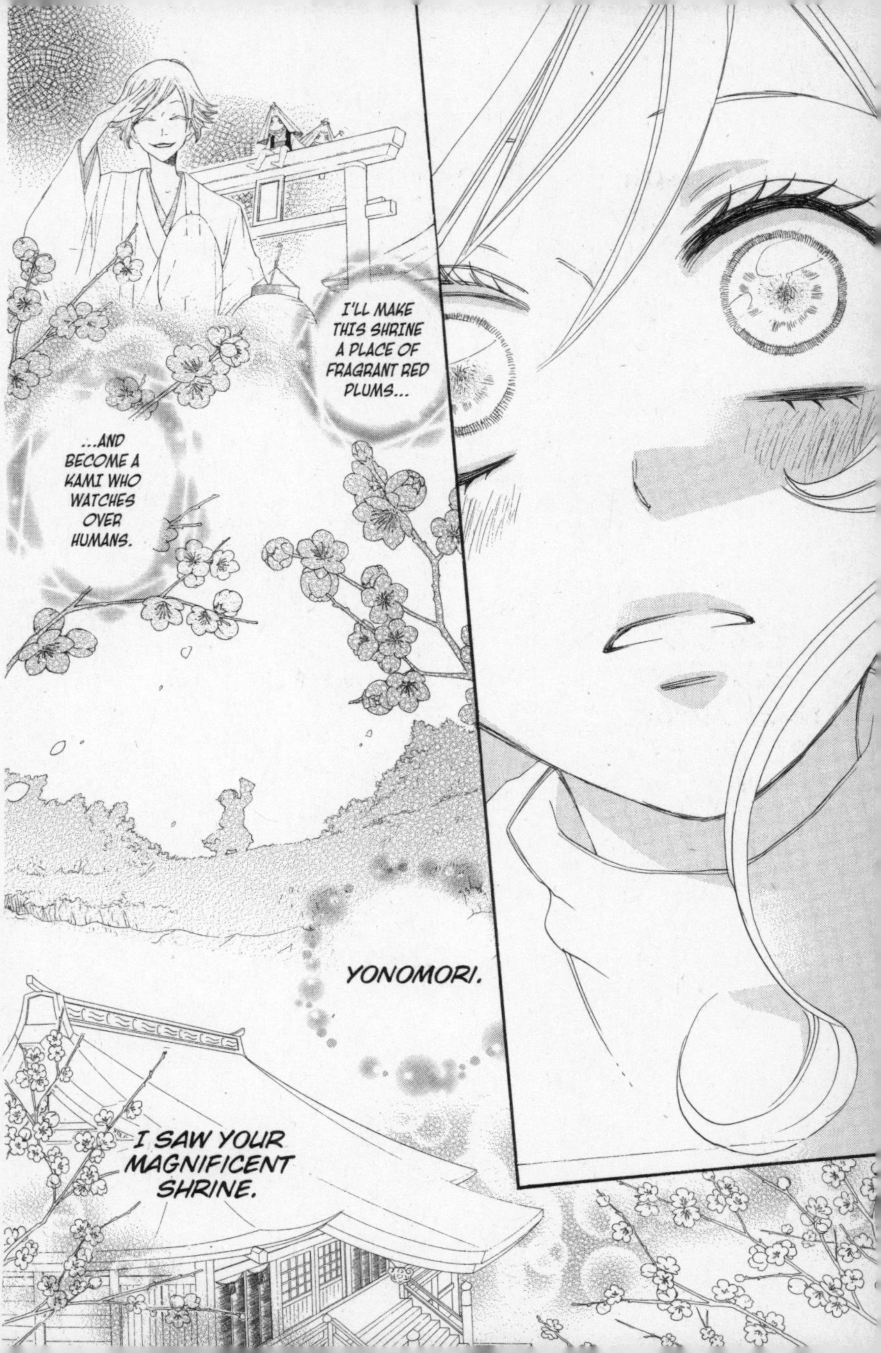
I'LL MAKE THIS SHRINE A PLACE OF FRAGRANT RED PLUMS...
...AND BECOME A KAMI WHO WATCHES OVER HUMANS.
YONOMORI.
I SAW YOUR MAGNIFICENT SHRINE.

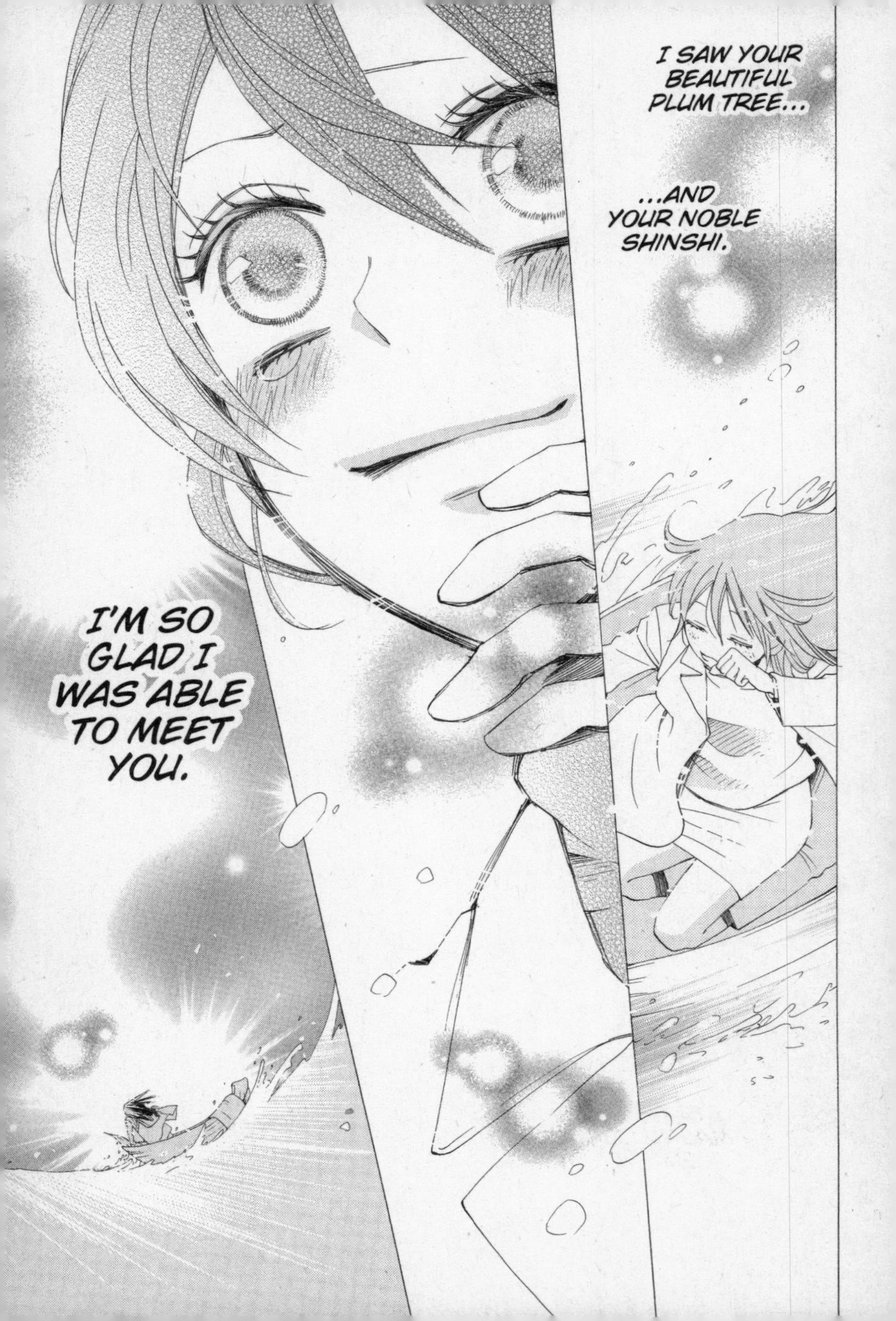
I SAW YOUR BEAUTIFUL PLUM TREE...
...AND YOUR NOBLE SHINSHI.
I'M SO GLAD I WAS ABLE TO MEET YOU.

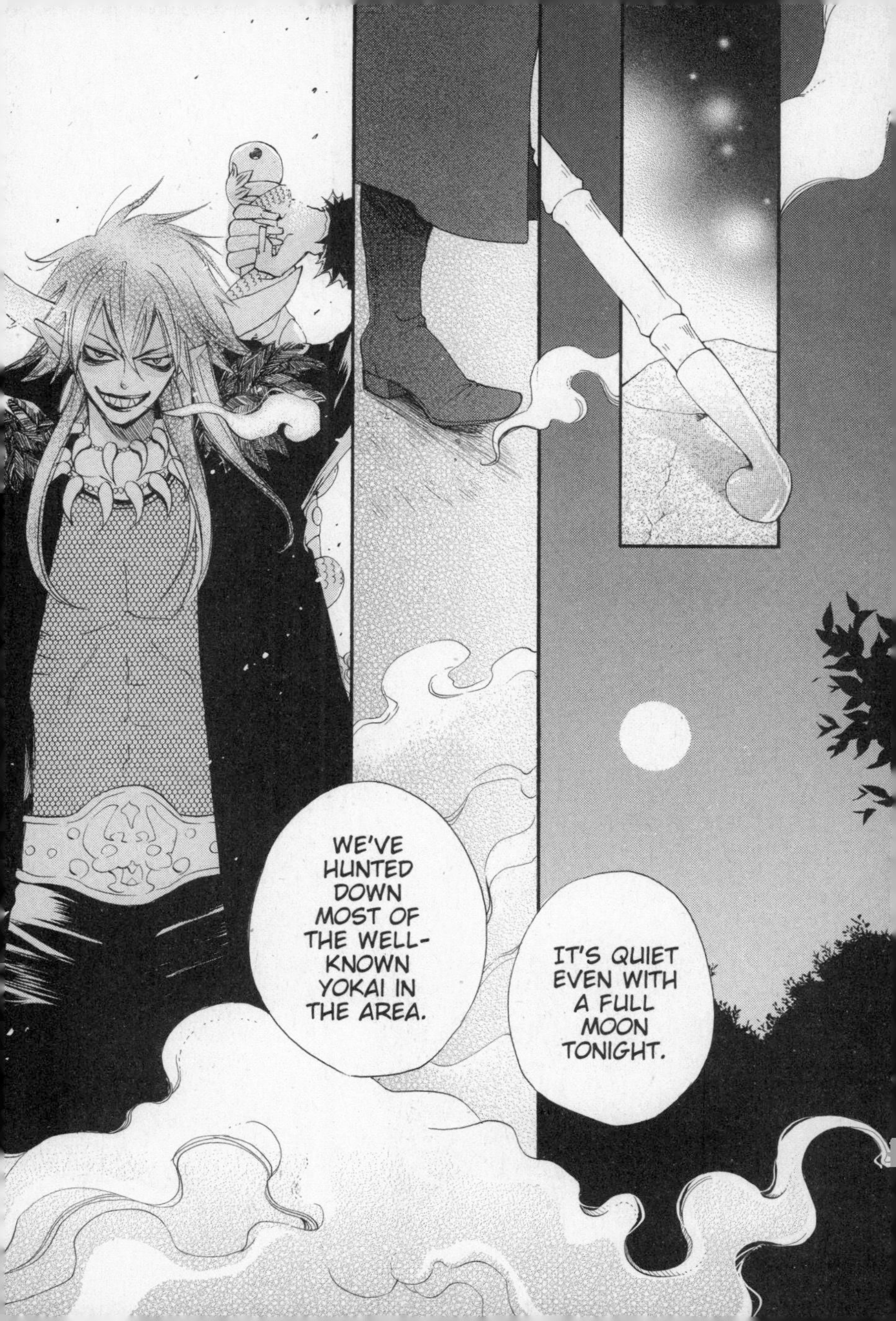
IT'S QUIET EVEN WITH A FULL MOON TONIGHT.
WE'VE HUNTED DOWN MOST OF THE WELL-KNOWN YOKAI IN THE AREA.

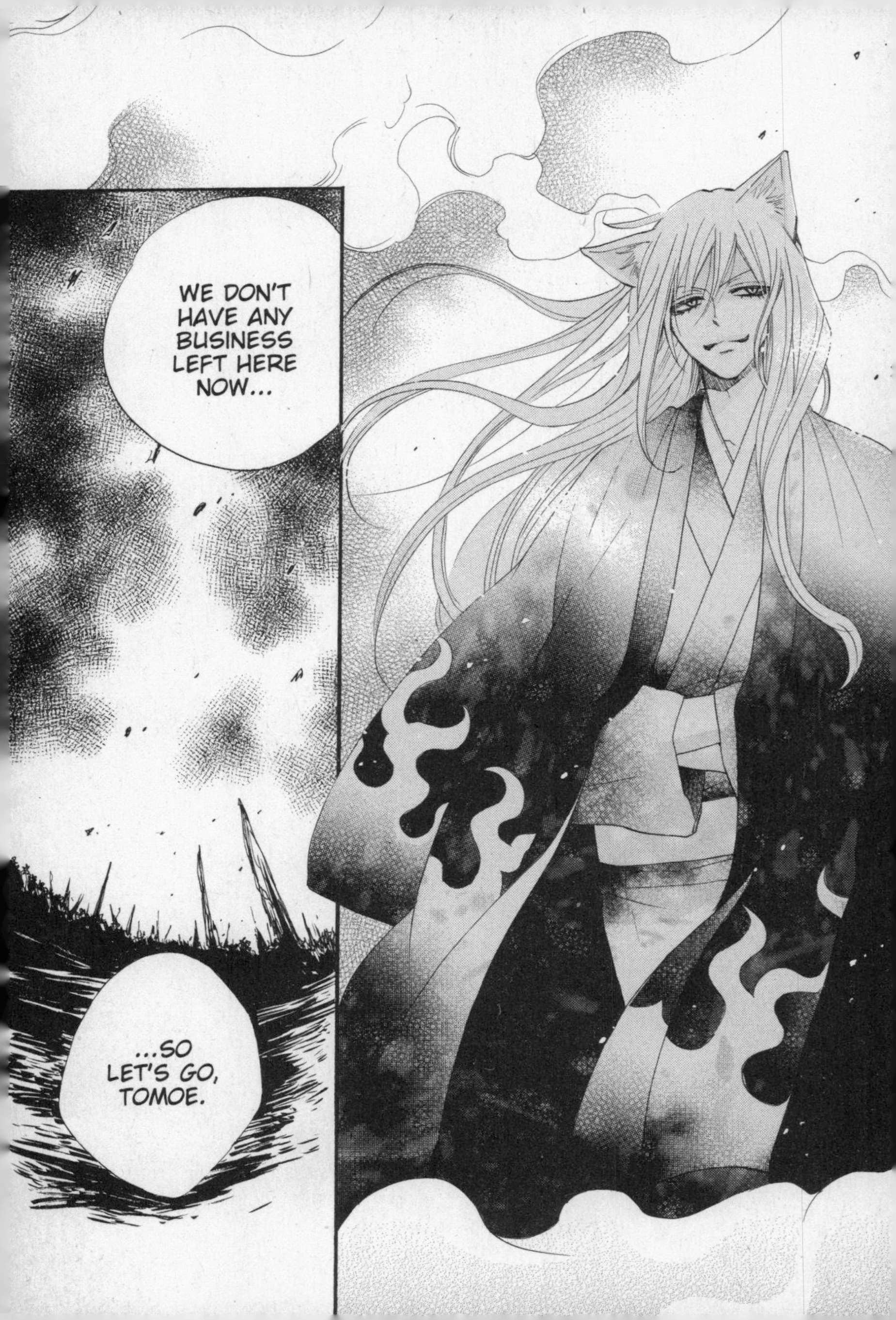
WE DON'T HAVE ANY BUSINESS LEFT HERE NOW...
...SO LET'S GO, TOMOE.

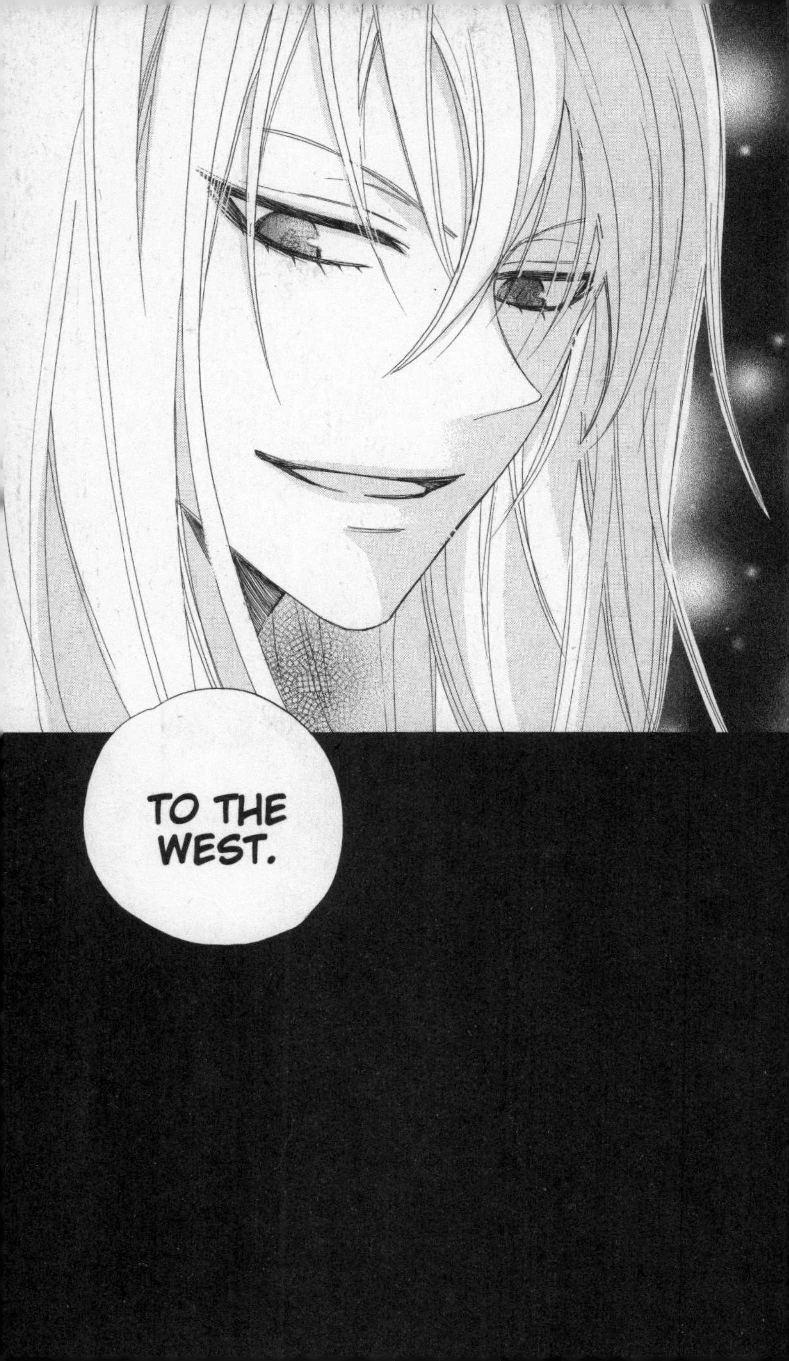
TO THE WEST.

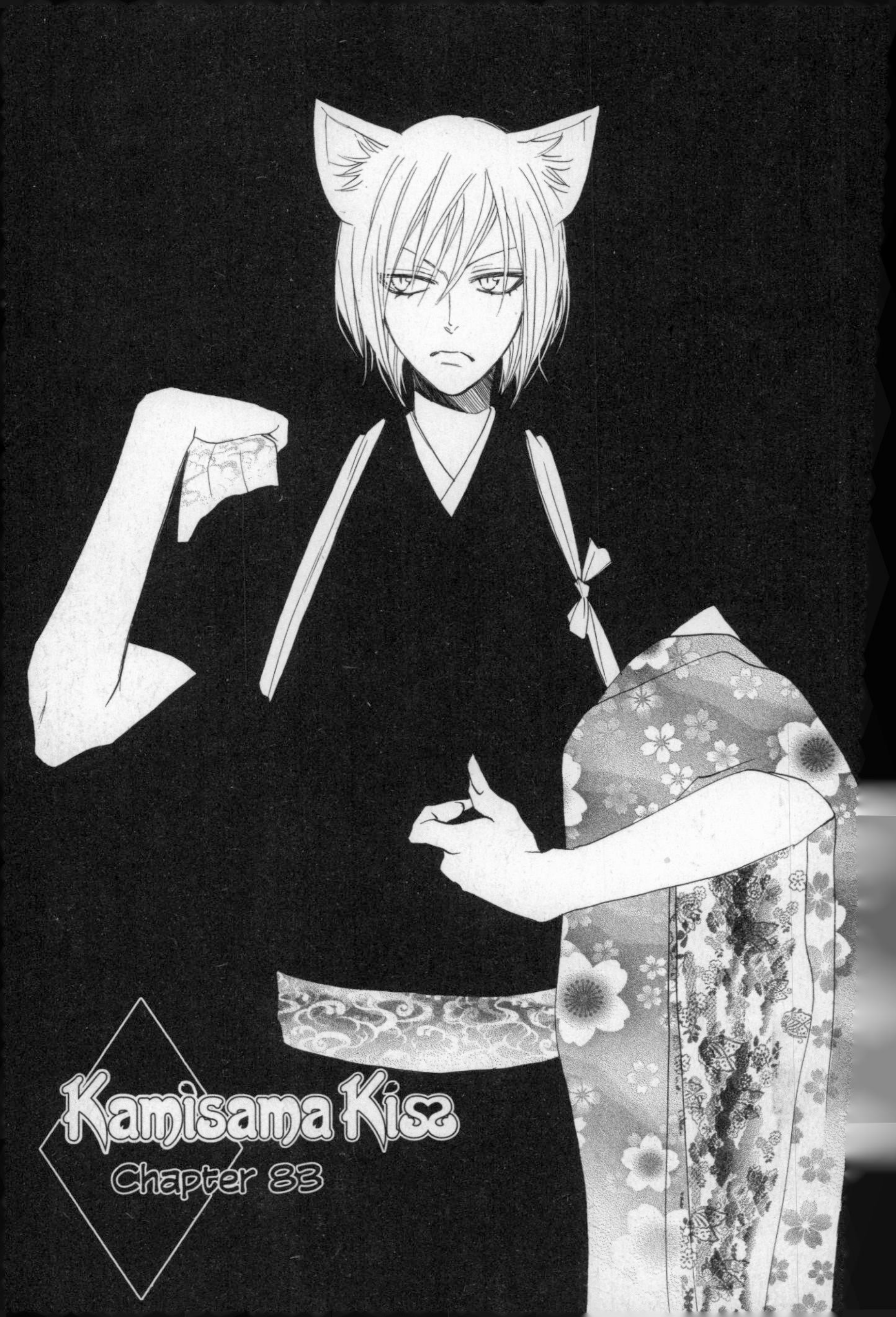
Kamisama Kiss
Chapter 83

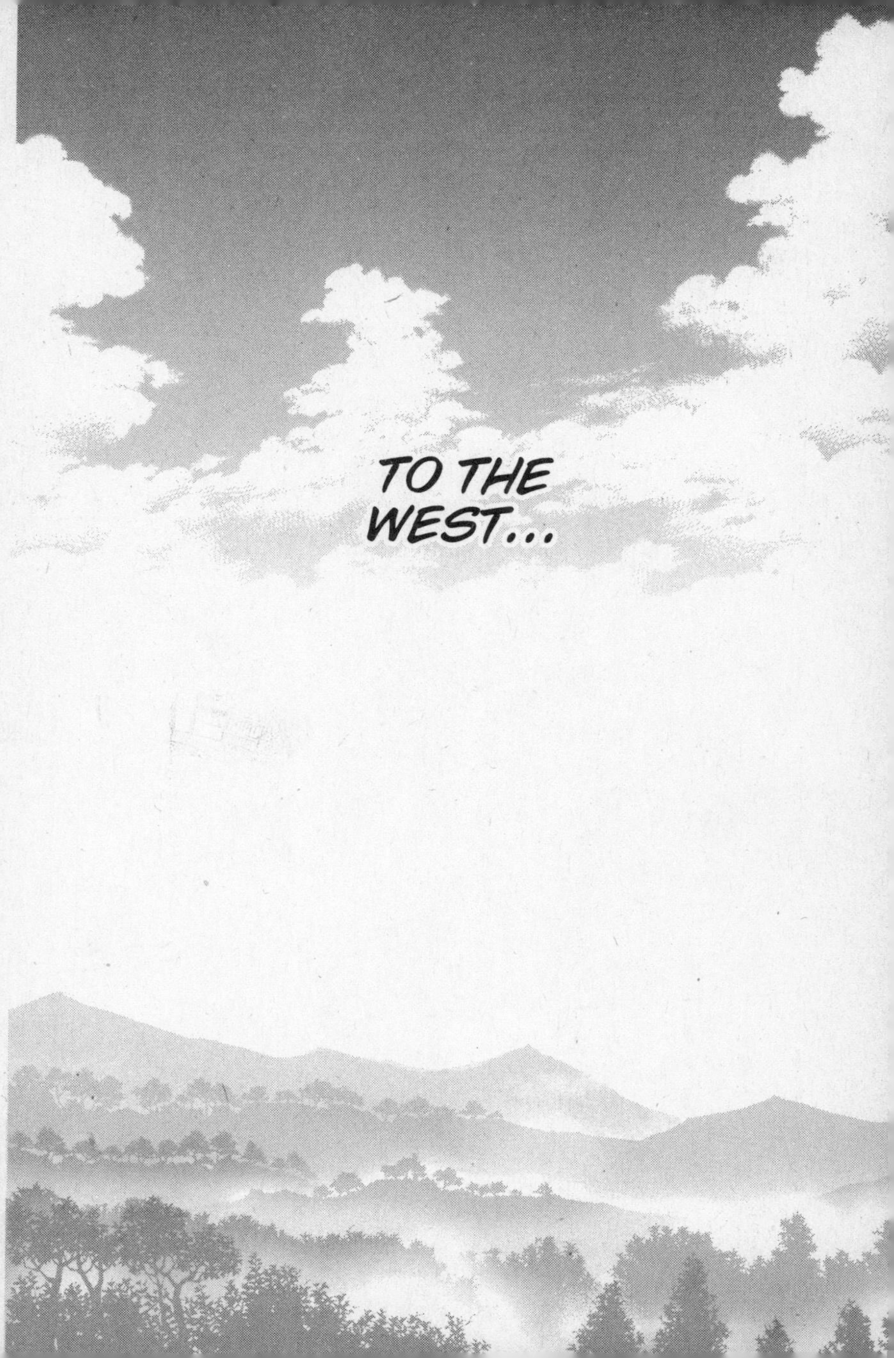
TO THE WEST...

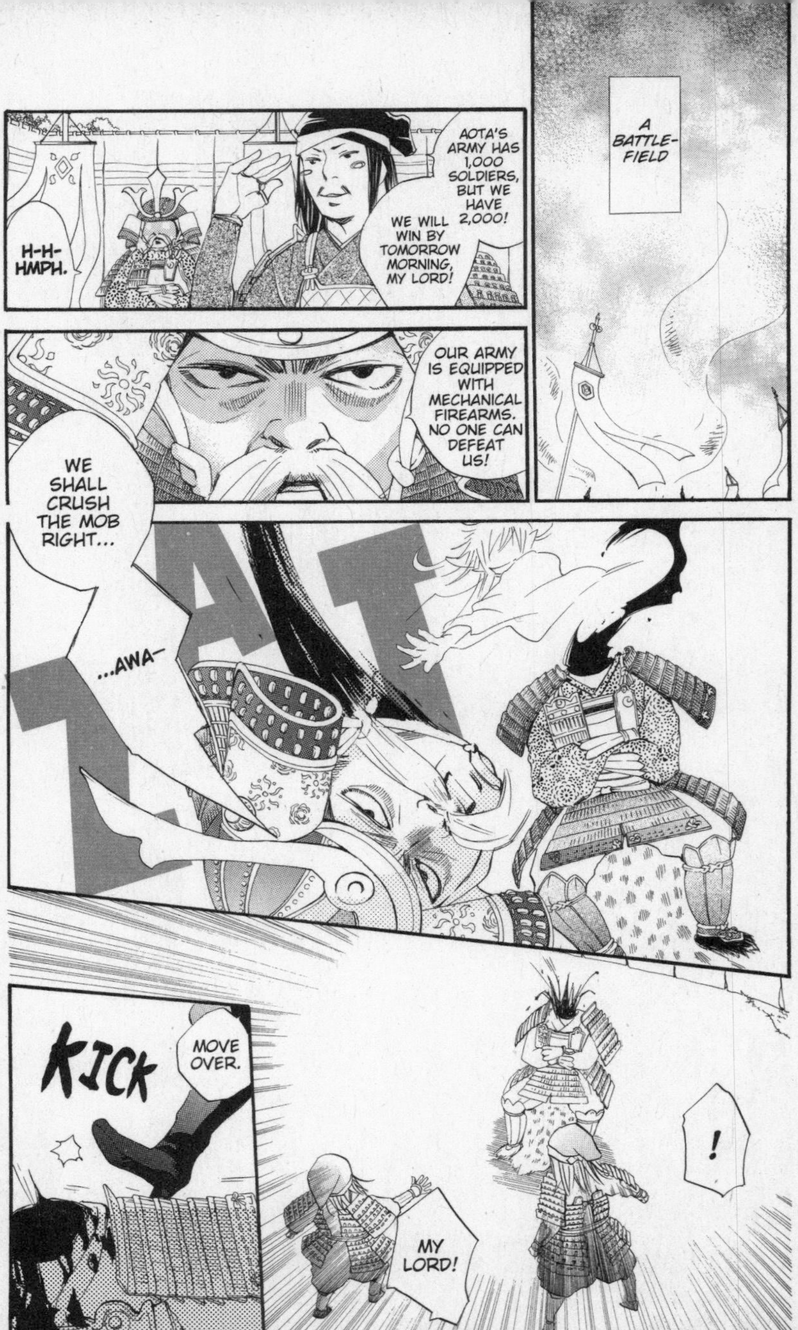
A BATTLE-FIELD
AOTA'S ARMY HAS 1,000 SOLDIERS, BUT WE HAVE 2,000!
WE WILL WIN BY TOMORROW MORNING, MY LORD!
H-H-HMPH.
OUR ARMY IS EQUIPPED WITH MECHANICAL FIREARMS. NO ONE CAN DEFEAT US!
WE SHALL CRUSH THE MOB RIGHT...
...AWA-
!
MY LORD!
MOVE OVER.
KICK

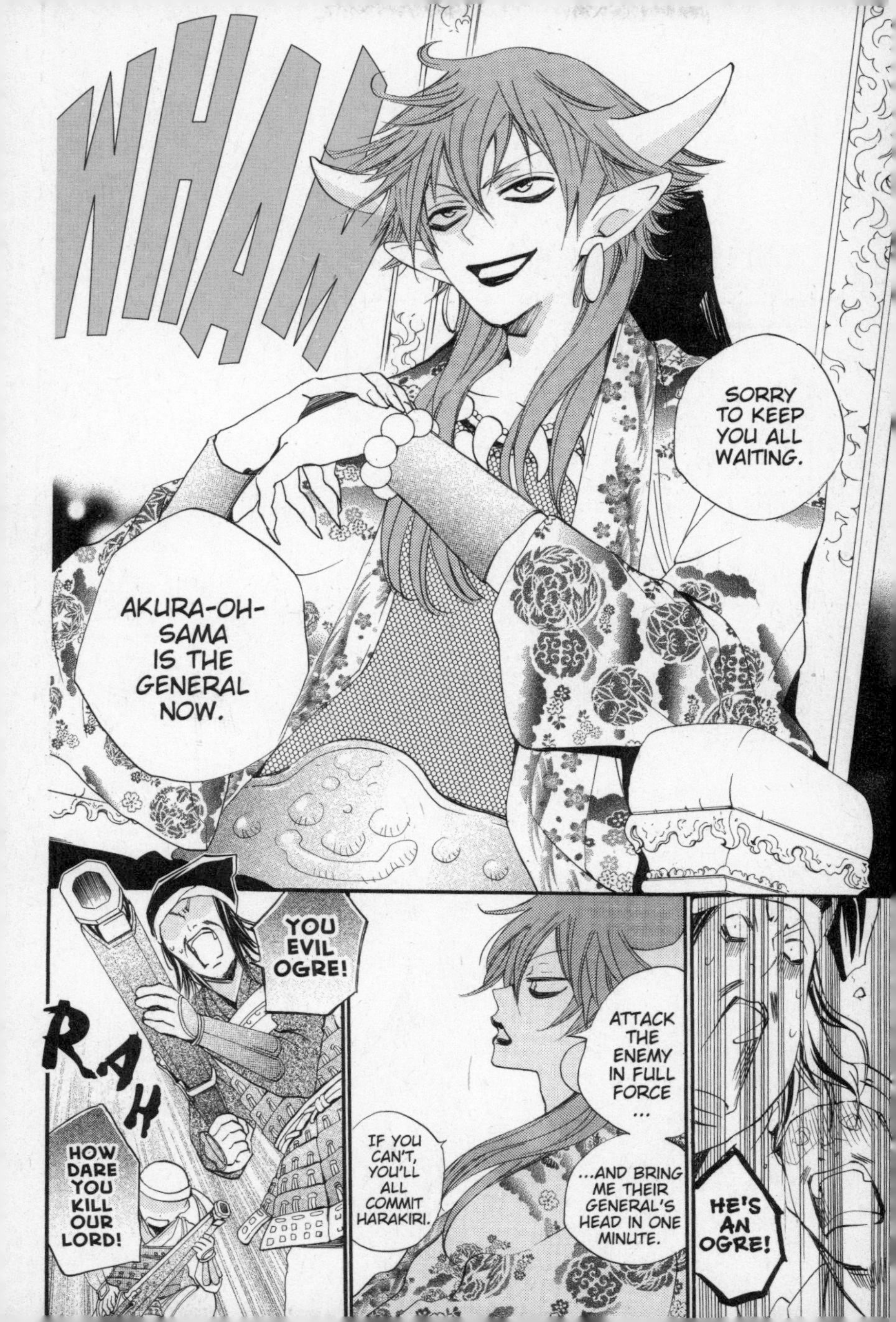
WHAM
SORRY TO KEEP YOU ALL WAITING.
AKURA-OH-SAMA IS THE GENERAL NOW.
HE'S AN OGRE!
ATTACK THE ENEMY IN FULL FORCE ...
...AND BRING ME THEIR GENERAL'S HEAD IN ONE MINUTE.
IF YOU CAN'T, YOU'LL ALL COMMIT HARAKIRI.
YOU EVIL OGRE!
RAH
HOW DARE YOU KILL OUR LORD!

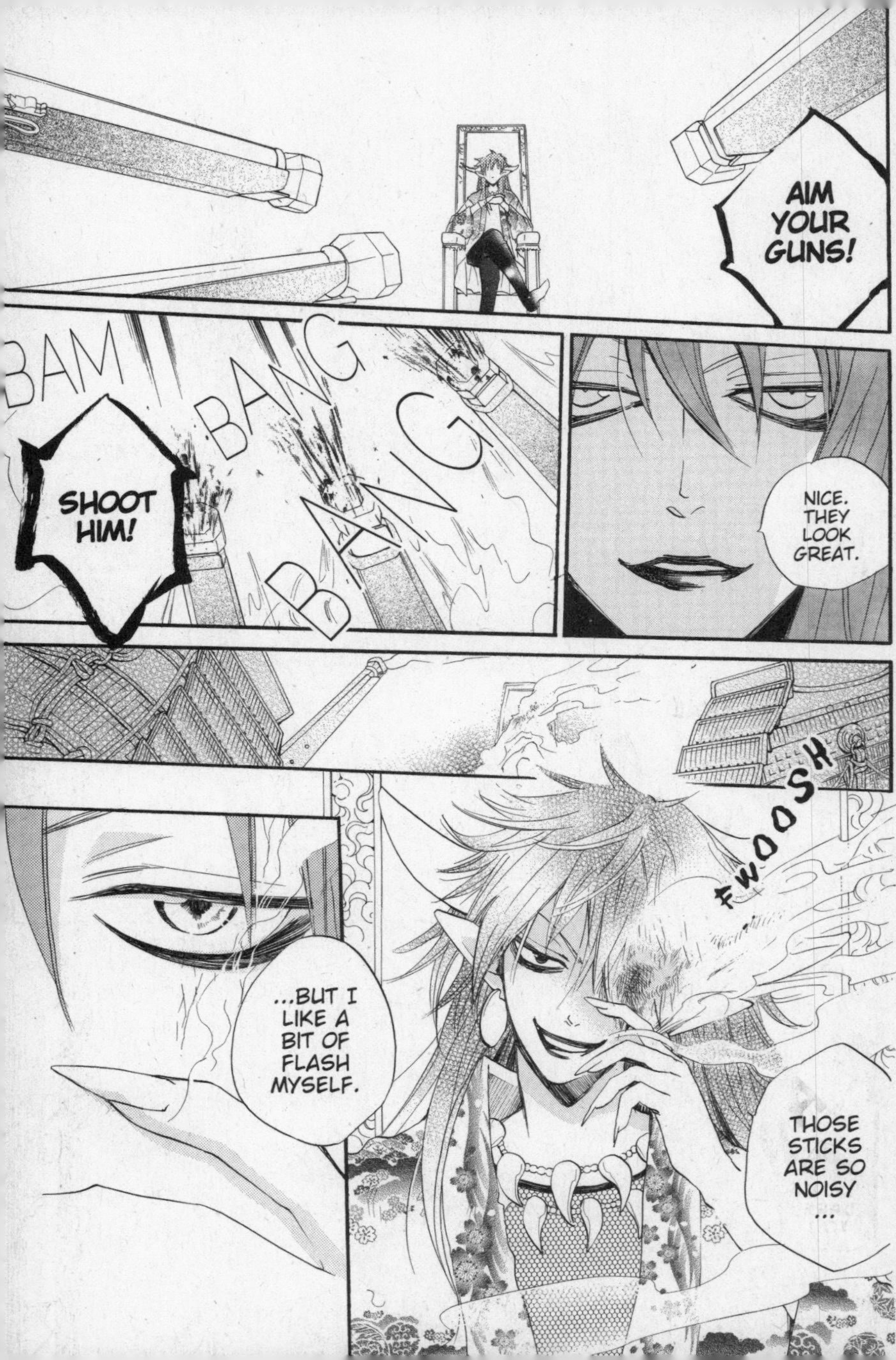
AIM YOUR GUNS!
NICE. THEY LOOK GREAT.
BANG
BANG
BAM
SHOOT HIM!
FWOOSH
THOSE STICKS ARE SO NOISY ...
...BUT I LIKE A BIT OF FLASH MYSELF.

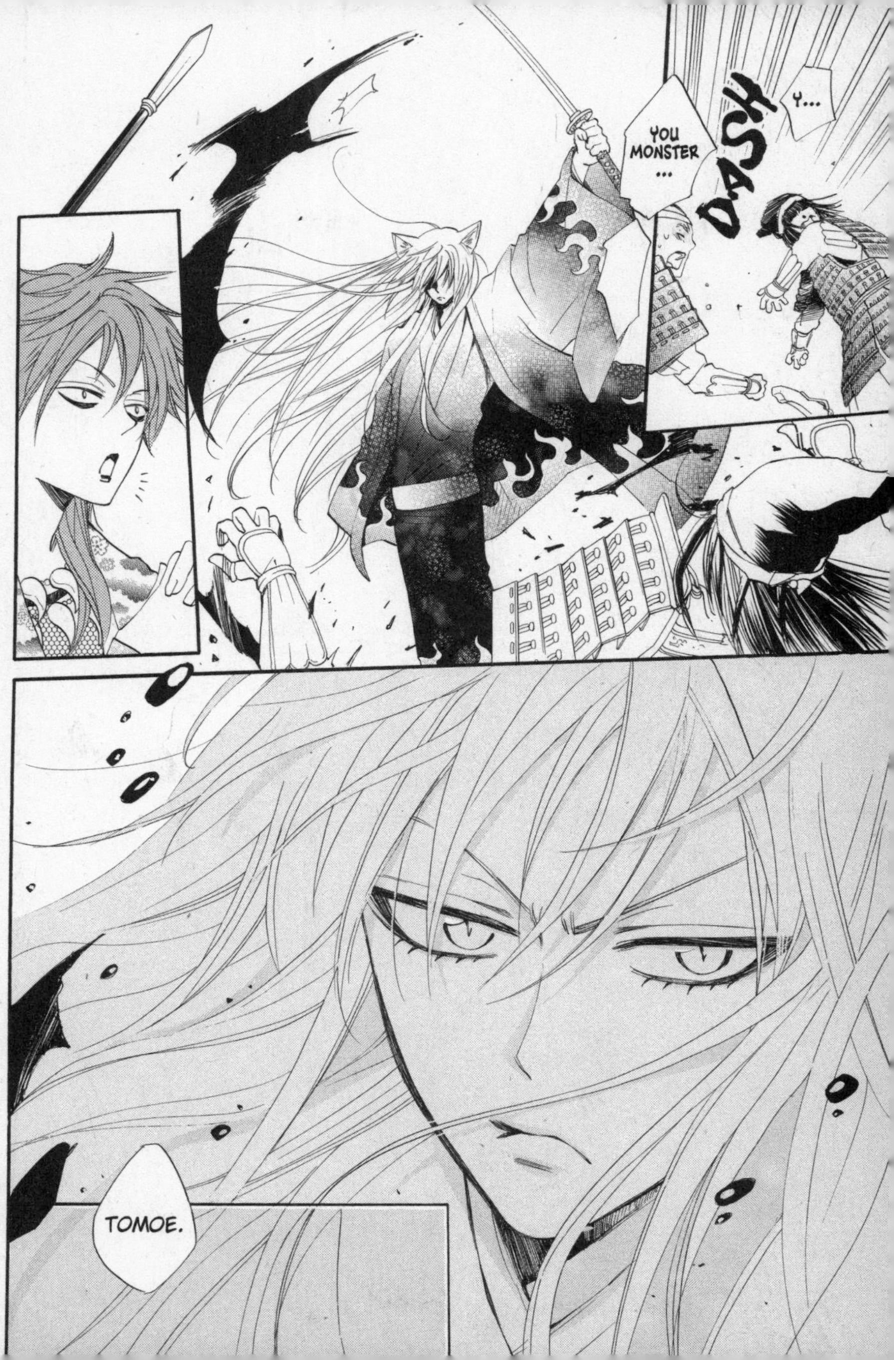
Y...
DASH
YOU MONSTER ...
TOMOE.

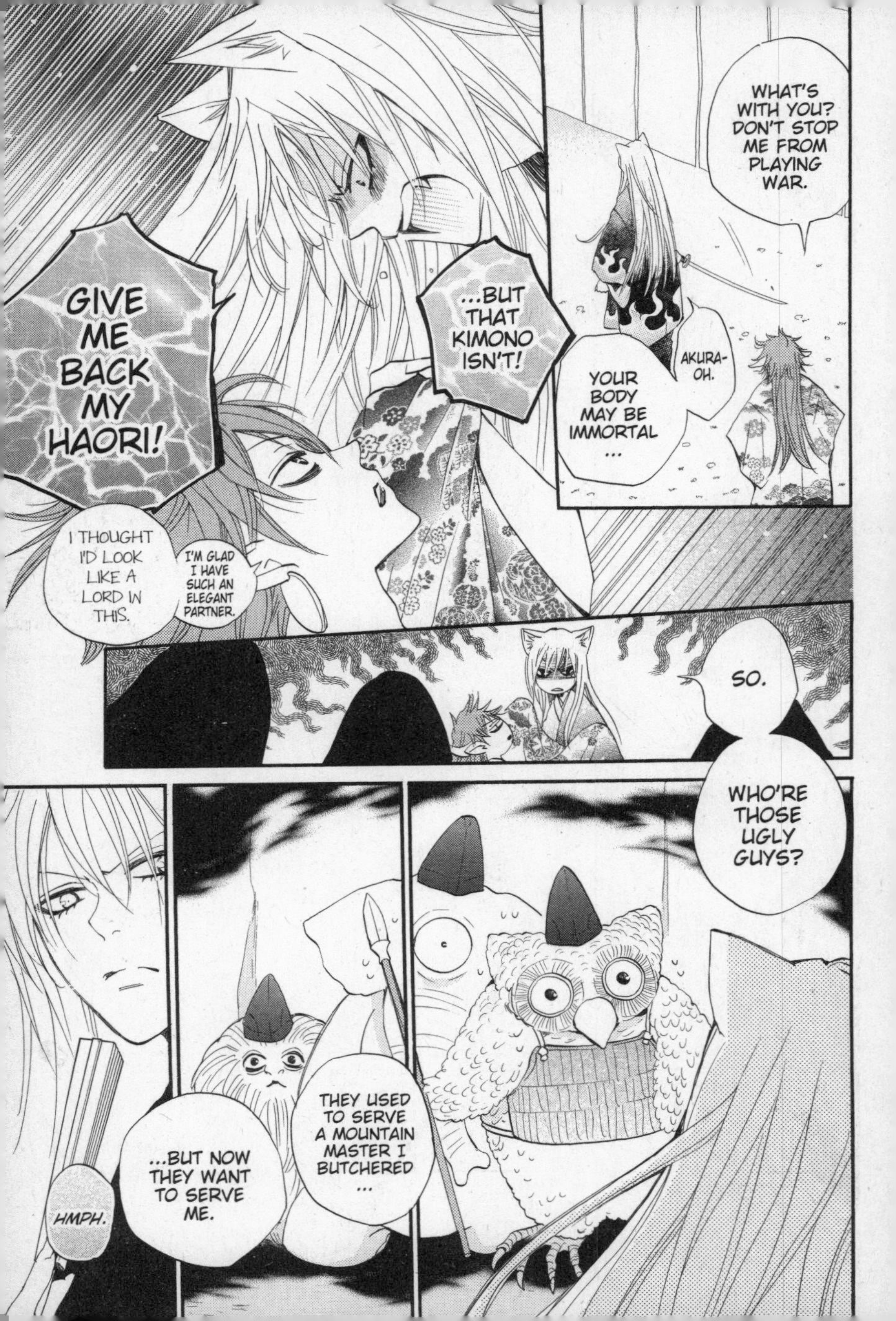
WHAT'S WITH YOU? DON'T STOP ME FROM PLAYING WAR.
AKURA-OH.
YOUR BODY MAY BE IMMORTAL ...
...BUT THAT KIMONO ISN'T!
GIVE ME BACK MY HAORI!
I'M GLAD I HAVE SUCH AN ELEGANT PARTNER.
I THOUGHT I'D LOOK LIKE A LORD IN THIS.
SO.
WHO'RE THOSE UGLY GUYS?
THEY USED TO SERVE A MOUNTAIN MASTER I BUTCHERED ...
...BUT NOW THEY WANT TO SERVE ME.
HMPH.

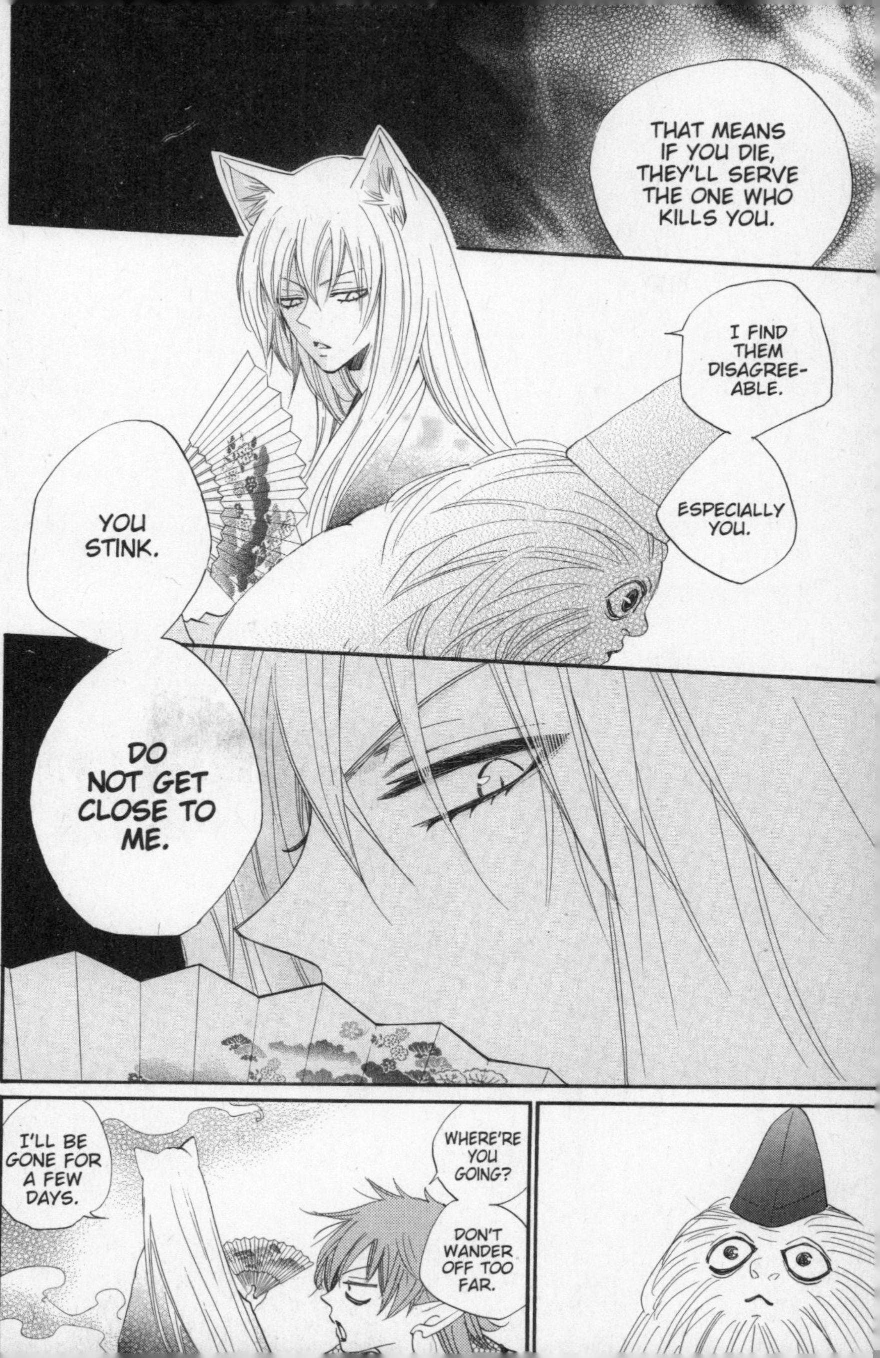
THAT MEANS IF YOU DIE, THEY'LL SERVE THE ONE WHO KILLS YOU.
I FIND THEM DISAGREE-ABLE.
ESPECIALLY YOU.
YOU STINK.
DO NOT GET CLOSE TO ME.
WHERE'RE YOU GOING?
I'LL BE GONE FOR A FEW DAYS.
DON'T WANDER OFF TOO FAR.

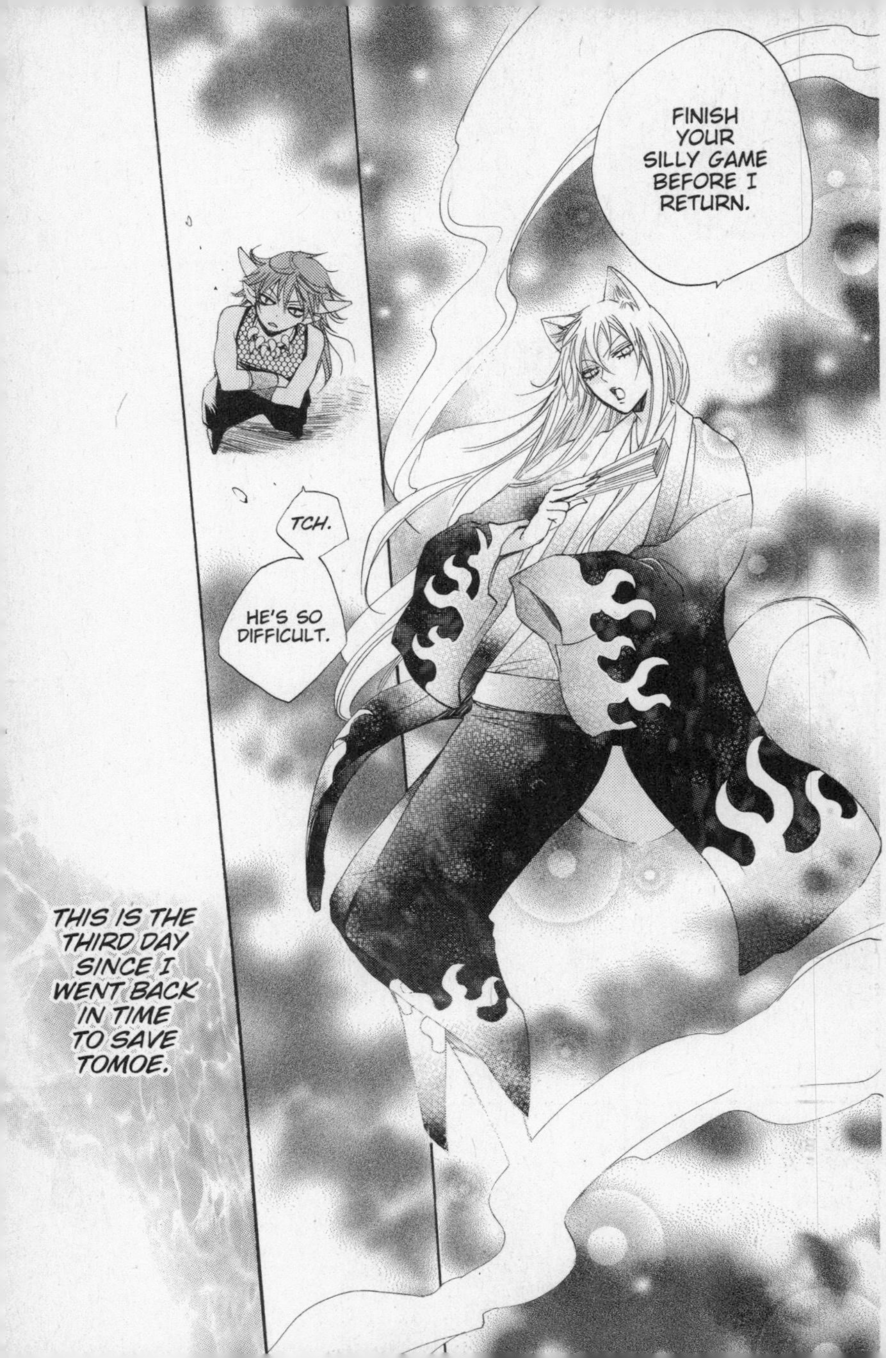
FINISH YOUR SILLY GAME BEFORE I RETURN.
TCH.
HE'S SO DIFFICULT.
THIS IS THE THIRD DAY SINCE I WENT BACK IN TIME TO SAVE TOMOE.

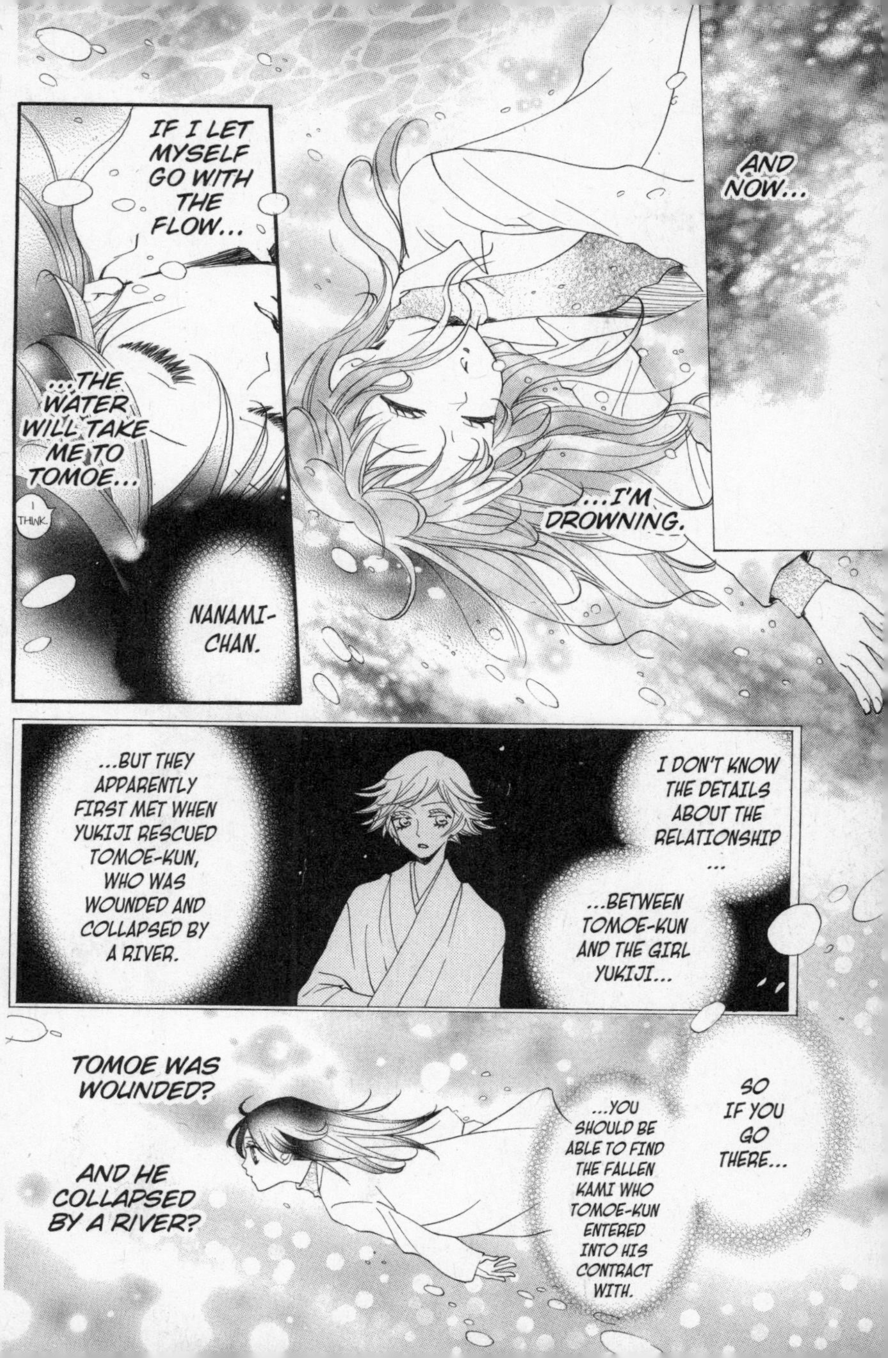
AND NOW...
...I'M DROWNING.
IF I LET MYSELF GO WITH THE FLOW...
...THE WATER WILL TAKE ME TO TOMOE...
I THINK.
NANAMI-CHAN.
I DON'T KNOW THE DETAILS ABOUT THE RELATIONSHIP ...
...BETWEEN TOMOE-KUN AND THE GIRL YUKIJI...
...BUT THEY APPARENTLY FIRST MET WHEN YUKIJI RESCUED TOMOE-KUN, WHO WAS WOUNDED AND COLLAPSED BY A RIVER.
SO IF YOU GO THERE...
...YOU SHOULD BE ABLE TO FIND THE FALLEN KAMI WHO TOMOE-KUN ENTERED INTO HIS CONTRACT WITH.
TOMOE WAS WOUNDED?
AND HE COLLAPSED BY A RIVER?

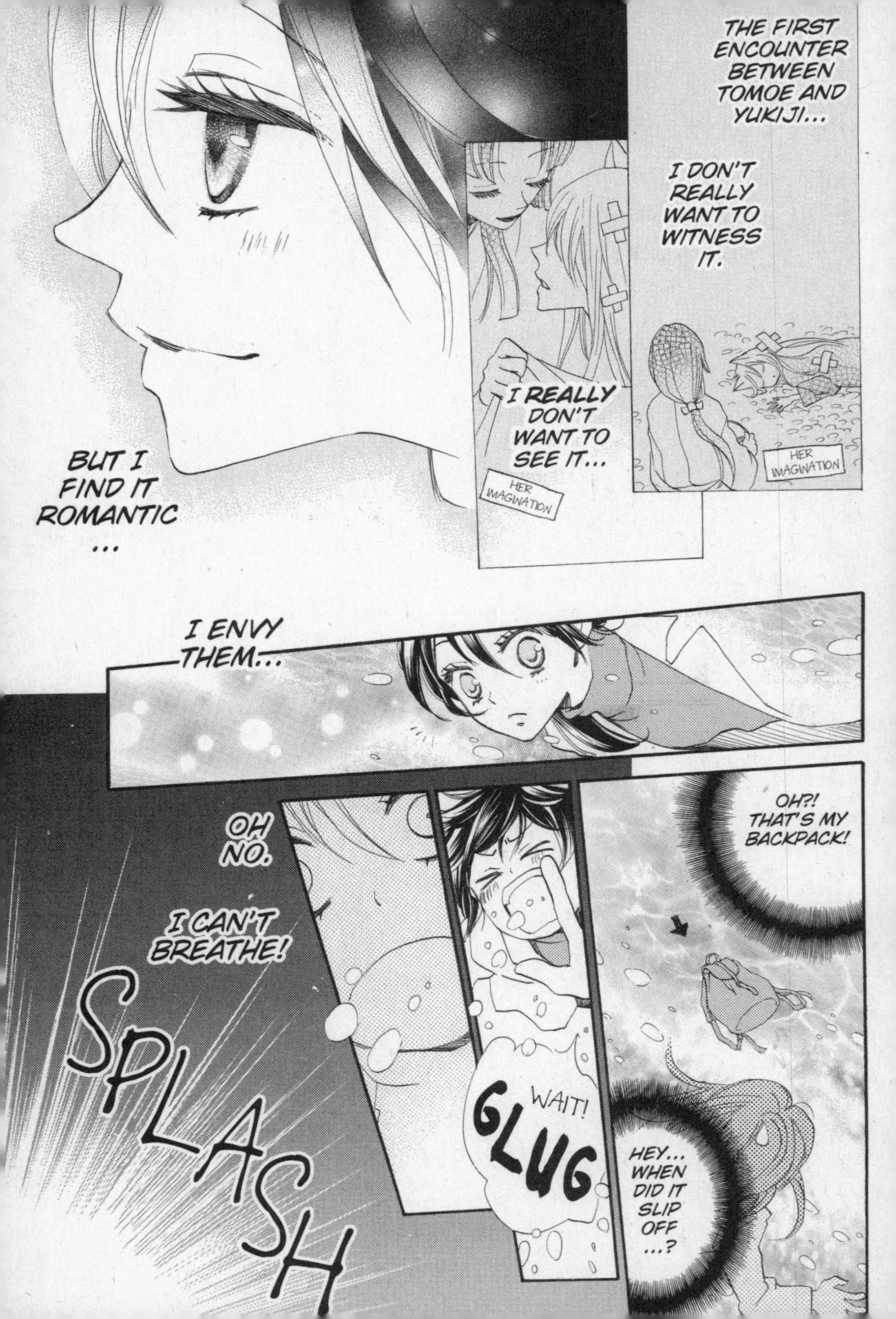
THE FIRST ENCOUNTER BETWEEN TOMOE AND YUKIJI...
I DON'T REALLY WANT TO WITNESS IT.
HER IMAGINATION
I REALLY DON'T WANT TO SEE IT...
HER IMAGINATION
BUT I FIND IT ROMANTIC ...
I ENVY THEM...
OH?! THAT'S MY BACKPACK!
HEY... WHEN DID IT SLIP OFF ...?
WAIT!
GLUG
OH NO.
I CAN'T BREATHE!
SPLASH

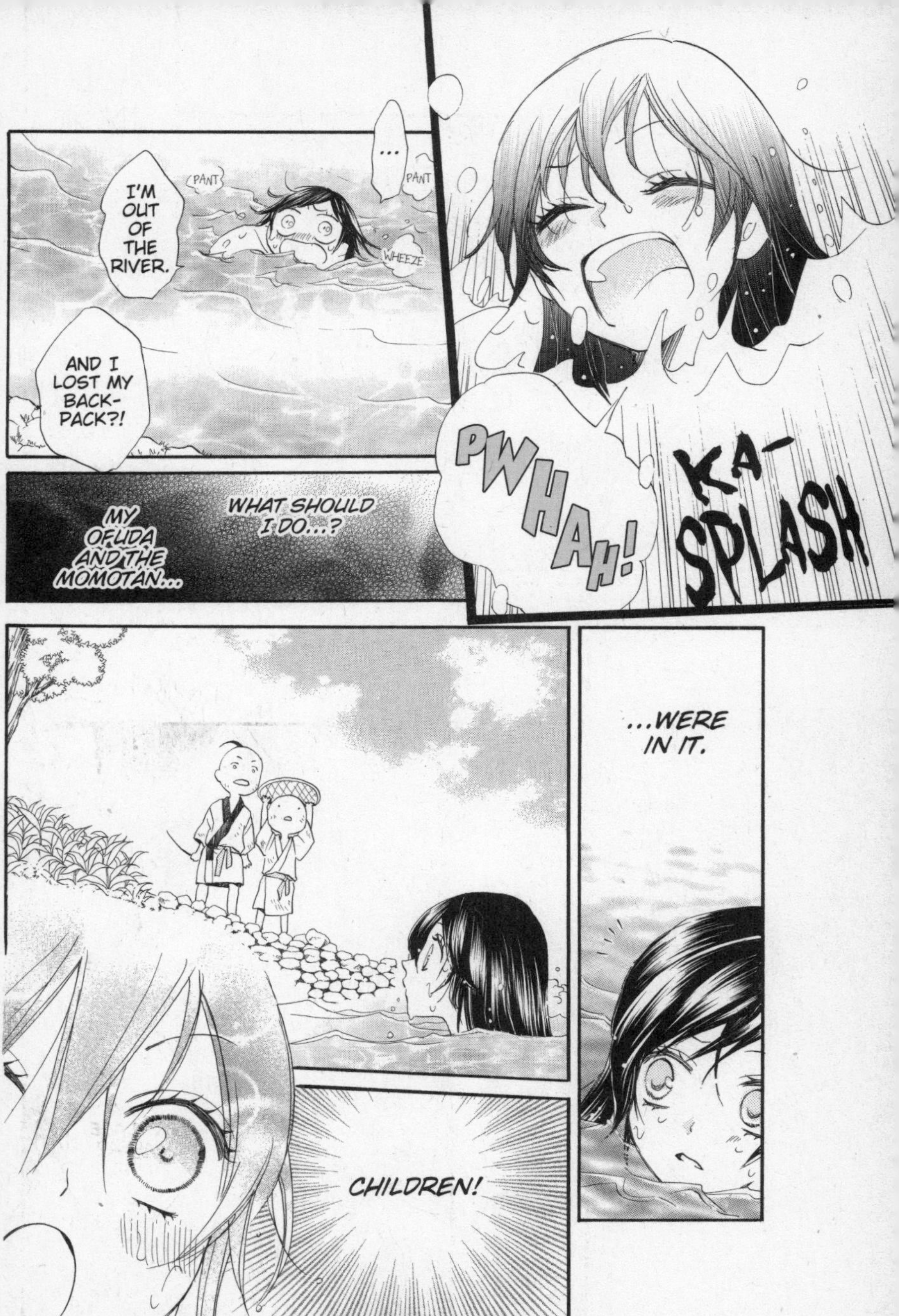
PWHAH!
KA-SPLASH
...
PANT
PANT
I'M OUT OF THE RIVER.
WHEEZE
AND I LOST MY BACK-PACK?!
WHAT SHOULD I DO...?
MY OFUDA AND THE MOMOTAN...
...WERE IN IT.
CHILDREN!

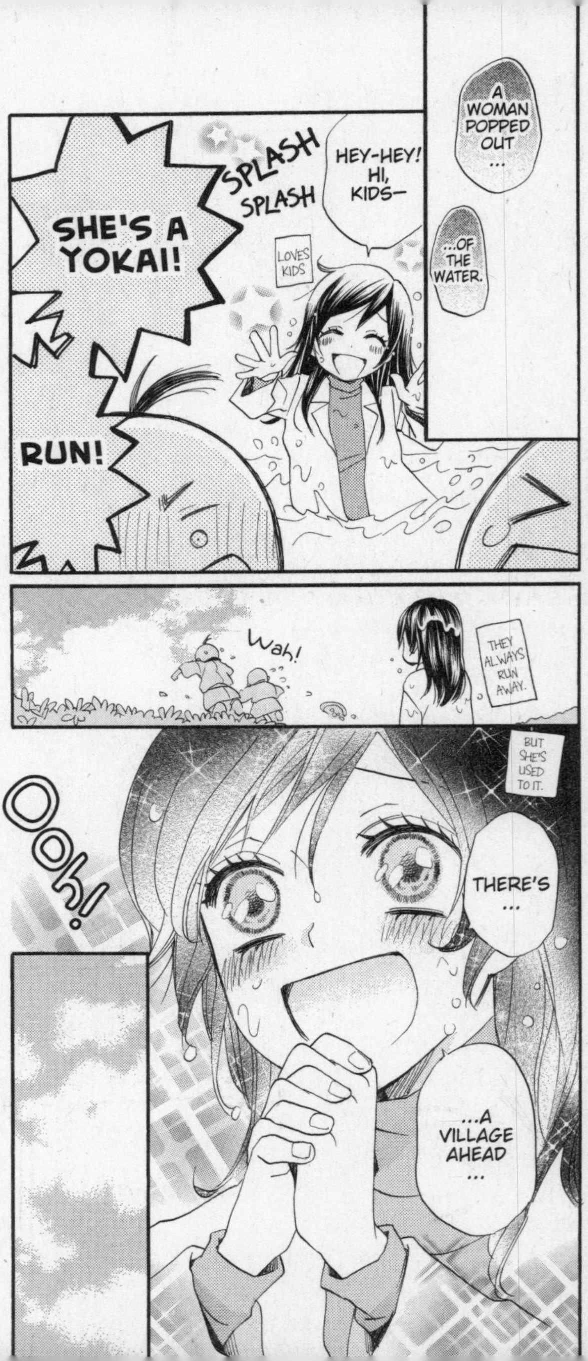
A WOMAN POPPED OUT ...
...OF THE WATER.
HEY-HEY! HI, KIDS—
SPLASH SPLASH
SHE'S A YOKAI!
LOVES KIDS
RUN!
THEY ALWAYS RUN AWAY.
Wah!
BUT SHE'S USED TO IT.
THERE'S ...
Ooh!
...A VILLAGE AHEAD ...

4

The Kamisama Kiss anime will already be broadcasting when this volume goes on sale.

Are people watching in areas where the anime airs?

THUMP THUMP

I'm thinking I gotta buy a Blu-ray player before the anime starts airing. My current DVD player is a little broken... I want to transfer the shows I've saved to discs, but I can't. I don't want to waste all the important shows I've recorded!

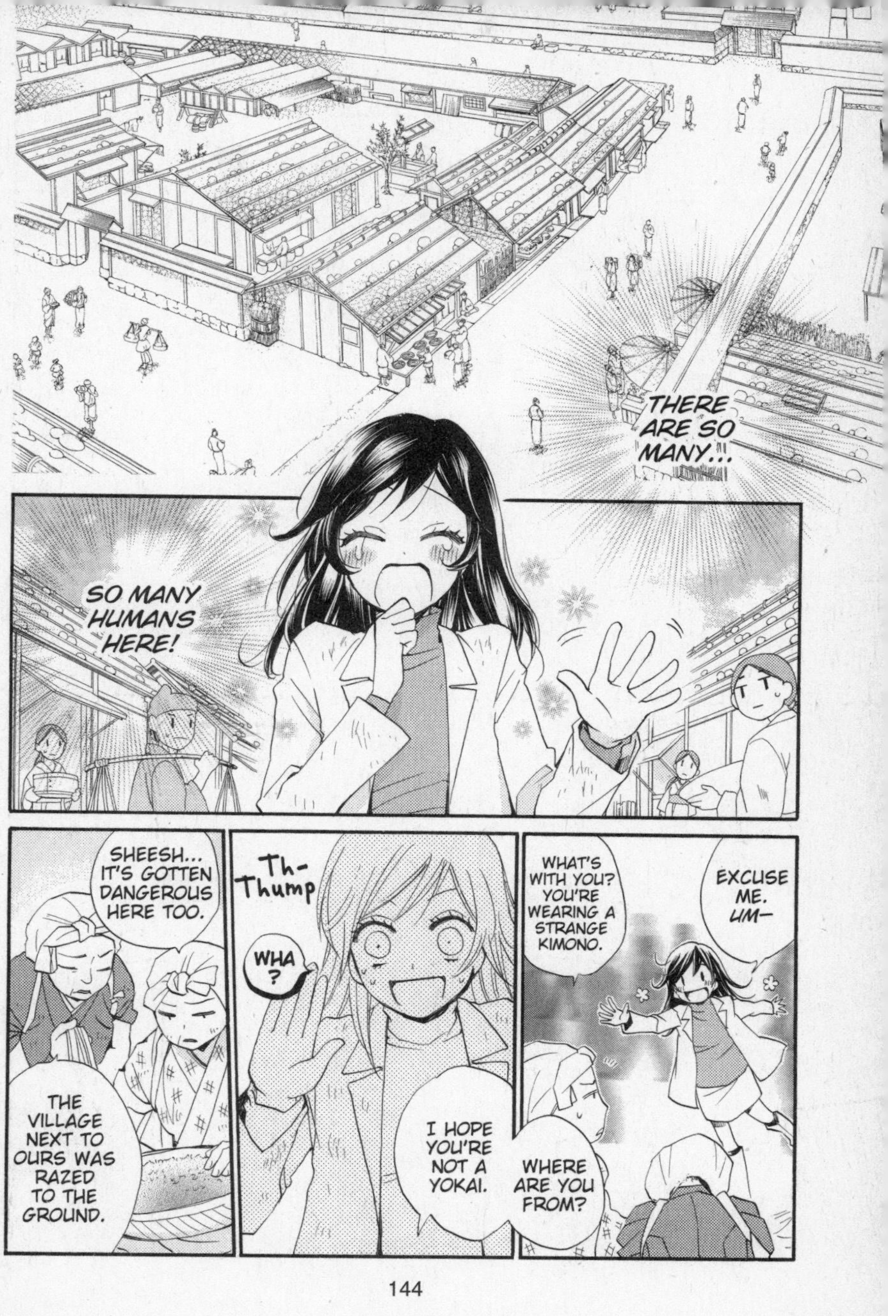
THERE ARE SO MANY...
SO MANY HUMANS HERE!
EXCUSE ME. UM—
WHAT'S WITH YOU? YOU'RE WEARING A STRANGE KIMONO.
WHERE ARE YOU FROM?
Th-Thump
WHA?
I HOPE YOU'RE NOT A YOKAI.
SHEESH... IT'S GOTTEN DANGEROUS HERE TOO.
THE VILLAGE NEXT TO OURS WAS RAZED TO THE GROUND.

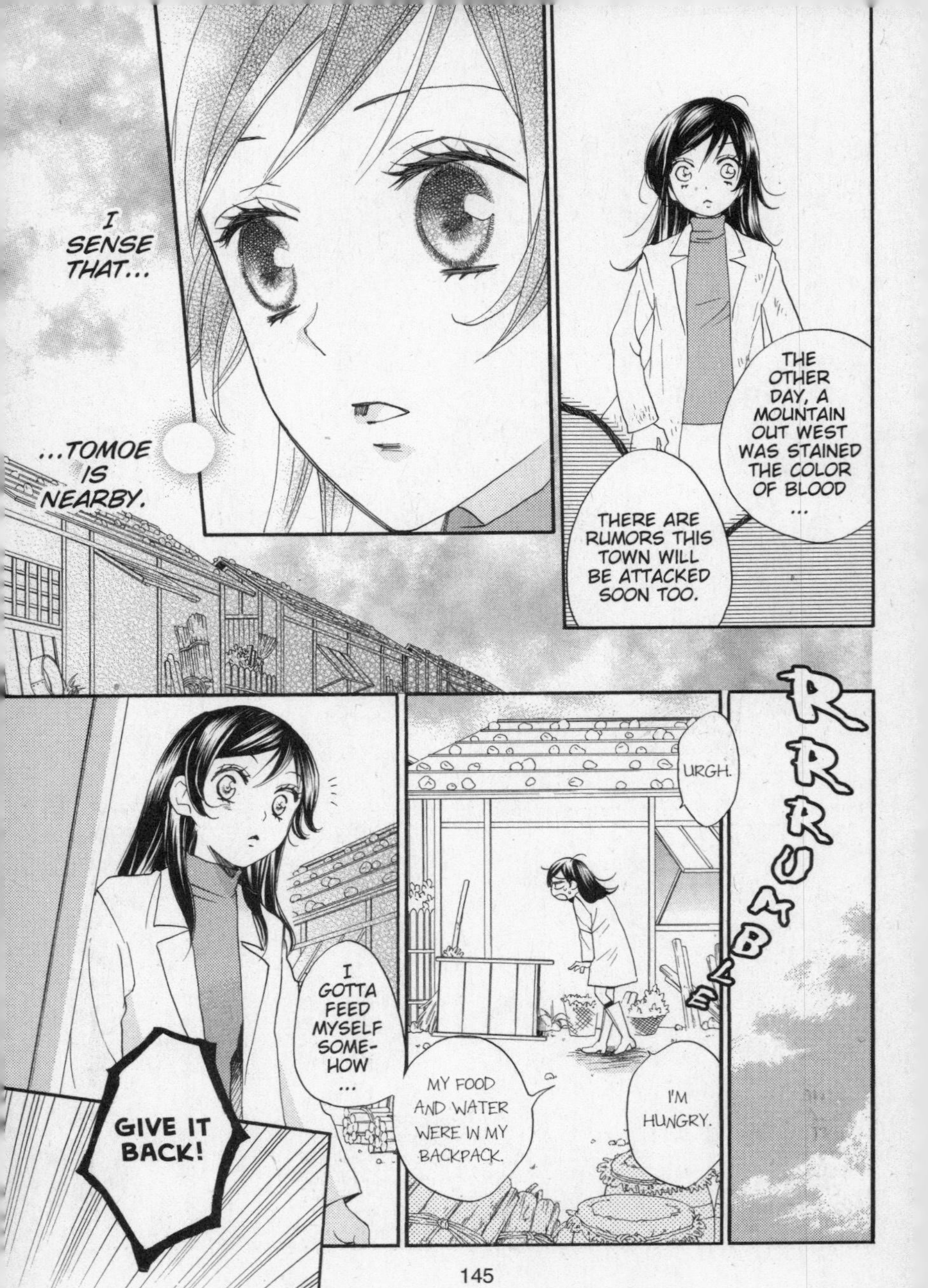
THE OTHER DAY, A MOUNTAIN OUT WEST WAS STAINED THE COLOR OF BLOOD ...
THERE ARE RUMORS THIS TOWN WILL BE ATTACKED SOON TOO.
I SENSE THAT...
...TOMOE IS NEARBY.
RRRUMBLE
URGH.
I'M HUNGRY.
MY FOOD AND WATER WERE IN MY BACKPACK.
I GOTTA FEED MYSELF SOMEHOW ...
GIVE IT BACK!

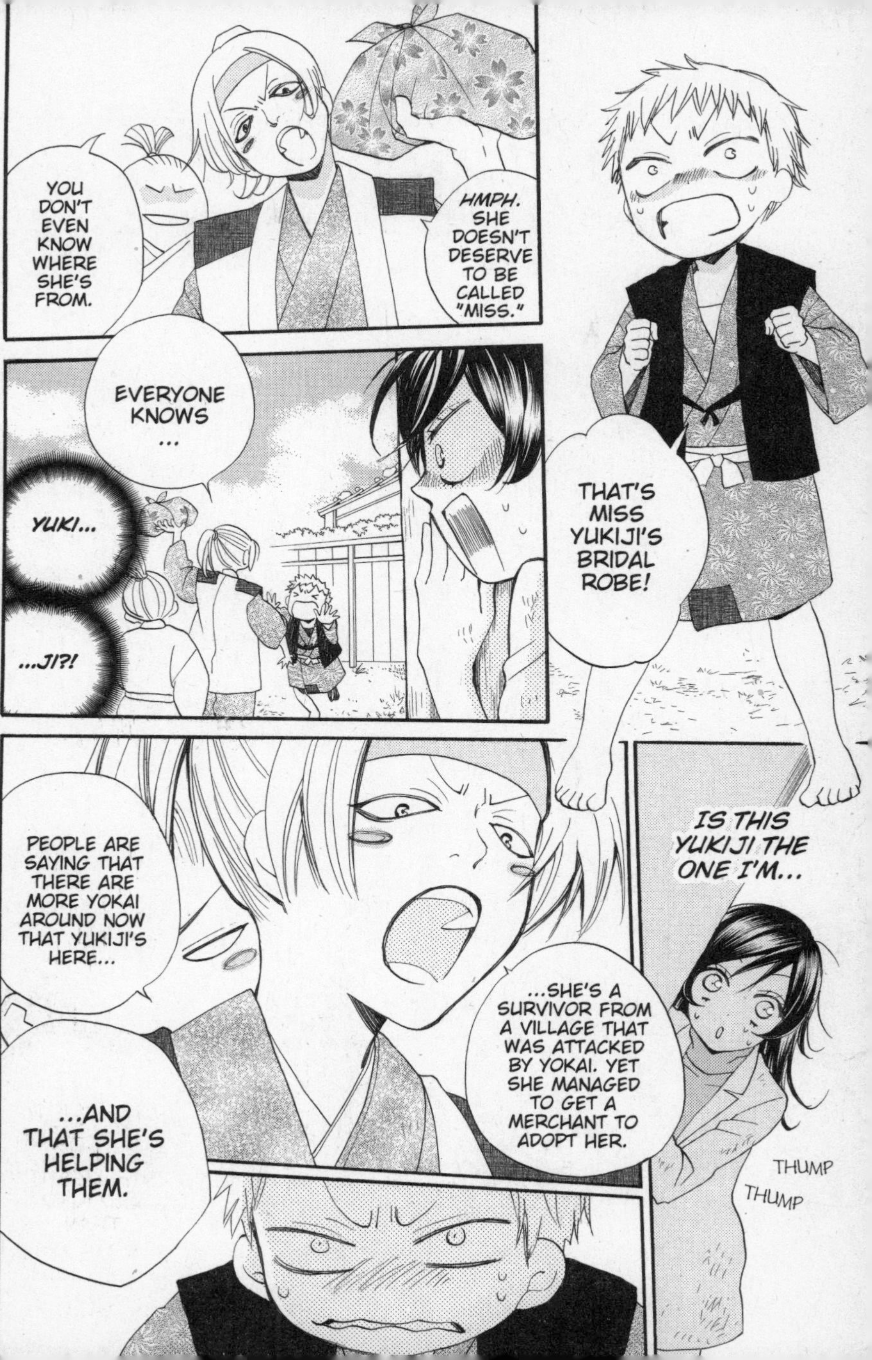
THAT'S MISS YUKIJI'S BRIDAL ROBE!
HMPH. SHE DOESN'T DESERVE TO BE CALLED "MISS."
YOU DON'T EVEN KNOW WHERE SHE'S FROM.
EVERYONE KNOWS ...
YUKI...
...JI?!
IS THIS YUKIJI THE ONE I'M...
THUMP
THUMP
...SHE'S A SURVIVOR FROM A VILLAGE THAT WAS ATTACKED BY YOKAI. YET SHE MANAGED TO GET A MERCHANT TO ADOPT HER.
PEOPLE ARE SAYING THAT THERE ARE MORE YOKAI AROUND NOW THAT YUKIJI'S HERE...
...AND THAT SHE'S HELPING THEM.

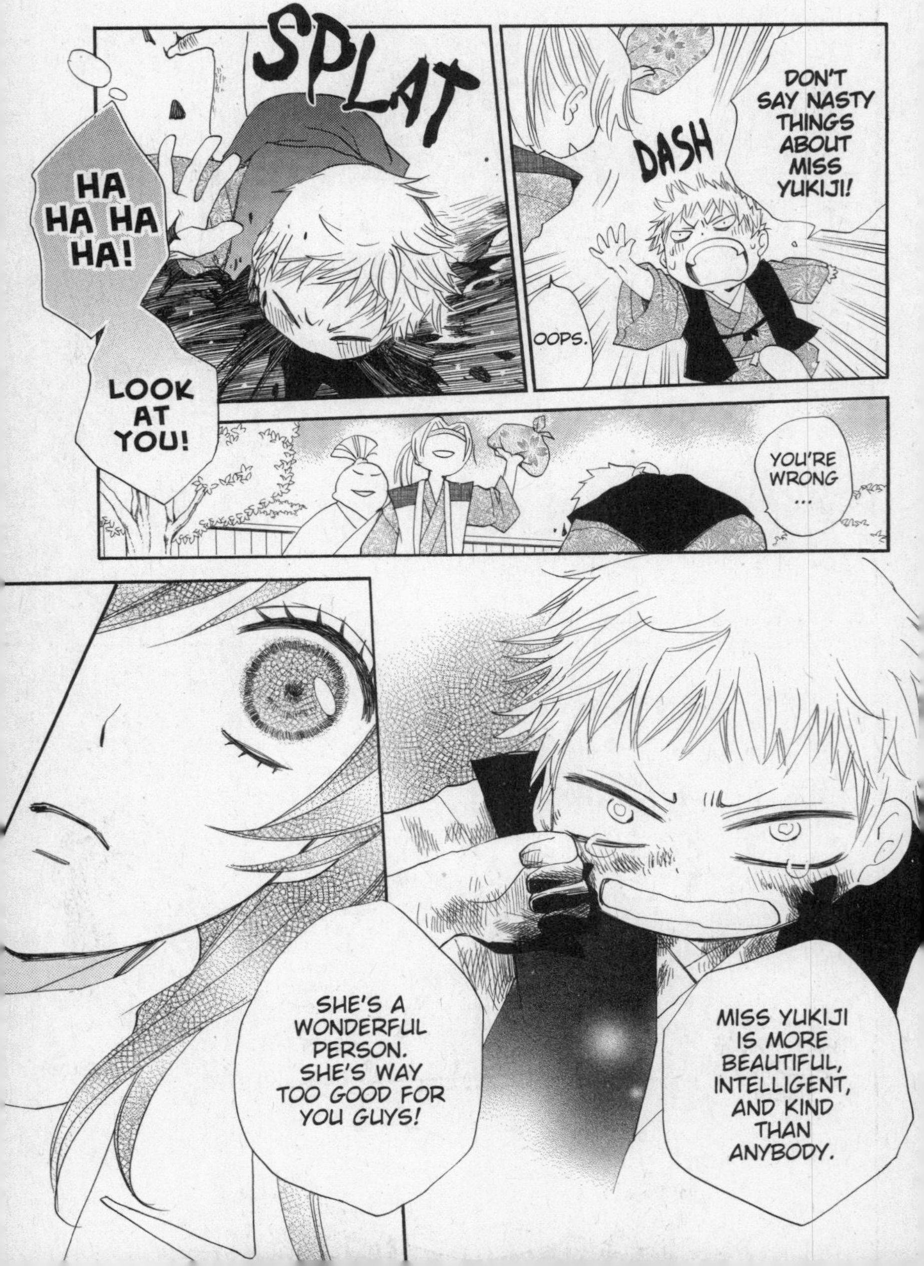
DON'T SAY NASTY THINGS ABOUT MISS YUKIJI!
DASH
OOPS.
SPLAT
HA HA HA HA HA!
LOOK AT YOU!
YOU'RE WRONG...
MISS YUKIJI IS MORE BEAUTIFUL, INTELLIGENT, AND KIND THAN ANYBODY.
SHE'S A WONDERFUL PERSON. SHE'S WAY TOO GOOD FOR YOU GUYS!

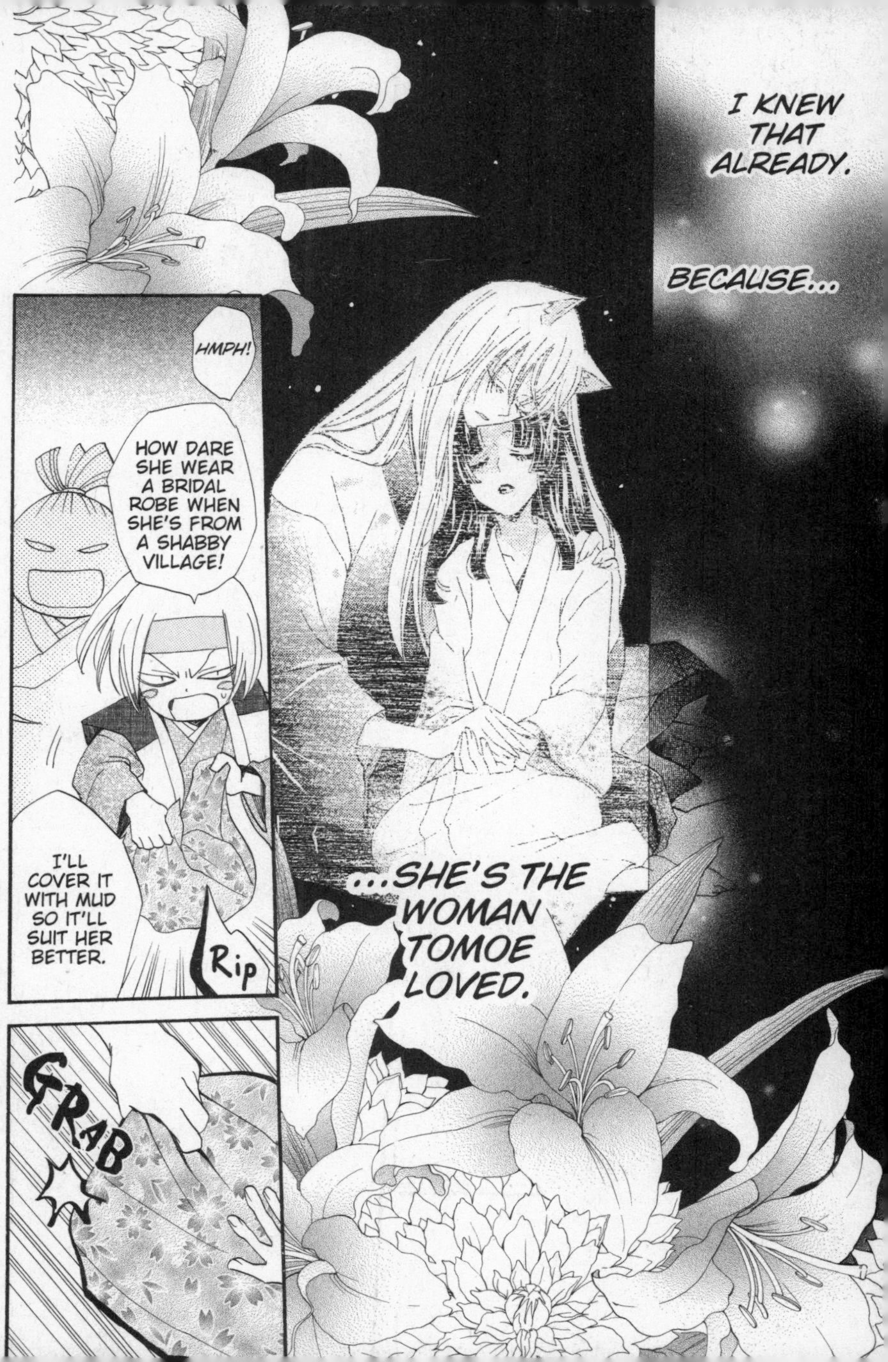
I KNEW THAT ALREADY.
BECAUSE...
...SHE'S THE WOMAN TOMOE LOVED.
HMPH!
HOW DARE SHE WEAR A BRIDAL ROBE WHEN SHE'S FROM A SHABBY VILLAGE!
I'LL COVER IT WITH MUD SO IT'LL SUIT HER BETTER.
Rip
GRAB

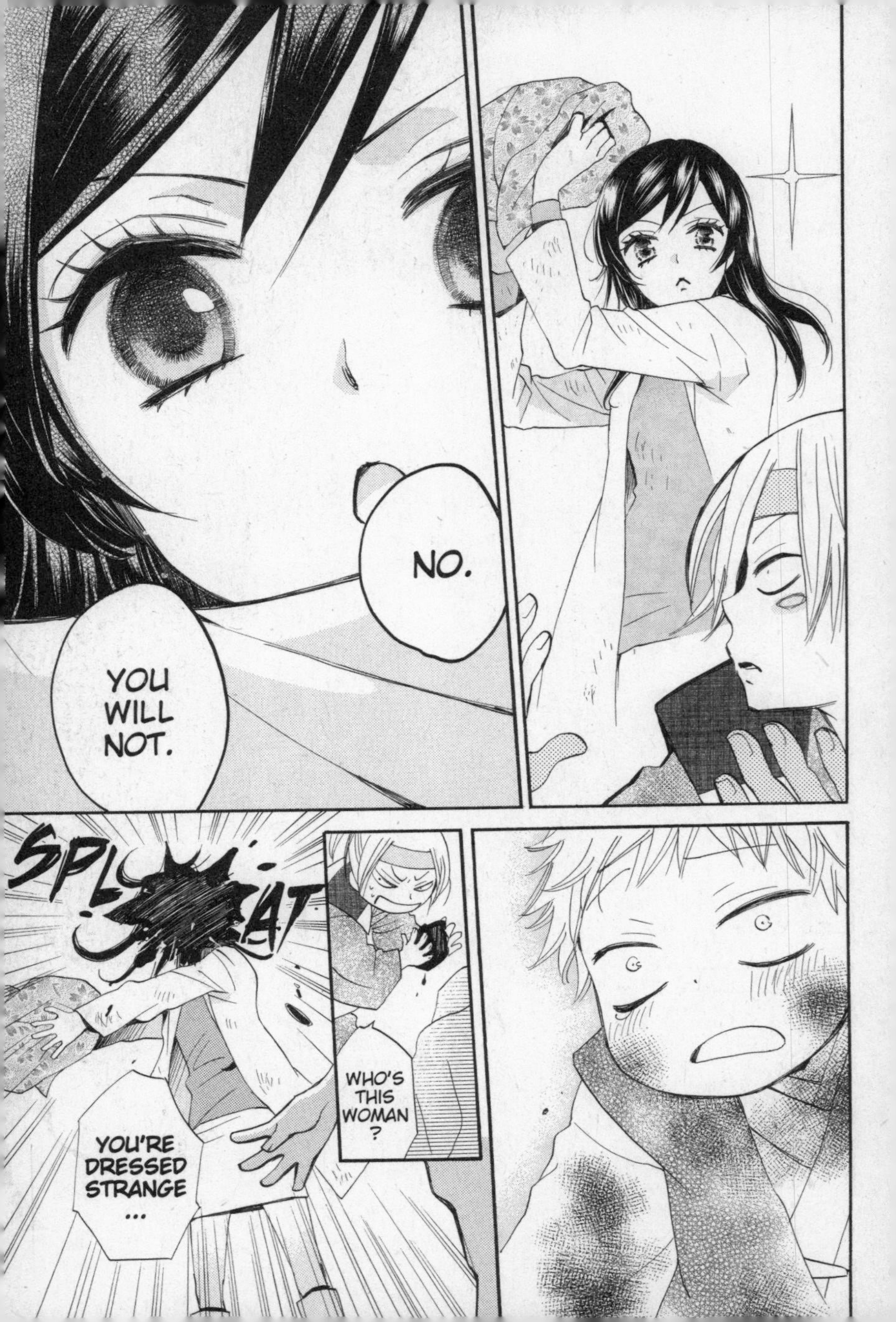
NO.
YOU WILL NOT.
WHO'S THIS WOMAN?
YOU'RE DRESSED STRANGE ...

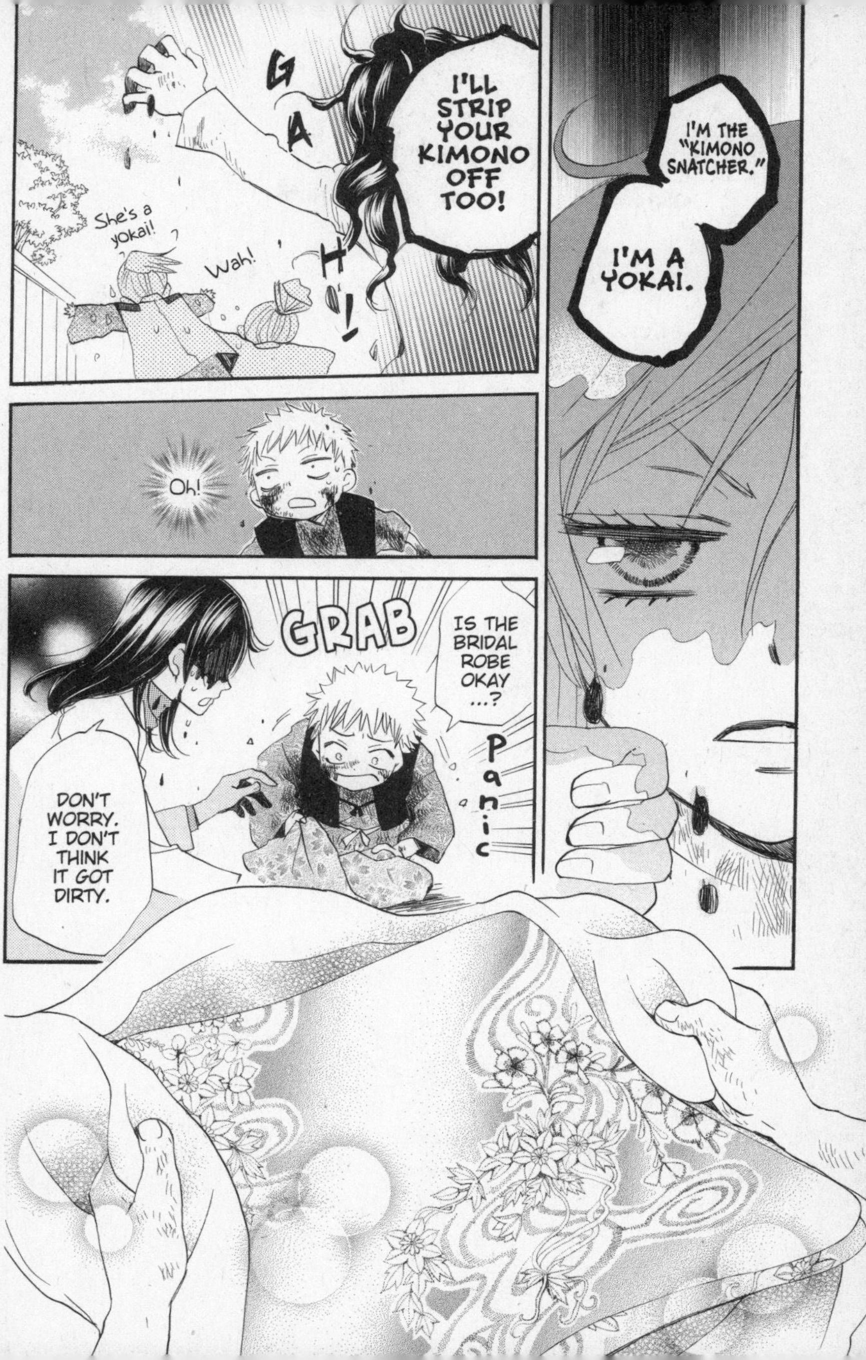
I'M THE "KIMONO SNATCHER."
I'M A YOKAI.
I'LL STRIP YOUR KIMONO OFF TOO!
GAH!!
She's a yokai!
Wah!
Oh!
GRAB
IS THE BRIDAL ROBE OKAY ...?
Panic
DON'T WORRY. I DON'T THINK IT GOT DIRTY.

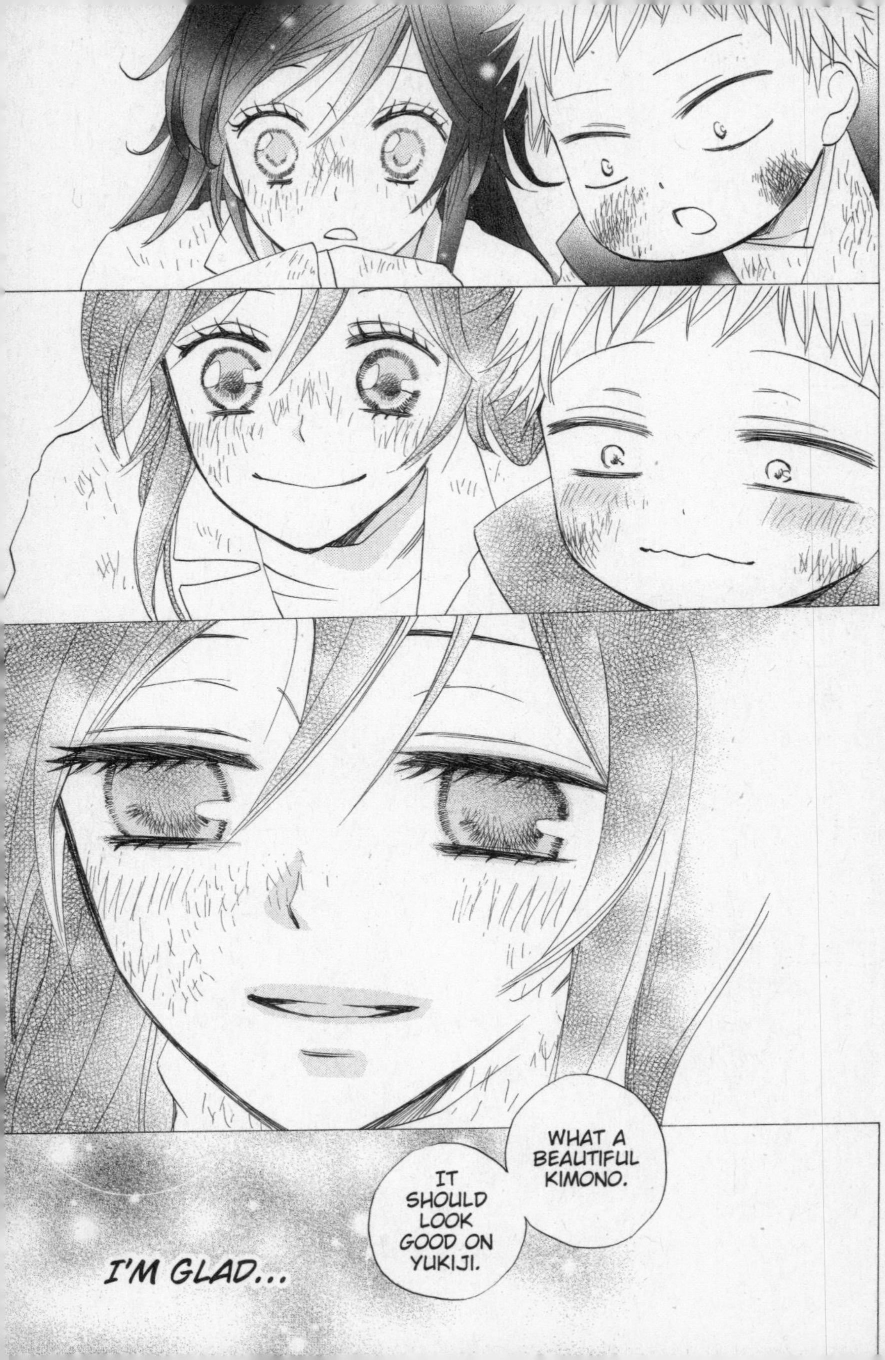
WHAT A BEAUTIFUL KIMONO.
IT SHOULD LOOK GOOD ON YUKIJI.
I'M GLAD...

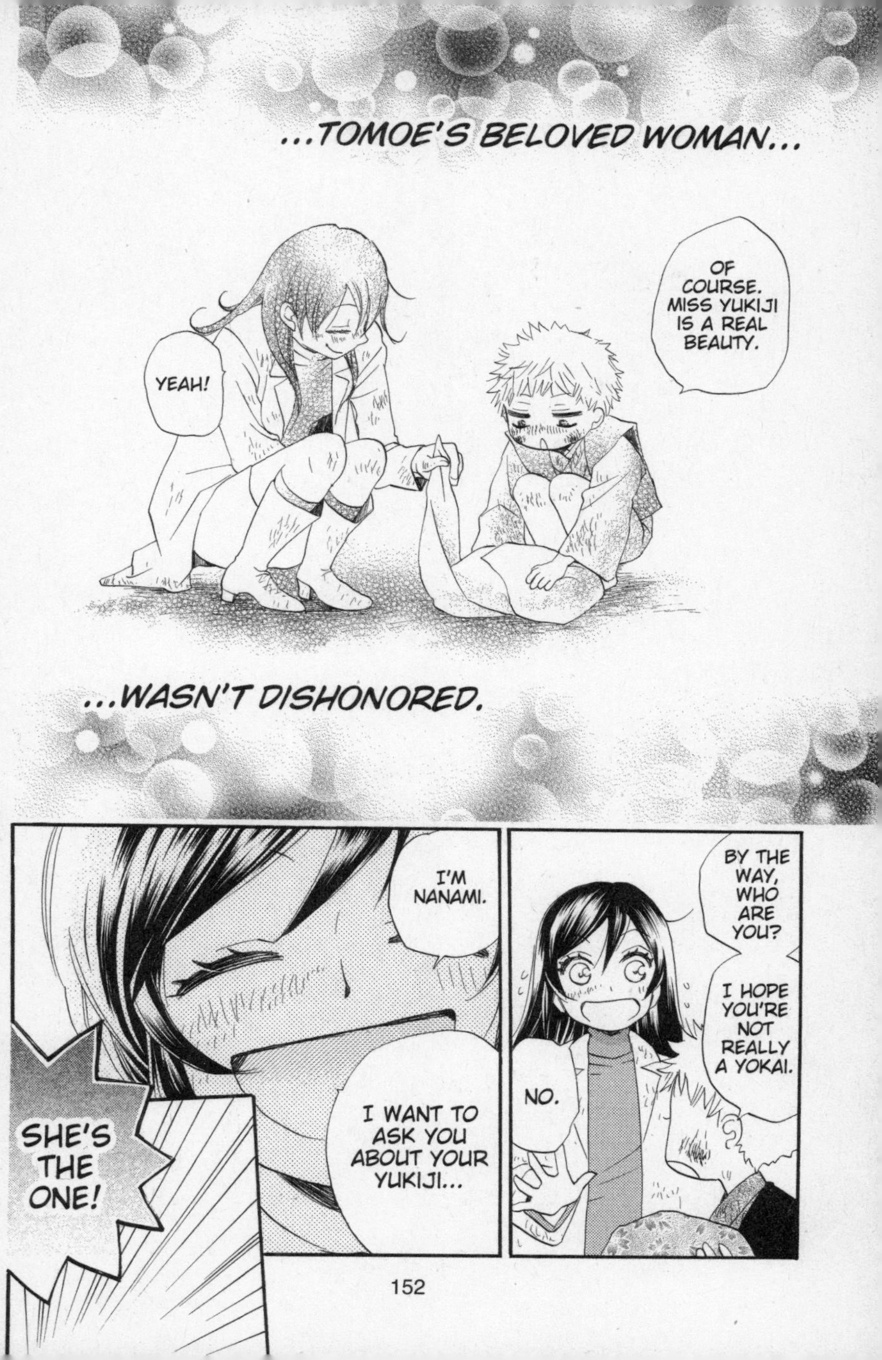
...TOMOE'S BELOVED WOMAN...
OF COURSE. MISS YUKIJI IS A REAL BEAUTY.
YEAH!
...WASN'T DISHONORED.
BY THE WAY, WHO ARE YOU?
I HOPE YOU'RE NOT REALLY A YOKAI.
NO.
I'M NANAMI.
I WANT TO ASK YOU ABOUT YOUR YUKIJI...
SHE'S THE ONE!

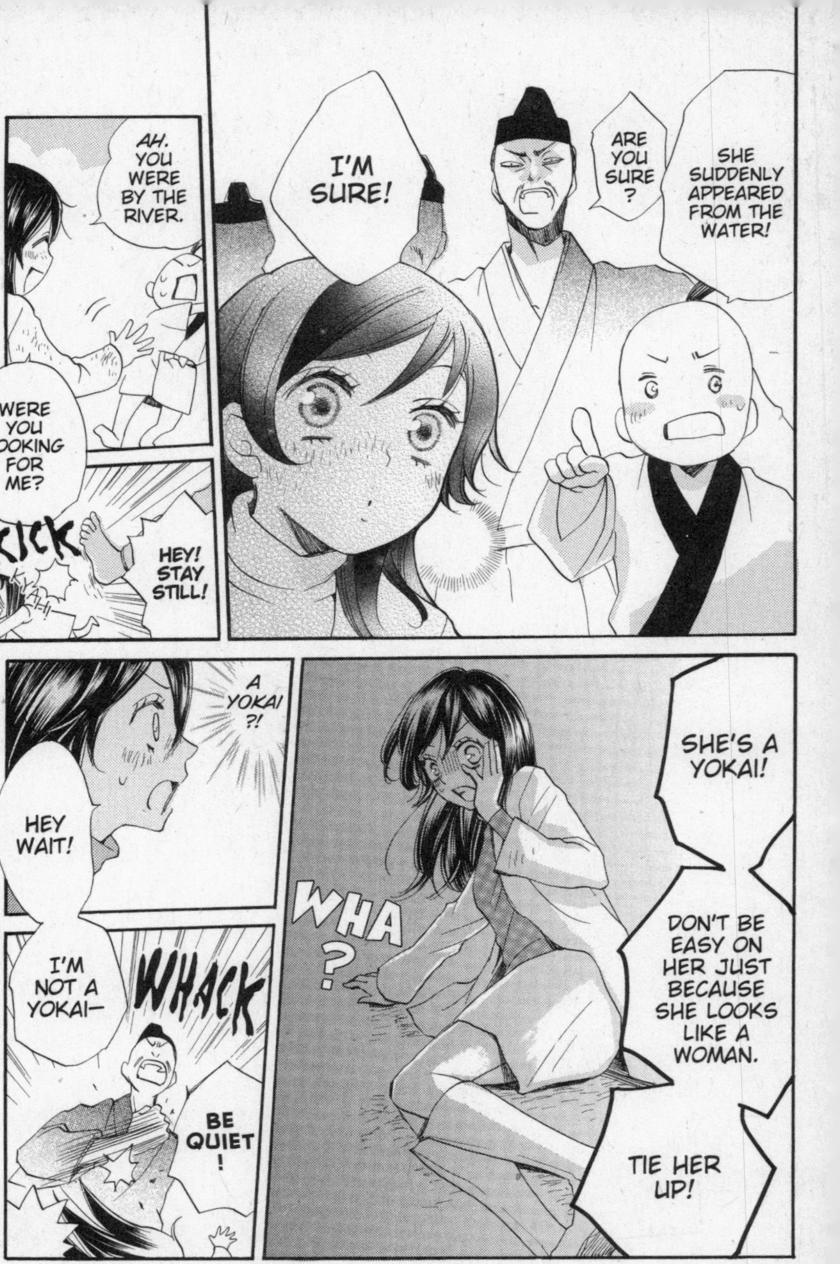
SHE SUDDENLY APPEARED FROM THE WATER!
ARE YOU SURE?
I'M SURE!
AH. YOU WERE BY THE RIVER.
WERE YOU LOOKING FOR ME?
HEY! STAY STILL!
KICK
SHE'S A YOKAI!
DON'T BE EASY ON HER JUST BECAUSE SHE LOOKS LIKE A WOMAN.
TIE HER UP!
WHA?
A YOKAI?!
HEY WAIT!
BE QUIET!
WHACK
I'M NOT A YOKAI—

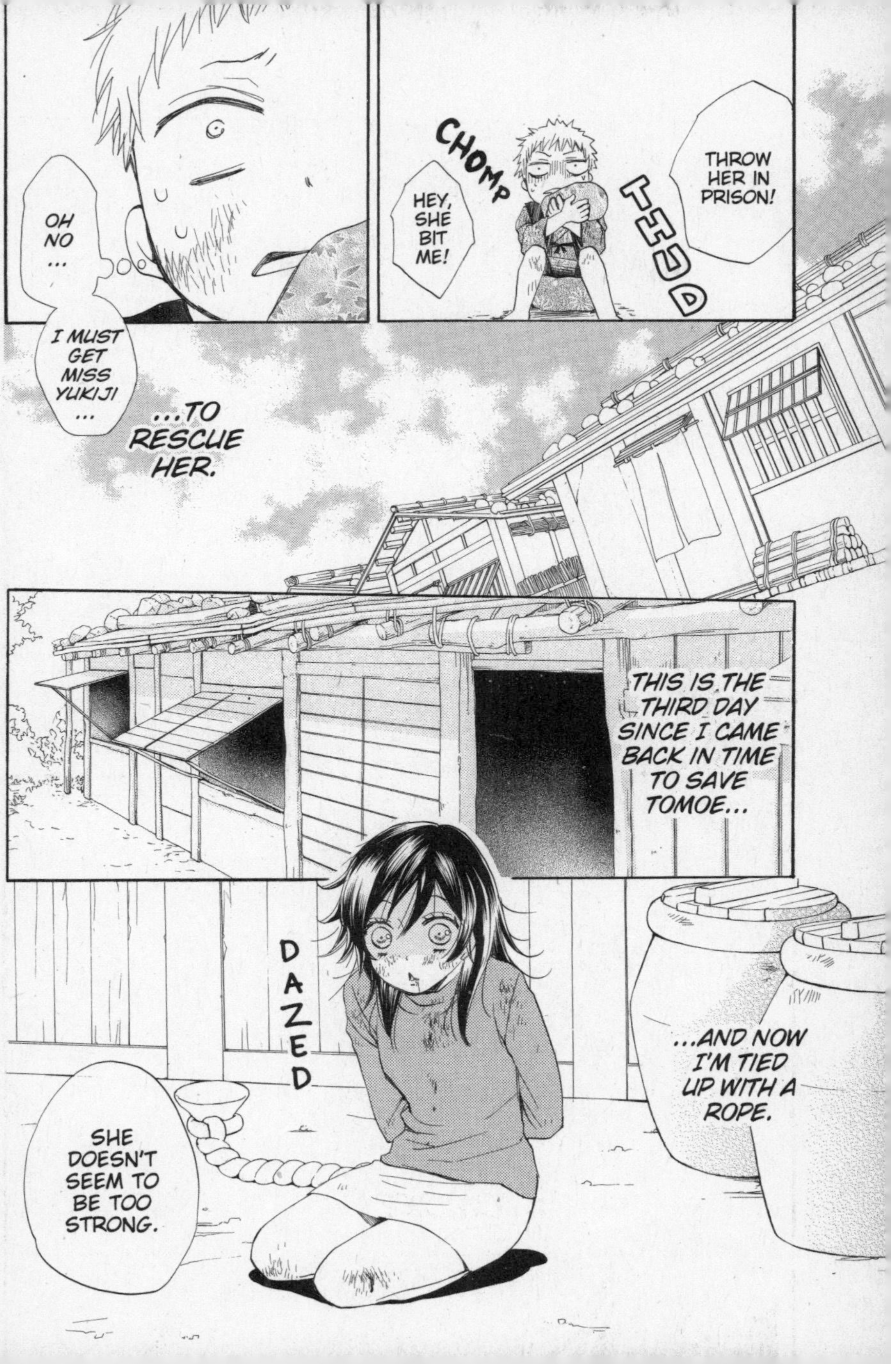
THROW HER IN PRISON!
THUD
CHOMP
HEY, SHE BIT ME!
OH NO ...
I MUST GET MISS YUKIJI ...
...TO RESCUE HER.
THIS IS THE THIRD DAY SINCE I CAME BACK IN TIME TO SAVE TOMOE...
...AND NOW I'M TIED UP WITH A ROPE.
DAZED
SHE DOESN'T SEEM TO BE TOO STRONG.

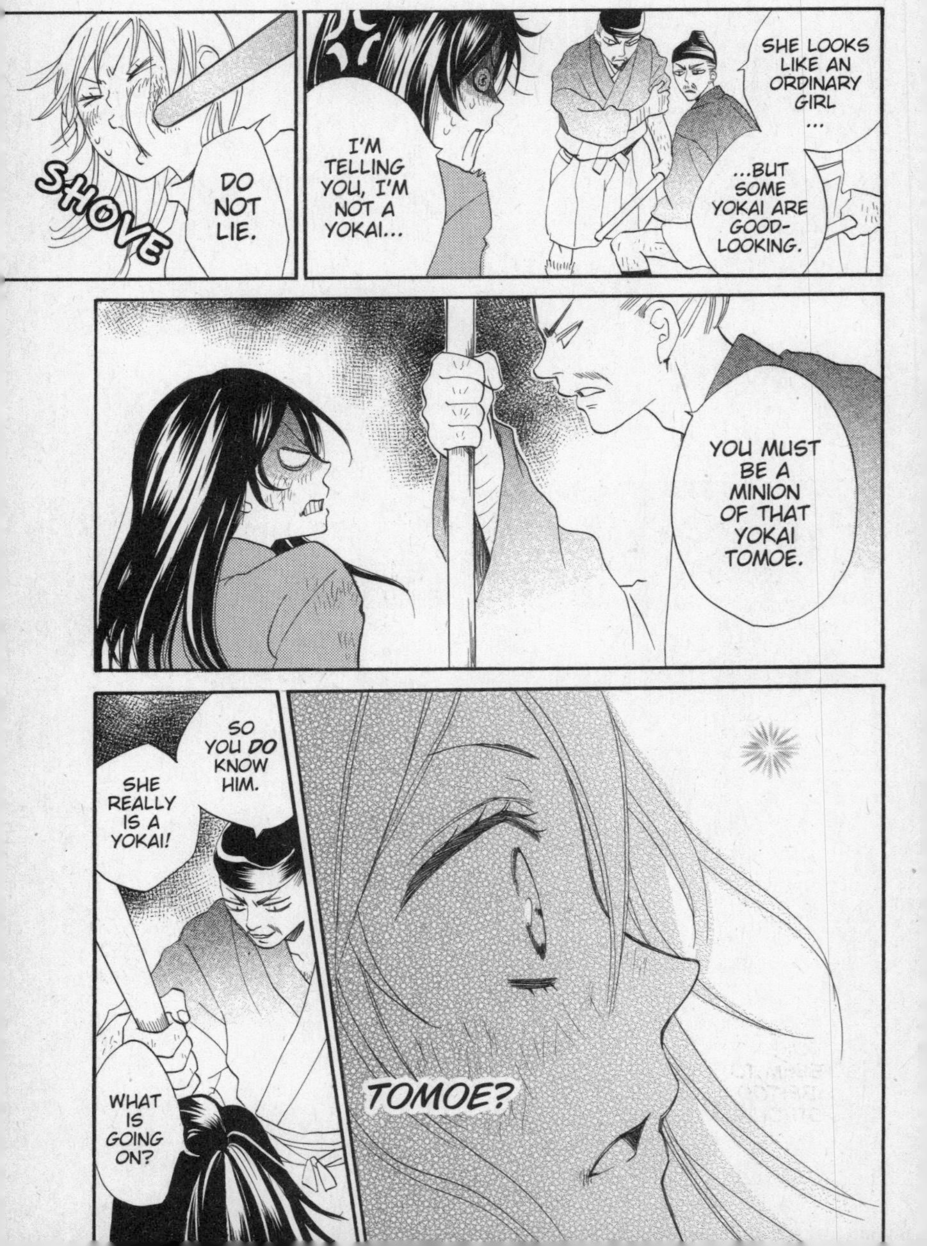
SHE LOOKS LIKE AN ORDINARY GIRL ...
...BUT SOME YOKAI ARE GOOD-LOOKING.
I'M TELLING YOU, I'M NOT A YOKAI...
DO NOT LIE.
SHOVE
YOU MUST BE A MINION OF THAT YOKAI TOMOE.
TOMOE?
SO YOU *DO* KNOW HIM.
SHE REALLY IS A YOKAI!
WHAT IS GOING ON?

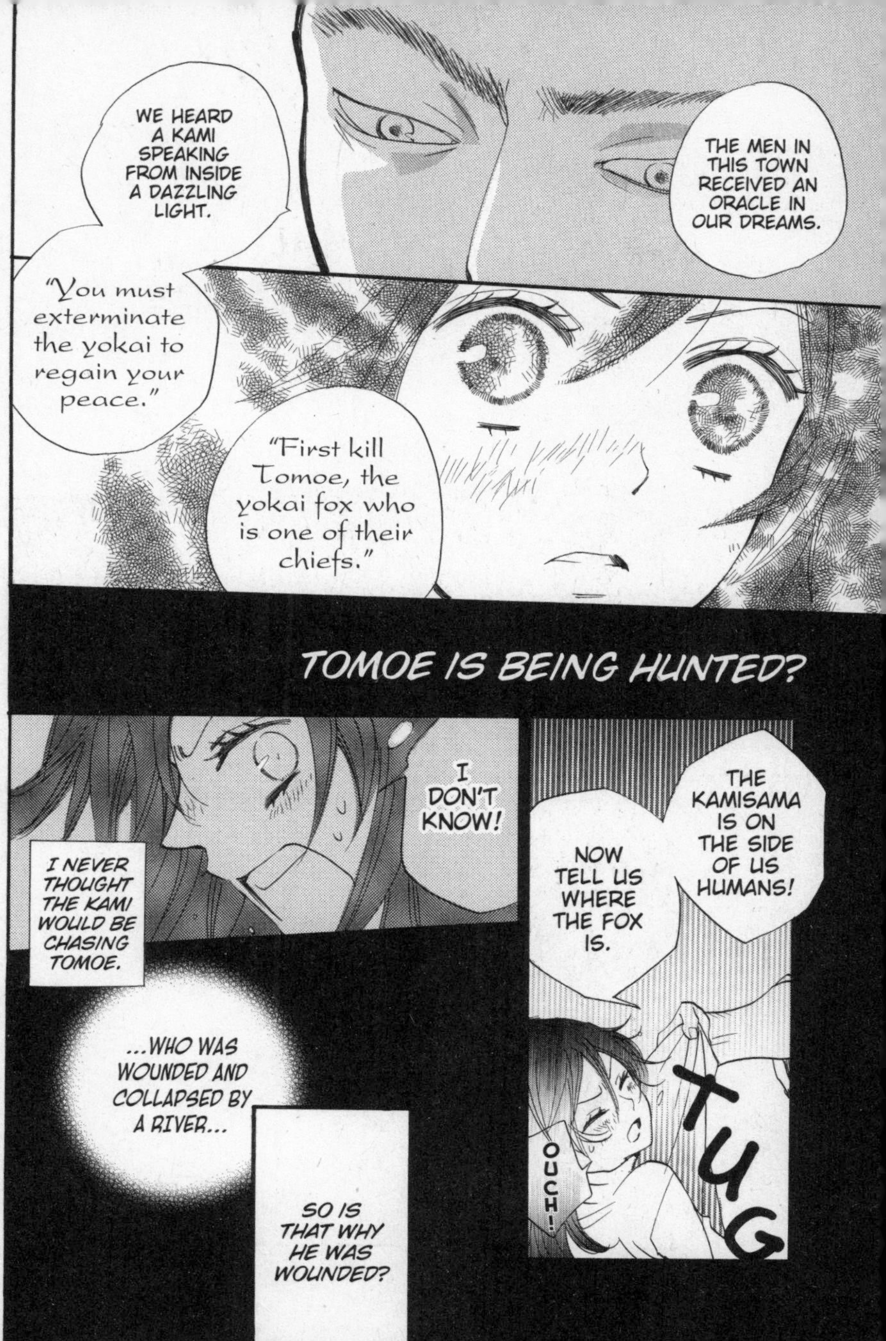
THE MEN IN THIS TOWN RECEIVED AN ORACLE IN OUR DREAMS.
WE HEARD A KAMI SPEAKING FROM INSIDE A DAZZLING LIGHT.
"You must exterminate the yokai to regain your peace."
"First kill Tomoe, the yokai fox who is one of their chiefs."
TOMOE IS BEING HUNTED?
THE KAMISAMA IS ON THE SIDE OF US HUMANS!
NOW TELL US WHERE THE FOX IS.
TUG
OUCH!
I DON'T KNOW!
I NEVER THOUGHT THE KAMI WOULD BE CHASING TOMOE.
...WHO WAS WOUNDED AND COLLAPSED BY A RIVER...
SO IS THAT WHY HE WAS WOUNDED?

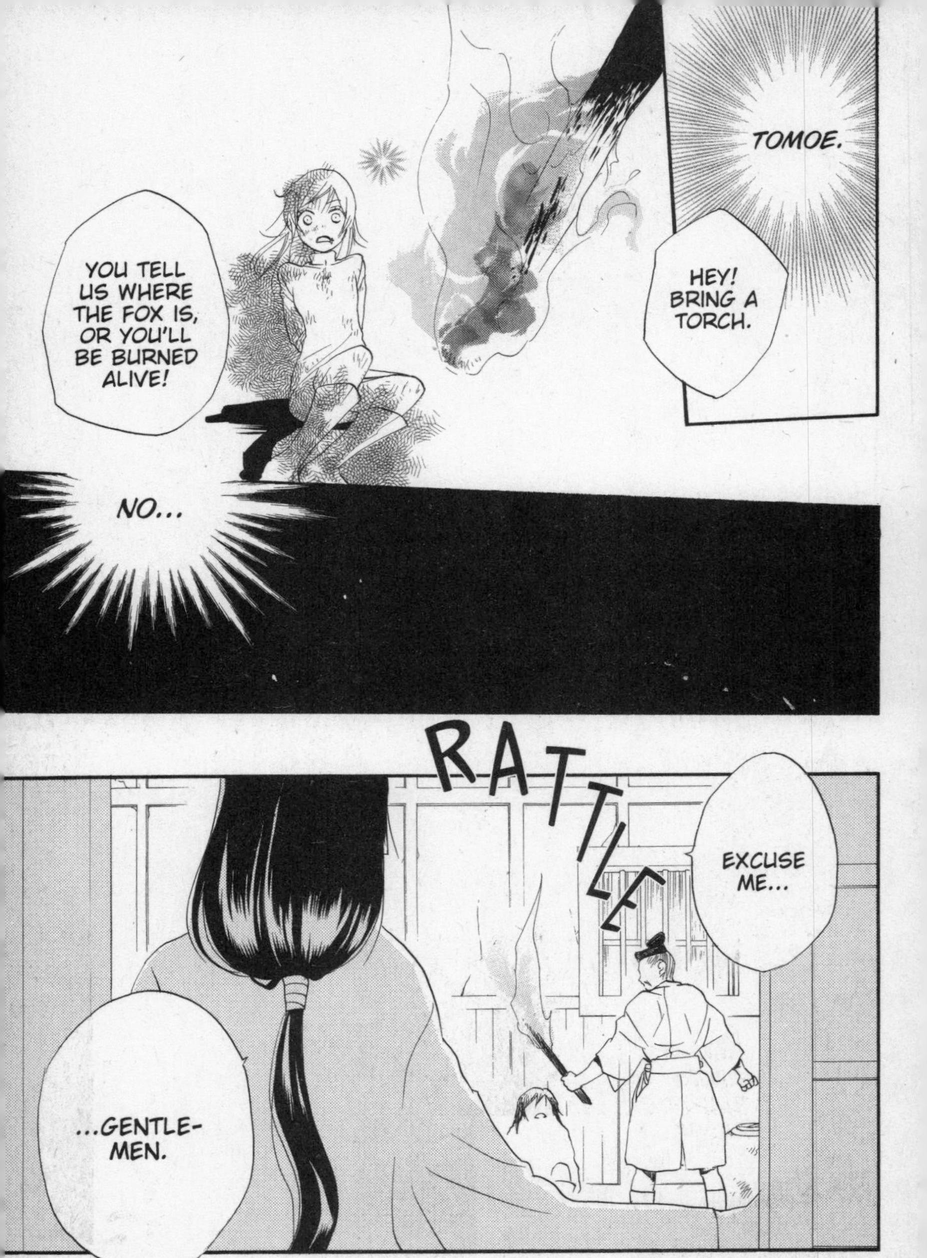
TOMOE.
HEY! BRING A TORCH.
YOU TELL US WHERE THE FOX IS, OR YOU'LL BE BURNED ALIVE!
NO...
RATTLE
EXCUSE ME...
...GENTLE-MEN.

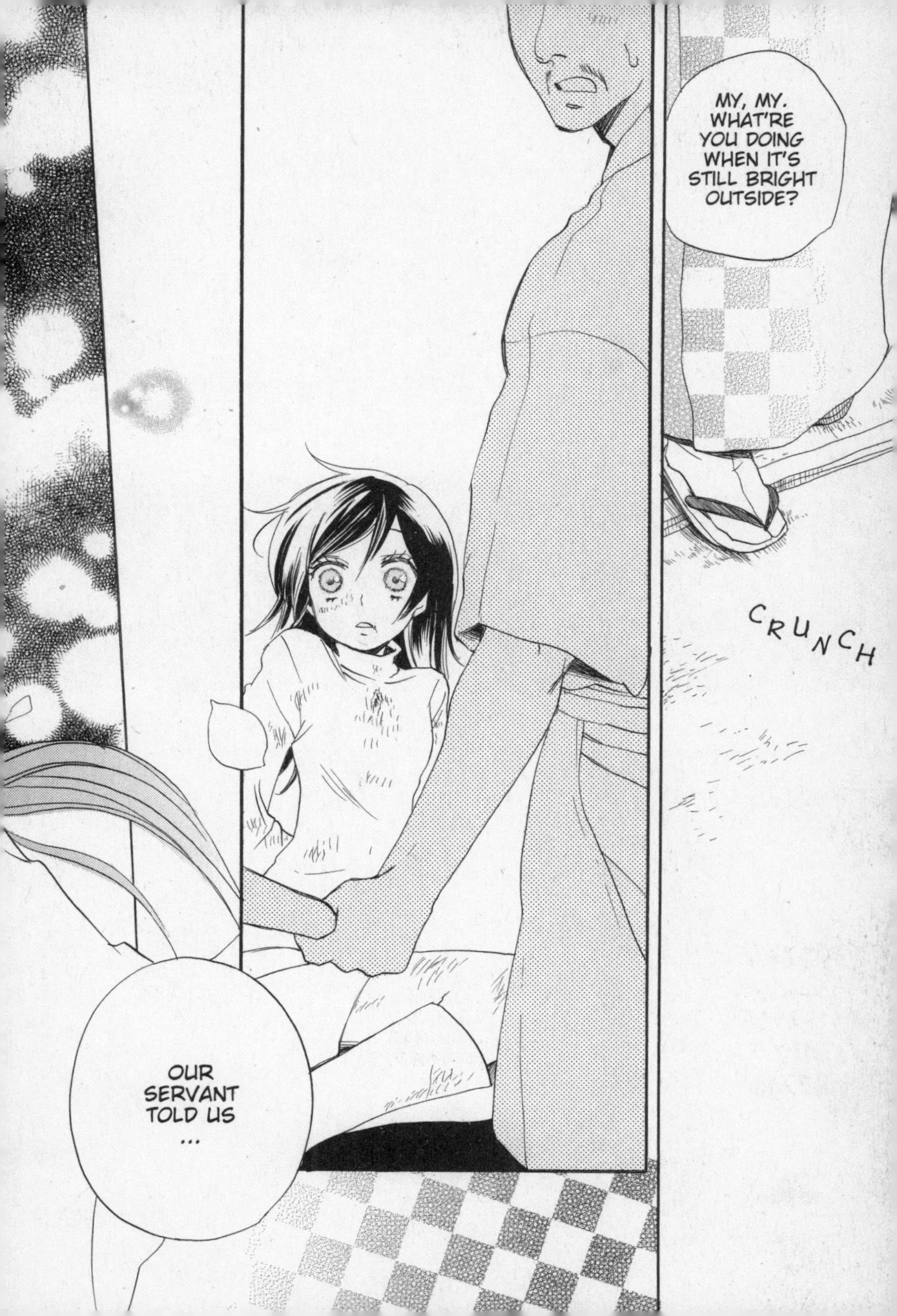
MY, MY. WHAT'RE YOU DOING WHEN IT'S STILL BRIGHT OUTSIDE?
CRUNCH
OUR SERVANT TOLD US ...

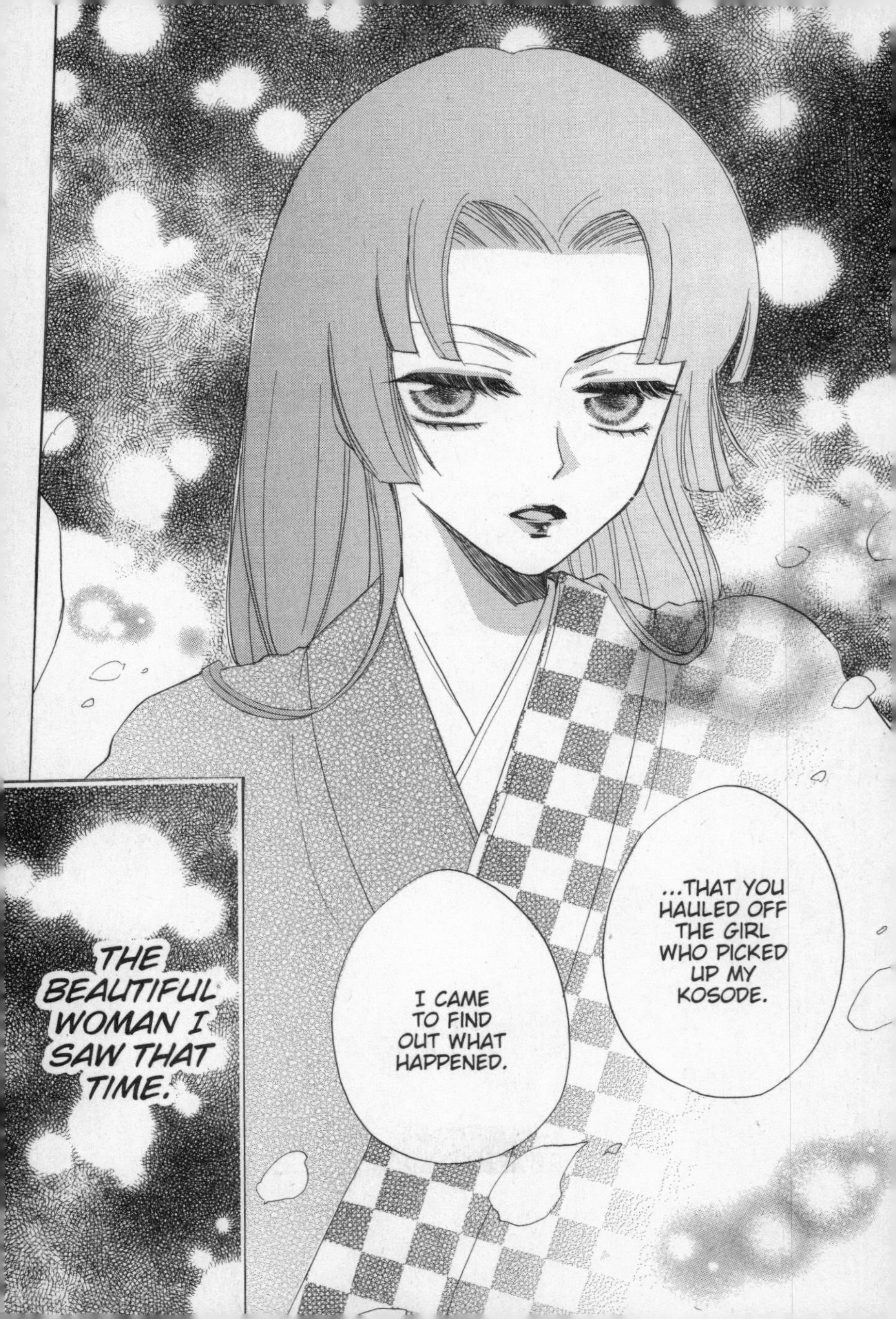
...THAT YOU HAULED OFF THE GIRL WHO PICKED UP MY KOSODE.
I CAME TO FIND OUT WHAT HAPPENED.
THE BEAUTIFUL WOMAN I SAW THAT TIME.

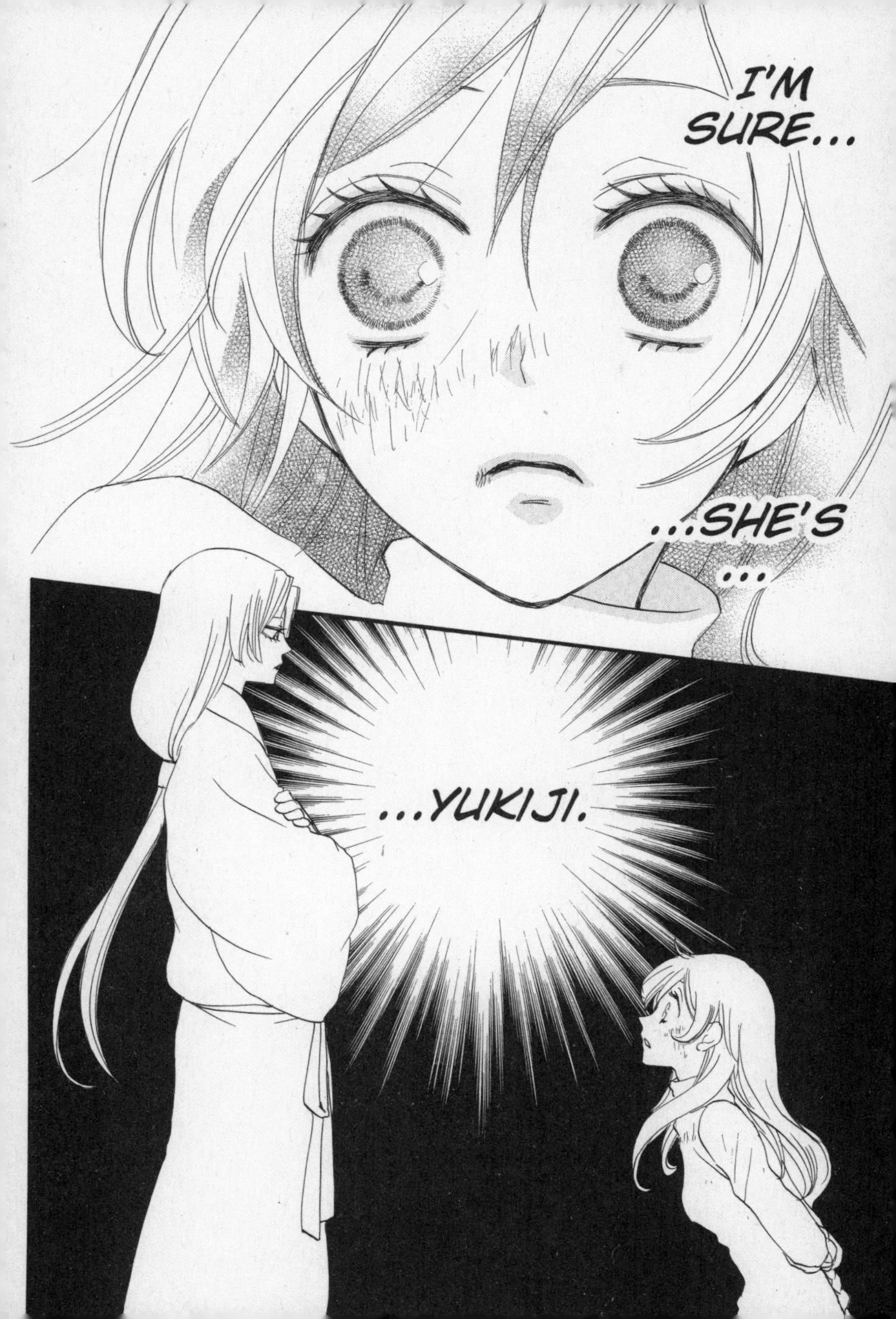
I'M SURE...
...SHE'S ...
...YUKIJI.

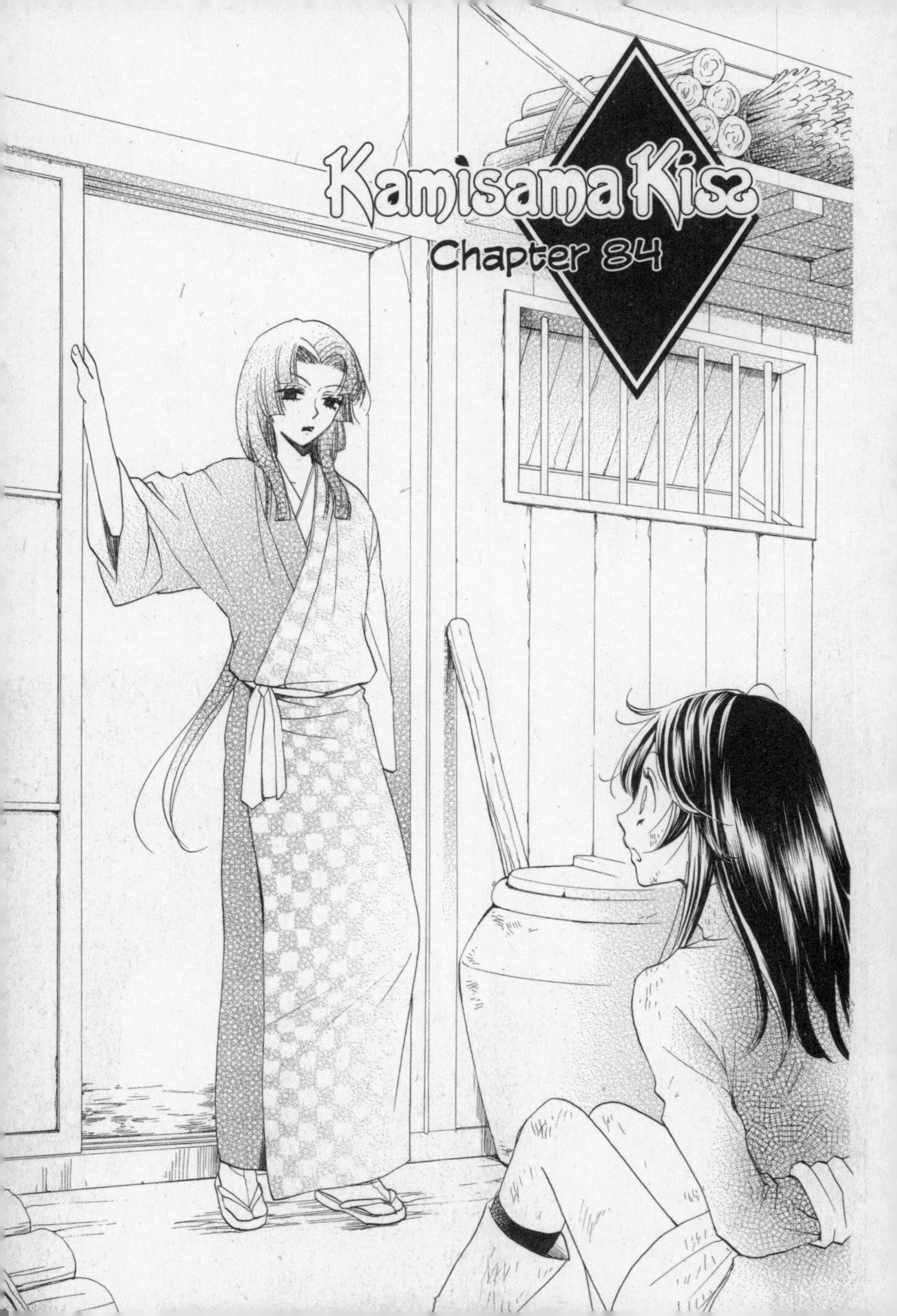
Kamisama Kiss
Chapter 84

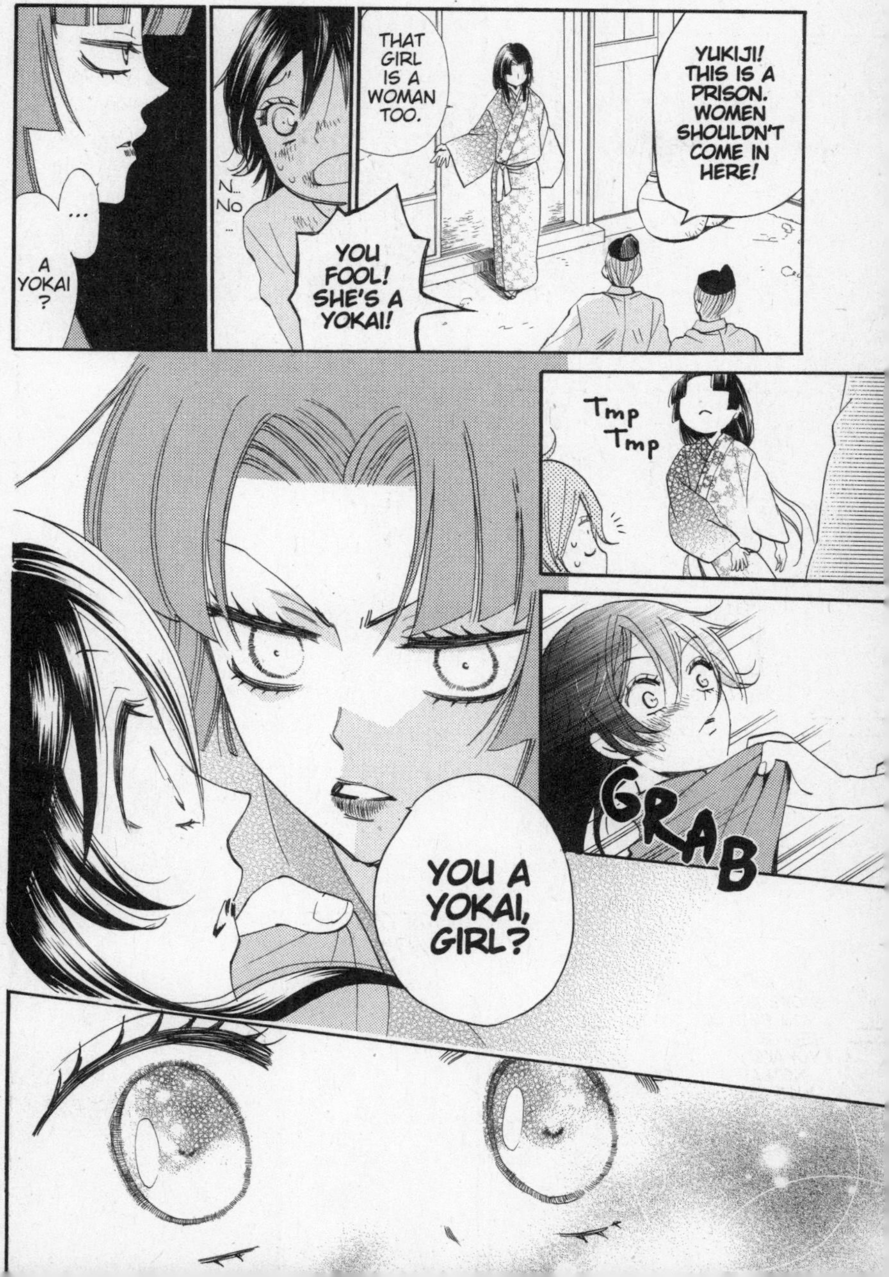
YUKIJI! THIS IS A PRISON. WOMEN SHOULDN'T COME IN HERE!
THAT GIRL IS A WOMAN TOO.
N... No ...
YOU FOOL! SHE'S A YOKAI!
...
A YOKAI ?
Tmp Tmp
GRAB
YOU A YOKAI, GIRL?

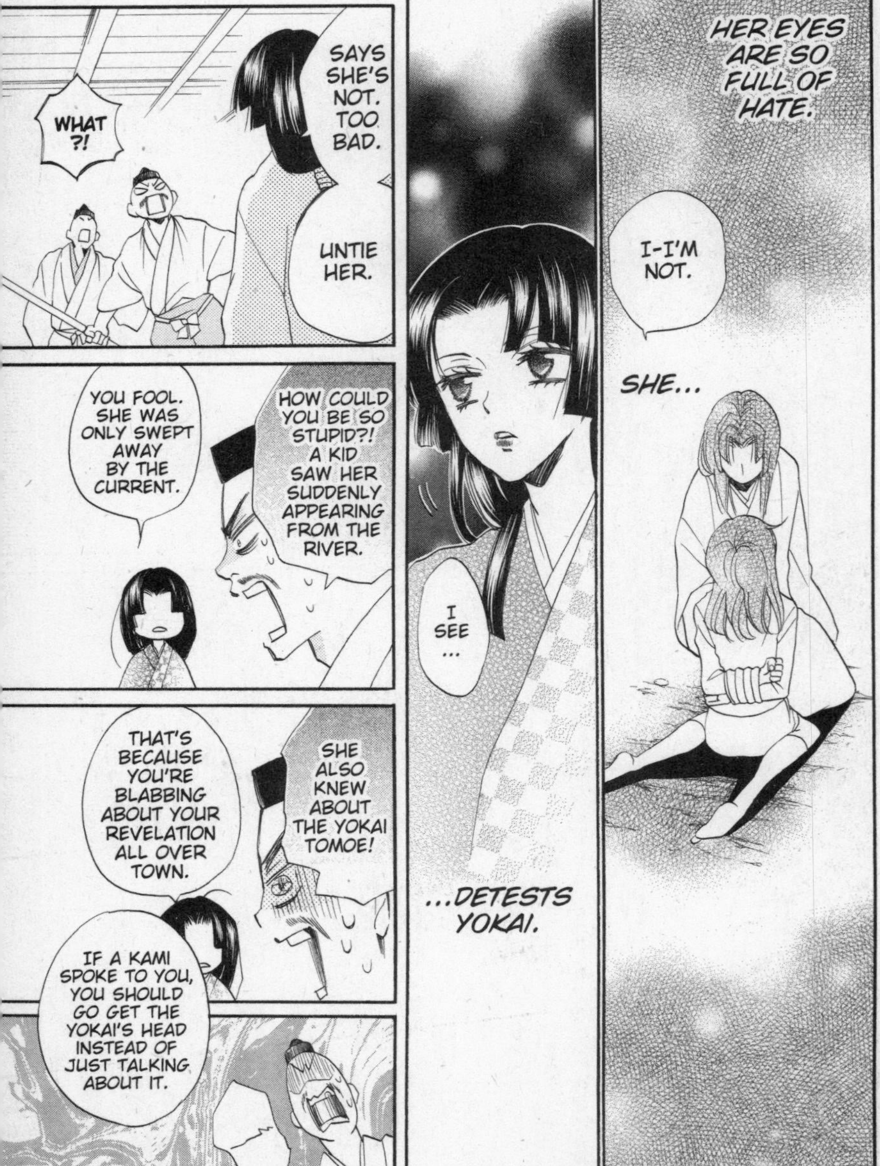
HER EYES ARE SO FULL OF HATE.
I-I'M NOT.
SHE...
I SEE ...
...DETESTS YOKAI.
SAYS SHE'S NOT. TOO BAD.
UNTIE HER.
WHAT ?!
HOW COULD YOU BE SO STUPID?! A KID SAW HER SUDDENLY APPEARING FROM THE RIVER.
YOU FOOL. SHE WAS ONLY SWEPT AWAY BY THE CURRENT.
SHE ALSO KNEW ABOUT THE YOKAI TOMOE!
THAT'S BECAUSE YOU'RE BLABBING ABOUT YOUR REVELATION ALL OVER TOWN.
IF A KAMI SPOKE TO YOU, YOU SHOULD GO GET THE YOKAI'S HEAD INSTEAD OF JUST TALKING ABOUT IT.

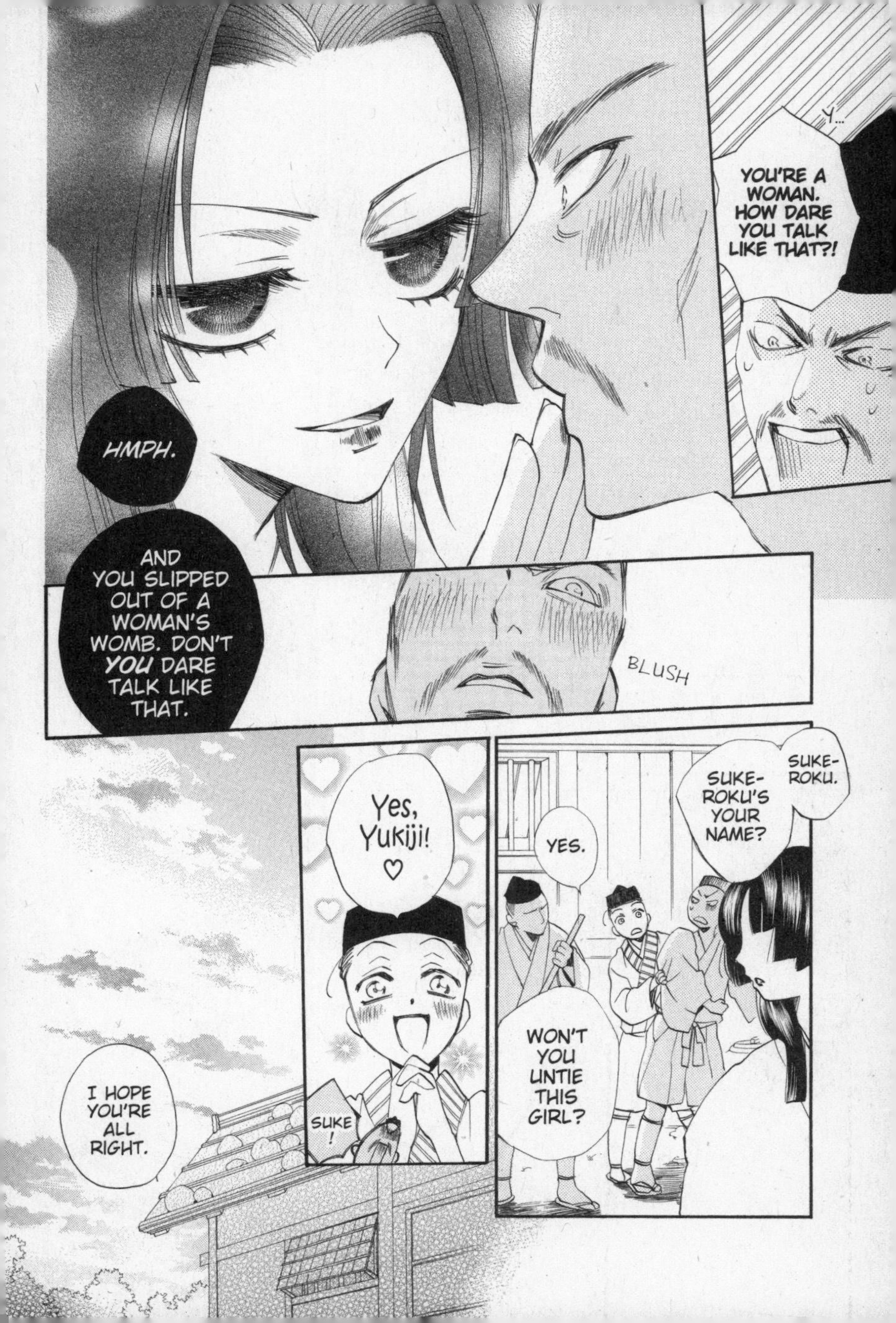
Y...
YOU'RE A WOMAN. HOW DARE YOU TALK LIKE THAT?!
HMPH.
AND YOU SLIPPED OUT OF A WOMAN'S WOMB. DON'T *YOU* DARE TALK LIKE THAT.
BLUSH
SUKE-ROKU.
SUKE-ROKU'S YOUR NAME?
YES.
WON'T YOU UNTIE THIS GIRL?
Yes, Yukiji! ♡
SUKE!
I HOPE YOU'RE ALL RIGHT.

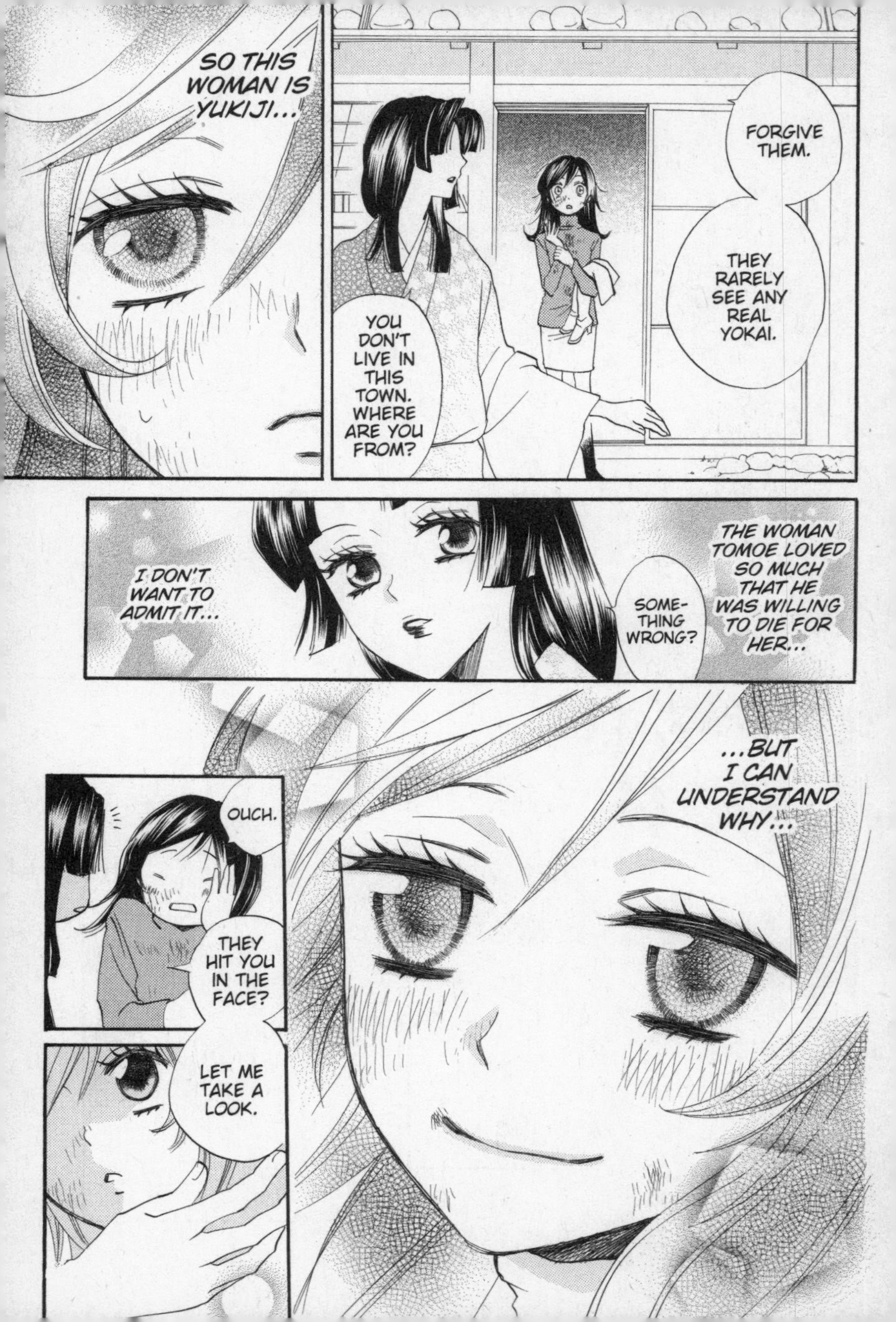
FORGIVE THEM.
THEY RARELY SEE ANY REAL YOKAI.
YOU DON'T LIVE IN THIS TOWN. WHERE ARE YOU FROM?
SO THIS WOMAN IS YUKIJI...
THE WOMAN TOMOE LOVED SO MUCH THAT HE WAS WILLING TO DIE FOR HER...
SOME-THING WRONG?
I DON'T WANT TO ADMIT IT...
...BUT I CAN UNDERSTAND WHY...
OUCH.
THEY HIT YOU IN THE FACE?
LET ME TAKE A LOOK.

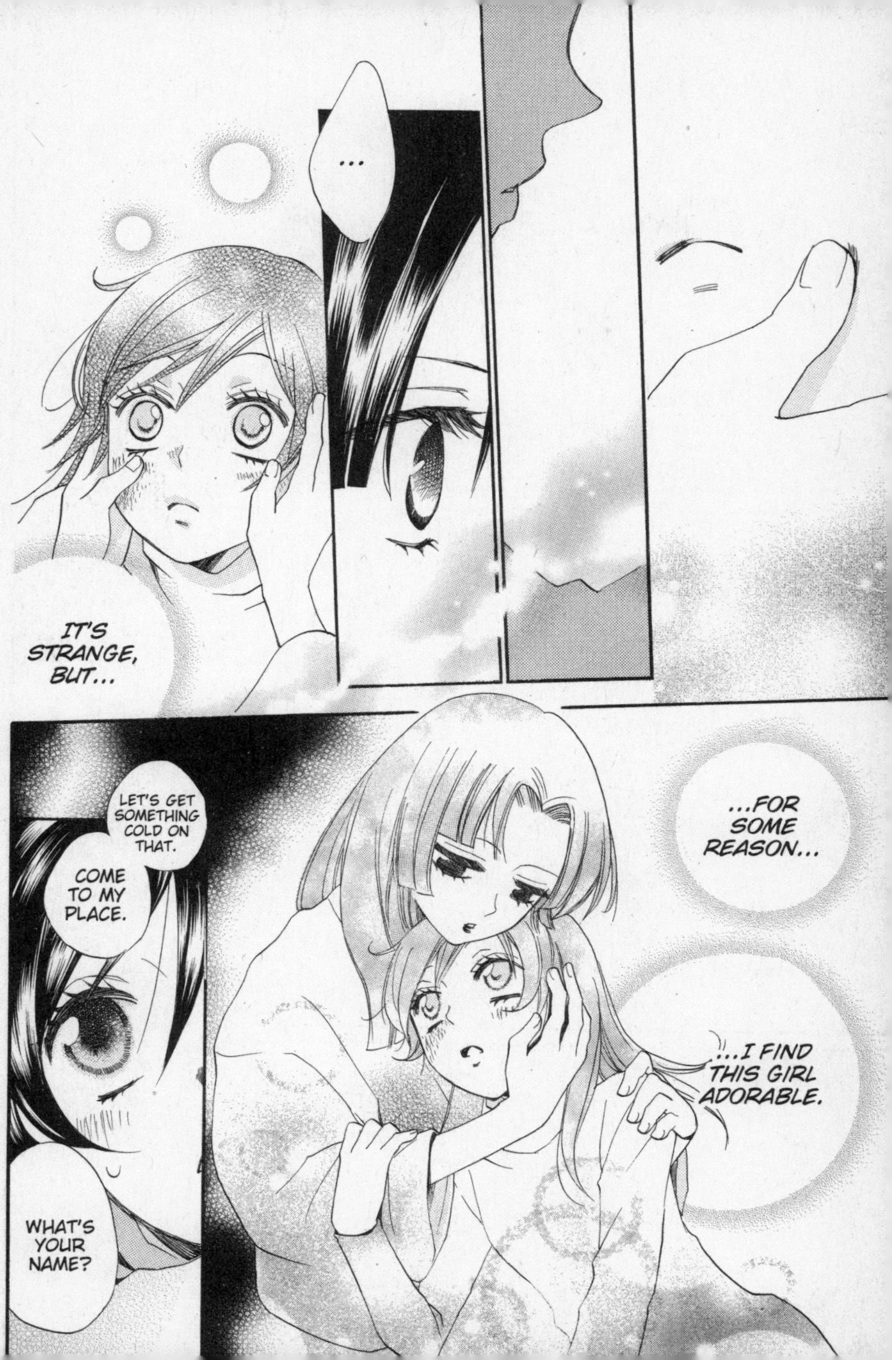
...
IT'S STRANGE, BUT...
...FOR SOME REASON...
...I FIND THIS GIRL ADORABLE.
LET'S GET SOMETHING COLD ON THAT.
COME TO MY PLACE.
WHAT'S YOUR NAME?

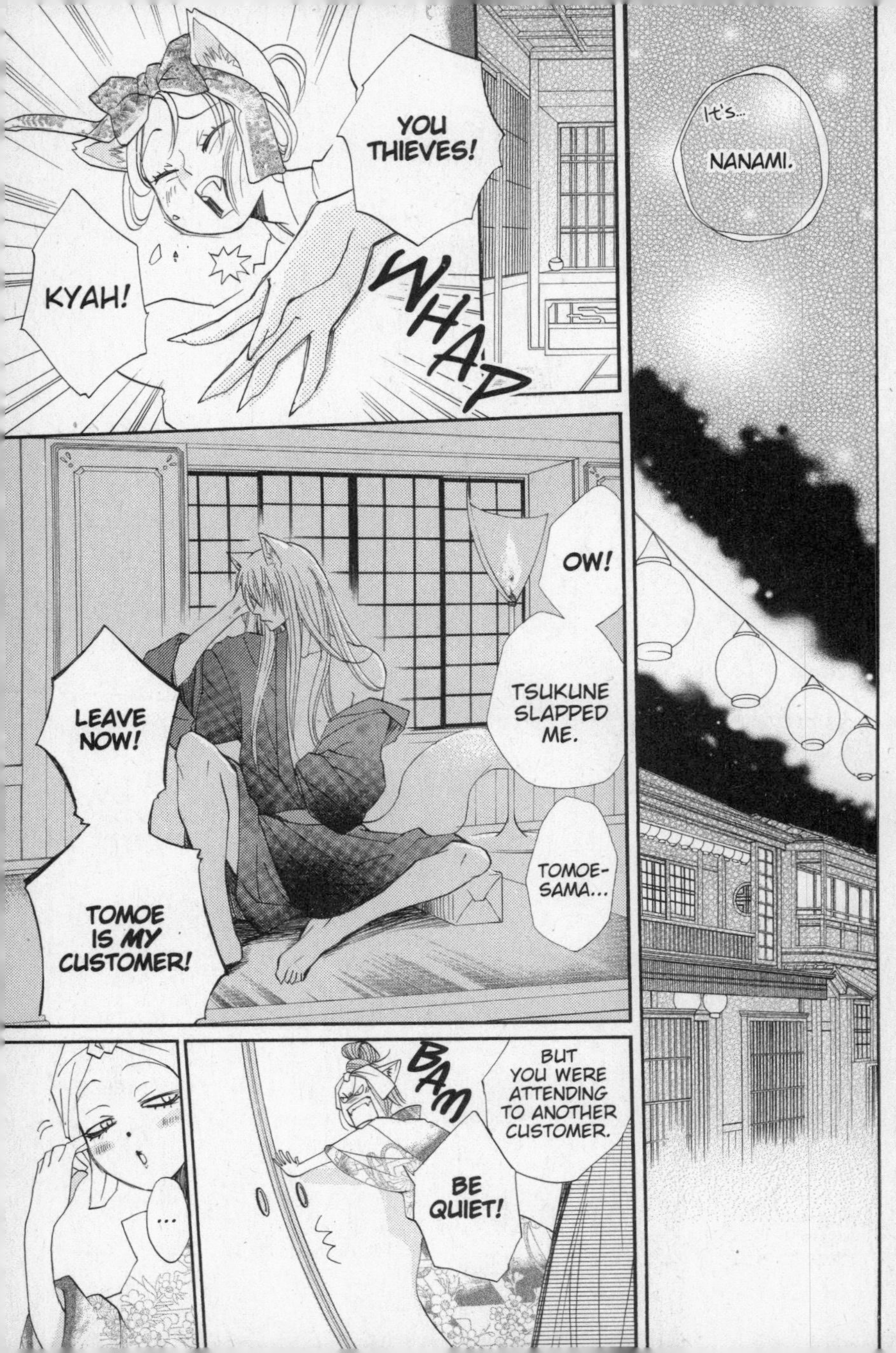
It's...
NANAMI.
YOU THIEVES!
WHAP
KYAH!
OW!
TSUKUNE SLAPPED ME.
TOMOE-SAMA...
LEAVE NOW!
TOMOE IS MY CUSTOMER!
BAM
BUT YOU WERE ATTENDING TO ANOTHER CUSTOMER.
BE QUIET!
...

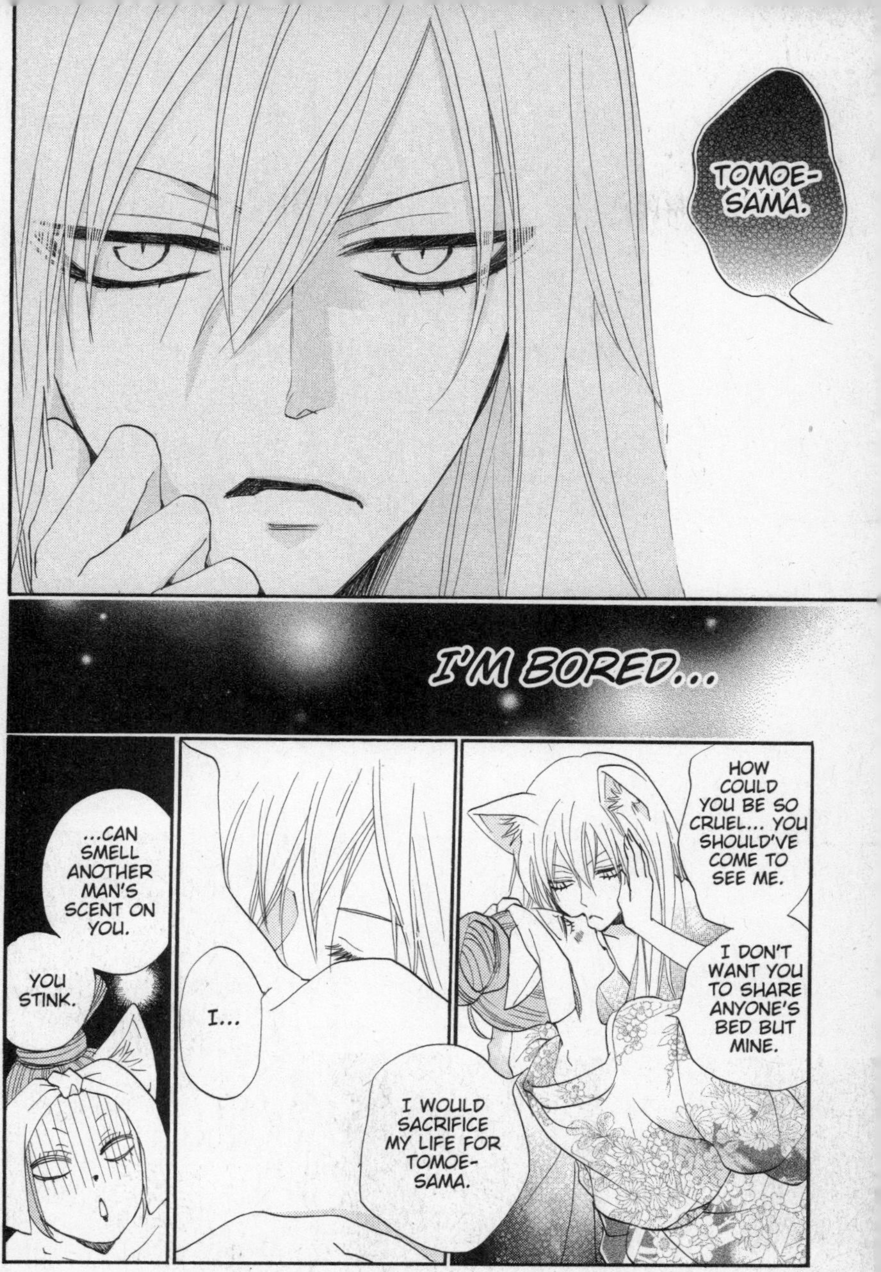
TOMOE-SAMA.
I'M BORED...
HOW COULD YOU BE SO CRUEL... YOU SHOULD'VE COME TO SEE ME.
I DON'T WANT YOU TO SHARE ANYONE'S BED BUT MINE.
I...
I WOULD SACRIFICE MY LIFE FOR TOMOE-SAMA.
...CAN SMELL ANOTHER MAN'S SCENT ON YOU.
YOU STINK.

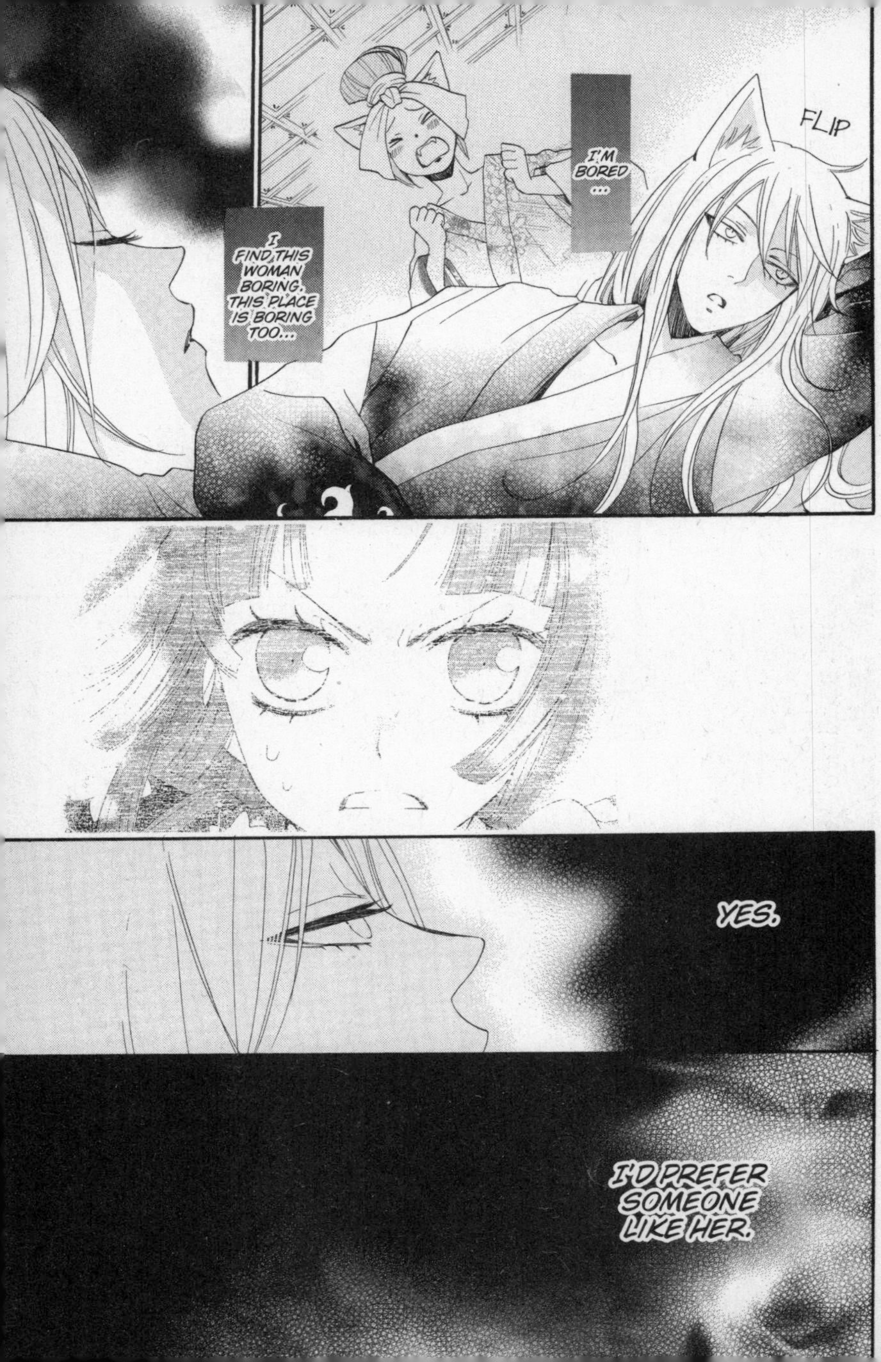
FLIP
I'M BORED...
I FIND THIS WOMAN BORING. THIS PLACE IS BORING TOO...
YES.
I'D PREFER SOMEONE LIKE HER.

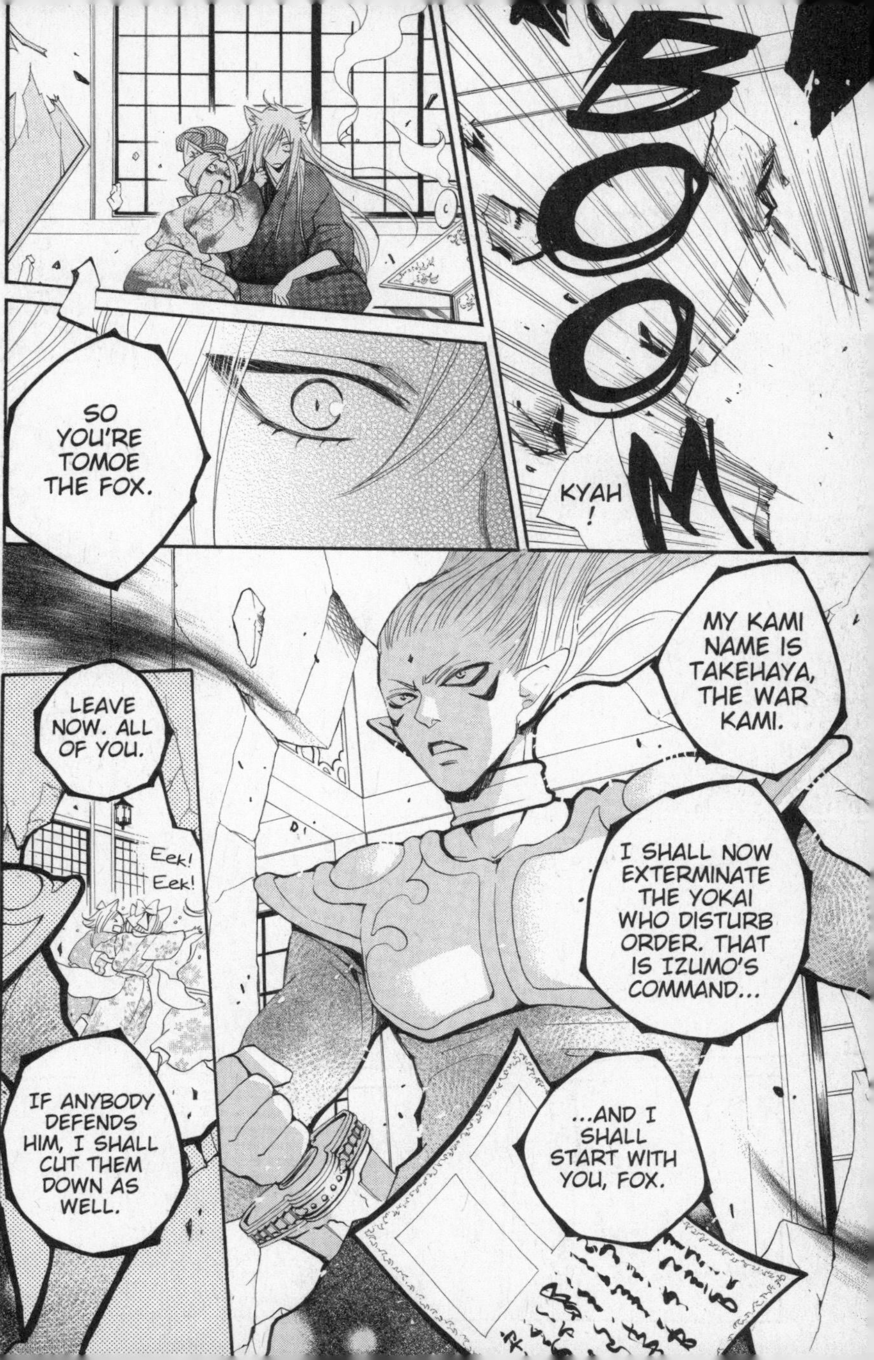
BOOM
KYAH!
SO YOU'RE TOMOE THE FOX.
MY KAMI NAME IS TAKEHAYA, THE WAR KAMI.
I SHALL NOW EXTERMINATE THE YOKAI WHO DISTURB ORDER. THAT IS IZUMO'S COMMAND...
...AND I SHALL START WITH YOU, FOX.
LEAVE NOW. ALL OF YOU.
Eek! Eek!
IF ANYBODY DEFENDS HIM, I SHALL CUT THEM DOWN AS WELL.

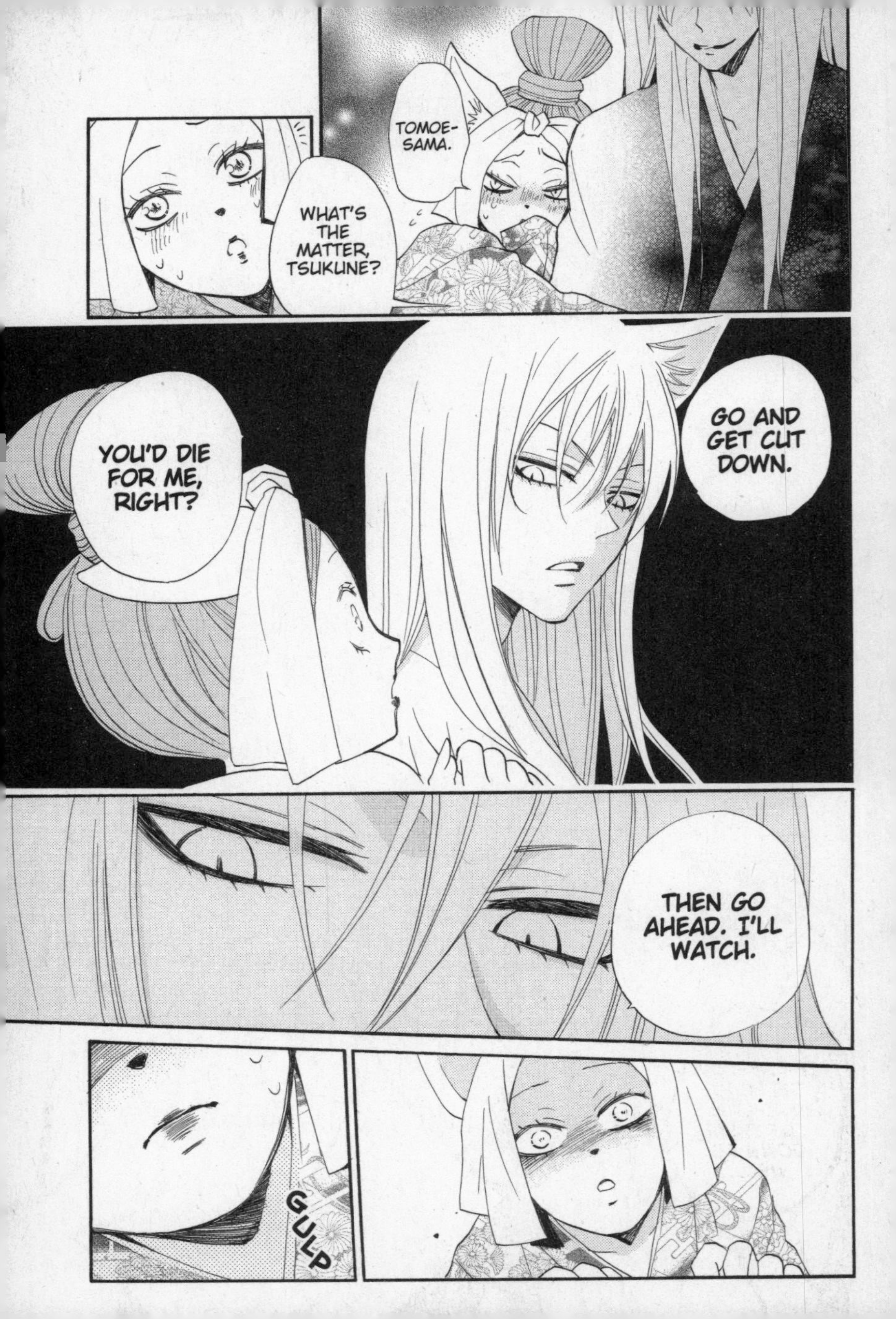
TOMOE-SAMA.
WHAT'S THE MATTER, TSUKUNE?
GO AND GET CUT DOWN.
YOU'D DIE FOR ME, RIGHT?
THEN GO AHEAD. I'LL WATCH.
GULP

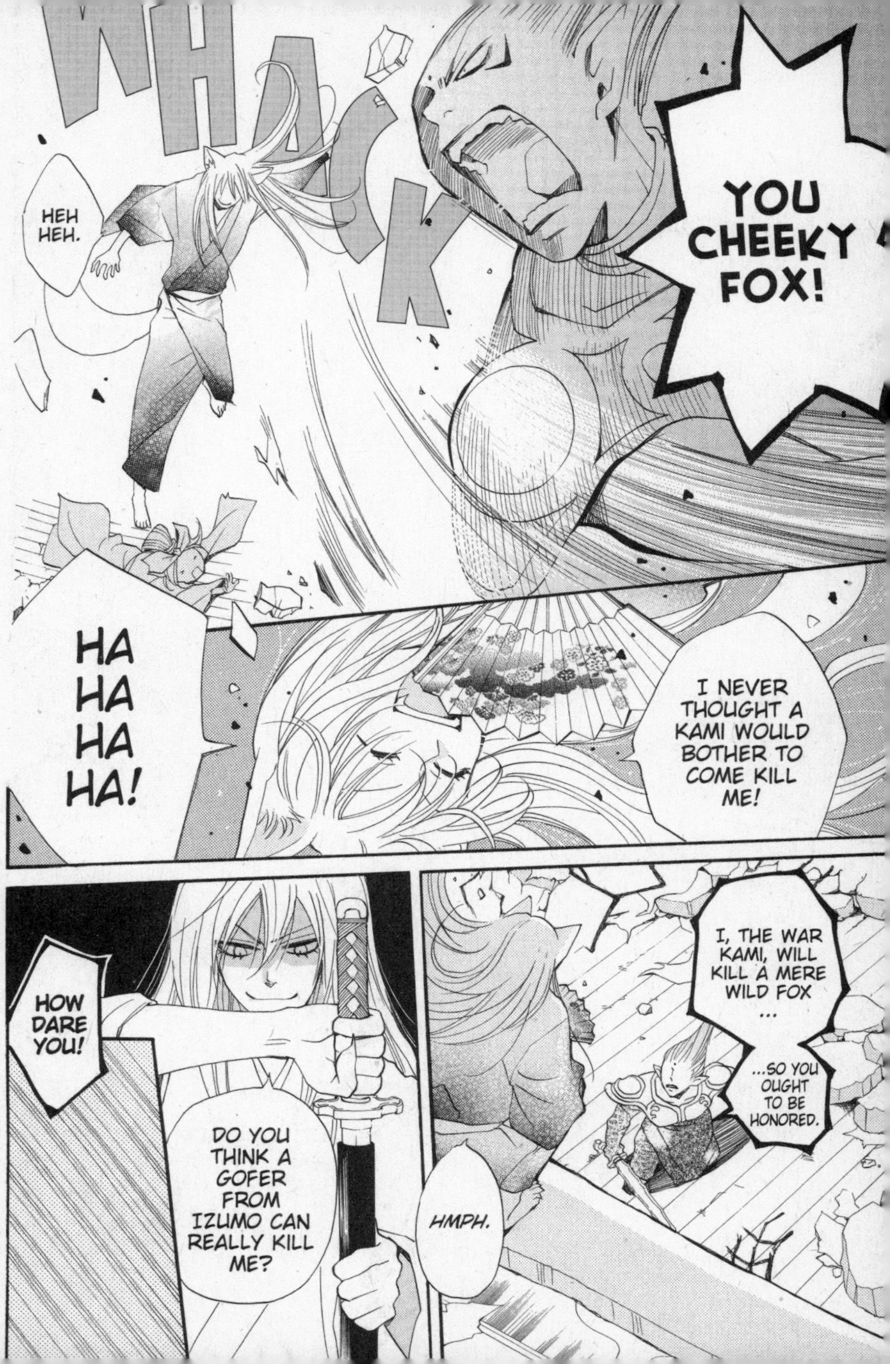
YOU CHEEKY FOX!
WHACK
HEH HEH.
I NEVER THOUGHT A KAMI WOULD BOTHER TO COME KILL ME!
HA HA HA HA!
I, THE WAR KAMI, WILL KILL A MERE WILD FOX ...
...SO YOU OUGHT TO BE HONORED.
HMPH.
HOW DARE YOU!
DO YOU THINK A GOFER FROM IZUMO CAN REALLY KILL ME?

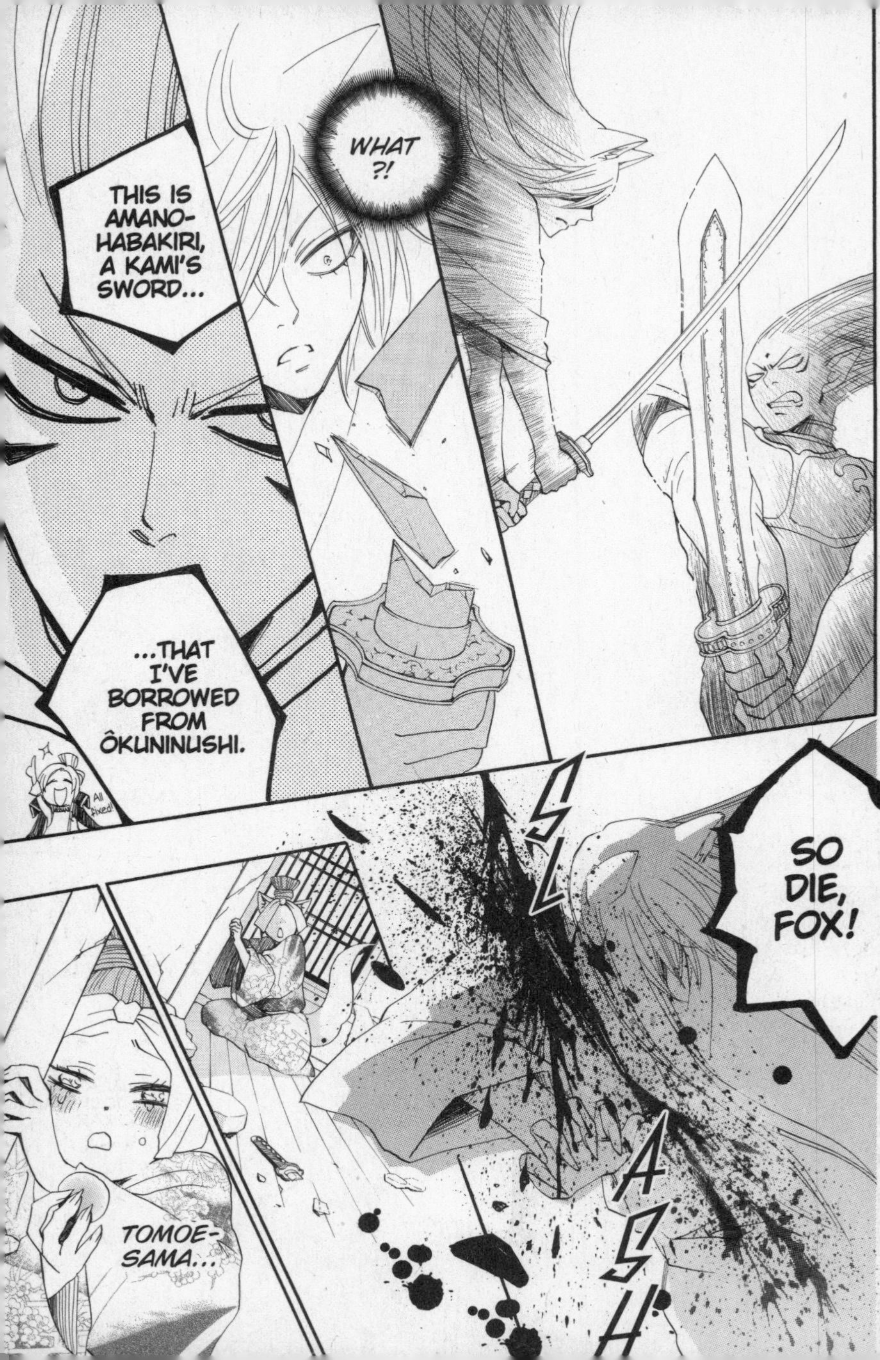
WHAT ?!
THIS IS AMANO-HABAKIRI, A KAMI'S SWORD...
...THAT I'VE BORROWED FROM ÔKUNINUSHI.
All fixed!
SO DIE, FOX!
SLASH
TOMOE-SAMA...

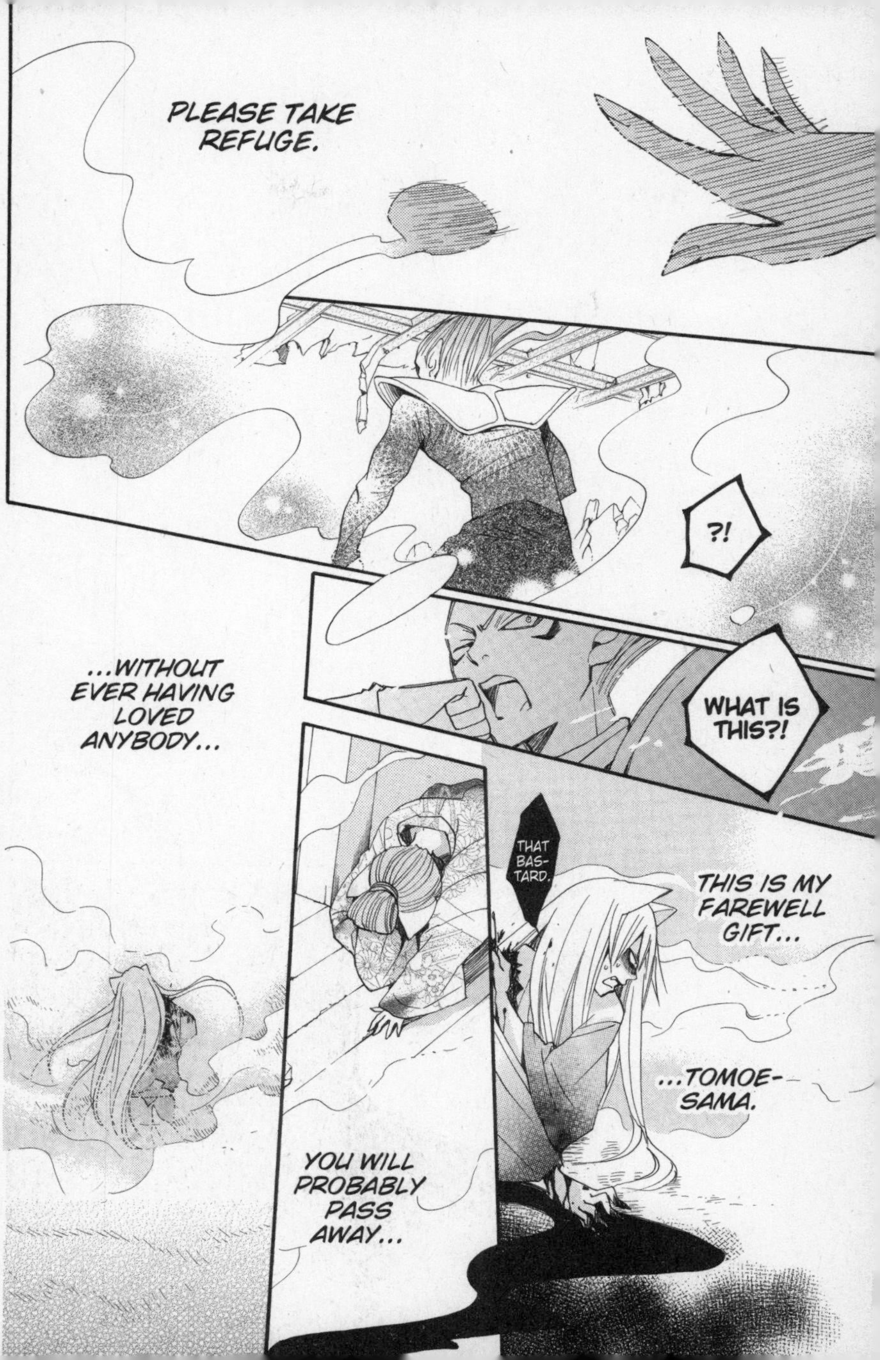

PLEASE TAKE REFUGE.
?!
WHAT IS THIS?!
THAT BASTARD.
THIS IS MY FAREWELL GIFT...
...TOMOE-SAMA.
YOU WILL PROBABLY PASS AWAY...
...WITHOUT EVER HAVING LOVED ANYBODY...

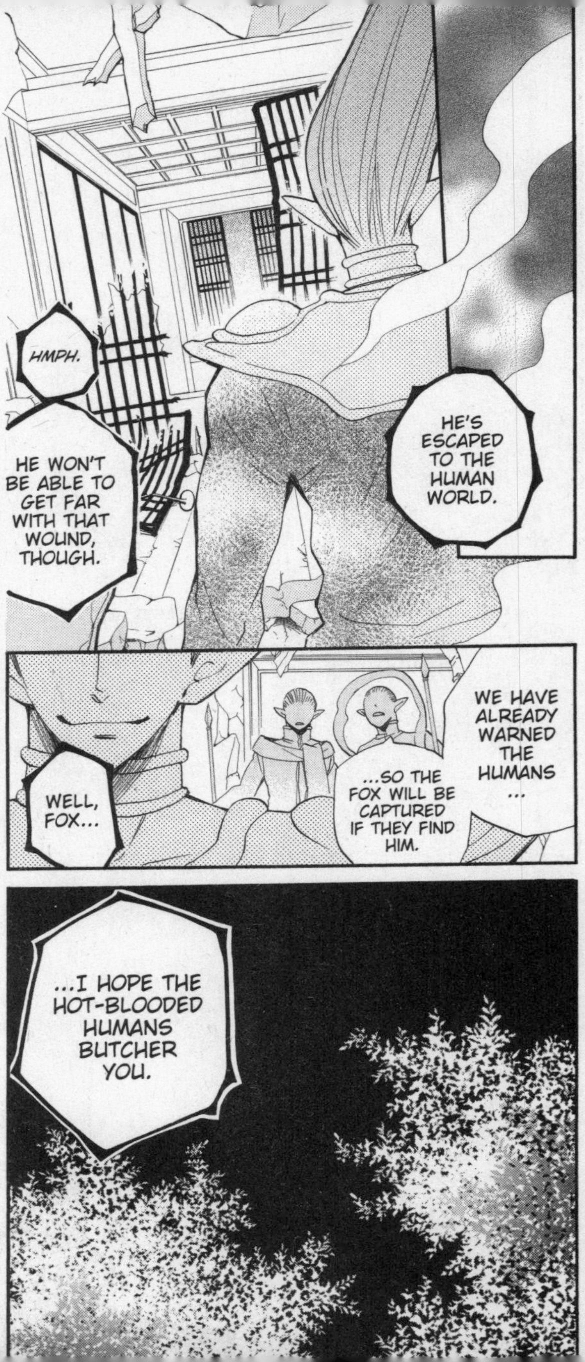
HE'S ESCAPED TO THE HUMAN WORLD.
HMPH.
HE WON'T BE ABLE TO GET FAR WITH THAT WOUND, THOUGH.
WE HAVE ALREADY WARNED THE HUMANS...
...SO THE FOX WILL BE CAPTURED IF THEY FIND HIM.
WELL, FOX...
...I HOPE THE HOT-BLOODED HUMANS BUTCHER YOU.

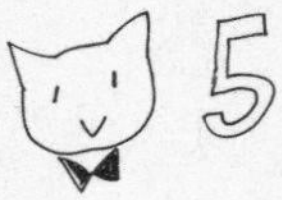
5

Thank you for reading this far and coming along with me!

I'll be very happy if we can meet again in volume 15!

See you again!

Love love!

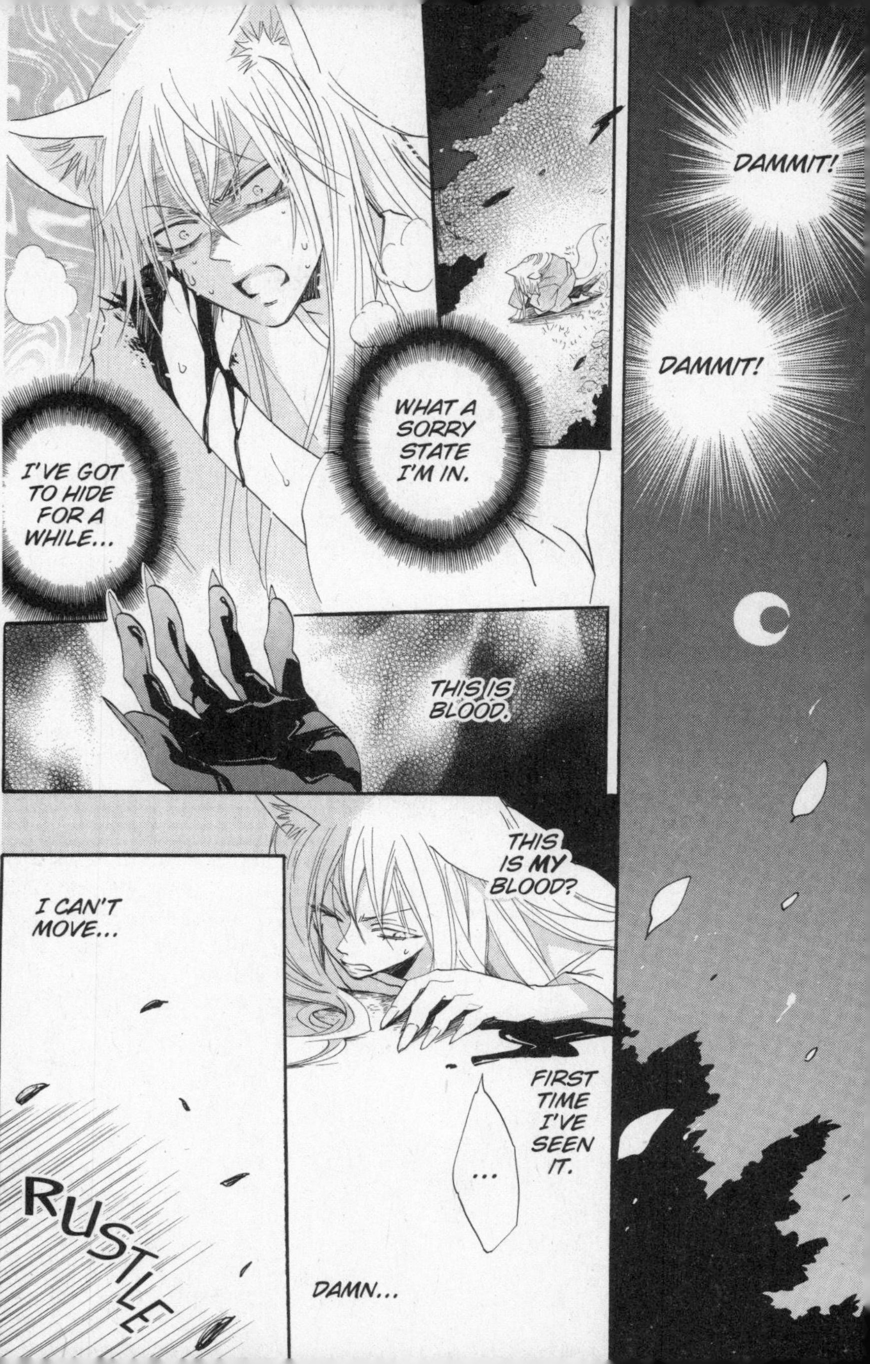
DAMMIT!
DAMMIT!
WHAT A SORRY STATE I'M IN.
I'VE GOT TO HIDE FOR A WHILE...
THIS IS BLOOD.
THIS IS MY BLOOD?
FIRST TIME I'VE SEEN IT.
...
I CAN'T MOVE...
RUSTLE
DAMN...

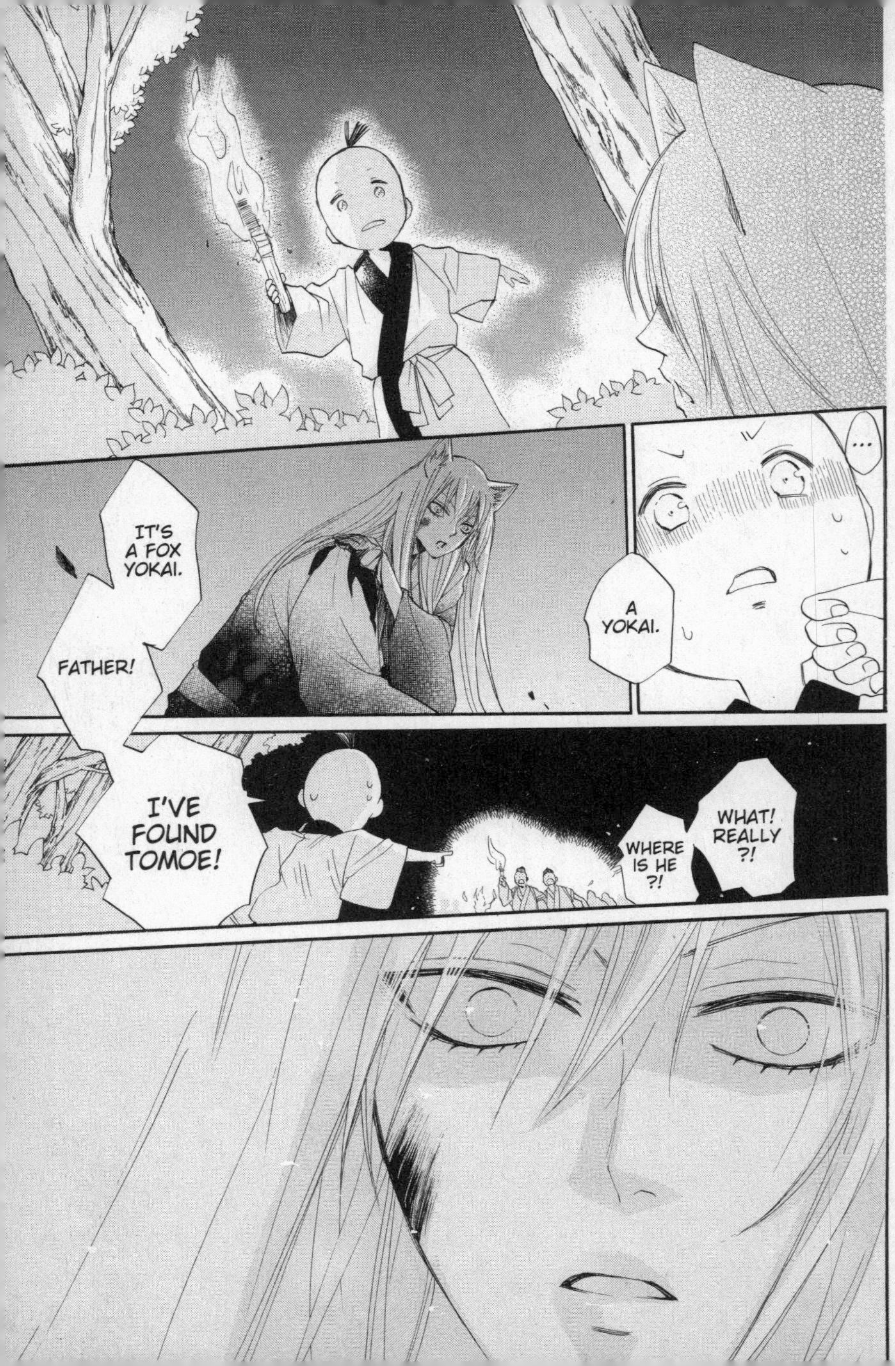
...
A YOKAI.
IT'S A FOX YOKAI.
FATHER!
I'VE FOUND TOMOE!
WHAT! REALLY ?!
WHERE IS HE ?!

MY EYES ARE BLURRY.
AM I GONNA DIE...
...SNAPPED ...
...BY THESE HUMAN WORMS ...?

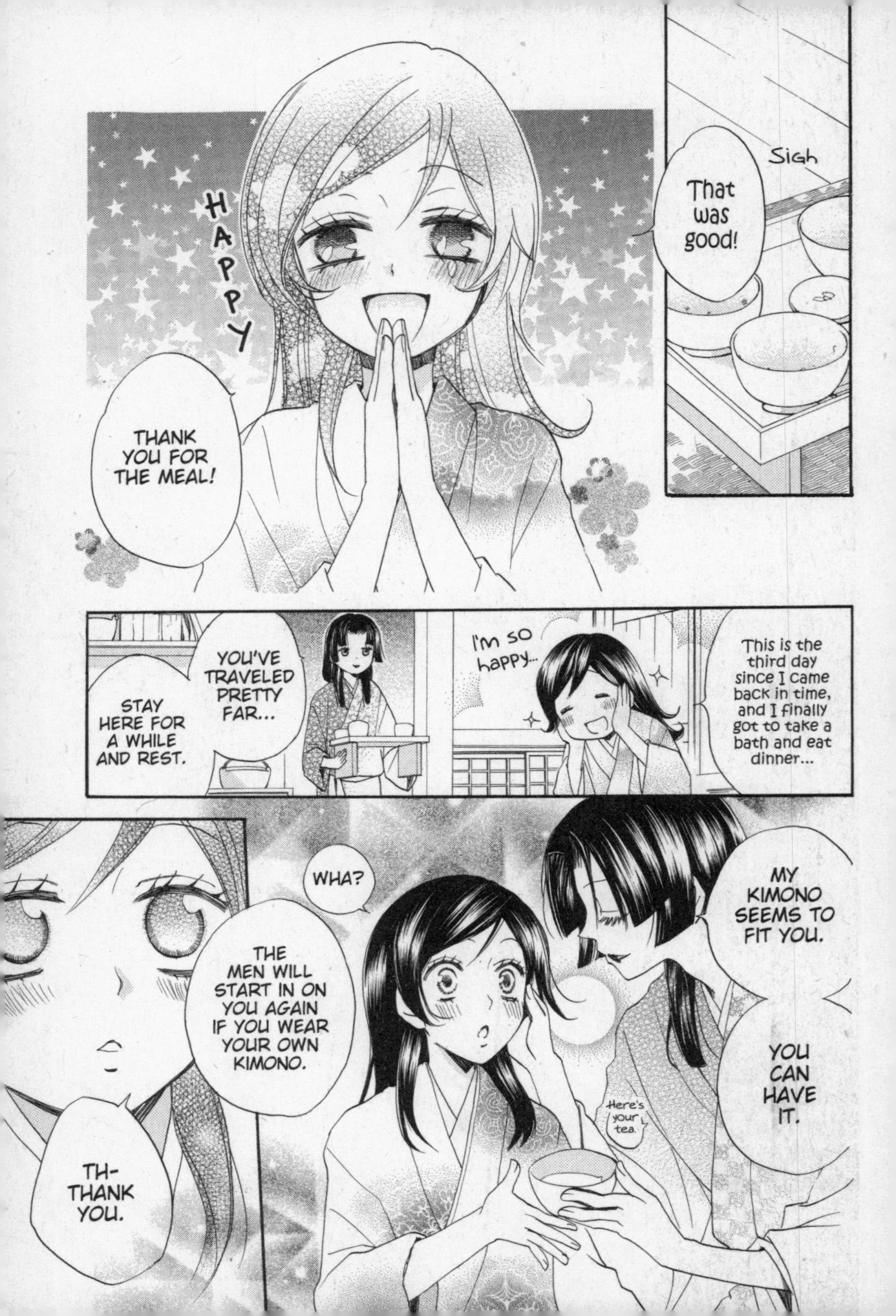
Sigh
That was good!
HAPPY
THANK YOU FOR THE MEAL!
This is the third day since I came back in time, and I finally got to take a bath and eat dinner...
I'm so happy...
YOU'VE TRAVELED PRETTY FAR...
STAY HERE FOR A WHILE AND REST.
MY KIMONO SEEMS TO FIT YOU.
YOU CAN HAVE IT.
WHA?
THE MEN WILL START IN ON YOU AGAIN IF YOU WEAR YOUR OWN KIMONO.
Here's your tea.
TH-THANK YOU.

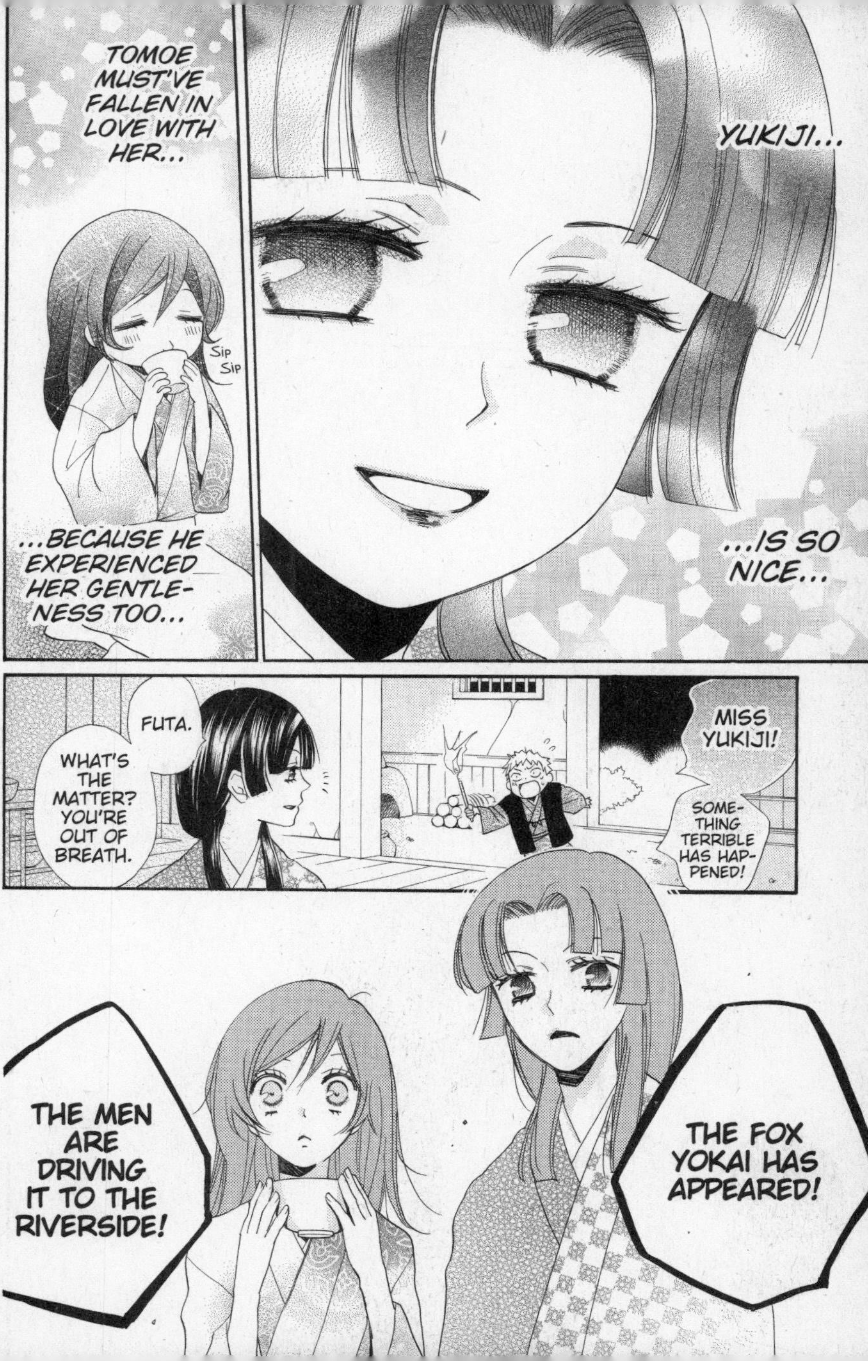
YUKIJI...
...IS SO NICE...
TOMOE MUST'VE FALLEN IN LOVE WITH HER...
Sip Sip
...BECAUSE HE EXPERIENCED HER GENTLENESS TOO...
MISS YUKIJI!
SOMETHING TERRIBLE HAS HAPPENED!
FUTA.
WHAT'S THE MATTER? YOU'RE OUT OF BREATH.
THE FOX YOKAI HAS APPEARED!
THE MEN ARE DRIVING IT TO THE RIVERSIDE!

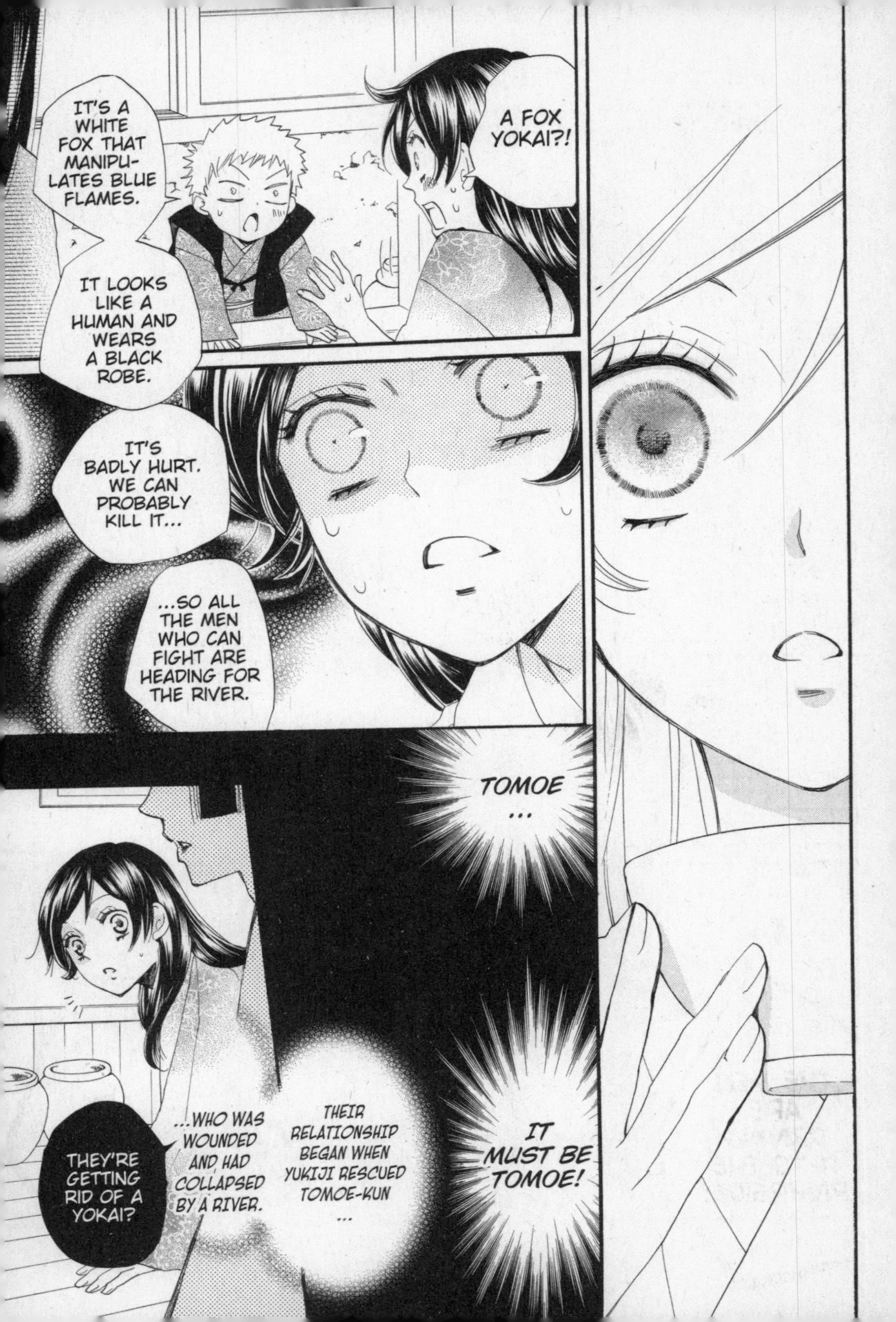
A FOX YOKAI?!
IT'S A WHITE FOX THAT MANIPU-LATES BLUE FLAMES.
IT LOOKS LIKE A HUMAN AND WEARS A BLACK ROBE.
IT'S BADLY HURT. WE CAN PROBABLY KILL IT...
...SO ALL THE MEN WHO CAN FIGHT ARE HEADING FOR THE RIVER.
TOMOE ...
IT MUST BE TOMOE!
THEIR RELATIONSHIP BEGAN WHEN YUKIJI RESCUED TOMOE-KUN ...
...WHO WAS WOUNDED AND HAD COLLAPSED BY A RIVER.
THEY'RE GETTING RID OF A YOKAI?

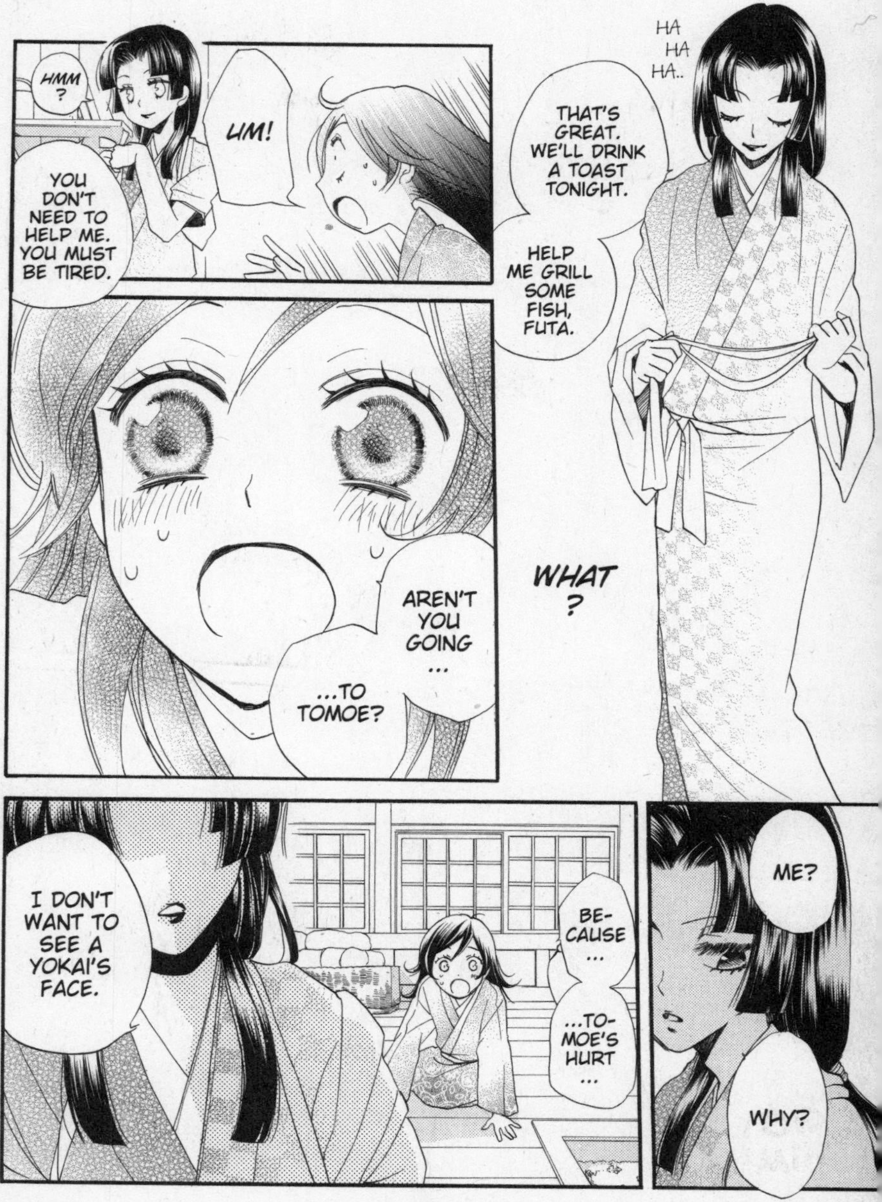
HA HA HA..
THAT'S GREAT. WE'LL DRINK A TOAST TONIGHT.
HELP ME GRILL SOME FISH, FUTA.
WHAT?
UM!
HMM?
YOU DON'T NEED TO HELP ME. YOU MUST BE TIRED.
AREN'T YOU GOING...
...TO TOMOE?
ME?
WHY?
BE-CAUSE...
...TO-MOE'S HURT...
I DON'T WANT TO SEE A YOKAI'S FACE.

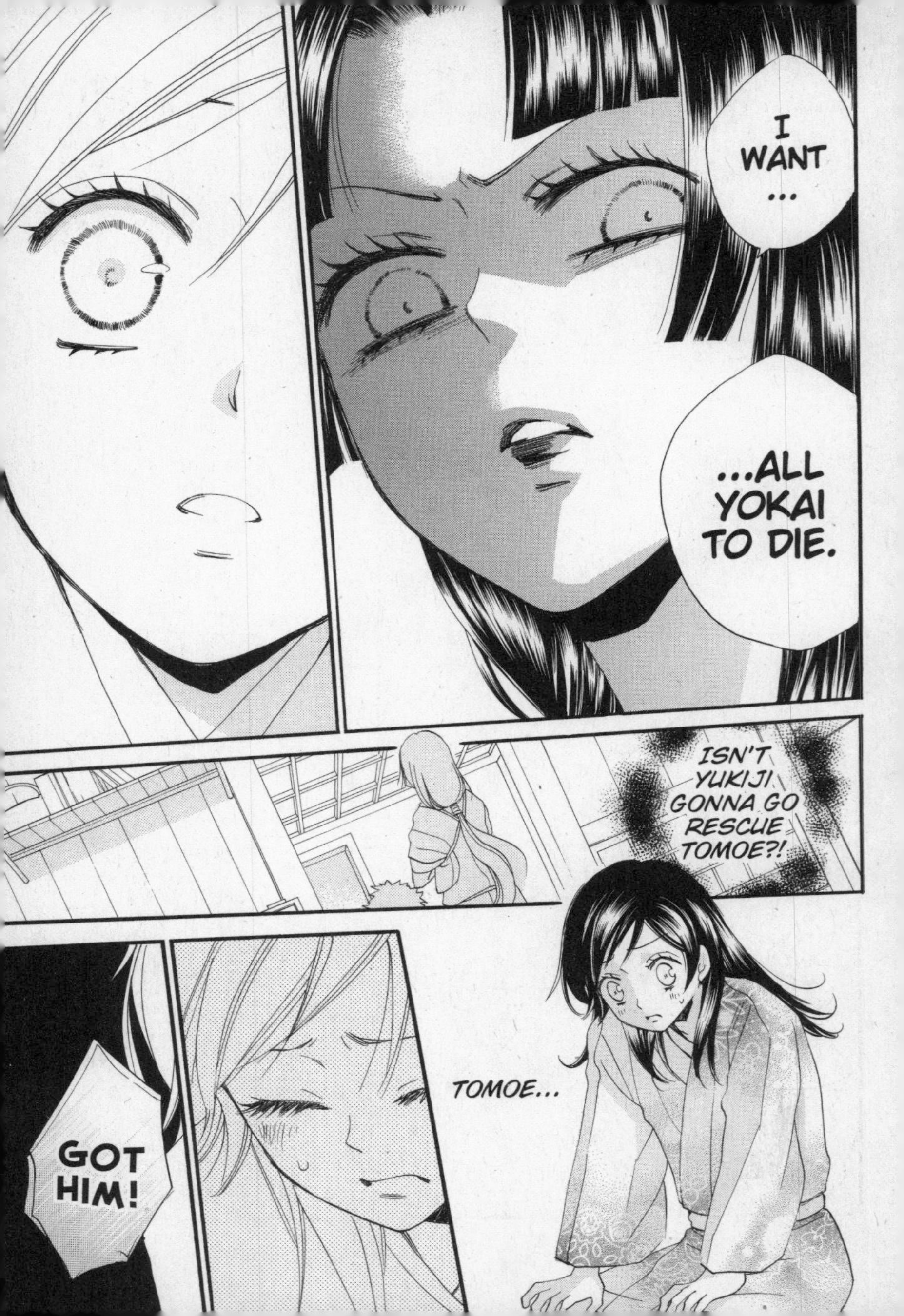
I WANT...
...ALL YOKAI TO DIE.
ISN'T YUKIJI GONNA GO RESCUE TOMOE?!
TOMOE...
GOT HIM!

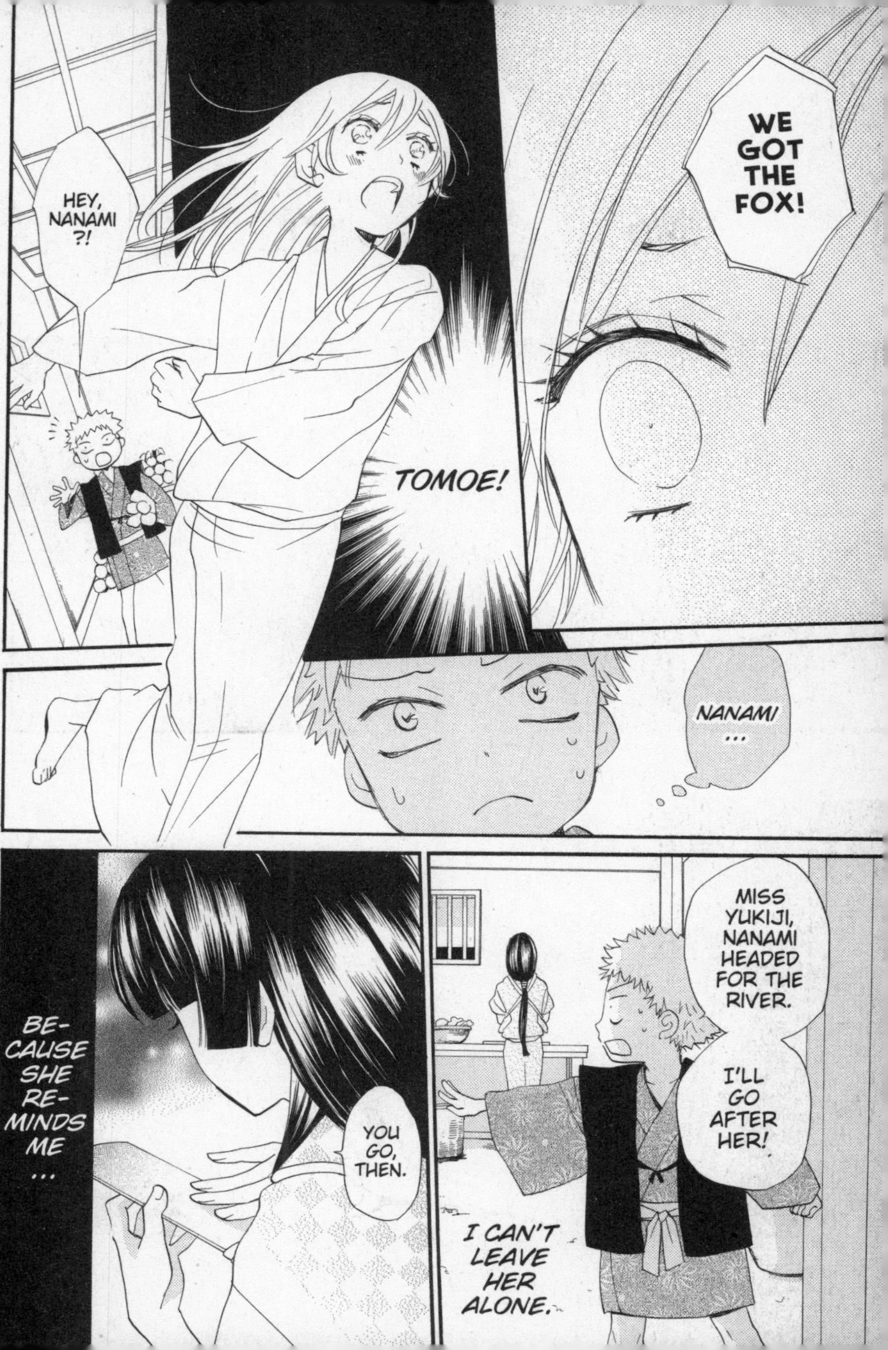
WE GOT THE FOX!
TOMOE!
HEY, NANAMI?!
NANAMI...
MISS YUKIJI, NANAMI HEADED FOR THE RIVER.
I'LL GO AFTER HER!
I CAN'T LEAVE HER ALONE.
YOU GO, THEN.
BE-CAUSE SHE RE-MINDS ME...

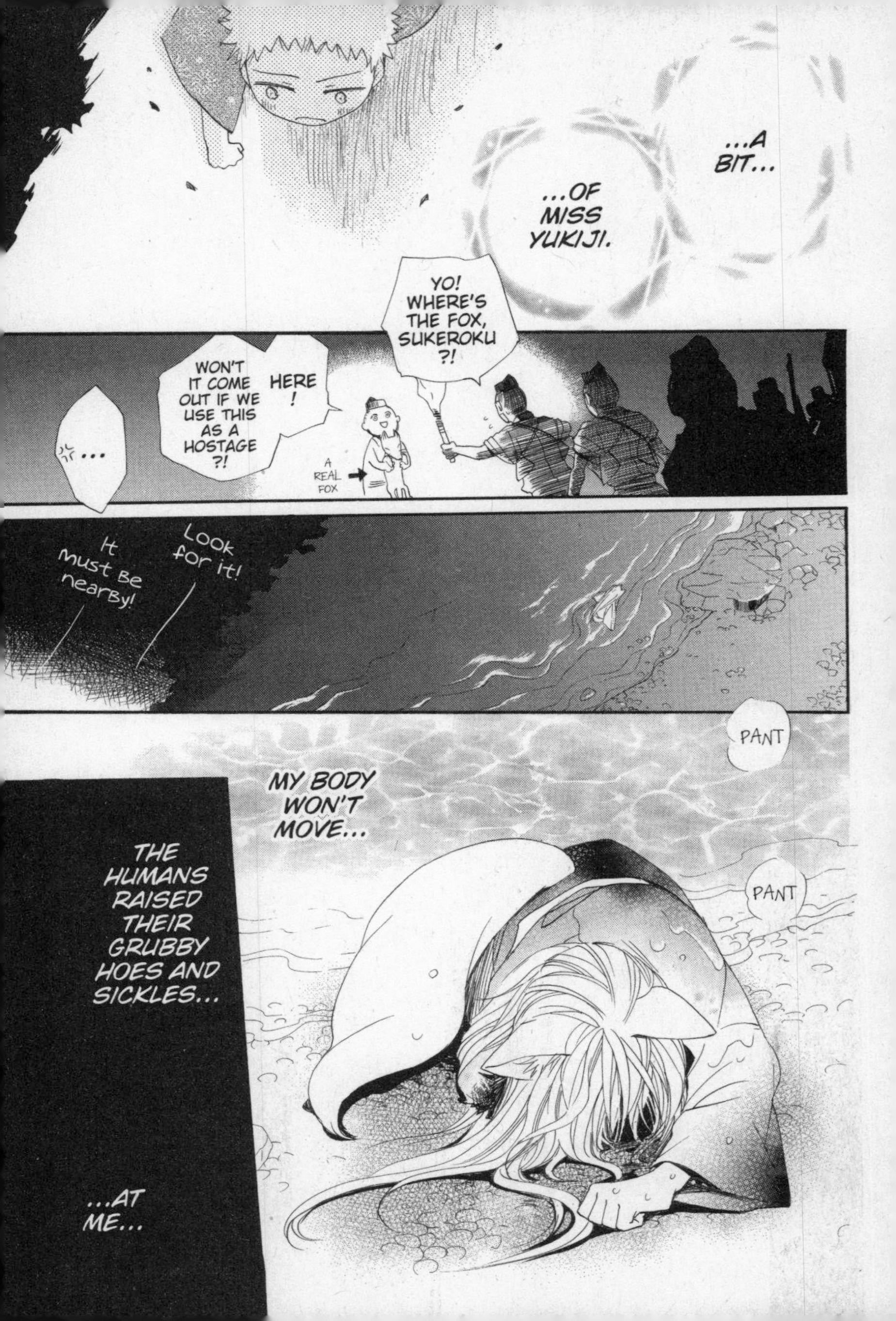
...A BIT...
...OF MISS YUKIJI.
YO! WHERE'S THE FOX, SUKEROKU ?!
HERE!
WON'T IT COME OUT IF WE USE THIS AS A HOSTAGE ?!
A REAL FOX
...
Look for it!
It must be nearby!
PANT
MY BODY WON'T MOVE...
PANT
THE HUMANS RAISED THEIR GRUBBY HOES AND SICKLES...
...AT ME...

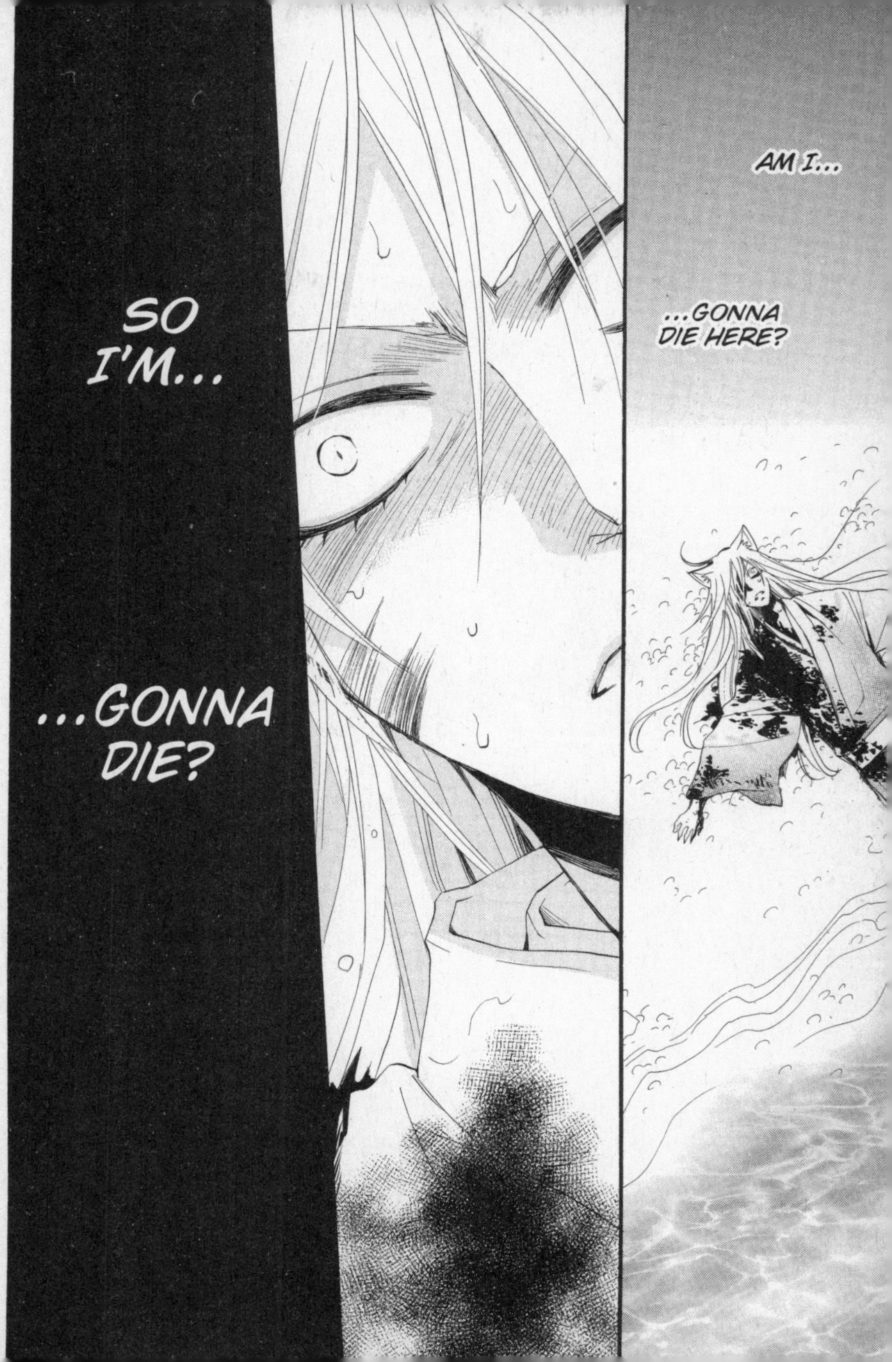
AM I...
...GONNA DIE HERE?
SO I'M...
...GONNA DIE?

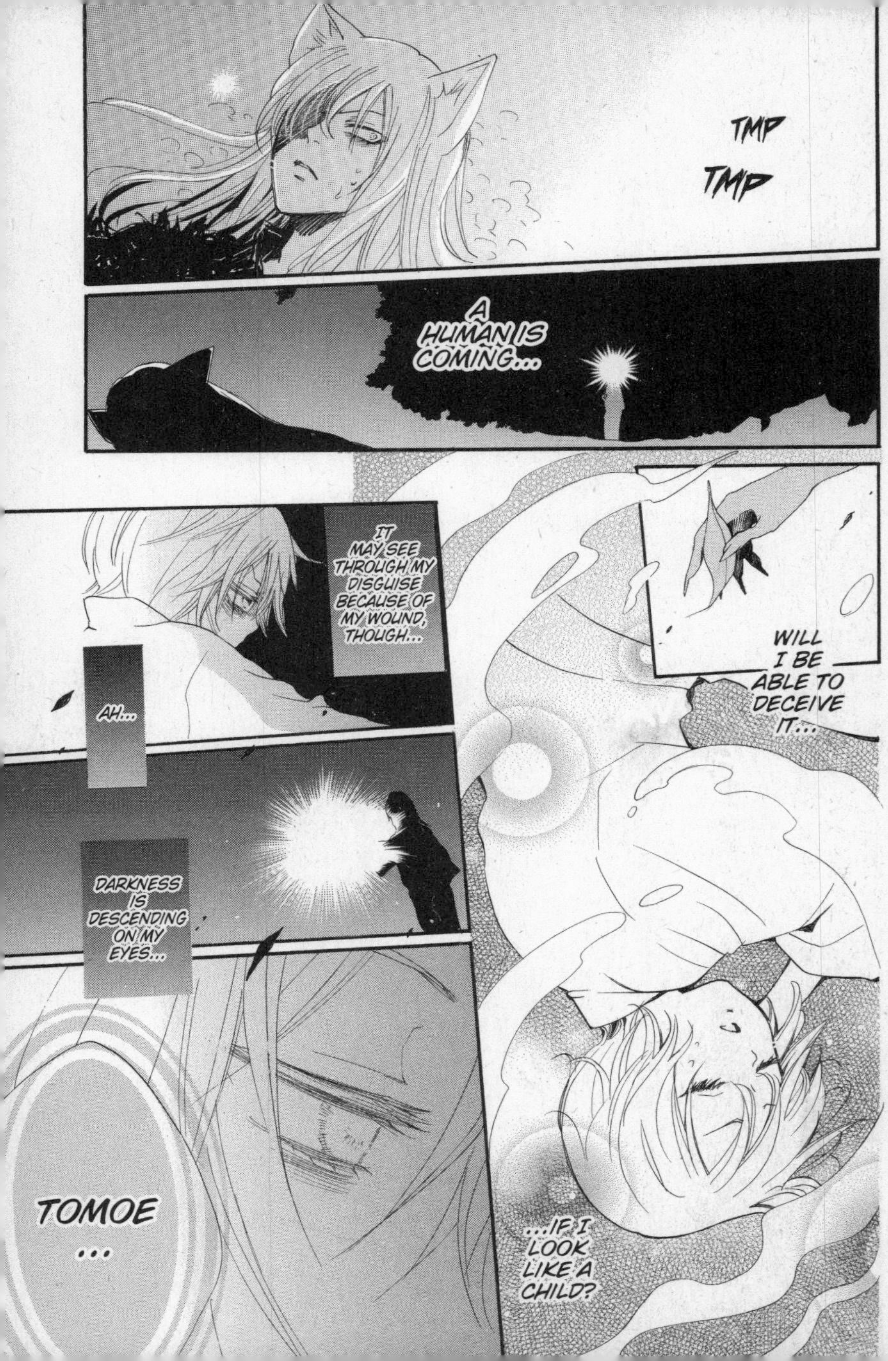
TMP
TMP
A HUMAN IS COMING...
WILL I BE ABLE TO DECEIVE IT...
...IF I LOOK LIKE A CHILD?
IT MAY SEE THROUGH MY DISGUISE BECAUSE OF MY WOUND, THOUGH...
AH...
DARKNESS IS DESCENDING ON MY EYES...
TOMOE ...

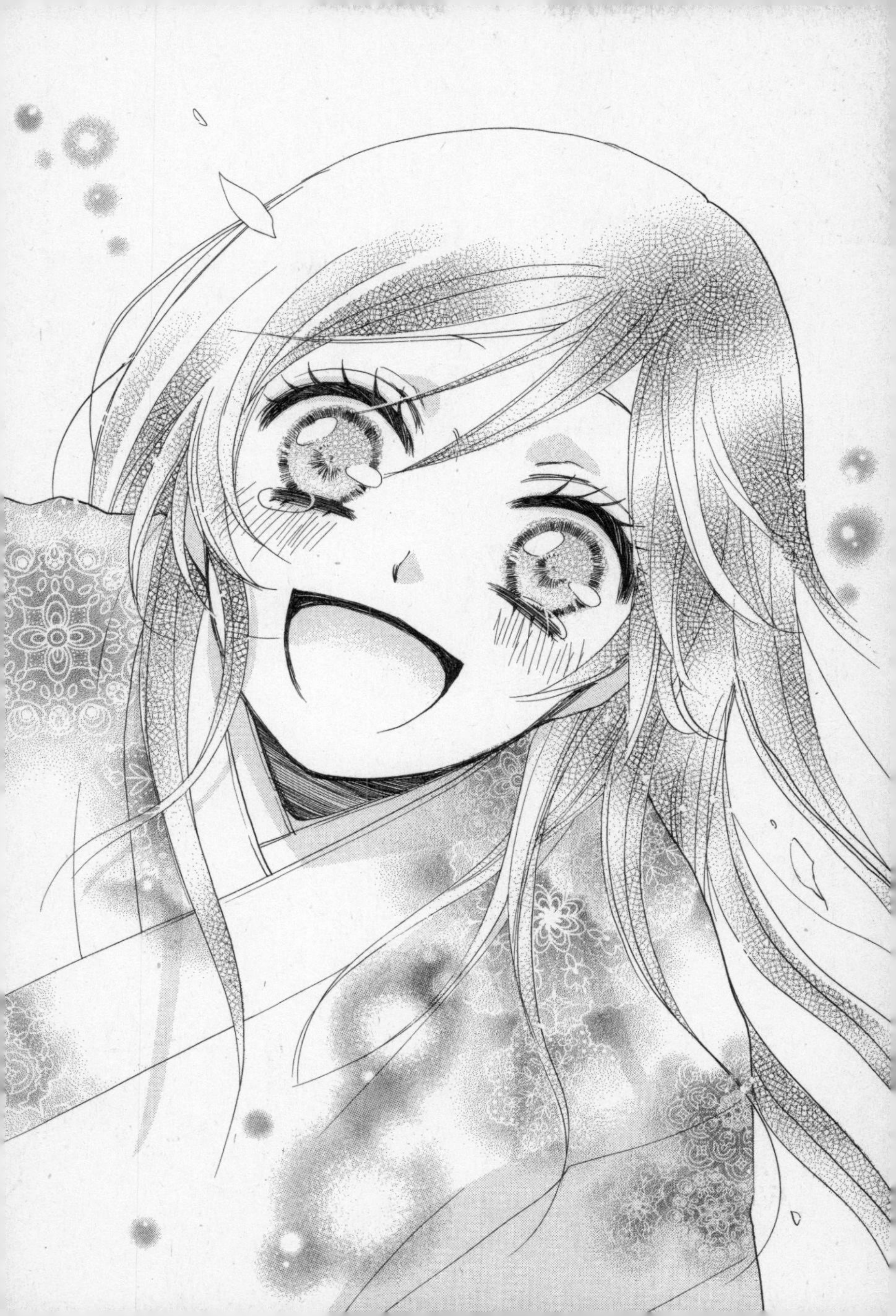

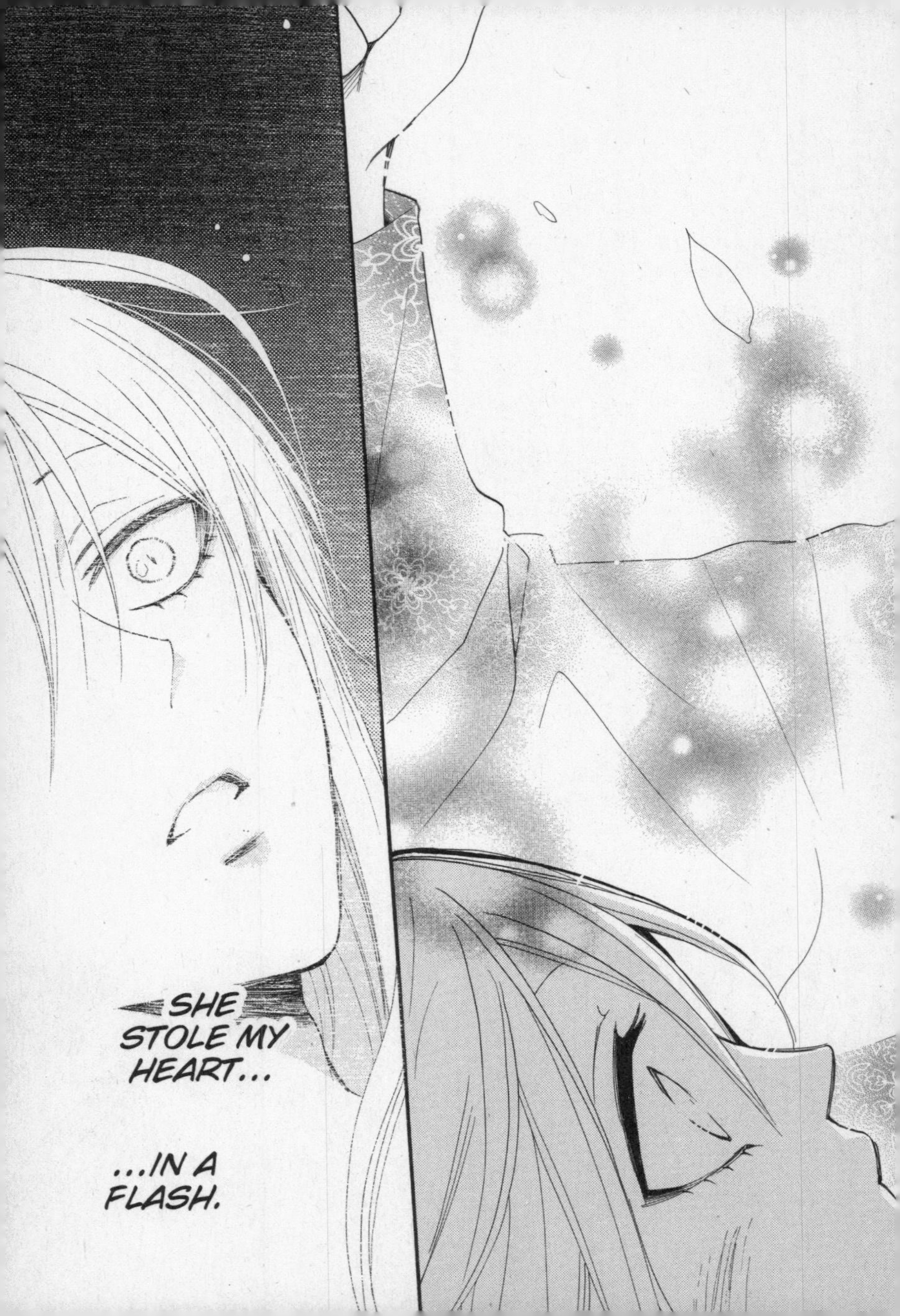
SHE STOLE MY HEART...
...IN A FLASH.

YES.
I RECOGNIZE HER EYES.
YOU'LL BE FINE ...
...TOMOE ...
THE FIRST WOMAN...
...I EVER WANTED...

# The Otherworld

*Ayakashi* is an archaic term for yokai.

*Kami* are Shinto deities or spirits. The word can be used for a range of creatures, from nature spirits to strong and dangerous gods.

*Onibi-warashi* are like will-o'-the-wisps.

*Ryu-oh* is a title that literally means "dragon king."

*Shikigami* are spirits that are summoned and employed by *onmyoji* (Yin-Yang sorcerers).

*Shinshi* are birds, beasts, insects or fish that have a special relationship with a kami.

*Tochigami* (or *jinushigami*) are deities of a specific area of land.

# Honorifics

*-chan* is a diminutive most often used with babies, children or teenage girls.

*-dono* roughly means "my lord," although not in the aristocratic sense.

*-kun* is used by persons of superior rank to their juniors. It can sometimes have a familiar connotation.

*-san* is a standard honorific similar to Mr., Mrs., Miss, or Ms.

*-sama* is used with people of much higher rank.

# Notes

**Page 6, panel 4: Torii**
*Torii* is a Shinto archway or gate.

**Page 43, panel 3: Tatami mats**
Traditional Japanese flooring. The mats are made from straw but are stiff and very heavy.

**Page 46, panel 4: Kami pillar**
There used to be a custom of offering "human pillars" as sacrifices when huge structures (such as bridges, dykes, and castles) were built. This was done as a prayer to the kami that the structures would not be destroyed by disasters or enemy attacks. The human pillars were buried alive or drowned.

**Page 134, panel 3: Harakiri**
Ritual suicide by slitting the stomach. Traditionally used by samurai to regain honor in the face of defeat or some disgrace. It is also known as *seppuku*.

**Page 137, panel 2: Haori**
A lightweight silk jacket that is worn over a kimono. It is traditionally a part of a man's formal outfit.

**Page 159, panel 1: Kosode**
A basic Japanese robe worn by both women and men, as either an inner or outer garment. The name means "small sleeves."

**Page 173, panel 3: Amano-habakiri**
A sword said to be used by the kami Susano-oh to defeat Yamata no orochi, the eight-headed monster serpent. The name means "Heavenly Serpent Slayer." Susano-oh is Amaterasu, the sun kami's younger brother, and one of his daughters married Ôkuninushi. The sword is said to have chipped when it chopped the serpent's tail. That is why Ôkuninushi says the sword has been "all fixed."

Julietta Suzuki's debut manga *Hoshi ni Naru Hi* (The Day One Becomes a Star) appeared in the 2004 *Hana to Yume Plus*. Her other books include *Akuma to Dolce* (The Devil and Sweets) and *Karakuri Odette*. Born in December in Fukuoka Prefecture, she enjoys having movies play in the background while she works on her manga.

# KAMISAMA KISS
## VOL. 14
### Shojo Beat Edition

### STORY AND ART BY
## Julietta Suzuki

English Translation & Adaptation/Tomo Kimura
Touch-up Art & Lettering/Joanna Estep
Design/Yukiko Whitley
Editor/Pancha Diaz

KAMISAMA HAJIMEMASHITA by Julietta Suzuki
© Julietta Suzuki 2012
All rights reserved.
First published in Japan in 2012 by HAKUSENSHA, Inc., Tokyo.
English language translation rights arranged with
HAKUSENSHA, Inc., Tokyo.

Printed in Canada

Published by VIZ Media, LLC
P.O. Box 77010
San Francisco, CA 94107

10 9 8 7 6 5 4 3
First printing, February 2014
Third printing, December 2017

www.viz.com          www.shojobeat.com

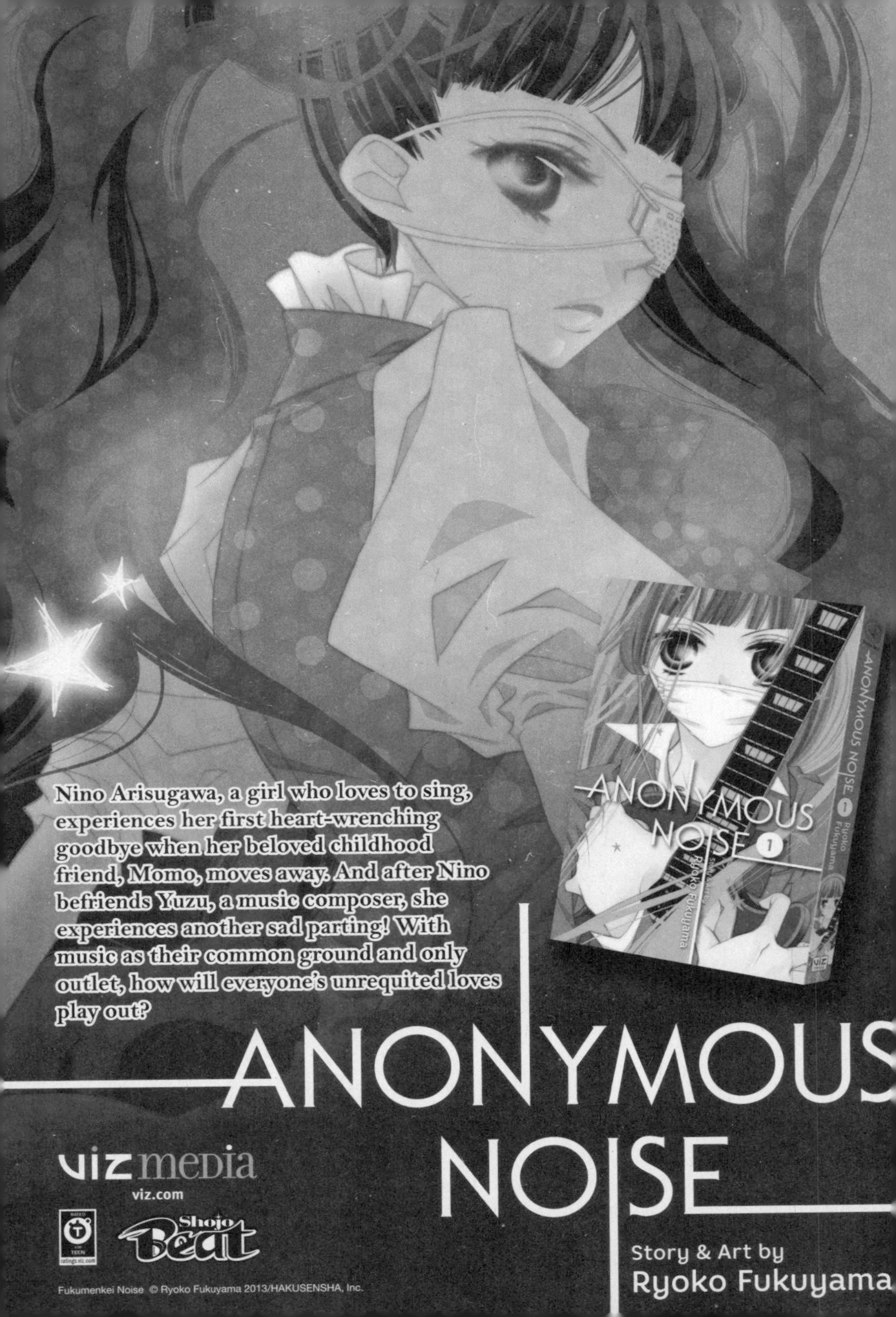
ANONYMOUS NOISE 1
Ryoko Fukuyama
Nino Arisugawa, a girl who loves to sing, experiences her first heart-wrenching goodbye when her beloved childhood friend, Momo, moves away. And after Nino befriends Yuzu, a music composer, she experiences another sad parting! With music as their common ground and only outlet, how will everyone's unrequited loves play out?
ANONYMOUS NOISE
viz media
viz.com
Shojo Beat
Story & Art by
Ryoko Fukuyama
Fukumenkei Noise © Ryoko Fukuyama 2013/HAKUSENSHA, Inc.

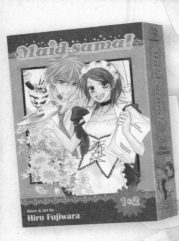

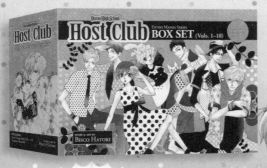

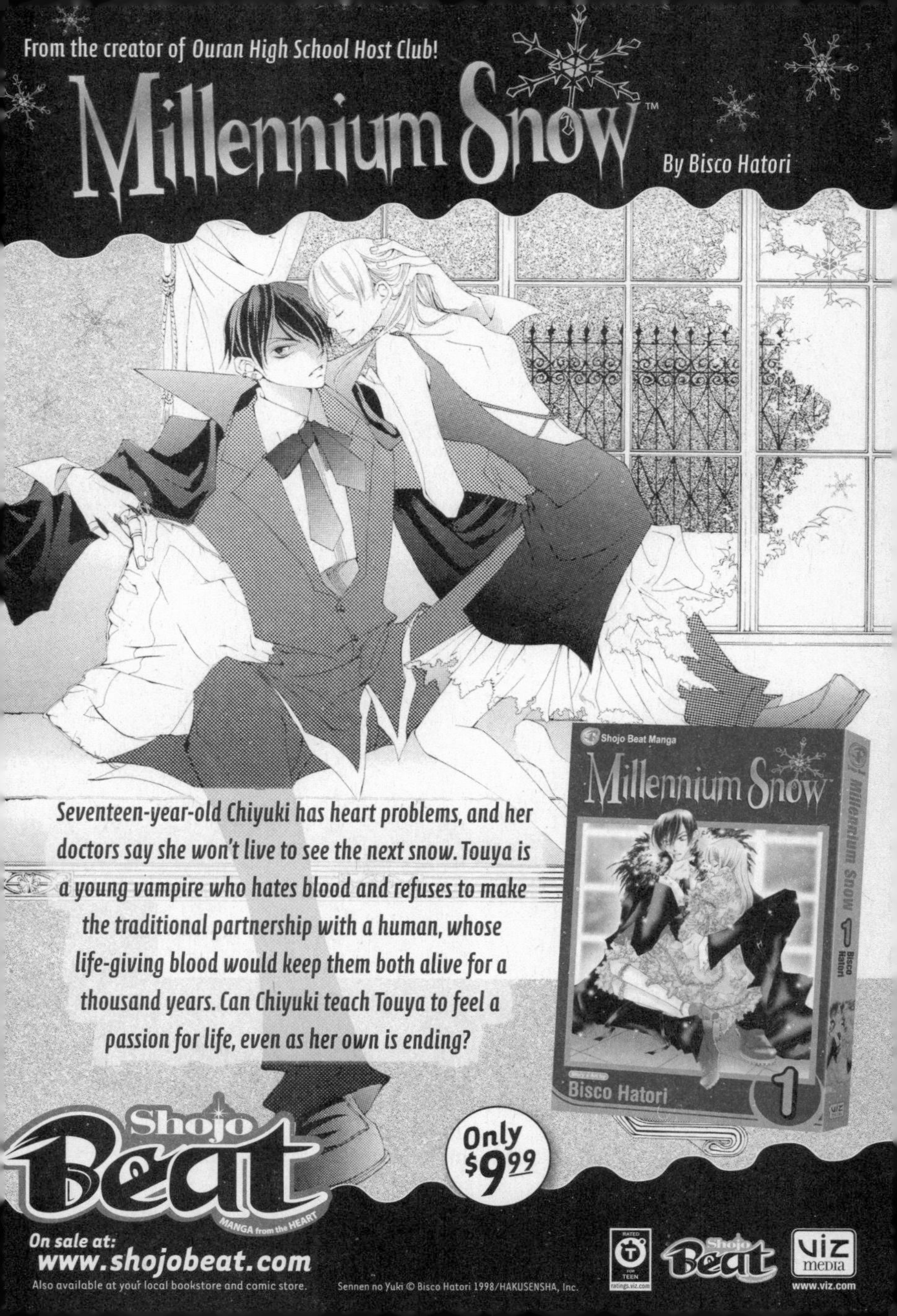
From the creator of Ouran High School Host Club!
Millennium Snow™
By Bisco Hatori
Shojo Beat Manga
Millennium Snow
Millennium Snow 1 Bisco Hatori
Bisco Hatori
1
Seventeen-year-old Chiyuki has heart problems, and her doctors say she won't live to see the next snow. Touya is a young vampire who hates blood and refuses to make the traditional partnership with a human, whose life-giving blood would keep them both alive for a thousand years. Can Chiyuki teach Touya to feel a passion for life, even as her own is ending?
Shojo Beat
MANGA from the HEART
Only $9.99
On sale at:
www.shojobeat.com
Also available at your local bookstore and comic store.
Sennen no Yuki © Bisco Hatori 1998/HAKUSENSHA, Inc.
RATED T FOR TEEN
ratings.viz.com
Shojo Beat
VIZ media
www.viz.com

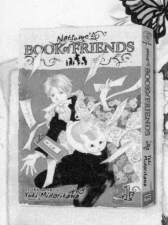
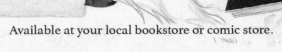

# This is the last page.

In keeping with the original Japanese comic format, this book reads from right to left—so action, sound effects, and word balloons are completely reversed. This preserves the orientation of the original artwork—plus, it's fun! Check out the diagram shown here to get the hang of things, and then turn to the other side of the book to get started!